AF806813

The International Library of Bioethics

Founding Editors

David N. Weisstub
Thomasine Kimbrough Kushner

Volume 109

Series Editor

Dennis R. Cooley, North Dakota State University, School of Humanities, Fargo, ND, USA

Editorial Board

Terry Carney, Faculty of Law Building, University of Sydney, Sydney, NSW, Australia

Marcus Düwell, Universiteit Utrecht, Utrecht, The Netherlands

Elizabeth Heitman, Southwestern Medical Center, University of Texas, Dallas, TX, USA

David Augustin Hodge, National Center for Bioethics, Tuskegee University, Tuskegee Institute, AL, USA

Søren Holm, Centre for Social Ethics and Policy, The University of Manchester, Manchester, UK

Nora L. Jones, Center for Urban Bioethics, Temple University, Philadelphia, PA, USA

Gerrit Kimsma, Radboud UMC, Nijmegen, The Netherlands

Daniel P. Sulmasy, Edmund D. Pellegrino Center for Clinical, Washington, DC, USA

The *International Library of Bioethics* comprises international and interdisciplinary volumes on foundational and applied issues in bioethics. The series focuses on perennial topics of aging, mental health, preventive medicine, medical research issues, end of life, biolaw, and other areas of bioethics, whilst expanding into other current and future questions involving the living world. The *International Library of Bioethics* examines the role of bioethics against the background of increasing globalization and interdependency of the world's cultures and government.

The series explores meaningful ways to answer the questions of how to direct biotechnology to human and other living things' ends, how to deal with changed values in the areas of religion, society, and culture, and how to formulate a new way of thinking. That is, to create a new, practical bioethics.

The international Library of Bioethics welcomes book proposals representing the broad interest of the series' focus. We especially encourage proposals addressing aspects of changes in biological and medical research and clinical health care, health policy, medical and biotechnology, and other applied ethical areas involving living things, with an emphasis on those interventions and alterations that force us to re-examine foundational issues.

José-Antonio Seoane · Oscar Vergara
Editors

The Discourse of Biorights

European Perspectives

Springer

Editors
José-Antonio Seoane
School of Law
University of A Coruña
A Coruña, Spain

Oscar Vergara
School of Law
University of A Coruña
A Coruña, Spain

ISSN 2662-9186 ISSN 2662-9194 (electronic)
The International Library of Bioethics
ISBN 978-3-031-66803-6 ISBN 978-3-031-66804-3 (eBook)
https://doi.org/10.1007/978-3-031-66804-3

This book is a result of the research project "The discourse of biorights: philosophical and legal bases for its foundation, characterization, and implementation" (DER2014-52811), funded by the Spanish Ministry of Economy and Competitiveness, and of the Research Group "Philosophy, Constitution and Rationality" within the Programme for research groups with growth potential (ED431B 2023/59), financially supported by the Xunta de Galicia (Spain).

© The Editor(s) (if applicable) and The Author(s), under exclusive license to Springer Nature Switzerland AG 2024
Chapters 1, 12, and 18 are licensed under the terms of the Creative Commons Attribution 4.0 International License (http://creativecommons.org/licenses/by/4.0/). For further details see license information in the chapters.

This work is subject to copyright. All rights are solely and exclusively licensed by the Publisher, whether the whole or part of the material is concerned, specifically the rights of translation, reprinting, reuse of illustrations, recitation, broadcasting, reproduction on microfilms or in any other physical way, and transmission or information storage and retrieval, electronic adaptation, computer software, or by similar or dissimilar methodology now known or hereafter developed.
The use of general descriptive names, registered names, trademarks, service marks, etc. in this publication does not imply, even in the absence of a specific statement, that such names are exempt from the relevant protective laws and regulations and therefore free for general use.
The publisher, the authors and the editors are safe to assume that the advice and information in this book are believed to be true and accurate at the date of publication. Neither the publisher nor the authors or the editors give a warranty, expressed or implied, with respect to the material contained herein or for any errors or omissions that may have been made. The publisher remains neutral with regard to jurisdictional claims in published maps and institutional affiliations.

This Springer imprint is published by the registered company Springer Nature Switzerland AG
The registered company address is: Gewerbestrasse 11, 6330 Cham, Switzerland

If disposing of this product, please recycle the paper.

Preface

Discussion about the value and protection of human life and health has increased in the last decades. The progress in biomedical and biotechnological research has opened new questions about the boundaries of life and made possible the evolution of science and technology with a remarkable consequence: the epistemological inability of the traditional scientific concepts and methodological tools to assess and understand these transformations, as well as the normative inadequacy of the current regulations, to identify.

Biorights arise as a category dealing with basic and human rights issues within the biomedical and biotechnological context, devoting special attention to the rights to life, health, integrity, freedom of religion, privacy, personal data protection, equality and non-discrimination and freedom of research, as well as new claims to join this catalogue of rights usually linked to technological progress. As such rights, biorights are not analysed solely from a legal standpoint, but also from the bioethical and biopolitical ones, aiming to show a broader perspective focused on the European context.

The book *The Discourse of Biorights. European Perspectives* contributes to defining the foundations, the concept, and the characteristics of biorights. Firstly, establishing what should be considered a human or fundamental bioright and, quite the opposite, what should be considered a simple expectation or claim unworthy of legal protection. Secondly, which are their main features and legal powers of their holders. Thirdly, finding out how biorights affect the theory of human rights and health justice. Furthermore, some European case law and domestic legislation are examined in order to assess how theoretical contributions fit the legal praxis and how courts and legislative and administrative powers deal with these biomedical and technological issues.

The different approaches included in the book confirm how manifold is the concept of biorights. Regardless of the specific biolegal conception addressed in every chapter (a comprehensive overview in Valdés & Lecaros (ed.) 2019; Valdés 2021), the book aims to deepen and continue with the work started years ago by some scholars (Rendtorff & Kemp 2000; Rendtorff 2015).

Framing the topic by making a case for a rights-based theory for health justice is José-Antonio Seoane's aim (Chap. 1). The author justifies the choice of rights and law as an appropriate and even essential normative foundation and, after some conceptual clarifications, examines the key elements and the philosophical foundation of the aforementioned rights-based theory, implemented through a two-tiered or two-level model.

Tomás de Domingo Pérez (Chap. 2) suggests that a fundamental rights-based theory is an appropriate basis for biorights, but only if their core content is guaranteed. This guarantee cannot be provided by the principle of proportionality, as the author shows by means of the right to physical integrity. However, guaranteeing the core content of rights requires a teleological approach which enables them to be harmonised.

Encarnación Fernández Ruiz-Gálvez (Chap. 3) explores in more detail the connection between the capabilities approach and an appropriate concept of health already studied in Chap. 1 in order to address the problem of health inequalities, particularly those of vulnerable groups. Conceiving social equity as a part of a broader problem of social justice, the author identifies nine determinants of health and formulates nine social policy strategies to address them.

On the basis of vulnerability as an ontological condition of the human being, and not merely an existential one, Claudio Sartea (Chap. 4) holds that it is possible to support and understand biorights as the requests of an indigent being, which requires preventing discrimination between healthy and sick people.

The meaning and scope of one of the classical features of rights, inalienability, is discussed by Noelia Martínez-Doallo (Chap. 5). Using bodily rights as a model, the author tries to show how moral and legal discourses approach this issue, how they deal with it differently, and how relevant the consequences may be.

The next two chapters deal with one of the most salient bioethical and biolegal principles: respect for persons and autonomy. María Jesús Vázquez Lobeiras (Chap. 6) challenges some cases of a bioethical application of the Kantian-inspired principle of autonomy and, based on Onora O'Neill's anti-individualist approach, suggests a more accurate interpretation of this concept which highlights the close interaction between information, autonomy and trust in the doctor-patient relationship.

In addition, Joaquim Gomes (Chap. 7) also thoroughly explores the principle of patient autonomy, considered both historically and analytically, focusing on the requirement for patient competence and the process of decision-making through advance directives, in particular in the context of the challenge of new technologies.

The existence of new rights related to the development of different technologies are examined in three of these chapters. The application of AI to neurotechnology involves a number of risks to human dignity, described by Daniel García San José (Chap. 8). One of the proposed remedies, the creation of new neuro-rights, is deemed unsuitable not so much because of the inflation of rights, but rather because they would only safeguard the rights of those who have been born. Moreover, the author holds that rights are neither a sufficient nor an adequate regulation. In his opinion, the best approach would be a set of universal principles ensuring their implementation through a special UN rapporteur.

The acknowledgement of cognitive freedom as a new bioright over any form of interference in the mind (mental integrity) is examined by Paolo Sommaggio (Chap. 9). Firstly, he questions developing this right based on the model of the right to property, because it is troublesome that mental states can be objects, neither private, if there is no free will, nor communal. In his view, the only appropriate approach is to consider the relation between the person and his/her deep self as a relationship of enjoyment of an object that cannot be considered entirely one's own. Cognitive freedom or mental integrity would therefore be acknowledged as a fundamental right, Chile being an example of the first steps in this direction.

What regulatory paradigm for new technologies should be developed in the light of the new rights is the topic addressed by Silvia Salardi (Chap. 10), who underlines that the access to human enhancement technologies by consumers exposes them to significant risks that are not well controlled and should be improved in order to achieve legal and reasonable solutions.

A reflection on new legal paths for classical rights at start of life is the next subjection for reflection. The need to envisage the international proscription of surrogacy is the main point of Alfonso Ballesteros' analysis of European Court of Human Rights case law (Chap. 11). Although it does not expressly acknowledge it, this case law legitimates surrogacy to a large extent. The author refutes this conclusion, arguing that the human person should not be on sale and there can be no right to have a child, because it undermines his/her dignity. He holds that, as the gestation process is segmented in surrogacy, only adult rights seem to matter and little attention is paid to the commodification of women.

Oscar Vergara (Chap. 12) also approaches the issue of surrogacy, but from the two most salient methodologies in biomedical ethics, principlism and casuistry, and concludes that none of them gives compelling answers. For this reason, the author approaches the question from a narrative point of view, considering this viewpoint makes it possible to highlight some issues that are usually overlooked, and which would contribute to shedding light on this question.

The legitimacy of circumcision is analysed and questioned by Agustín Motilla (Chap. 13), since it may clash with contemporary concerns for the protection of minors. Although this practice, unlike female mutilation, has hardly any medical contraindications and has a strong community component, the author underlines that its admissibility requires it to be carried out under appropriate surgical conditions.

Conscientious objection in the context of health services is the issue examined by Rosana Triviño-Caballero (Chap. 14). Reviewing an old legislative reform that restricted healthcare for undocumented immigrants in Spain, the author argues for a broad concept of conscientious objection that encompasses positive and not just negative actions, as is usually done, and also considers whether it may include the disobedience of healthcare professionals towards a restrictive legislation.

A new right to cross-border healthcare, formulated in a European directive and transposed into law in several countries, is discussed by Ana Ylenia Guerra Vaquero and Ana María Marcos del Cano (Chap. 15). The authors highlight the paradox of the Spanish case, where health care is provided to foreigners in Spain or to Spaniards abroad, while within Spain there are hindrances to health care for its own nationals, such as when requesting health care outside one's own autonomous community or when requesting a change of health centre.

A thorough review of the legislation of EU states with regard to the processing of health data in terms of secondary use for research is presented by Olga Tzortzatou-Nanopoulou et al. (Chap. 16). Besides this broad outlook, the authors' main concern is how it affects rights, in particular in relation to the General Data Protection Regulation (Regulation (EU) 2016/679).

Another biolegal perspective on the massive use of personal data in the field of health is provided by Maria Leonor Teixeira (Chap. 17), who attempts to reach a balance between the advantages for biomedical research and the serious dangers in relation to the privacy of patients and research subjects.

End-of-life rights are also evolving, since some Western countries have shaped the provision of death on request, in certain circumstances, as a legal right, implying a public obligation to dispense death. Using Spanish legislation on euthanasia as a paradigmatic case, Carolina Pereira-Sáez (Chap. 18) reflects on this bioright as a new right, belonging to a new and distinct category of rights, not just a further generation continuing the previous ones. She firstly focuses on the claim that this new bioright is grounded in the classic rights of previous generations. Then, she analyses the relevant features of this new bioright, that are also found in other new rights. Finally, she points out some implications of these new rights on our understanding of law: new rights are part of a Law that is also new.

Finally, Patrizia Borsellino (Chap. 19) gives a history-based defence of euthanasia. She shows how the process of dying has gone from being considered as something that is foreign to medicine to the implementation of palliative care, in conjunction with the strengthening of the autonomist paradigm. The author illustrates this shift using the evolution of legislative and case law in Italy, while regretting the lack of a further move towards admitting new lawful end-of-life scenarios, including euthanasia.

A Coruña, Spain

José-Antonio Seoane
Oscar Vergara

References

Rendtorff, J.D., and P. Kemp. 2000. *Basic Ethical Principles in European Bioethics and Biolaw* (vol. I). Barcelona and Copenhagen: Institut Borja de Bioética & Centre for Ethics and Law.

Rendtorff, J.D. 2015. Update of European bioethics: basic ethical principles in European bioethics and biolaw. *Bioethics Update* 1: 113–129.

Valdés, E. and J. A. Lecaros (eds.). 2019. *Biolaw and policy in the twenty-first century*. Cham: Springer.

Valdés, E. 2021. *Biolaw: Origins, doctrine and juridical applications on the biosciences*. Cham: Springer.

Contents

About the Editors

José-Antonio Seoane is Full Professor of Philosophy of Law and Coordinator of the Research Group *Philosophy Constitution, and Rationality* at the Universidade da Coruña, Spain, where teaches in the Faculties of Law, Health Sciences, Computing Science, and Humanities.

He is a member of the Spanish Bioethics Committee and Chair of the Bioethics Expert Group of the Spanish National Transplantation Organization.

His recent publications on bioethical issues include P. Serna, J-A. Seoane (ed). *Bioethical decision making and argumentation*, Springer, 2016; El marco normativo de la investigación en personas con demencia (N Álvarez-Lata, coauthor). *Revista de Derecho Privado y Constitución* 36, 2020: 131–177 Bioética, Biopolítica, Bioderecho. In *Pedagogía de la Bioética* (N Terribas, E Busquets, eds.). Lectio, 2021, 183–192; Lex artis, *Anuario de Filosofía del Derecho* 38, 2022, 275–300; Uterus transplantation as a surgical innovation (A Pérez-Blanco et al, coauthorship). *Bioethical Inquiry*, online: 29 June 2023; Deliberación bioética y Derecho. *Argumenta Philosophica* 2/2023: 39–58; Aspectos ético-legales del asesoramiento genético. In *Consultas de alto riesgo de tumores digestivos* (S Carballal Ramil, J Cubiella Fernández, dir.). Panamericana, 2024, 17–29; Legislative debates on death with dignity and euthanasia. An approach to the Spanish situation. In *Debating Laws. Studies on parliamentary justification of legislation* (AD Oliver-Lalana, ed.). Springer, 2024, 85–113.

Oscar Vergara is currently Associate Professor of Philosophy of Law at the Universidade da Coruña, Spain, and a member of the Philosophy, Constitution and Rationality Research Group at the same University. Previously has been professor at the Universidad de Piura, Peru.

He is the author and editor of several national and international publications in his field of specialization. In the area of bioethics, it is noteworthy the book *Método y razón práctica en la ética biomédica [Method and Practical Reason in Biomedical Ethics]*, Granada, Comares, 2018. Other significant papers in this field are: To be alive when dying: moral catharsis and hope in patients with limited life prognosis, *Medicine, Health Care and Philosophy* 24, 2021: 517–527; The Dramatic Essence of the Narrative Approach, *Theoretical Medicine and Bioethics* 39, 2018: 361–374; Autonomy, Monomania and Free Development of Personality in the Clinical Relationship. To what extent can the autonomous person be protected?, *Ramon Llull Journal of Applied Ethics* 13, 2022: 27–51; Pacto de silencio y derecho a la información en pacientes gravemente enfermos. Escribiendo el último capítulo de la vida [Conspiracy of Silence and Right to Information in Critically Ill Patients. Writing the last chapter of life], *Revista de Bioética y Derecho* 52, 2021: 45–60; Ética biomédica y prudencia [Biomedical Ethics and Prudence], *Cuadernos de Bioética* XXVI–87, 2015: 267–277.

He is currently a member of the Ethics Committee of the Spanish Association of Coloproctology and a member of the Advisory Committee of the journal *Cuadernos de bioética*. He also teaches in different university degrees on subjects related to bioethics.

Contributors

Alfonso Ballesteros University Miguel Hernández, Elche, Spain

Carla Barbosa Biomedical Law Center, University of Coimbra, Coimbra, Portugal;
Jean Monnet Center of Excellence "Building the Age of a Lawful and sustainable Data-Use" (BALDUS), Universitá Degli Studi di Perugia, Perugia, Italy;
Department of Health, Ethics & Society—CAPHRI School, FHML, Maastricht University, Maastricht, Netherlands

Patrizia Borsellino University of Milano-Bicocca, Milan, Italy

Gauthier Chassang Inserm UMR1295 Centre for Epidemiology and Research in Population Health (CERPOP), Faculty of Medicine, University of Toulouse III Paul Sabatier, Toulouse, France;
Unesco Chair "Ethics Science and Society", E2S, Federal University of Toulouse, Toulouse, France;
Ethics and Biosciences Platform—Genotoul Societal, GIS Genotoul, Toulouse, France

Tomás de Domingo Pérez Universidad Miguel Hernández, Elche, Spain

Aliuska Duardo-Sánchez Department of Public Law, Social and Legal Sciences Applied to New Technosciences, University of the Basque Country (UPV/EHU), Basque Country, Spain;
Department of Legal Philosophy, Faculty of Law, Universidad Nacional de Educación a Distancia (UNED), Madrid, Spain

Silja Elunurm Secondary Data Use, Estonian Next Generation National Health Information System development project, Estonian Ministry of Social Affairs, Tallin, Estonia;

Regulatory and Legal, Migrevention, Tartu, Estonia;
Health Founders Estonia Consortium, Tartu, Estonia

Encarnación Fernández Ruiz-Gálvez Universidad de Valencia, Valencia, Spain

Daniel García San José University of Seville, Seville, Spain

Christine Dalebø Gjerdevik PwC, Oslo, Norway

Joaquim Gomes Judge of Court of Appeal of Porto, Member of Portuguese Data Protection Authority, Porto, Portugal

Ana Ylenia Guerra Vaquero Universidad Nacional de Educación a Distancia, Madrid, Spain

Radek Halouzka ELSI Services and Research, Biobanking and BioMolecular Resources Research Infrastructure—European Research Infrastructure Consortium (BBMRI-ERIC), Graz, Austria;
Masaryk Memorial Cancer Institute, Brno, Czech Republic;
Faculty of Medicine, Masaryk University, Brno, Czech Republic;
National Centre of Nursing and Other Health Professions, Brno, Czech Republic

Mette Hartlev Faculty of Law, University of Copenhagen, Copenhagen, Denmark;
National Committee on Health Research Ethics, Copenhagen, Denmark

Ragnhild Angell Holst Norwegian Directorate of Health, Oslo, Norway

Dorota Krekora-Zajac ELSI Services and Research, Biobanking and BioMolecular Resources Research Infrastructure—European Research Infrastructure Consortium (BBMRI-ERIC), Graz, Austria;
Zając & Partners Law Firm L.P. Advocates and Legal Counsels, Warsaw, Poland;
Department of Comparative Civil Law, Faculty of Law and Administration, University of Warsaw, Warsaw, Poland

Jan Kuráň Masaryk Memorial Cancer Institute, Brno, Czech Republic

Teodora Lalova—Spinks Clinical Pharmacology and Pharmacotherapy research group, Department of Pharmaceutical and Pharmacological Sciences, KU Leuven, Leuven, Belgium;
Center for IT & IP law (CiTiP), KU Leuven, Leuven, Belgium

Maria Luisa Lavitrano School of Medicine and Surgery, Universita' Degli Studi di Milano—Bicocca, Milan, Italy

Matteo Macilotti Faculty of Law, University of Trento, Trento, Italy;
Italian node, Biobanking and BioMolecular resources Research Infrastructure of Italy (BBMRI.it), Milan, Italy

Marina Makri Biomedical Research Foundation of the Academy of Athens, Athens, Greece;
Faculty of Medicine, Aristotle University of Thessaloniki, Thessaloniki, Greece

Ana María Marcos del Cano Universidad Nacional de Educación a Distancia, Madrid, Spain

Noelia Martínez-Doallo Universidade da Coruña, A Coruña, Spain

Signe Mežinska ELSI Services and Research, Biobanking and BioMolecular Resources Research Infrastructure—European Research Infrastructure Consortium (BBMRI-ERIC), Graz, Austria;
Faculty of Medicine, University of Latvia, Riga, Latvia;
Institute of Clinical and Preventive Medicine, University of Latvia, Riga, Latvia

Fruzsina Molnár-Gábor Faculty of Law/BioQuant, University of Heidelberg, Heidelberg, Germany

Agustín Motilla Universidad Carlos III, Getafe, Spain

Carolina Pereira-Sáez Universidade da Coruña, A Coruña, Spain

Susanne Rebers Netherlands Cancer Institute, Amsterdam, Netherlands;
ELSI, Health-RI, Utrecht, Netherlands

Jane Reichel Faculty of Law, Stockholm University, Stockholm, Sweden;
Center for Research Ethics & Bioethics, Uppsala University, Uppsala, Sweden

Silvia Salardi University of Milano-Bicocca, Milan, Italy

Claudio Sartea University of Perugia, Perugia, Italy

José-Antonio Seoane University of A Coruña, A Coruña, Spain

Santa Slokenberga Faculty of Law, Uppsala University, Uppsala, Sweden

Paolo Sommaggio University of Padova, Padova, Italy

Tom Southerington School of Law, University of Turku, Turku, Finland;
Finnish Biobank Cooperative—FINBB, Turku, Finland;
Medical Research Ethics Committee, Turku University Hospital, Turku, Finland

Maria Leonor Teixeira Public Prosecutor, Porto, Portugal

Rosana Triviño-Caballero Department of Public Health and Maternal & Child Healthcare, Faculty of Medicine, Universidad Complutense de Madrid, Madrid, Spain

Olga Tzortzatou-Nanopoulou Biomedical Research Foundation of the Academy of Athens, Athens, Greece;
ELSI Services and Research, Biobanking and BioMolecular Resources Research Infrastructure—European Research Infrastructure Consortium (BBMRI-ERIC), Graz, Austria

María Jesús Vázquez Lobeiras Universidad de Santiago de Compostela, Santiago de Compostela, España

Ruth Vella Falzon University of Malta, Msida, Malta

Oscar Vergara University of A Coruña, A Coruña, Spain

Alexandra Ziaka Biomedical Research Foundation of the Academy of Athens, Athens, Greece;
Tilburg Institute on Law, Technology & Society, Tilburg University, Tilburg, Netherlands

Chapter 1
A Rights-Based Theory for Health Justice

José-Antonio Seoane

Abstract Health is a universal need and good that deserves protection, even if there is no consensus on its meaning and scope. Nonetheless, this chapter makes a case for a rights-based theory of health care, considering that its protection should be deemed a public duty of justice. In order to deploy such a theory, the chapter starts by justifying the choice of rights and law as an appropriate and even essential normative foundation. It continues with some conceptual clarifications and examines the key elements and the five-fold philosophical foundation of the rights-based theory. Then it discusses how the theory can be implemented through a two-tiered or two-level model. Finally, the chapter concludes with a brief recapitulation of some of these aspects.

Keywords Capabilities approach · Fundamental rights · Law · Needs · Recognition · Secure functionings

Despite being one of the most basic human needs (Doyal and Dough 1991, 4 and 50 ff.) and an individual and societal good, health is not guaranteed for everyone, everywhere. There are significant health disparities among persons and communities, although only some of them are health inequalities that can be deemed to be health injustice or inequity. This should be a main concern of a theory of health justice that aims to define how a society and its normative systems should deal with health inequalities.

The purpose of this chapter is to address this concern by making a case for a rights-based theory for health justice. I begin by justifying the choice of (1) rights and law as an appropriate and even essential normative foundation. I then examine (2) the key subjective and objective elements of the rights-based theory and its philosophical foundation. Then I discuss (3) how the theory can be implemented through a two-tiered or two-level model. Finally, I conclude with a (4) brief recapitulation of some of these aspects.

J.-A. Seoane (✉)
University of A Coruña, A Coruña, Spain
e-mail: jose.antonio.seoane@udc.es

© The Author(s) 2024

J.-A. Seoane and O. Vergara (eds.), *The Discourse of Biorights*, The International Library of Bioethics 109, https://doi.org/10.1007/978-3-031-66804-3_1

1.1 Why Rights?

The societal and individual value of health justifies it being acknowledged and protected as a basic right. Rights set the worth of health and give good arguments for achieving health justice. From a descriptive standpoint, they are a core feature in the constitutional rule of law and express justified claims concerning justice at a national and international level. From a prescriptive standpoint, rights' features turn them into the most convincing normative proposal for the protection of health.

1.1.1 The Political Context

In order to be fair, any decision on allocating goods and burdens in health field has to consider the context in which it is implemented and therefore the two main processes of transformation of our contemporary political systems: constitutionalisation and the crossing of the State boundaries, mainly as globalisation. In both processes rights play a significant role as a core element in the constitutional rule of law and international justice.

The first factor is constitutionalisation. After the Second World War, a new ethical, political and legal shaping of our societies arose in Europe: Constitutions appeared as an axiological order which imbues every sphere of social life. The legal-political model of the previous centuries, the legislative rule of law, is exhausted and replaced by the constitutional rule of law, which demands another theoretical answer (Alexy 1987, 405–408; Ferrajoli 2008, 33 ff.). The Constitution is considered a legal, valid and enforceable norm that holds legal supremacy within legal system, and constitutional norms are value-laden norms that often appear as principles thus demanding a practical legal reasoning and balancing. Besides establishing the limits of power, the Constitution guarantees its core values through all-pervading basic rights, which have a double dimension: individual or subjective, as individual liberties, and objective or institutional, as architectural elements of the legal order, foundations of the political community, and guiding criteria to achieve constitutional goals.

The second factor is the tendency to supersede the boundaries of the State, mainly the globalisation of Law (Ferrarese 2012). In the classical model, legal features depend on political ones and the rule of law is characterised by legislative norms (Kelsen 1960, §§ 36 ff.; Bobbio 1979). Nevertheless, sovereignty is no longer such an absolute power and the domestic legal system is no longer the only one within its territory. An *ad extra* or supra-national trend and an *ad intra* or infra-national trend show that sovereignty and territoriality, distinctive factors of the State, are eroded and redefined. In the end, international consensus about rights and democracy strengthens the relationship of globalisation and constitutionalisation (Ferrajoli 2007, 552 ff.) and explains post-national multilevel constitutionalism (Pernice 2006).

1.1.2 The Contribution of Law

Every society aims to protect life and health as basic goods through informal or non-institutional ways, such as social forms, habits, traditions, or morals, and institutional ways, with the law being the most important. Nonetheless, agreement on the importance of life and health fades when defining their meaning and protection. This axiological pluralism gives rise to reasonable disagreements about right and wrong (Rawls 1993), which can be resolved through dialogue or rational practical discourse characteristic of deliberative democracies (Habermas 1997). However, after such a dialogue there may be various correct discursive outcomes. Since a just society cannot allow life and health to remain unprotected until the optimal answer is achieved through ideal unlimited argumentation, certain procedures and bodies—mainly legislative and adjudicative or judicial—are necessary to put an end to this deliberative phase, guide its realisation and guarantee reaching a decision. At this point, the institutional dimension becomes important and leads to a normative system able to offer a correct response that resolves the controversy.

The so-called problem of knowledge can be solved through law, which eliminates uncertainty, confirms the recognition of our basic values or goods through its legal formulation, and prevents force or private justice from being the criterion for decision-making. Law also addresses the problem of organisation, coordinating personal expectations to foster social cooperation, which alleviates the inadequacy of individual initiative and spontaneous cooperation to achieve certain ends and moral goods. Finally, it protects our fragility, resolves conflicts and ensures effectiveness through its normativity or binding force, enforcing compliance with its provisions. Since the legal recognition of life or health as shared values does not imply global or unanimous agreement on their scope, nor that the legal norms regulating them will always be respected and complied with, law also responds to the problem of enforcement by ultimately relying on coercion, i.e. the possibility of the legitimate exercise of force to ensure obedience and the application of the law (Alexy 1996, 220–221).

1.1.3 Rights

To renounce the regulation of community life by law would mean anarchy, and in anarchy rights would not be guaranteed. The necessity of law can therefore be substantiated by rights (Alexy 1996, 221), understood as a rational basis for justified claims to actually enjoy something (Shue 1996, 14–15). The vocabulary of rights expresses the demands and implications of the relationship of justice, of what is fair from the point of view of the other to whom something is owed or due (Finnis 2011, 205). Moreover, the suitability of rights for a theory of health justice is confirmed by their characters. The first feature is universality. Human rights are bestowed by virtue of being a person, without further requirement, and they universally reflect and ensure values. As they are *universalia iuris materialis*, rights have to be present at all times and in all places to address health issues. In addition to the objective universality, i.e. universal content, rights are also universal from a subjective perspective, both in relation to their holders (every person) and their recipients or addressees (*erga omnes* effectiveness, i.e. individuals, groups, and governments) (Alexy 1995, 101–110). Further features confirm the suitability of rights: their moral validity, their fundamental character, their enforceability, and their priority. Human and fundamental rights identify, assert, and ensure the basic conditions for a decent life through justified and enforceable claims. From a normative point of view, rights are the result of a public deliberation and ratify the unity of practical reason through a threefold dimension: (1) moral, which expresses the most valuable goods and capabilities in society; (2) legal, through their inclusion in the highest domestic and international legal norms, constitutions or covenants, as applicable and binding legal norms to public powers and citizens; and (3) political, regarding their condition as objective or institutional norms: they conflate the legal order and the political community structure, guide the intervention of public powers and represent the main criteria of legitimacy for power. Therefore, they are not just moral expectations but have a legal and enforceable character. Finally, another two features are conclusive for health justice. Since rights provide social benefits, it is not possible to enjoy them if they are just bestowed; they need positive and active interventions as a result of being granted. Furthermore, rights have a previously mentioned twofold dimension: subjective or individual powers and objective or institutional elements. Fundamental rights are a core element of the rule of law that establishes the foundations of the political community: in a negative sense, rights limit political powers, which must neither infringe on them nor discourage their exercise; and in a positive sense, rights guide policies and political actions, which should foster their exercise.

Human rights and fundamental rights both belong to a broader legal category, i.e. subjective rights, understood as legal positions and relations that guarantee individuals some legal goods issued in legal norms (Alexy 2002, 111 ff.; Pariotti 2013, 3–6). Both categories have been analytically differentiated regarding the normative source of recognition and the right-holder scope (Pariotti 2013, 3–6). Human rights are subjective rights recognised by international legal instruments to every person whilst fundamental rights are recognised in domestic—or regional, as in Europe—legal systems by Constitutions, requiring in some cases the possession of some conditions—e.g. citizenship. Nonetheless, following on the above, fundamental rights are to be preferred because they better translate the meaning of the contemporary transformations of legal and political systems and the contribution of law through methodological and institutional guarantees. This institutional turn (Shue 1996, 166 ff.) provides a degree of efficiency unachievable for ethics or politics alone. Furthermore, fundamental rights add positivity and enhance constitutional protection, certainty and enforceability, and they deploy their binding legal force and ensure its observance and enforceability within the political framework of the rule of law, providing efficiency.

1.2 Elements

1.2.1 The Right Holder: Human Being

The anthropological standpoint for the rights-based theory for health justice is to acknowledge that the human condition is fragile, biologically finite and not free from disease. We appreciate our lives more for our actions and achievements than for their length (Callahan 2009), according to our condition of end-oriented beings, since every individual tries to overcome his/her vulnerability and limitations transforming his/her needs into opportunities in life. We are able to deliberate, make value judgments and plans and pursue our goals through our emotional and rational grammar (Nussbaum 2001), but we are also needy beings, dependent on others and limited by internal and external aspects (MacIntyre 1999). We are both active beings, even though agency does not have full mastery of our lives, and passive beings, suffering and subjected to the contingency of what happens to us (τύχη) beyond our intervention and control (Nussbaum 1986).

Therefore, human beings are interdependent, combining autonomy with vulnerability and dependence. The former enables us to exercise our capacities in order to become the authors of our lives through our own decisions and actions, to be accountable for them and to deserve moral appreciation; the latter shows that care and support are needed to deal with our life. If autonomy expresses the individual character of our decisions and actions, dependence exemplifies how our answers cannot be merely individual since they are based on significant memberships and bonds that define us. Our personality and our identity are partially shaped by our relations in a context of recognition, community and dialogue.

1.2.2 The Object: Health

Health is both a universal need for a fulfilling human life and a value appreciated by individuals and communities whose meaning has changed throughout history. Traditionally, it has been dialectically characterised by its opposed concept, disease. In primitive culture, exemplified by the narrative of the great Mediterranean religions, the notion of health was understood as 'grace', while disease was grasped as 'disgrace'. In Ancient culture, when reality was interpreted in terms of nature, health was conceived as 'order' (κόσμος) and disease as 'disorder' (χάος). In the Modern era, especially since the Eighteenth Century, health ceased to be primarily a matter of fact and became an axiological issue; therefore, health meant 'happiness' or 'fortune', whilst disease denoted 'unhappiness' or 'misfortune' (Gracia 1998). In the twentieth century, the notion of health endorsed by the World Health Organization in the preamble of its Constitution as "a state of complete physical, mental and social well-being and not merely the absence of disease or infirmity" (World Health Organization 1946) stands out. Nonetheless, five objections can be raised:

epistemological, as it refers to an idealised idea of health and not to what people interpret or experience as such; moral, in the sense of moralising health and blaming individuals for their unhealthiness and therefore unsupportive of lifestyles; political, because such an ambitious conception of health generates unattainable growth of public policies on disease prevention and health protection (Camps 2001, 98–102) and because it does not seem possible to find a definition of well-being consistent with a plurality of conceptions of the good life, which is a characteristic of modern democratic societies; social, because this broad definition carries the danger of overly medicalising social problems (Peter 2001, 161; Huber et al 2011); and legal, because of the impossibility of achieving its guarantee and realisation through law.

Therefore, more balanced and feasible conceptions are brought forward nowadays (Leonardi 2018). This is the case of the WHO's biopsychosocial definition of health in terms of functioning and capabilities, and as a result of the interaction of the individual with his or her environment (World Health Organization 2001), or the positive and complex concept of health as the ability to adapt and direct control of oneself with regards to the physical, emotional and social challenges of life (Huber et al. 2011). Health is valuable insofar as it enables us to pursue our vital goals and to interact in society; it means an opportunity, a possibility of life (Daniels 2008) or, even better, a human basic capability (Nussbaum 2011a; Ruger 2010; Venkatapuram 2011). This sounder conception of health includes physical health or survival, mental health, which is part of the second most basic human need, autonomy (Doyal and Dough 1991, 56–66 and 61–66), and the social or collective point of view, allowing health needs to be analysed in the context of the social, economic, political and legal system and to be considered a common good, not just an individual good.

The above, though, is not enough. Health should be conceived within a framework, because having these opportunities to pursue health autonomously requires a minimum context of equality, as it does not depend on individual action alone (See *infra* Chap. 3). The degree of inequality substantially determines levels of health, the disparity of which affects the whole of society and not just the least advantaged (Wilkinson and Pickett 2010). Since health is a consequence of the conditions in which a person lives, it is understandable that health inequity, i.e. unfair and avoidable differences in people's health status, has been explained by the social determinants of health, that is, the non-medical factors that influence health outcomes, or the conditions in which people are born, grow up, live, work and age, and the broad set of forces and systems that shape their daily lives, including economic policies and systems, development agendas, social norms, social policies and political systems (World Health Organization-Commission on Social Determinants of Health 2009; Pan American Health Organization 2019). Therefore, as health influences other needs, capacities and rights, health justice must be concerned with both health and the underlying determinants of health (Committee on Economic, Social and Cultural Rights 2000, point 4 in fine). Furthermore, individual and collective factors other than social determinants of health that influence personal health must not be ignored (World Health Organization 2001; Ruger 2010, 99–103, 152–154; Preda and Voigt 2015). In conclusion, personal health is the result of the interaction of four determining factors: biological endowments and needs, individual behaviours, the physical environment and social conditions (Ruger 2010; Venkatapuram 2011, 19, 71, 106, 234).

1.2.3 *The Foundations*

The validity and feasibility of rights as a means of health protection requires a philosophical and political foundation that underpins their interpretation, application and development. In order to fulfil this goal a philosophical-political foundation based on five pillars, in harmony with the notion of health outlined above, is proposed. It starts with an axiological revision of the notion of need and continues with the theories of recognition, which have underlined the importance and precedence of justice as recognition before the deliberation on distributive justice. The notion of health capability is then supported by the capabilities approach and the reinforcement of the secure functionings approach—already adopted by the capabilities approach (Nussbaum 2011a, 73–74)—as security, must accompany justice and ensure the durability of the exercise of capabilities, as well as adding new capabilities to the catalogue. Finally, a political conception of care that raises its degree of normativity and consolidates its nature of public duty, and not merely an individual one, is proposed in line with a rights-based theory.

1.2.3.1 A Value-Laden Conception of Need

Needs are widely used as a criterion for health justice (Walzer 1983). However, several criticisms undermine their suitability: the difficulty of determining what the basic needs are; the variability of individual and social needs, the existence of false or imposed needs; their passive character, linked to human shortcomings and limitations instead of considering us as end-oriented beings; their negative character, insofar as interventions are oriented towards eliminating deprivation or liberating from need; or their paternalistic character, since the satisfaction of needs does not necessarily require the intervention or action of the subject. A further criticism must be added: the notion of need alone is not enough, for it must be connected to the teleological character of our decisions and specify what something is needed for and the moral importance of the end to be achieved (Frankfurt 1988, 104–107).

Therefore, the notion of need should be connected with health agency (Ruger 2010) and medical necessity (Callahan 2009, 144–200, specially 171 ff.) as well as other philosophical approaches—mainly the capabilities and the secure functionings approaches—(other proposal in Reader 2006) in a twofold way. Firstly, autonomy as one of the two most basic human needs, understood as a negative and positive freedom and supported by a range of valuable opportunities for action and a prior set of social conditions for fulfilling those needs (Doyal and Gough 1991, 89 ff., 98, 109 ff.). Secondly, along with this link to human agency and relational autonomy is a descriptive-normative conception of need (Wiggins 1998, 25). What we need would not be simply that without which it is not possible to live or subsist (Shue 1996), but that without which good cannot be or come to be (Aristotle 1933, V, 1015a 20–25), it is not possible to flourish, to pursue one's ends and have a fulfilled life (Anscombe 1958, 7).

1.2.3.2 The Theories of Recognition

The rights-based approach gives precedence to theories of recognition (Honneth 1996, 2003; Fraser 2003, 2008; Ricoeur 2005), because the distributive paradigm could obscure institutional context, and justice should address not just allocation but also the institutional conditions for exercising and developing individual capacities. Recognition must be prior to allocation, and such precedence empowers people (Young 1990, 15–38), reinforces participation and improves the justification of the distribution, since it makes it possible to include everybody in the deliberation about the conditions of justice (Fraser 2008, 6 ff., 55 ff., 108–118).

Recognition expands into two main meanings and dimensions (Ricoeur 2005, 1–22; Ikäheimo, Laitinen, 2009, 33–56). (1) The subjective or individual recognition, which entails the identification, or knowledge, of one's capacities and attributes, besides the recognition and acceptance by means of self-confidence, self-respect and self-esteem (Honneth 1996; Ricoeur 2005, 1–22, 247 ff.). (2) The intersubjective recognition that determines the aforementioned: being recognised by others is necessary to complete one's own identity and to recognise oneself (Honneth 1996; Taylor 1989, 1994). There are three levels of mutual recognition: love, legal recognition, and social esteem, whose denial establishes different issues of justice (Honneth 1996, 92 ff.).

The rights-based health justice does not address all these forms, since rights focus on mutual recognition and thus, in its second way, legal recognition. Individual recognition and the two other ways of intersubjective recognition affect the development and enforcement of legal recognition, but do not reach its level of enforceability.

It has been proposed that the inherent-rights approach, typical of post-World War II declarations of rights, be complemented by a politics of 'socio-cultural recognition' prior to distribution (Hayden 2012, 570, 574–576). A more interesting contribution points to the presence of the idea of debt at the origin of reciprocal recognition (Ricoeur 2005, 12), whereby duties, because of their relation to rights and their categorical and universal character, can be understood as enforceable and direct duties of justice, which is a normatively relevant feature of legal recognition. The other levels of inter-subjective recognition—love and social esteem or solidarity—are a matter of degree, whereas respect and legal recognition are not: all human beings, by the mere fact of being human beings, regardless of their individual qualities, deserve recognition and respect for their rights. Thus, any exclusion or dispossession of rights represents a form of disrespect that must be qualified as unjust (Honneth 1996, 131 ff.). This confirms that the central normative categories of justice as recognition are not identity, fair distribution or equality, but dignity and respect (Honneth 2007b), understood as necessary conditions for fair intersubjective relations and a remedy to the reification or instrumentalisation of persons and their treatment as commodities or interchangeable objects (Honneth 2007a).

The status model of recognition considers recognition as a matter of social justice that operates as a normative criterion for assessing injustice (Fraser 2008, 12 ff. and 48 ff.), places every individual on a fair and equal level and allows for actions independent of the individual's opinion or judgement: conditions denying a fair social participation, in spite of individual acceptance, are unjust and should be ruled out (Fraser 2003, 26 ff. and 48 ff.). Those features make it a promising approach related to other philosophical pillars of the rights-based theory, mainly secure functionings, and it is especially appropriate for dealing with the social determinants of health, guiding the implementation of public health measures, and addressing structural injustice (Young 2011).

1.2.3.3 The Capabilities Approach

The capabilities approach (Sen 1999; Sen 2009; Nussbaum, 2006; Nussbaum 2011b; Ruger 2010; Venkatapuram 2011, 113–142) asserts that the purpose of any political, ethical, and legal measure in health issues is based on the notion of 'capability', aimed at providing people with the necessary means to choose from, and act among, different valuable and real options. In this sense, the capabilities approach is related to the aforementioned notion of value-laden necessity, but complements it with those of health capability, health functioning and health agency (Ruger 2010, 83, 141 ff.).

Capabilities are understood as combined capabilities, i.e. an individual's internal capabilities and adequate external conditions, which should be constructed as opportunities that let each individual freely establish his/her own idea of good in order to pursue it within a basic background of equal opportunity—or capability–, and not in one of results—or functioning. The central human capabilities have been framed in ten categories, that can be translated into different fundamental or human rights (Vizard 2021) that define basic social justice: (1) Life. (2) Bodily health. (3) Bodily integrity. (4) Senses, imagination, and thought. (5) Emotions. (6) Practical reason. (7) Affiliation. (8) Other species. (9) Play. (10) Control over one's environment: (a) political, and (b) material (Nussbaum 2011a, 33 ff.).

Health is a prominent capability. Understood as bodily health, meaning being able to enjoy good health, including reproductive health; being adequately nourished; and having adequate shelter (Nussbaum 2011a, 33). More precisely, health has been defined as a person's ability to attain or exert a cluster of basic human activities, or the capability to accomplish a cluster of basic or vital capabilities or functionings (Venkatapuram 2011, 42–43 and 109), the global aim of health protection being to ensure the capability to have good health or 'to be healthy' (Ruger 2010, 3; Venkatapuram 2011, 143 ff.), to have the ability to achieve certain health functionings and the freedom to achieve them (Ruger 2010, 81).

Health is a significant part of other capabilities that should ensure a dignified human life and leads us to a relational notion of health, which links it to other capabilities, functionings and rights, giving it not only value per se but also an instrumental value. The importance of health to the exercise of the other capacities does not require conceiving it as a *primus inter pares* meta-capability that blurs the other capabilities (Richardson 2016, 3 ff.), nor as something all-encompassing or as a capability integrated by the other capabilities, even if it is necessary for all of them (Tengland 2016, 17–18) and other functionings (Ruger 2010, 81).

The capabilities approach connects goods, values and rights through the notion of capability, proposing medical necessity and medical appropriateness as objective criteria for access to health care (Ruger 2010, 143), and incorporating, through health agency, the ability to achieve health outcomes by means of free choices and voluntary action and the role of individual responsibility (Ruger 2010, 82).

1.2.3.4 The Secure Functionings Approach

A theoretical complement comes from the secure functionings approach (Wolff and de-Shalit 2007; Wolff 2011, 146–169; Wolff 2012), which stresses the importance of a secure and lasting implementation of capabilities and rights. Since fair health protection must not be reduced to ensure a certain level of functioning at any particular time, this approach underlines the prospects for sustaining that level and guaranteeing health 'capability security' (Wolff and de-Shalit 2007, 64 ff.). Furthermore, it consists of having 'genuine opportunities' and not just 'formal opportunities' (Wolff and de-Shalit 2007, 80) and providing secure reasonable options for choosing and acting, while avoiding either the exposure to extreme risks or the sacrifice of other capabilities or functionings (Wolff and de-Shalit 2007, 61–64). This is the meaning of a 'genuine opportunity for secure functioning' (Wolff and de-Shalit 2007, 37, 74).

The notion of health security has four dimensions: vulnerability, control, resilience, and fear or anxiety (Wolff 2011, 138–144). The relational character of health, capabilities and rights also appears with 'corrosive disadvantages', which have negative effects on other functionings, and 'fertile functionings', which spread their good effects overs several categories, either directly or by reducing risk to other functionings (Wolff and de-Shalit 2007, 10, 121–122).

To have a limited number of genuine opportunities for secure functioning gives rise to social injustice and disadvantage, which can be triggered by shortcomings in the internal resources, the external resources or the social framework. The internal resources are internal capabilities, whereas the external resources and the social framework are equivalent to the external conditions. Instead of policies oriented towards personal enhancement or resources, the intervention here aims to improve people's status or social position. This perspective links secure functionings with the aforementioned theories of recognition, since the policies and strategies for addressing disadvantages and injustice should focus on the status enhancement instead of personal enhancement, cash compensation, or targeted resource enhancement (Wolff and de-Shalit 2007, 173–177).

Another contribution of this approach is the addition of new categories to the list of central human capabilities. (11) Doing good to others or being able to care for others and to express gratitude. (12) Living in a law-abiding fashion, i.e. being able to live within the law; not being forced to break the law, cheat, or to deceive other people or institutions. (13) Understanding the law, its demands, legal rights, duties, powers, and opportunities, which requires an accessible legal system approach (Wolff and de-Shalit 2007, 50 ff.). Thus, the discourse of justice is complemented with the discourse of care, particularly in the 11th category, while categories 12 and 13 highlight the importance of knowledge and the respect for the normative and institutional framework of human action as well as the adoption of a legal approach.

1.2.3.5 A Political Theory of Care

Since human beings are dependent on others to develop their basic capabilities, individuals need to care and be cared for (Engster 2007). Along with human interdependence and sociability, the relevance of health care is reinforced by its status as a basic goal and duty of medicine (Callahan (dir.) 1996) and other healthcare professions.

Care consists of a cluster of practices and values. Like health, care is neither a commodity (Held 2006, 51–56, 108 ff.; Tronto 2013) nor a consumption good defined by market criteria and achievable only for people who can afford it. Furthermore, care should not be understood just as an attitude, a motivation, or a virtue, because this conception can reduce care as a matter of gratitude and generosity and place it just in private or familial realms (Tronto 2013). Care is different from benevolence, a familial virtue, and it is better characterised as a social relation than an individual disposition (Held 2006, 42, 51–56).

There is no logical opposition between care and justice. In a democratic society care matters to everyone, regardless of gender (Gilligan 1982), and healthcare becomes a political responsibility that encompasses a set of public practices, even while maintaining its private dimension. Since health is a universal need philosophically translated into a capability, healthcare becomes a basic duty of justice, enforceable and deserved by everyone. There can be care without justice, but not justice without care (Held 2006, 17).

This political conception means that healthcare should be understood neither as a commodity nor as a family gift, but as an entitlement. Care is a complex process with four steps: caring about, caring for, care-giving and care-receiving, and even a fifth phase: caring with (Tronto 2013, 22–23), that can also be expressed in terms of care rights: (1) a right to receive care: everyone is entitled to receive adequate care; (2) a right to give care: everyone is entitled to participate in relationships of care that give meaning to their lives; and (3) a right to decide how to care and be cared for: everyone is entitled to participate in the public process about how society should ensure the first two premises (Tronto 2013, 153 ff.).

1.3 Implementation

1.3.1 Health as a Right: A Right to Healthcare

In the international field the acknowledgement of health as a right can be found as early as in the preamble of the WHO's constitution (1946), confirmed two years later (1948) in the Universal Declaration of Human Rights (article 25.1). A more accurate legal status for the right to health in international human rights law was stated by the International Covenant on Economic, Social and Cultural Rights of 1966 (article 12) and confirmed, among others, by the International Convention on the Elimination of All Forms of Racial Discrimination of 1965 (article 5); the Convention on the Elimination of all Forms of Discrimination Against Women of 1979 (articles 12 and 14); the Convention on the Rights of the Child of 1989 (article 24); or the Convention on the Rights of Persons with Disabilities of 2006 (article 25). References to the right to protection of health can also be found in regional human rights, as in the European Social Charter of 1961 (revised in 1996: article 11), as well in soft law regulations such as UNESCO's Universal Declaration on Bioethics and Human Rights of 2005 (especially article 10 in relation to articles 3, 11, and 14). Furthermore, the right to healthcare is included in the Charter of Fundamental Rights of the European Union of 2001 (article 35).

In the national field the right to health care is included in Constitutions and domestic legislative norms and case-law tied to human dignity and other fundamental rights. This is the case for the Italian Constitution (1947), acknowledging healthcare as a fundamental right of the individual and a collective interest (article 32, related to articles 2 and 3), and the Spanish Constitution (1978), including a right to health protection (article 43.1 related to article 10.1 and 15).

In light of the aforementioned some conclusions are drawn. Although the expression 'right to health' is commonly used both in legal and ordinary language, the legally accurate expression is 'right to healthcare', since this right is not to be understood as a right to be healthy but to enjoy some freedoms and entitlements that enable people to be healthy and flourish (Committee on Economic, Social and Cultural Rights, 2000, point 8). In addition, the right to healthcare has to be considered as a fundamental right, connected to other rights and freedoms that shape it (Committee on Economic, Social and Cultural Rights, 2000, point 8) and support constitutional democracy (Ferrajoli 2007, 398 ff, specially 408–412); it is actionable and enforceable and, despite the social and economic hindrances, must not be underestimated and unprotected (Alexy 2002, 334–348). All human rights are universal, indivisible, and interdependent and interrelated (Vienna Declaration and Programme of Action (1993), point 5), and every right, either liberty or social or political, implies costs and requires provisions (Holmes and Sunstein 1999; Ferrajoli 2007, 67–71) in order to be guaranteed.

The right to healthcare is thus presented as an inclusive right, connected to many factors that determine a healthy life, mainly the underlying determinants of health (Committee on Economic, Social and Cultural Rights 2000, point 14 *in fine*; United

Nations High Commissioner for Human Rights–World Health Organization 2008, 6), which shows the suitability of the notions of health capability and, even more, corrosive disadvantages and fertile functionings.

1.3.2 *Two Levels of Health Justice and Rights*

Health justice is translated into the language of rights as a secure health capability, i.e. what each human being deserves throughout the sustained exercise of his/her basic capabilities (Seoane 2019). The relational character of rights connects the right to healthcare with other rights in order to ensure a secure health capability (Cohen and Ezer 2013, 7–19).

The rights-based proposal for health justice is supported by a sufficientarian approach, since the goal is not avoiding inequality nor that everyone has the same, or too little, but that each should have enough (Frankfurt 1987, 2005), even in terms of health well-being (Powers and Faden 2006, 50). Health is understood as a non-positional capability (Nielsen and Axelsen 2017, 56) that requires a minimum threshold of capabilities and rights for everyone but also admits different or unequal levels above this critical threshold.

Health protection refers to two dimensions of justice which must be correctly ordered. Firstly, justice as recognition, and only then, secondly, distributive justice. The latter is concerned with correcting inequalities and ensuring an adequate allocation of goods, resources or benefits, on the basis of capabilities. But first how this distribution is carried out and who participates as recipient and decision-maker must be answered. Therefore, a two-tiered health system (Rid 2017, 44–45) or two levels of heath justice and rights are to be distinguished (Committee on Economic, Social and Cultural Rights 2000, point 43; Eleftheriadis 2012, 268–285): a first level of justice as recognition, in order cover everyone, including minorities; and a second level of distribution through public deliberation.

1.3.2.1 Core Obligations

The core obligations refer to justice as recognition and broaden the scope of healthcare granting rights' subjective universality. This basic level, which is broader than the right to health care, could be summarised trough three overall aspects related to biological and physical human needs—mainly related to survival, as a platform for pursuing a flourishing human life–, fundamental interests of a human agent—to shape and pursue valuable ends—and fundamental interests of a social being—to pursue one's valuable ends within a community—(Axelsen and Nielsen 2017, 113). The lack of health not only harms physical integrity through disease, suffering or pain, but also entails situations of humiliation and exploitation that erode dignity itself, which is the foundation of rights (Committee on Economic, Social and Cultural Rights 2000, points 3 and 11; Eleftheriadis 2012, 282). In short, it protects basic categorical values and constitutional rights that are morally claimable and legally enforceable, establishing a threshold below which dignity and rights are infringed.

In this level, the right to health care imposes three types of obligations on the State: to respect, to protect, and to fulfil, ensuring the availability, accessibility, acceptability, and quality of the essential elements of health (Committee on Economic, Social, and Cultural Rights 2000, points 33 and 43, and point 11, respectively).

A prominent domestic legal example of these core obligations is the fundamental right to the guarantee of a subsistence minimum (*Existenzminimum*), recognized in 2010 by the German Federal Constitutional Court (BVerfGE 125, 175; cf. also Deutscher Ethikrat 2011, 78–81), derived from human dignity (article 1(1) of the German Basic Law) in combination with the principle of the social welfare state (article 20(1) of the German Basic Law).

1.3.2.2 Progressively Realized Set of Goals

The progressively realized set of goals refers to distributive justice and is implemented through legally developed rights that are dependent on the socioeconomic background and the distributive choices in political and social deliberation (Committee on Economic, Social and Cultural Rights 2000, point 44; Eleftheriadis 2012, 282–283). To attain the highest possible level of health through a fair distribution of health capabilities, as a second step after recognition, requires the inclusion and participation of everybody in the deliberation.

A rights-based approach should be aware of some issues in order to guarantee a fair allocation in this level, only after fulfilling the core obligations of the first level. First, that mere equality of opportunity means that, in conditions of scarcity, not all rights can be satisfied simultaneously. If one eschews a strictly egalitarian principle whereby all rights are left equally unsatisfied, balancing will be necessary in order to determine which rights are respected in practice; the ranking of rights and the criteria for their satisfaction must be decided in a transparent procedure by democratically legitimised bodies. Secondly, that in a society based on the rule of law, rights and their corresponding obligations cannot be set off against each other on an interpersonal basis; the maximisation of medical benefits at the macrosocial level may infringe on the rights of individuals because an inter-individual valuation of life or health could involve an ethically and legally unacceptable consideration of the individual as a fungible entity, incompatible with human dignity. Finally, that even though efficiency is a worthy goal, it can only be achieved in connection with rights and a sound conception of health (Deutscher Ethikrat 2011, 61–72). Regarding the former, a majority or generalisation is not enough, since universalisation is required; regarding the latter, health benefits must be assessed in terms of individual capabilities and functionings.

1.4 Conclusion

Broadening the progressively realised goals (level 2) and turning them into core obligations (level 1) reflect the evolution of a society and its legal system towards a fair universal healthcare; and conversely, the legally unacceptable regression or reduction of rights to health illustrates the opposite process (Committee on Economic, Social and Cultural Rights 2000, point 32).

In order to comply with these obligations (Wolff 2012, 27–35) and avoid, among others, the 'bottomless pit objection' (Ruger 2010, 187 ff.), scientific and deliberative approaches through substantive and procedural principles to define medical appropriateness and medical necessities should play a key role. This means taking into account efficiency, but after justice and scientific medical decision; and also identifying and distinguishing central capabilities and needs belonging to the first level from those belonging to the second level, both at the macrolevel as well as at the meso- and micro-level, where individual autonomous decisions become proportionally more important (Ruger 2010, 172 ff., 187–192; Deutsche Ethikrat 2011, 71–72).

On the basis of a biopsychosocial concept of health and a relational concept of a human being, I have made a case for a rights-based theory for health justice underpinned by a political conception of healthcare and four other philosophical supports: a value-laden concept of health need, the theories of recognition, the capabilities approach, and the secure functioning approach. The result is a finite model of health care, limited in aspirations and thus economically more plausible but at the same time responsive to our need for good health with affordable, accessible, and sustainable healthcare goals (Callahan 2009, 143 ff.) instead of aiming at unlimited medical progress and technological innovation (Callahan 2009, 196, 203). Identifying a basic level, a minimum or a sufficient threshold below which the right to health and even other rights are violated translates the notion of justice as recognition and the legal meaning of dignity or decent minimum. In a negative sense, it avoids violation of rights and the risk of considering the right to health as a matter of degree, where everything is valid, it being only a question of more or less, as it could lead to the absolute denial of the right. In other words, the sufficient threshold of level 1 becomes an all or nothing question, while level 2 can be a more or less, or scalar, model (Selgelid 2016, 28–30).

This chapter is one of the results of the Research Group *Philosophy, Constitution and Rationality* within the Programme for research groups with growth potential (ED431B 2023/59), financially supported by the Xunta de Galicia (Spain).

References

Alexy, Robert. 1987. Rechtsystem und praktische Vernunft. *Rechtstheorie* 18: 405–419.

Alexy, Robert. 1995. Law, discourse, and time. *Archiv Für Rechts- und Sozialphilosophie* 64: 101–110.

Alexy, Robert. 1996. Discourse theory and human rights. *Ratio Juris* 9 (3): 209–235.
Alexy, Robert. 2002. *A theory of constitutional rights* (transl. J. Rivers). Oxford: Oxford University Press.
Anscombe, Elizabeth A. 1958. Modern moral philosophy. Philosophy XXXIII/124: 1–19.
Aristotle. 1933. *Metaphysics* (transl. H. Tredennick). Cambridge, Mass.: Harvard University Press.
Axelsen, David V. and Nielsen, Lasse. 2017. Essentially enough. Elements of a plausible account of sufficientarianism. In *What is enough? Sufficiency, justice, and health*, ed. Carina Fourie, Anette Rid, 101–118. Oxford: Oxford University Press.
Bobbio, Norberto. 1979. *Il positivismo giuridico*. Torino: Giappichelli.
Callahan, Daniel (dir.). 1996. The goals of medicine: setting new priorities. The Hastings Center Report 26/6: S1-S27.
Callahan, Daniel. 2009. *Taming the beloved beast. How medical technology costs are destroying our health system*, Princeton, N. J.: Princeton University Press.
Camps, Victoria. 2001. *Una vida de calidad. Reflexiones sobre bioética*. Barcelona: Ares y Mares.
Cohen, J., and T. Ezer. 2013. Human rights in patient care: A theoretical and practical framework. *Health and Human Rights* 15 (2): 7–19.
Committee on Economic, Social and Cultural Rights. 2000. *General Comment No 14. The Right to the Highest Attainable Standard of Health (Article 12 of the International Covenant on Economic, Social and Cultural Rights)*. Geneva: United Nations.
Daniels, Norman. 2008. *Just health: meeting health needs fairly*. New York: Cambridge University Press.
Deutscher Ethikrat. 2011. *Medical benefits and costs in health care. The normative role of their evaluation*. Berlin: Deutscher Ethikrat. https://www.ethikrat.org/fileadmin/Publikationen/Stellungnahmen/englisch/DER_StnAllokationEN_Online.pdf.
Doyal, Len, and Ian Gough. 1991. *A theory of human need*. London: Macmillan.
Eleftheriadis, P. 2012. A right to health care. *Journal of Law, Medicine & Ethics* 40 (2): 268–285.
Engster, Daniel. 2007. *The heart of justice. Care ethics and political theory*. New York: Oxford University Press.
Ferrarese, Maria Rosaria. 2012. *Prima lezione di diritto globale*. Roma-Bari: Laterza.
Ferrajoli, Luigi. 2007. *Principia iuris. Teoria del diritto e della democrazia, 2. Teoria della democrazia*. Roma-Bari: Laterza.
Ferrajoli, Luigi. 2008. *Diritti fondamentali. Un debatito teorico*. Roma-Bari: Laterza.
Finnis, John. 2011. *Natural law and natural rights*, 2nd ed. Oxford: Oxford University Press.
Frankfurt, Harry. 1987. Equality as a moral ideal. *Ethics* 98 (1): 21–43.
Frankfurt, Harry. 1988. Necessity and desire (1984). In *The importance of what we care about*, 104-116. Cambridge: Cambridge University Press.
Frankfurt, Harry. 2005. *On inequality*. Princeton, N. J.: Princeton University Press.
Fraser, Nancy. 2003. Social justice in the age of identity politics: Redistribution, recognition, and participation. In *Redistribution or recognition? A political-philosophical exchange*, Nancy Fraser and Axel Honneth, pp. 7–109. London: Verso.
Fraser, Nancy. 2008. *Scales of justice. Reimagining political space in a globalizing world*. New York: Columbia University Press.
Gilligan, Carol. 1982. *In a different voice: psychological theory and women's development*. Cambridge, Mass.: Harvard University Press.
Gracia, Diego. 1998. Historia de los conceptos de salud y enfermedad. In *Bioética clínica*, 19–31, Santa Fe de Bogotá: El Búho.
Habermas, Jürgen. 1997. *Between facts and norms. Contributions to a discourse theory of law and democracy* (1992). Cambridge: Polity.
Hayden, Patrick. 2012. The human right to health and the struggle for recognition. *Review of International Studies* 38: 569–588.
Held, Virginia. 2006. *The ethics of care: Personal, political, and global*. New York: Oxford University Press.

Holmes, Stephen, and Sunstein, Cass. R. 1999. *The cost of rights: why liberty depends on taxes*. New York-London: Norton.
Honneth, Axel. 1996. *The struggle for recognition. The moral grammar of social conflicts* (1992) (transl. J. Anderson). Cambridge, Mass.: The MIT Press.
Honneth, Axel. 2003. Redistribution as recognition: A response to Nancy Fraser. In *Redistribution or recognition? A political-philosophical exchange*, Nancy Fraser and Axel Honneth, 10–197. London: Verso.
Honneth, Axel. 2007a. *Reification: A Recognition-Theoretical View (2005)*. Oxford-New York: Oxford University Press.
Honneth, Axel. 2007b. *Disrespect: the normative foundations of critical theory*. Cambridge: Polity Press.
Huber, Machteld, et al. 2011. How should we define health. *British Medical Journal* 343: 235–237.
Ikäheimo, H., and Laitinen, A. 2009. Analyzing recognition: Identification, acknowledgement and recognitive attitudes towards persons. In *Recognition and Power. Axel Honneth and the tradition of the critical social theory*, ed. B. van den Brink, D. Owen, pp. 33–56. Cambridge: Cambridge University Press.
Kelsen, Hans. 1960. *Reine Rechtslehre*, 2nd ed. Wien: Deuticke.
Leonardi, Fabio. 2018. The definition of health: towards new perspectives. *International Journal of Health Services* 48: 735–748.
MacIntyre, Alasdair. 1999. *Dependent rational animals: why human beings need the virtues*. London: Duckworth.
Nielsen, Lasse, and David V. Axelsen. 2017. Capabilitarian sufficiency: capabilities and social justice. *Journal of Human Development and Capabilities* 18 (1): 46–59.
Nussbaum, Martha C. 1986. *The fragility of goodness. Luck and ethics in Greek tragedy and philosophy*. Cambridge, Mass.: Cambridge University Press.
Nussbaum, Martha C. 2001. *Upheavals of thought. The intelligence of emotions*. Cambridge, Mass.: Cambridge University Press.
Nussbaum, Martha C. 2006. *Frontiers of justice: disability, nationality, species membership*. Cambridge, Mass.-London: Belknap Press.
Nussbaum, Martha C. 2011a. *Creating capabilities: the human development approach*. Cambridge, Mass.-London: Belknap Press.
Nussbaum, Martha C. 2011b. Capabilities, entitlements, rights: supplementation and critique. *Journal of Human Development and Capabilities* 12 (1): 23–37.
Pan American Health Organization. 2019. *Just societies: Health equity and dignified lives*. https://iris.paho.org/handle/10665.2/51571.
Pernice, Ingolf. 2006. The global dimension of multilevel constitutionalism. A legal response to challenges of globalisation. In *Völkerrecht als Weltordnung/Common values in International Law. Festscshrift für Christian Tomuschat*, ed. P. M. Dupuy, B. Fassbender, M. N. Shaw, K. P. Sommermann, pp. 973–1006. Kehl am Rhein: N. P. Engel Verlag.
Peter, Fabianne. 2001. Health equity and social justice. *Journal of Applied Philosophy* 18 (2): 159–170.
Powers, Madison & Faden, Ruth. 2006. *Social justice. The moral foundations of public health and health policy*. New York: Oxford University Press.
Preda, Adina, and Kristin Voigt. 2015. The social determinants of health: why should we care. *American Journal of Bioethics* 15 (3): 25–36.
Rawls, John. 1971. *A theory of justice*. Cambridge, Mass.: Belknap Press.
Rawls, John. 1993. *Political liberalism*. New York: Columbia University Press.
Reader, Soran. 2006. Does a basic needs approach need capabilities? *The Journal of Political Philosophy* 14 (3): 337–350.
Richardson, Henry S. 2016. Capabilities and the definition of health: comments on Venkatapuram. *Bioethics* 30 (1): 1–7.
Ricoeur, Paul. 2005. *The course of recognition* (2004) (transl. D. Pellauer). Cambridge, Mass.: Harvard University Press.

Rid, Anette. 2017. Sufficiency, health, and health care justice. The state of the debate. In *What is enough? Sufficiency, justice, and health*, ed. Carina Fourie, Anette Rid, pp. 30–47. Oxford: Oxford University Press.
Ruger, Jennifer Prah. 2010. *Health and social justice*. Oxford-New York: Oxford University Press.
Selgelid, Michael J. 2016. Capabilities and incapabilities of the capabilites approach to health justice. *Bioethics* 30 (1): 25–33.
Sen, Amartya. 2001. *Development as freedom*, 2nd ed. Oxford-New York: Oxford University Press.
Sen, Amartya. 2009. *The idea of justice*. Cambridge, Mass.: Harvard University Press.
Seoane, José-Antonio. 2019. Health justice & rights. notizie di POLITEIA XXXV/133: 30–42.
Shue, Henry. 1996. *Basic rights: subsistence, affluence, and US foreign policy*, 2nd ed. Princeton: Princeton University Press.
Taylor, Charles. 1989. *Sources of the self: the making of the modern identity*. Cambridge, Mass.: Harvard University Press.
Taylor, Charles. 1994. The politics of recognition (1992). In *Multiculturalism. Examining the politics of recognition*, ed. Amy Gutmann, pp. 25–73. Princeton, NJ: Princeton University Press.
Tengland, Per-Anders. 2016. Venkatapuram's capability theory of health: a critical discussion. *Bioethics* 30 (1): 8–18.
Tronto, Joan C. 2013. *Caring democracy. Markets, equality, and justice*. New York: New York University Press.
United Nations High Commissioner for Human Rights–World Health Organization. 2008. *The right to health*. Fact Sheet No 31. Geneva: United Nations.
Venkatapuram, Sridhar. 2011. *Health justice. An argument from the capabilities approach*. London: Polity.
Vizard, Polly. 2021. The capability approach and human rights. In *The Cambridge handbook of the capability approach*, ed. Enrica Chiappero-Martinetti, Siddiqur Osmani, and Mazaffar Qizilbash, 624–642. Cambridge: Cambridge University Press.
Walzer, Michael. 1983. *Spheres of justice. A defense of pluralism and equality*. New York: Basic Books.
Wiggins, David. 1998. Claims of need. In *Needs, values, truth. Essays in the philosophy of value*, 3rd edition, pp. 1–57. Oxford: Oxford University Press.
Wilkinson, Richard, and Pickett, Kate. 2010. *The spirit level. Why greater equality makes societies stronger* (2009). New York: Bloomsbury.
Wolff, Jonathan. 2011. *Ethics and public policy. A philosophical inquiry*. London: Routledge.
Wolff, Jonathan. 2012. *The human right to health*. New York: Norton.
Wolff, Jonathan, and de-Shalit, Avner. 2007. *Disadvantage*. Oxford: Oxford University Press.
World Health Organization. 1946. *The World Health Organization's Constitution*. Geneva: World Health Organization. https://www.who.int/about/accountability/governance/constitution.
World Health Organization. 2001. *International Classification of Functioning, Disability and Health (ICF)*. Geneva: World Health Organization. https://www.who.int/classifications/international-classification-of-functioning-disability-and-health.
World Health Organization-Commission on Social Determinants of Health. 2009. *Closing the gap in a generation: Health equity through action on the social determinants of health (final report)*. Geneva: World Health Organization. https://www.who.int/publications/i/item/WHO-IER-CSDH-08.1.
Young, Iris Marion. 1990. *Justice and the politics of difference*. Princeton, N. J.: Princeton University Press.
Young, Iris Marion. 2011. *Responsibility for justice*. New York: Oxford University Press.

Open Access This chapter is licensed under the terms of the Creative Commons Attribution 4.0 International License (http://creativecommons.org/licenses/by/4.0/), which permits use, sharing, adaptation, distribution and reproduction in any medium or format, as long as you give appropriate credit to the original author(s) and the source, provide a link to the Creative Commons license and indicate if changes were made.

The images or other third party material in this chapter are included in the chapter's Creative Commons license, unless indicated otherwise in a credit line to the material. If material is not included in the chapter's Creative Commons license and your intended use is not permitted by statutory regulation or exceeds the permitted use, you will need to obtain permission directly from the copyright holder.

Chapter 2
On the Possibility of a Bioethics Based on Fundamental Rights

Tomás de Domingo Pérez

Abstract This work defends the possibility of a bioethics based on fundamental rights as an alternative to principlism. To do this, it is necessary to have a theory of fundamental rights in which these do not allow themselves to be harmed or restricted through the principle of proportionality, which is the dominant conception today. The delimitation of the content of each fundamental right and the regulation of its exercise in the real framework that contextualizes it constitute the most relevant tasks when it comes to solving practical problems in which fundamental rights are present. The chapter pays particular attention to the fundamental right to physical integrity within the framework of the Spanish constitutional system to show what the approach to a fundamental rights-based bioethics should be.

Keywords Fundamental rights · Neoconstitutionalism · Principle of proportionality · Right to physical integrity · Inalienability of fundamental rights · Regulation of the exercise of fundamental rights

2.1 Introduction

Among the main difficulties to giving a satisfactory answer to a large number of bioethical problems is moral pluralism, that is, the existence in a society of different conceptions of good or right, as well as different ways of establishing it generally or in relation to specific cases. Certainly, as Beauchamp and Childress point out, on these differences it is possible to identify norms that are examples of a common morality. Principlism itself, with the principles of autonomy, beneficence, non-maleficence and justice, which these authors advocate and which constitutes the dominant theoretical model in contemporary bioethics, is presented as an example of this (Beauchamp and Childress 2009, 2–5). However, the principlist model has been the object of numerous criticisms, for, among other reasons, the insufficient justification of its

T. de Domingo Pérez (✉)
Universidad Miguel Hernández, Elche, Spain
e-mail: t.domingo@umh.es

© The Editor(s) (if applicable) and The Author(s), under exclusive license to Springer Nature Switzerland AG 2024

J.-A. Seoane and O. Vergara (eds.), *The Discourse of Biorights*, The International Library of Bioethics 109, https://doi.org/10.1007/978-3-031-66804-3_2

principles and the so-called "intuitionist drift" to which it can lead (García Llerena 2012; Vergara Lacalle 2018, 16–28). One of the proposed alternatives is the recognition of human rights or fundamental rights -insofar as they are incorporated into national constitutions- as a basis for what has come to be called a fundamental rights-based biolaw.[1] Fundamental rights would constitute a "common morality", and they will not only determine the forbidden, but, as García Llerena points out, could even guide clinical decision making (Cf. García Llerena 2012, 197–222).

I would like to dedicate these pages to argue that an basic law bioethics can only be sustained solidly from a theory of fundamental rights that is based on the defence of its central position of these rights being an axiological foundation of the political community and, therefore, does not admit the possibility of its restriction through the use of the principle of proportionality. In my opinion only thus can fundamental rights be presented as a "common morality" capable of overcoming moral pluralism and offering practical guidelines for the regulation that corresponds to the legislator, as well as for practical-prudential decisions that constitute the last link in the process of realisation of the law. To avoid my reflections being excessively abstract, I will argue from the Spanish constitutional system of fundamental rights and take into account the fundamental right to physical integrity, which is so important to bioethical problems.

2.2 The Difficulty of a Fundamental Rights-Based Bioethics in the Current Context Presided by the Principle of Proportionality

The Constitutional State of Law that emerged from World War II places fundamental rights in a central position as the core of the common good and material pillar of the legal system (Cf. Häberle 2003, 7–11). The public authorities must not only refrain from injuring or restricting them, but they are "bound" by them, which translates into positive action aimed at making their respect and enjoyment effective. The guarantee of the essential content of the fundamental rights recognised in art. 53.1 of the Spanish constitution thus acquires a systemic importance, given that it marks a limit for the legislator -and for all public powers (Cf. Martínez-Pujalte 1997, 99–105)- making possible the basic idea of constitutionalism: the effective limitation of political power as regards respect for the fundamental rights of the person (Cf. Aragón 2007, 34; Pereira Menaut 2003, 27). Therefore, it makes sense, regardless of whether it is a more or less fortunate expression, that the term "neoconstitutionalism" be used to refer to the changes introduced by the Constitutional State of Law.

To the extent that fundamental rights are considered as something valuable or good, they constitute a point of connection between morality and law based on the

[1] . To the extent that bioethical problems imply a way of ordering coexistence, their legal relevance is pointed out and this explains why the term "biolaw" is preferred. About this denomination, cf. Ollero (2006), 15–23 and Aparisi (2007), 63–84.

legal system. Placing them as the axiological foundation of coexistence, the core of the justice to which any other collective good is subordinated, may be considered correct or not, but allows for moral assessments and guides legal practice according to a criterion that, in principle, is clearly established. However, this approach has been deeply altered by the irruption of the proportionality principle and this makes the possibility of an basic law bioethics considerably more difficult, as I will try to show below.

Neoconstitutionalism arises with the aim of avoiding supposed collective or individual goods without rank of fundamental right being wielded as valid reasons to injure or to restrict fundamental rights. All this implies a substantive theory of justice in which any rule or behaviour that attacks them is rejected as unjust. It is intended, therefore, to avoid the risk of relativisation of fundamental rights, even if this comes from the democratic legislature. Respect for the guarantee of the essential content of fundamental rights should be interpreted -if we want to be coherent with this conception- as an armour that the nation in its Constitution has used to grant rights to short-lived democratic majorities that aspire to introduce restrictions. However, the Constitutional Court and most scholars have rejected this conception and it supports the possibility that fundamental rights are restricted or injured on certain occasions for very qualified reasons. This idea, which is summarised by the Constitutional Court defending that there are no absolute or unlimited rights, seems to open the door to a consideration of all the circumstances of the cases without apriorisms of any kind. In this way, the legislature can adopt or allow the restriction of a fundamental right if it is adequate to achieve a constitutionally relevant good; if necessary, insofar as the injury or restriction of the fundamental right is deemed inevitable; and if it is proportional in the strict sense, which implies weighing -this subprinciple is known as "balancing"- whether the damage to the fundamental right is compensated by the benefits that the protection of the good in question entails.[2] The application of the principle of proportionality, as is well known, consists in the examination of these requirements.

If the restriction of fundamental rights is allowed, its axiological hierarchy, that is, its central position as core of the common good, is affected and it must be accepted that there may be good reasons to sacrifice what had been considered most valuable. It is true that such restrictions can be justified in light of very specific circumstances

[2]. García Amado (García Amado 2021, 62) is very critical of the assessment and also considers that going down this path means relativising fundamental rights. García Amado takes a position against balancing because he believes that, that way, it will always be possible to find arguments capable of justifying the injury to or restriction of fundamental rights. Perhaps Atienza (Atienza 2021, 79–100) is right when he states, following Alexy, that not every consideration that results in the injury of a fundamental right is rationally admissible. Hence, the main hermeneutical task consists of delimiting the content of the rights as a prior step to the study of when they have been legitimately exercised. And here the question can be raised of whether to limit the content of rights it is necessary to weigh, which is the position that Atienza seems to defend. However, this interpretation is hasty, because when this author states that to interpret the "essential content" of a right "I do not see how it can be done without balancing" p. 91), in reality I think he is referring to the problem of determining whether a right has been exercised legitimately, which is certainly an operation that requires evaluations that can lead to confusion with balancing.

that the law should take into consideration due to its practical-prudential nature. However, the possibility of a fundamental rights-based bioethics is blurred to the extent that the protection provided by fundamental rights becomes a "prima facie" protection, as is clearly seen in Alexy's theory of fundamental rights (Cf. Alexy 1997, 267–329).

The principle of proportionality involves the substitution within the framework of the Constitutional State of Law of a substantive theory of justice based on the absolute respect for fundamental rights by a procedural theory in which fundamental rights can be restricted, or not, according to how the circumstances of the case are assessed. This opens the door to an argumentative procedure in which, according to the circumstances, priorities can be established subject to review in conflictive situations. Paying attention to all the circumstances of each case must be valued positively (cf. Vergara 2014, 307–333). Nevertheless, it is necessary to be aware of the implications of the theory of fundamental rights that underlies this conception. The "prima facie" protection of fundamental rights is settled with a requirement of argumentation that does not prevent its restriction. Perhaps one of the cases that illustrates this conception most clearly is STC 215/1994, of 14 July. The Constitutional Court here examined a question of constitutionality raised by a judge that had to resolve the claim of the parents of a daughter with Down syndrome to proceed with her sterilisation in accordance with the provisions of the second paragraph of art. 428 of the old Penal Code. The judge raised the question because he considered that this precept was incompatible with the fundamental right to physical integrity (Article 15 CE), which was unequivocally admitted by the Constitutional Court. The Constitutional Court did not question whether the measure restricted the fundamental right. However, for the Constitutional Court the core of the question was to investigate whether the "self-determination" that was granted to able people could be extended to the mentally disabled. The Constitutional Court sought to ensure that a "good" enjoyed by the people who can give their consent extends to those who cannot provide it, and insists that the impossibility of supplying consent in the case of the mentally disabled would cause them serious harm: "But such objection [the impossibility of supplying the consent of the mentally disabled], which would exclude the incapable of an option that is granted to capable people, is unacceptable because, taken to its logical conclusion, it would lead to rejecting any medical treatment and, above all, to an ablatory surgical intervention essential for life or simply beneficial to the health of the seriously mentally deficient "(Legal basis 4).

Apart from the questionable interpretation of the right to physical integrity made by the Constitutional Court, an evident conclusion that should be noted from its argument: preserving the physical integrity of the mentally disabled is considered worse than sterilising them.[3] In other words, respecting a fundamental right that,

---

[3] . This positive assessment contrasts with the rejection of this practice that has finally led to its complete prohibition through law 2/2020, of December 16, which has deleted the second paragraph of art. 156 CP. The reform of the Penal Code of 2015 carried out by Law 1/2015, of March 30, already represented a notable restriction of it, but this Statute takes into account the International Convention on the Rights of Persons with Disabilities of 2006, and eradicates it completely, as was suggested by some authors since the 2015 reform itself (Martínez-Pujalte, 2015, 65–82). In the

in coherence with the basis of the Constitutional State of Law, should be seen as a matter of principle, the Constitutional Court gives a solution that depends on the weighting of the various goods at stake, one of which is the fundamental right. This way, in my opinion, prevents the fundamental rights representing an orientation for solving bioethical problems to the extent that their strength depends on the criteria that at any moment are established by the legislature.[4] Indeed, from the moment at which the possibility of restricting fundamental rights is admitted in accordance with the requirements of the principle of proportionality, the position of the Constitutional Court as guarantor of rights is clearly affected. It is true that the Constitutional Court can review the decision of the legislature and determine if a restrictive measure is justified or if, on the contrary, there is a disproportionate sacrifice of the right. But then, why should the assessment of the Constitutional Court be imposed on the legislature when it comes to deciding the opportunity to introduce restrictions that the Constitution has not banned, given that the legislative has the democratic backing of "current" citizens, who may also have chosen their representatives to promote these restrictive policies? In my opinion, if you want to be faithful to the original values on which the Constitutional State of Law is based, the Constitutional Court can only have real meaning as the ultimate guarantor of fundamental rights, because to respect and to protect them is considered a value to preserve beyond the conjunctural will of the political representatives of the citizens.[5] But what is interesting here is that a fundamental rights-based bioethics is only possible if fundamental rights are presented as an insurmountable barrier, as a matter of principle whose respect marks a limit, on the one hand, and an orientation, on the other, at the time of addressing bioethical problems and, in particular, examining legislation. However, as often happens when a person or a group courageously defend some values, fear may give rise to taking dogmatic positions in their defence alien to the necessary prudence demanded by practical problems. In this sense, it can give the impression that the solution proper to the "balancing" that introduces the principle of proportionality -and that is observed in STC 215/1994- represents a legal conception inspired by a consequentialist utilitarian moral; For its part, the defence of the right to physical integrity as a matter of principle would seem to come from a non-consequentialist moral conception typical of Kantian deontologism. This impression is not correct, at least regarding the requirement of respect for fundamental rights that I believe it is necessary to claim. In my opinion, it is possible to combine the defence of the central position of the fundamental rights recognised and granted in the Constitutional State

preamble to the law, reference is made to the serious anomaly in terms of respect for human rights that this practice entails.

4 . STC 19/2023, of March 22, which resolves the unconstitutionality appeal presented by the Vox parliamentary group in the Congress of Deputies against Organic Law 3/2021, of March 24, which regulates euthanasia, constitutes a very clear example of what I am pointing out.

5 . This is the core of the debate that was held within the Constitutional Court in STC 198/2012, of November 6, and which in my opinion is far from being closed. On the occasion of the examination of whether there is a constitutional concept of marriage, the magistrates openly disagreed on the margin of constitutional interpretation available to the legislature and on the role that the Constitutional Court itself should play.

of Law and the prudence required by practical problems, especially those related to bioethics. This is the path that a fundamental rights-based bioethics must aspire to constitute as a viable alternative to principlism. In what follows I will try to establish what could be the keys of a theory of fundamental rights that allows this objective to be achieved and I will examine again the right to physical integrity from this perspective.

2.3 Keys to a Fundamental Rights-Based Bioethics Possible in the Light of the Right to Physical Integrity

Fundamental rights have limits, but, consistent with the guarantee of their essential content, if we want to preserve their axiological position, we must maintain that they can not be injured or restricted as long as they are exercised legitimately. Therefore, two tasks can be identified that must be conveniently specified. On the one hand, the delimitation of the content of fundamental rights and, once this question is clarified, the determination of how to establish that a right has been legitimately exercised.

2.3.1 The Delimitation of the Content of the Fundamental Right to Physical Integrity

The claim that fundamental rights have limits means that each fundamental right protects a certain legal good, usually a sphere of personality and/or human activity. Constitutional texts tend to recognize fundamental rights without including excessive detail regarding their contents, and public authorities, especially the legislative, play an essential role in delimiting them. In order to develop it, the data provided by the Constitution itself must be taken into account, both those that derive from the literal tenor of the precepts in which each fundamental right is explicitly recognised and those deriving from a systematic interpretation of the Constitution. From there, the delimitation of the content opens many interpretative possibilities about the human person, which undoubtedly constitutes the ontological reference of law, becomes very important. It is difficult to understand the content of some fundamental rights without an anthropological investigation (Cf. Marías 1983, 9–13, 71–78).[6] At this point we cannot aspire to univocal responses, to demonstrations typical of the exact sciences, but this should not lead to sterile scepticism, but to trust in the capacity of human reason to find plausible arguments. As Ollero rightly states, "a right can only be delimited based on an implicit theory of justice, capable of ruling when our

[6]. In the search for this ontological referent it has been usual to appeal to the notion of human nature. In any case, without needing to refer to "human nature", Ortega's analytical theory of human life discovers a structure necessary to analyze any human life, and within that analytical structure we can find what Marías has called the "empirical structure" of human life.

relationships with others can or cannot be considered adjusted. This explains the controversial nature of establishing its scope" (Ollero 2006, 119). In this delimiting task, in which practical reason makes sense, the Constitutional Court has the last word in assessing whether the legislator's interpretation is adequate or, on the contrary, improperly restricts the fundamental right. Bearing in mind what has just been said, I will reexamine the fundamental right to physical integrity in order to criticise the approach of the Constitutional Court in STC 215/1994 and to show how the problems could be approached and solutions found from a bioethics oriented on a theory of fundamental rights committed to its defence against possible restrictions.

An examination of this right from a teleological perspective makes it possible to disagree with the interpretation made by the Constitutional Court in STC 215/1994. On the one hand, we must bear in mind the literal wording of the precept that relates to this right to "maintain the integrity of the body, or, in other words, the right to preserve, in the face of interference from others, the totality of the bodily functions and organs and the external body appearance" (Martínez-Pujalte 2011, 169). This is an interpretation that coincides with the position maintained by the Constitutional Court in STC 207/1996, of December 16, in which it is defined as "the right of the person to corporal safety, that is, his right to not suffer injury or damages in his body or external appearance without his consent" (FJ 2). But, on the other hand, the literal interpretation must be complemented with a teleological inquiry if one does not wish to incur a "literalism" that leads to absurd conclusions. Indeed, in STC 215/1994, the Constitutional Court makes an argument that allows the conclusion that, if the consent of the mentally disabled were not replaced, they would be deprived of any medical intervention aimed at preserving their health. It is observed that the Court does not appreciate a difference between an intervention aimed at sterilising a person and another whose purpose, for example, is to cure a cancer. Undoubtedly, there may be situations in which it is debatable whether a measure is truly therapeutic, but the discrepancies in this area arise after the distinction between an intervention aimed at improving the body or protecting health or even life itself, and one that has nothing to do with this. In this sense, sterilisation may try to justify itself for various reasons, but there is no doubt that it violates physical integrity by depriving the person of one of his or her essential physical abilities.[7] On the other hand, curing a mentally disabled person of cancer not only does not mean an injury to their right to physical integrity, but quite the opposite. The teleological perspective allows us to understand the differences between these situations. But to finish delimiting this right properly, it is necessary to clarify the role played by consent in relation to interventions on one's own body.

To finish adequately delimiting this right, it is important to clarify the role that consent plays in relation to interventions on one's own body (Cf. Ortiz Fernández 2021). This is a question that has gained renewed importance in view of the arguments developed by the Constitutional Court in STC 19/2023 to specify the scope of the fundamental right to life, since the constitutionality of euthanasia has been justified,

---

[7]. For that reason art. 149.1 CP punishes as a crime of injury anyone who by any means or procedure causes "impotence, sterility..." to a penalty of between six and twelve years in prison.

among other reasons, due to the existence of a supposed right to "self-determination" that at first appeared linked to the fundamental right to physical integrity.[8]

In normal situations the intervention on the body can be rejected or allowed by its passive subject. Now, this does not mean that each person has an absolute capacity of decision over their body. If this were the case, the restrictive measures of organ trade could not be justified, nor would it make sense to punish freely consensual injuries inflicted by a third party. Neither the literal nor the teleological perspective allow the understanding of the right to physical integrity as a right to disposition over one's own body (Martínez-Pujalte 2011, 170 and ss). However, this does not mean that the right holder does not have the freedom to refuse medical treatment, even if it is appropriate according to the medical criteria to achieve the cure, without having to give religious or ideological reasons. Informed consent is part of the content of the right to physical integrity as established by STC 37/2011, of March 28: "The patient's consent to any intervention on their person is something inherent, among others, to their fundamental right to physical integrity, to the power that this implies to prevent any non-consensual intervention on one's own body, which cannot be unjustifiably limited as a consequence of a situation of illness. It is a faculty of self-determination that legitimises the patient, in the use of their freedom of will, to freely decide on therapeutic measures and treatments that may affect their integrity, choosing between the various possibilities, consenting to their practice or rejecting them" (legal basis 5). The opinion of the Court is complemented by the reference to the fact that the consent can only be exercised, in one way or another, if there is adequate medical information about the therapeutic measures, which is a guarantee for the effectiveness of the principle of freedom of the patient's will. On the other hand, it is interesting to point out -for what will be said later- that the Constitutional Court also admits in relation to this dimension of the right to physical integrity, the possibility of introducing duly justified restrictions, in line with the dominant theory of fundamental rights.

When the aim is to cure or prevent diseases by intervening on the body, physical integrity is favoured, but the consent of the affected person must be obtained. However, I consider it an unjustified leap in argument to understand that the right to physical integrity (and, much more so, the right to life) recognises as such a right to individual "self-determination". In my opinion, if the will of the person who refuses medical treatment is not respected, the intervention could be interpreted as degrading treatment prohibited by art. 15 of the Spanish constitution. Therefore, in the case of people with a disability, to the argument that attacking physical integrity is not the same as curing, we should add the importance of accompanying them in order to obtain their consent to any treatment along the lines set out by the reform of the Civil Code introduced by Statute 8/2021, of June 2, without forgetting that the impossibility of providing consent must not be confused with an explicit rejection of it. In the first case it seems clear that bodily interventions aimed at curing or protecting the health

[8]. The connection between the justification of the constitutionality of euthanasia and the right to self-determination has been explicitly recognised by the Constitutional Court in STC 38/2023, of April 20, point 4.

of the patient would be fully justified,[9] while it would be doubtful in the second case, since it would be necessary to examine whether this rejection is motivated by the impossibility of understanding the meaning of the therapeutic measure, in which case forced intervention would in no way constitute degrading or humiliating treatment.

If the intervention is not aimed at preserving health, in my opinion, the absence of consent forbids it completely and, consequently, sterilisation -to refer to the case of STC 215/1994- of mentally disabled people represents an injury to the right to physical integrity proscribed by the Constitution. This conclusion is not altered by the fact that consented sterilisation is lawful conduct. Purely, it is a decriminalised behaviour that is tolerated, as can be seen from a joint reading of arts. 149.1 and 156 of the current Penal Code. This nuance is important, since it underlines that the legislator renounces punishing it as an exception to the general rule that marks the irrelevance of consent to injuries inflicted by third parties. The violation of the right to physical integrity does not necessarily imply that "it is possible to claim the criminalisation of voluntary sterilisation, since not every violation of a fundamental right must necessarily be constitutive of crime" (Martínez-Pujalte 2011, 172). There may be situations in which it is considered that certain personal interests weigh on the individual in such a way that the possibility of injurious solutions to a fundamental right are not criminally opposed by the legislature. The issue takes on a different aspect and is open to debate from the moment such interventions are paid for by the National Health System,[10] and pathologies that affect health are not included.

I have pointed out that in the absence of an explicit refusal on the part of the patient, the measures aimed at preserving health and, therefore, life can not only be justified, but imposed from the perspective of a fundamental rights-based bioethics that respects fundamental rights.[11] Nevertheless, very complex situations can arise, largely due to advances in medicine. Is keeping a person in an irreversible coma with serious brain damage alive healing? And, on the other hand, what are the right means to keep a person alive? These two questions are enough in themselves to show some

[9] . In STC 38/2023, of April 20, the Court admitted the legality of the COVID vaccination of an Alzheimer's patient against the will of her son, at the time her legal representative, using as the main argument that, in the absence of the possibility of obtaining the consent of the affected person, "the mission of the person called to provide support is not to replace the convictions of the person with disabilities with their own but to ensure respect for the «will, desires and preferences of that person». Beyond this vicarious action, as spokesperson for the wishes of the affected person, the decision-making capacity of the person providing support is limited to the search for the realisation of the interest of the affected person, which must respond, as has already been said, to objective criteria that are fully auditable by the judicial authority" (legal basis 6). Subsequently, the benefit of vaccination to the patient's health is justified, concluding that vaccination did not represent an injury to her fundamental right to physical integrity.

[10] . RD 1010/2006, of September 15, which establishes the portfolio of common services of the National Health System and the procedure for its updating. Within point 5.3.7 dedicated to "Family planning", point 5.3.7.3 includes the "realisation of tubal ligations and vasectomies".

[11] . The Statute 41/2002, of November 14, allows in art. 9.2 b) the intervention "when there is a serious immediate risk to the physical or mental integrity of the patient and it is not possible to obtain their authorisation, consulting, when circumstances permit, their relatives or the persons linked in fact to them".

of the problems that can arise here and in which I can not stop with the attention that the question requires. Basic law bioethics should be guided by the respect for human life, which should be extreme in the case of the most vulnerable people. If these people had anticipated possible future situations in which they would reject certain therapeutic measures, the right to physical integrity would force respecting their will.[12] In the absence of manifestations one way or the other, this type of situation can be interpreted in different ways, but the recognition and defence of the right to life can only lead to caring for them and to dedicating the necessary public resources to it. However, when, to keep a person alive, it is necessary to use artificial means with no hope of improving their situation, the situation causes them unbearable pain, or the patient has entered into a situation of agony that makes implies their near future death -to mention some of the many situations that may arise- the principle of dignity may advise limiting the therapeutic effort so as not to reach what is called therapeutic obstinacy or in dysthanasia. The difference between some situations and others requires an examination of the cases from a teleological perspective. In those cases in which one must decide whether to artificially prolong life or not -regardless of the difficulty involved in determining when these cases exist- the requirement of respect for the right to life and to physical integrity does not lead to doing everything possible to keep a person alive using any means, since it is necessary to insist that death does not imply "per se" an injury to the right to life, but that it is a part of life itself (cf. SPAEMANN 2007, 114–116).[13] Therefore, in my opinion, in these cases the will to limit the therapeutic effort could be decided by a representative of the patient or even by the doctors who attend them without it being interpreted as an injury to the right to physical integrity or to the right to life of the patient who is in that state.[14]

2.3.2 The Restrictions on and the Problem of the Legitimate Exercise of Fundamental Rights

The study of the right to physical integrity has made it possible to differentiate interventions aimed at preserving health from those that do not meet that end. On the other hand, it has become clear that the rejection of a treatment does not contravene

---

[12]. The Statutes that since 2010 have been approved in various autonomous regions of Spain regulating the rights of the persons in the process of death try to guarantee respect for the will of those who are in such a situation.

[13]. This author emphasises that prolonging life at any price is leading to more and more people who have to die without ever having seen a dying person, which is something unnatural that causes a "great fear of death" (p. 115). It is important to let people die in a dignified way, because "when dying is no longer understood or assumed as a part of living, then the culture of death opens up" (p 116).

[14]. Given this possibility, it is important to exercise caution to avoid abusing the most vulnerable people, as was observed by the European Court of Human Rights in the case of *Pretty v. United Kingdom*, of April 29, 2002.

the right to physical integrity, and that neither respect for this right nor the right to life necessarily leads to using all the means that scientific advances offer to preserve biological life These conclusions are reached through a teleological interpretation of this right. To show finally that a fundamental rights-based bioethics requires reinforcing the idea that fundamental rights do not admit restrictions, it is convenient to return to the thesis that there are no unlimited rights and that, therefore, the refusal of a treatment or intervention must be respected unless other constitutionally relevant interests overrule it, as stated in STC 37/2011. It is evident that we are faced with the possibility of resorting to the principle of proportionality to introduce restrictive measures. In principle, it is possible to think of situations in which you have to intervene on someone´s body against their will. This is foreseen, for example, by Spanish statute 41/2002 art. 9.2 a), which authorises physicians to intervene in favour of the health of a patient without having their consent -it can be inferred that even with their opposition- "when there is a risk to public health for health reasons established by Law. In all cases, once the pertinent measures have been adopted, in accordance with the provisions of Organic Law 3/1986, they shall be communicated to the judicial authority within a maximum period of 24 h, provided that they provide for the mandatory placement of persons". It seems that the legislature is thinking about the hypothesis of an epidemic situation with serious risk to public health.[15]

The COVID pandemic has required careful thought about the justification for mandatory vaccination. In the case of Spain, as is known, a voluntary vaccination strategy was chosen, but the European Court of Human Rights has admitted the possibility of mandatory vaccination as long as there is legal authorisation, a legitimate purpose, and the need for intervention (STEDH, Vavřička and others v. the Czech Republic, April 8, 2021, cited in STC 38/2023, point 4). Undoubtedly, the threats that epidemics pose to public health allow us to imagine situations in which resorting to mandatory vaccination is considered. However, as the Constitutional Court itself points out, "the legal treatment of vaccination is more complex than suggested by the dilemma posed by the appellant between a legal regime of 'mandatory' and another of 'voluntariness', since there are intermediate legal systems, such as the recommendation by the public authority of certain vaccines considered essential, which are incorporated into an official calendar and on which the consequent benefit activity is developed (this system in which the so-called nudging or spur techniques are currently incorporated), or the conversion of vaccination into a necessary condition to obtain a benefit or service or to carry out a certain activity (a modality that can be considered as a system of 'indirect obligation')" (STC 38/2023, point 5). Therefore, we can imagine an extreme situation in which, should mandatory vaccination be necessary it would not even be enough to confine people who refuse to be vaccinated and they must be intervened on. It is difficult to think of a similar situation, since it

[15] . In accordance with the provisions of art. 9.2 a) of Statute 41/2002, mandatory vaccination in the event of an epidemic would be justified, while the same would not happen if the risk to public health were potential. In this regard, cf. Bioethics Committee of Spain, "Ethical-legal issues of vaccine rejection and proposals for a necessary debate", at http://assets.comitedebioetica.es/files/documentacion/es/cues-etico-legales-rechazo-vacunas-proposals-debate-necessary.pdf, pp. 20–23 (last consulted September 19, 2023).

has not even occurred with the COVID pandemic, but it is worth asking whether in these cases we would be facing a justified injury to the fundamental right to physical integrity. In order to give a response to this question, it is necessary to introduce clarifications related to the theory of fundamental rights.

Facing a contagious disease, medicine must try to cure the patient and, within the framework of policies aimed at preserving public health, prevent the disease from spreading and affecting other people. Vaccination of the population may be an essential measure to prevent the spread of the disease, or the need for the measure may be discussed. To dispel these doubts, it would be necessary to analyse different extremes, including whether the measure is adequate, necessary and proportional in the strict sense. It gives the impression that the argumentative channels of the principle of proportionality are imposed; However, this situation presents the peculiarity that it is a factual reality which prevents the full enjoyment of a fundamental right.

I will better illustrate the problem posed by these "factual" situations through other examples. Rodríguez-Toubes uses the case of two castaways who compete for a single lifeguard to show that conflicts between fundamental rights are inevitable. According to him, "both have an equal right to life, and to fight to defend it even if doing so endangers the life of the other. There is a conflict of rights, which in no way is only apparent" (Rodríguez-Toubes 2000, 150). Undoubtedly, both have the right to life and, therefore, neither has the right to kill the other, although if someone did it would be impossible not to appreciate a state of necessity that would exempt him from criminal responsibility. Now, imagine that their degree of civilization is such that they give up fighting to climb a piece of wood—as in the movie Titanic—that only one of them can sustain and that, finally, the forces fail and one of the two dies. In my opinion, there is no conflict between rights, but a factual situation that prevents both living due to a lack of means.

Another factual impossibility -although of another nature[16]- can be observed in the event that a Seventh-day Adventist working in a factory requests rest on Saturday and, after the appropriate study of the petition, the employer finds that for the productive process it is essential that the worker must come to work that day. The reality of the productive process prevents him from enjoying rest that day and it would not be correct to interpret this situation as a restriction -though justified- of his right. Unlike the epidemic or a flood, in this case the factual circumstance that prevents the exercise of the right is shaped by socio-cultural (Sunday rest is the result of catholic tradition) and technical-organisational (the machines that are part of the productive process within the framework of productive organisation) factors.

The difference between the example of the right to religious freedom and that posed by forced vaccination in the case of an epidemic is that, since the right to physical integrity is a right in which the "defence" stands out against non-consent interventions, it might seem that the restriction is more evident than when a person cannot rest on a Saturday for work reasons. However, we are not faced with any

[16]. I would divide the factual situations that can condition and even make impossible the exercise of fundamental rights into circumstances of a physical-natural, technical, organisational or social nature.

restriction, but rather with factual circumstances that contextualise the exercise of fundamental rights. It is convenient to deepen the explanation of why it is not appropriate to speak of restrictions, which leads to the problem of the legitimate exercise of fundamental rights.

Once the content of a fundamental right has been delimited, it may happen that, in certain circumstances, its exercise, even if it consists of the same behaviour, is legitimate and in other situations it is not. To fully understand this idea, one must start from the very concept of a fundamental right. Leaving aside some analytical problems, a fundamental right constitutes a good, a sphere of the personality and/or of the human activity that the Constitution recognises as valuable to the individual and also to the community.[17] Why does the fundamental right represent a good for the individual? Obviously, because it helps them to develop their personality freely within the framework of the society in which they live and in which rights are recognised and protected. This leads to an important conclusion: fundamental rights are exercised in the world (understood as the society in which one lives), but they do not constitute an instrument to create a world in our image and likeness. In other words, the physical and social reality constitutes a context that cannot fail but to be taken into account when assessing the legitimate exercise of fundamental rights. Physical reality and social structures are not rigid, they evolve, but they do not stop having profiles and being valid for a while. In the same way, we must affirm that human beings have different ways of being in the world, fundamental rights being an instrument to be able to make their own way of life that derives from the personal condition of the human being a reality. All these factors must be taken into account to determine when a right is exercised legitimately, because we must agree with Ollero that when we affirm our right to something we do not limit ourselves to expressing our desire, but we are also saying that "the enjoyment of that something respects my existential connection with others, which does not destroy it but allows me to adjust my behaviour to theirs" (Ollero 1996, 401–402).

Indeed, fundamental rights cannot be interpreted as instruments to break social structures by imposing our own vital options, because if this were possible, it would be difficult for them to be considered "goods" and much less the foundation of political order and social peace, to use the terminology of art. 10.1 of the Spanish constitution. The exercise of fundamental rights must be integrated into the social context in which it is performed, which undoubtedly requires achieving an adjustment between what protects the fundamental right and respect for reality that includes the social structures that form part of it. It is normal for there to be imbalances that, to a large extent, reflect or may respond to conflicts of values. Buildings, institutions, typical relationships, gastronomy, etc., are often the result of the vision of the world that the social majority has had throughout history. What happens then to the individual who belongs to a minority with a substantially different way of life and one, perhaps, incompatible

[17] . In my opinion, there is no doubt that within the framework of the Constitutional State of Law, fundamental rights are also collective goods, otherwise it would not make sense for the constitution to grant them the central position that it grants them in the terms that it does in constitutions such as the German and the Spanish. For a refutation to Robert Alexy's opposition between individual rights and collective goods (Cf. De Domingo 2011, 10–14).

with some of these realities that make up the social structure? Requiring them to respect these structures, even if this supposes the rejection of their convictions, could lead one to think that the thesis I am maintaining is markedly conservative. To refute this objection, it must be observed that fundamental rights are exercised in a given reality and in a specific social context, but they also help to shape it and promote its transformation. This idea means that the exercise of a fundamental right cannot be legitimate if it is incompatible with a constitutionally acceptable social institution or with the normal development of collective life; But the central position that fundamental rights occupy, the obligation of public authorities to ensure that their respect is real and effective, requires that everything possible be done so that reality and social structures are transformed and embrace the peculiar form to be in the world of each one through the exercise of their fundamental rights. These can be, therefore, a factor of social transformation and not a social dissolvent. But to finish developing this idea it is necessary to point out that when, through the action of the public authorities or of the individuals acting on the context trying to make the exercise or the respect demanded by a fundamental right possible but this is not possible, the situation should not be considered as a restriction of the fundamental right, but a factual impossibility of exercising it. Consequently, an epidemic whose solution would only be possible through mandatory vaccination through bodily intervention represents a dramatic factual situation to stop the spread of a disease. There is, therefore, an undoubted difference between an injury or restriction of fundamental rights that is presented as the result of an extreme factual situation, which not even a regulation can avoid, and a position that openly admits of the possibility of injuring or restricting fundamental rights to protect other legal rights through recourse to the principle of proportionality. In the first case, beyond the "extreme situations", the demands of the adjustment lead to the problem of adequately regulating the exercise of fundamental rights to make their effective enjoyment possible, which is also consistent with the literal tenor of art. 53.1 of the Spanish constitution. In the second case, the way is opened for fundamental rights to be relativised, which, among other things, greatly hinders the possibility of having an alternative fundamental rights-based bioethics to principlism.

2.4 Conclusion

The theory of fundamental rights requires conceptual clarifications that may influence the response given to specific cases. That is why the theoretical approach from which the cases are confronted is so important. The theory of fundamental rights that I propose advocates to delimit its content and examine the legitimacy of its exercise through prudential deliberation with the existential context in which it takes place. Admitting in general that fundamental rights may be injured or restricted means extending the impossibility of exercising rights or preserving them beyond situations in which factual circumstances prevent it, which blurs the theory of justice of neoconstitutionalism and prevents a fundamental rights-based bioethics. Therefore, respect for fundamental rights must become a matter of principle in the face of any bioethical problem. This thesis, axiologically strong, not only does not close the way to prudence, but rather demands it to a greater extent. Prudence is necessary in delimiting the content of fundamental rights, since this cannot be carried out in the abstract, but by understanding, in the light of concrete cases, the profiles of each good protected by fundamental rights. It is also important to regulate the exercise of fundamental rights, a task that acquires a renewed importance insofar as it must show that regulation responds to the needs of adjustment to the existential context, and not to incorporating restrictions. And it is also important to discover in front of each concrete case whether a right has been exercised legitimately and, therefore, deserves to be respected, or if it is facing a restriction that should be rejected. Bioethics raises extremely difficult problems but reaffirms itself in the central position of fundamental rights as the basis of a fundamental rights-based bioethics that is the way forward to achieve its solution.

References

Alexy, Robert. 1997. *Teoría de los derechos fundamentales*. Translation by Ernesto Garzón Valdés. Madrid: Centro de Estudios Constitucionales.

Aparisi, Ángela. 2007. Bioética, bioderecho y biojurídica (Reflexiones desde la filosofía del derecho). *Anuario De Filosofía Del Derecho* 24: 63–84.

Aragón, Manuel. 2007. La Constitución como paradigma. In *Teoría del neoconstitucionalismo. Ensayos escogidos*, presentation by Miguel Carbonell, ed. Miguel Carbonell. Madrid: Trotta.

Atienza, Manuel. 2021. Carta sobre la ponderación. In Manuel Atienza Rodríguez y Juan Antonio García Amado. *Debates iusfilosóficos. Sobre ponderación, positivismo jurídico y objetivismo moral*. Lima: Palestra, 79–100.

Beauchamp, T.L., and J. Childress. 2009. *Principles of biomedical ethics*. New York: Oxford University Press.

De Domingo Pérez, Tomás. 2011. La teoría de la justicia del neoconstitucionalismo: los derechos fundamentals como núcleo del bien común, 5–29. In Antonio Luis Martínez-Pujalte and Tomás de Domingo Pérez. *Los derechos fundamentales en el sistema constitucional: teoría general e implicaciones prácticas*. Granada: Comares.

Colisiones entre principios y ponderación en la teoría de los derechos fundamentales de Robert Alexy: una aproximación crítica. 2015. In *El neoconstitucionalismo en la teoría de la argumentación de Robert Alexy*, Ed. Alejandra Flores, María Elósegui y Enrique Uribe, 95–136. México: Porrúa.

García Amado, Juan Antonio. 2021. Sobre ponderaciones. Debatiendo con Manuel Atienza. Manuel Atienza Rodríguez y Juan Antonio García Amado. *Debates iusfilosóficos. Sobre ponderación, positivismo jurídico y objetivismo moral*. Lima: Palestra, pp. 37–78.

García-Llerena, Viviana. 2012. *De la bioética a la biojurídica: El principialismo y sus alternativas*. Comares: Granada.

Häberle, Peter. 2003. *La garantía del contenido esencial de los derechos fundamentales*. Translation by Joaquín Brage Camazano, presentation and preliminary study by Francisco Fernández Segado. Madrid: Dykinson.

Marías, Julián. 1983. *Antropología metafísica*. Madrid: Alianza Editorial.

Martínez-Pujalte, Antonio Luis. 1997. *La garantía del contenido esencial de los derechos fundamentales*. Foreword by Andrés Ollero Tassara. Madrid: Centro de Estudios Constitucionales.

El contenido esencial del derecho a la integridad física y la esterilización de personas con discapacidad intelectual. 2011. In Antonio Luis Martínez-Pujalte and Tomás de Domingo Pérez. *Los derechos fundamentales en el sistema constitucional: teoría general e implicaciones prácticas.* Granada: Comares, pp. 165–180.

Derechos fundamentales y discapacidad. 2015. Foreword by Alberto Durán. Madrid: Cinca.

Ollero, Andrés. 1996. *¿Tiene razón el Derecho?* Foreword by Gregorio Peces-Barba, Madrid: Congreso de los Diputados.

Bioderecho. Entre la vida y la muerte. 2006. Cizur Menor: Aranzadi.

Ortiz Fernández, Manuel. 2021. *El consentimiento informado en el ámbito sanitario: responsabilidad civil y derechos constitucionales.* Madrid: Dykinson.

Pereira Menaut, Antonio-Carlos. 2003. *Rule of Law o Estado de Derecho.* Madrid: Marcial Pons.

Rodríguez-Toubes, Joaquín. 2000. *Principios, fines y derechos fundamentales.* Madrid: Dykinson.

Spaemann, Robert. 2007. ¿Matar, o dejar morir? Translation by José María Barrio Maestre. Cuadernos de Bioética. XVIII. 2007/1ª: 107–116.

Vergara, Óscar. 2014. Casuismo, ética biomédica y derecho. *Persona y Derecho* 71: 307–333.

Método y razón práctica en la ética biomédica. 2018. Granada: Comares.

Chapter 3
Social Determinants of Health and the Indivisibility of Social Justice

Encarnación Fernández Ruiz-Gálvez

Abstract The work starts from a holistic conception of health as a reality shaped by the interaction of multiple factors; (i) genetic / biological, (ii) individual behavioural / lifestyles, and (iii) environmental, including both the physical environment and social circumstances. The social "determinants" of health (SDH) approach underlines the importance of the social environment, that is, the influence that social structures and the position that each person occupies in the social system have on health and illness. SDH generate deep inequalities in health between the different social groups and between the different countries. This is one of the most important social justice issues facing modern societies and the globalized world. Hence, since the end of the 1970s in the series of international conferences on health promotion, to guarantee equity has been considered a priority objective of health policies. The principle of Health in All Policies is a corollary of the SDH approach. So that the merit of this approach lies, inter alia, in highlighting the indivisibility of the various dimensions of social justice.

Keywords Social determinants of health · Capabilities approach · Health equity · Social justice

3.1 Introduction

The observation of the deep inequalities in health (as measured by life-expectancy at birth, infant mortality, morbidity, etc.) between the different social groups and between the different countries has attracted the attention of scientists and after of public policies and international organizations (specially, WHO) on the so-called 'social determinants of health' (SDH).

The social determinants of health are the conditions in which people are born, grow, live, work and age. These circumstances are shaped by the distribution of

E. Fernández Ruiz-Gálvez (✉)
Universidad de Valencia, Valencia, Spain
e-mail: encarnacion.fernandez@uv.es

© The Editor(s) (if applicable) and The Author(s), under exclusive license to Springer Nature Switzerland AG 2024

J.-A. Seoane and O. Vergara (eds.), *The Discourse of Biorights*, The International Library of Bioethics 109, https://doi.org/10.1007/978-3-031-66804-3_3

money, power and resources at global, national and local levels (www.who.int/social_determinants/sdh_definition/en/index.html). This approach does not deny the importance of access to medical care (which is undoubtedly one of the social determinants of health), but it also highlights the influence of non-medical social and economic factors in the health of the population. Social determinants of health largely, though not exclusively, shape the opportunities for people to enjoy good health, that is to live a long and healthy life, and even shape their opportunities to adopt healthy lifestyles.

The relevance of this issue from the point of view of public policies is framed in the context of a comprehensive and social conception of health (and health policies) and connects with what today is a priority goal of health policies: the achievement of health equity.

Indeed, the so-called social determinants of health are mostly responsible for health inequalities within and between countries. These inequalities constitute *inequities* because they are not only unnecessary and avoidable but unfair and unjust as well (Whitehead 1990, p. 5). These health inequities are one of the most important social justice issues facing contemporary societies and the globalized world.

Although the usual terminology is social 'determinants' of health, it seems more appropriate to speak of social 'conditioning factors' of health. In this sense Valls-Llobet (2009, p. 104) writes: "I do not agree that there are determinants of health, neither genetic nor acquired. Neither in adult life, nor in intrauterine life. Nor do I believe that there are psychological determinants. But biological, hormonal, psychological and social conditions. And although there are small spaces of freedom, for centuries humanity and especially women have had very few spaces and possibilities to exercise it".

3.2 Towards a Holistic and Social Conception of Health

The concept of health, as so many others, is an open concept that varies with the historical evolution and the evolution of social circumstances, with different conceptions of it. Thus we can distinguish, among others, a biomedical model and a social, or more exactly biopsychosocial, model of health; a conception of health as well-being and a vision of it as a basic capability of human beings.

3.2.1 From the Biomedical Model to the Biopsychosocial Model

Traditionally, the biomedical model identified health with the absence of disease. And, in turn, it conceived the disease as a deviation from the biological norm, with a unique etiology, whose clearest paradigm was infectious diseases, each caused by a bacterium, fungus or virus. The mechanistic view of the human body favours that the disease has been interpreted as an abnormality (Izquierdo 1998, pp. 63–4).

Instead of this partial view of health and disease, the social model highlights the role played by social and socio-economic factors in the promotion of health and the causation of disease and also relates these factors themselves to the broader social structure.

The biomedical model is blamed for paying too much attention to diseases and their remedy, forgetting questions such as “why good health is important for people, what good health means to them, and what the broader social context is in which the pursuit of health and the response to disease are shaped” (Peter 2001, p.161).

The biomedical model would not correspond to reality, since health and illness are the result of the interaction of various conditioning factors that "act at the same time and with varying degrees of intensity, which mutually reinforce or neutralize each other and whose consequences are alterations in physical and mental health" (Valls-Llobet 2018, p. 36). Such factors are mainly of four types: (i) genetic / biological, (ii) individual behavioural/ lifestyles, and (iii) environmental, including both the physical environment and social circumstances. The SDH approach underlines the importance of the latter, of the social environment, that is, the influence that social structures and the position that each person occupies in the social system have on health and illness.

This comprehensive understanding of health as a result of the interaction of diverse factors implies overcoming the limitations inherent in the research method of modern science that is characterized by abstraction, by narrowing the object of study, focusing on a single aspect of reality (Heidegger 1977; Zubiri 1963, pp. 243 ff.; Ballesteros 2001, pp.19 ff.). Therefore "western medical science has been built isolating the problems, with the supposed desire to study them better" (Valls-Llobet 2009, p. 75). Consequently, the balance between biological, psychological, social and environmental causes of diseases is still invisible to many health professionals and to public health questionnaires.

In this regard, it has been important scientific achievements that we have begun to study diseases in relation to the environment and working conditions. However, less progress has been made in the study of the gender conditioning of health. The decision of the USA National Investigation Health in 1993, including women in the research studies has been an important step in the road towards equal opportunities in health, but it has only been applied in 25 or 30% of the studies published in the last 15 years and, in addition, there are very few investigations carried out with a gender perspective, studying at the same time the conditions of life and work and the social environment of women and men (Valls-Llobet 2018, p. 39).

3.2.2 *From Well-Being to Health as Basic Human Capability*

On the other hand, a broad concept of health is based not only on the absence of disease, but consists of a well-being situation that we associate with our own human dignity. In this sense, article 25 of Universal Declaration of Human Rights explicitly connects health with well-being. Likewise, the Constitution of the World Health Organization declares in its Preamble: "Health is a state of complete physical, mental and social well-being and not merely the absence of disease or infirmity".

Consistently with this, the right to health protection includes not only medical care, but also public health actions aimed at (i) prevention of disease (cancer screening, vaccinations); at (ii) health protection (food and environmental security, occupational health); and even at (iii) promotion of individual and collective health (prenatal care, childhood health programs, health literacy, healthy aging programs, etc.).

This broad concept of the right to health protection is what the WHO Constitution proclaims in its Preamble, according to which "the enjoyment of the highest attainable standard of health is one of the fundamental rights of every human being without distinction of race, religion, political belief, economic or social condition". In the same sense, article 12 of the International Covenant on Economic, Social and Cultural Rights establishes that "the States Parties to the present Covenant recognize the right of everyone to the enjoyment of the highest attainable standard of physical and mental health".

Within the framework of an integral conception of health, it is evident that although medical care can prolong survival and improve prognosis after serious illnesses, more important for the health of the population as a whole are the social and economic conditions that make people sick and in need of medical attention. Thus, the relevance of the so-called social determinants of health opens up. However, and this must be remembered from the beginning, universal access to medical care is undoubtedly one of the social determinants of health. The importance of health care is therefore not excluded, but "a wider responsibility [is necessary] for creating healthy societies" (Wilkinson and Marmot 2003, pp. 7–9).

The SDH approach highlights that health is a reality conditioned by the physical and social environment: socio-economic situation, level of education, place of residence and housing, employment situation and working environment, social and family relationships, gender, political and environmental factors, as well as accessibility to social and health services.

This approach highlights the important connections that exist in modern societies between health and broader economic and social objectives. Health promotion is not solely the responsibility of the health sector, but goes beyond healthy lifestyles, to well-being and enabling environments. Therefore, health and well-being of the population are inseparable objectives and fundamental characteristics of a successful, integrated and just society.

However, the model that identifies health and well-being poses certain difficulties (Peter 2001, p. 161): (i) The difficulty to distinguish health from other components of well-being and to understand those situations in which a certain well-being can be achieved despite having bad health or, vice versa, those in which health is good but well-being is low. (ii) Secondly, it is not clear how to define well-being in a way that is compatible with the plurality of conceptions about the good life that exist in our democratic societies. (iii) And third, such a broad conception of health can lead to an excessive medicalization of social problems, presenting the social promotion of health as a technical problem with technical solutions rather than as a political problem with a political solution.

In addition, the concept of well-being is an open concept susceptible of diverse interpretations, but which tends to be identified with the utilitarian conception of it, according to which well-being is defined in terms of some mental characteristic (pleasure, happiness, satisfaction of desires). Sen maintains that well-being understood in utilitarian terms is not an adequate criterion of justice, nor an adequate criterion to evaluate equality and inequality. And this is because the representation of individual well-being as an internal characteristic (pleasure, happiness, satisfaction of desires) does not account for the real life of people, especially in the case of people in situations of persistent adversity and deprivation. They often accept their situation and try to enjoy small things. "Equal happiness can go with widely divergent fulfilment of needs" (Sen 1992, pp. 2; 6–7; and Chaps. 3 and 4, pp. 39 ff.).

From what has been said, it follows that the utilitarian conception of well-being is not appropriate to address the problems of equity in health, nor to define the concept of health. For this purpose, the capabilities approach is much more appropriate (Sen 1999, 2009; Nussbaum 2006, 2011). The idea underlying this approach is that for the political evaluation of either inequality, poverty, sexual discrimination or well-being, freedom, quality of life, development, as well as justice and social ethics, the relevant information is not the individual utility or welfare, nor the resources to which people have access, but what people can *do* and *be* with those resources. This is what Sen calls capability: the actual, effective ability of a person to do valuable acts or reach valuable states of being (*functionings*). For this approach, what is decisive and what needs to be promoted directly are not the *functionings* but the corresponding basic capabilities (the capabilities to function). Sen illustrates it with the well-known example that fasting is not the same as starving. "The distinction is obviously important in many social contexts: we may, for example, try to eliminate involuntary hunger, but not wish to forbid fasting" (Sen 1993, p. 40). This is related to the relevance of choice in our lives.

Sen often mentions good health as an example of basic functioning (Sen 1993, p. 31). Therefore, public policies should promote the corresponding capability, so that the overall objective of health interventions should be to guarantee the ability to have health or to be healthy (Venkatapuram 2011, pp. 143ss.). But in addition, health is in itself a fundamental capability required to function in society (Sen 1999), a basic capability of human beings (Nussbaum 2006, 2011, pp. 53–55), a possibility or opportunity of life that enables us to pursue our life goals and interact in the social context. In particular, health has been defined as "a person's ability to achieve or exercise a cluster of basic human activities", or as "the ability to achieve a basic cluster of beings and doings—or having the overarching capability, a meta-capability, to achieve a set of central or vital inter-related capabilities and functionings" (Venkatapuram 2013, p. 271), among others, the ability to participate fully in the workforce and in the democratic political process (Braveman et al. 2011a, pp. 149–150).

In addition, "[t] he fair protection of health can not be limited to guaranteeing a certain level of functioning at the present time, but it also requires its maintenance over time, guaranteeing the health capability security". Accordingly, the right to health protection would consist of the 'right to a secure health capability' (Seoane 2016, p. 47 and *passim*).

Understood in this way, health appears as a good both individually and socially. Given the biological individuality of each human being, there is no doubt that health has an undeniable individual aspect, it is a universal human need, an individual good that has a component of natural gift and a component of personal motivation (Martínez Part 2016, p. 137). But health is also a social good. It is a great resource of society and an asset for economic and social development, for whose care, protection and promotion society must procure the means. "As collective goals, good health and well-being for all should be given high priority at local, national, regional and international levels" (*Rio Political Declaration on Social Determinants of Health*, 2011). Likewise, the Shanghai Declaration of 2016 reaffirms that health is "a shared social goal and a political priority for all countries".

Health protection and promotion is a basic component of sustainable human development (Sen 1999). Indeed one of the Sustainable Development Goals established in the United Nations 2030 Agenda is "ensure healthy lives and promote well-being for all at all ages". In the same sense, the *Shanghai Declaration* recognizes that health and wellbeing are essential to achieving sustainable development, and particularly to achieving the United Nations Development Agenda 2030 and its Sustainable Development Goals.

Thus, health is necessary and valuable for both individuals and communities. Consequently, its protection is a basic duty of justice and not a commodity that only those who can afford it can enjoy (Seoane 2016, p. 50). Hence the importance of the principle of health equity, an issue that we address in the next section.

3.3 Health Inequalities and Health Equity

The 1978 Declaration of Alma-Ata reaffirmed the essential value of equity in health, as well as the series of international health promotion conferences from the 1986 Ottawa Charter to the Shanghai Declaration adopted during the 9th Global Conference on Health Promotion (Shanghai. 21–24 November 2016).

The integral vision of the right to health protection, which is not limited to medical care, but also requires the prevention of illness and protection and even the promotion of health, so that each person enjoys 'the highest attainable standard of health', carries a concern for equity in the sense that all human beings have the real ability (the 'capability' in the sense of Sen and Nussbaum) to achieve 'the highest attainable standard of health', without social circumstances operate as an obstacle to it.

In this regard, the Committee on Economic, Social and Cultural Rights, in its General Comment No. 14, holds that the right to health of the article 12 of ICESCR is "not to be understood as a right to be healthy". Rather, it is "the right to a system of health protection which provides equality of opportunity for people to enjoy the highest attainable level of health".

In this context, the notion of social determinants of health that refers to social circumstances that favour health (favourable environments) or, on the contrary, that are harmful to health, acquires political relevance. The social determinants generate important health inequalities and explain most of the health inequities.

"*Health inequalities*" is the terminology widely used internationally to refer mainly, though not only, to socioeconomic inequalities in health. In the United States, however, the expression "*health disparities*" is used more frequently, with which ethnic or racial inequalities are often alluded to, although not only to them. With these nuances, both denominations can be considered as equivalent.

Nevertheless, what has a certain complexity is to specify its meaning. Disparities/inequalities in health can be characterized (Braveman et al. 2011a) as a subset of health differences whose specific features would be those of being systematic, plausibly avoidable and adversely affecting socially disadvantaged groups. According to this definition, health disparities do not refer generically to all health differences, not even to all health differences that deserve special attention from public policies, but only those that adversely affect socially disadvantaged groups. The elderly usually have worse health than the other adults; skiers are at greater risk of long-bone fractures than non-skiers. These would be examples of health differences that would not be considered health disparities, as they are not associated with social injustice. Furthermore, the authors argue that if a more socially advantaged group has worse outcomes in a given health indicator (e.g., higher incidence of breast cancer in White women than in African-American women, or shorter life expectancy among men with respect to women), this may be an issue of public health importance, but it "would not be a social injustice and, therefore, not a health disparity or equity issue" (p. 152), since Whites are in a more advantageous social position than African-Americans and, more importantly, in many health indicators, including mortality from breast cancer, White women are healthier than African-Americans (Henry J. Kaiser Family Foundation 2009). Also, although men have shorter life expectancy, women have worse health, which, in part at least, reflects their subordinate social position.

If the expression 'health disparities' is interpreted as any health differences between different population groups, then it would encompass the whole scope of epidemiology, which is the study of the distribution of diseases and risk factors among different populations. On the contrary, the aforementioned authors prefer to reserve that denomination for those health differences that are relevant from the point of view of social justice. Simply put, health disparities/inequalities are that socially disadvantaged groups have worse health (Braveman et al. 2011a, p. 153).

Hence, these health disparities/inequalities are qualified as *inequities* (Whitehead 1990, p. 5), term that makes explicit the moral dimension of the problem and which allows to distinguish unequivocally inequalities (health differences thought to reflect social injustice) of the remaining health differences.

Indeed, health inequalities are politically, socially and economically unacceptable, unfair and largely avoidable. Hence a priority goal of health policies is to ensure equity, reducing social inequalities in health as unnecessary, unjust and avoidable.

Nonetheless, the problem that arises is to clarify the reason why these social inequalities in health are unjust. Peter's response to the question raised is that social inequalities in health are unjust insofar as they result from an unjust basic structure of society in the sense of Rawls, which benefits the better off groups to the detriment of the worse off groups, undermining the fundamental equality of all members of society and even the social bases for self-respect (Peter 2001, pp. 164–167). This thesis uses Rawls's theory of justice as a framework of reference, but goes beyond it, since, as it is known, for Rawls the basic structure of society affects the distribution of material resources and thus the opportunities that people have to carry out their life plans and even influences the development of personal skills and talents (1993, p. 270). However, Rawls does not address the issue of how social arrangements affect people's health and life expectancy, which is precisely what empirical studies about social inequalities in health show.

However, Braveman et al. (2011a, pp. 150–151) argue that it is not necessary to prove the existence of a causal relationship between social disadvantage and health disparities. Whether or not this causal link exists, health inequalities are especially unfair because they adversely affect groups who are already disadvantaged socially, placing them at a greater disadvantage, which makes it potentially more difficult for these people to overcome their socially disadvantaged situation, since poor health is an obstacle to it. That is, health inequalities reinforce or aggravate social disadvantage and vulnerability and this is what makes them relevant to social justice, although the causes of these health disparities have not been established conclusively, because controversies persist about the undoubted strength (or not) of the evidences that support the causal role of some social factors (Braveman and Gottlieb 2014).

Health equity is social justice in health. It consists of the commitment to reduce (and ultimately eliminate) health disparities. It's about equalizing opportunities to be healthy. Braveman et al. (2011a, p. 151) underline that, coherently with the bioethical principles of beneficence and non-maleficence, equity requires concerted efforts to improve the situation of those who were worse off to start, within a general strategy of improving everyone' health. Reduction in health disparities by improving the health of the socially disadvantaged (never worsening advantaged groups' health) is the measure of progress towards health equity.

Peter (2001, pp. 162–164) distinguishes between a direct approach and an indirect approach to health equity. The first conceives health equity as an end in itself, independent of, although parallel to justice in other spheres, such as income or education. In contrast, the indirect approach conceives the search for health equity as embedded in and interlinked with the general objective of seeking social justice, placing emphasis on broader social processes, on 'upstream' influences on people' health (p. 160). The SDH' approach relates to this indirect approach to health equity, which is more apt to understand the inherent complexity of health, without confining it to a sphere of its own and independent of all other social spheres (Peter 2001, p. 164).

According to this approach, health equity is indivisible and inseparable from social justice as a whole. Ensuring social justice is an indispensable component of any effort to achieve health equity. Social justice that requires jointly addressing issues of distribution and recognition. The resources necessary for health (not only medical care, but also the nonmedical social determinants of health, including living and working conditions) must be distributed equitably. Health equity has to go beyond medical care. Justice in the distribution of wealth, opportunities and privileges is a requirement of health equity.

But, in addition to distribution, recognition is also a matter of social justice. Recognition implies the normative requirement of participatory parity, which acts as a normative criterion for evaluating injustices (Fraser 2009). Conditions that deny equity in social participation are unfair and must be eliminated (Fraser 2003). Furthermore, "the recognition must be prior to the distribution and such precedence improves the justification of the distribution, since it makes possible the inclusion of all in the deliberative determination of the conditions of justice in health" (Seoane 2016, p. 49). In this regard, the Committee on Economic, Social and Cultural Rights, in its General Comment No. 14, includes within the normative content of the right to health of article 12 of ICESCR "the participation of the population in all health-related decision-making at the community, national and international levels".

Equity in participation can help to avoid perpetuating feelings of exclusion among the most vulnerable and generating trust (Benjamin 2015). The 2015 American Public Health Association report on health equity tells a very significant story in this regard. Multomah County Health Department in Oregon designed a program to reduce the rates of perinatal problems (preterm births and infant mortality) in the native communities. But the lack of trust of the communities turned out to be an obstacle to the implementation of the program. So, health workers let go of their predetermined agenda and decided to listen to communities and to engage in an open and honest dialogue about the role of government in perpetuating inequalities. The outcome was a new project, this time a truly community-driven project, which was launched in 2011: Future Generations Collaborative, in which recognition of the role of oppression and historical trauma is essential to shaping effective health interventions.

In response to the growing concern over persistent and increasing health inequities, WHO set up the Commission on Social Determinants of Health in 2005 to offer advice on how to mitigate them. The Commission Final Report, published in August 2008, entitled *Closing the gap in a generation. Health equity through action on the social determinants of health*, emphasizes that the objective pursued is to achieve health equity and that the strategy proposed to achieve it is to act on the social determinants of health.

The World Health Assembly, meeting in May 2009, adopted the resolution *Reducing health inequities through action on the social determinants of health* (WHA 62.14), in which it took note of the recommendations of the Commission on Social Determinants of Health.

With this background, the World Conference on Social Determinants of Health held in Rio de Janeiro in October 2011 adopted the *Rio Political Declaration on social determinants of health*, which expresses the "determination to achieve social and health equity through action on social determinants of health and well-being by a comprehensive intersectoral approach".

3.4 Social Environment and Health Outcomes

The empirical studies about the incidence of the social environment on health have identified and systematized the diverse social conditioning factors of health.

1. The first and most general is the socioeconomic position (reflected by, e.g., income, wealth, educational attainment and employment).

Poverty has adverse effects on health. This is something that has been observed over the centuries (Rosen 2015; Hamlin 2010). And not only extreme poverty, but also relative poverty as well (Shaw et al. 2006, pp. 196–223). Being much poorer than most people in the society in which they live (income below 60% of the national average) often denies people access to decent housing, education, transportation and other vital factors for full participation in society (Wilkinson and Marmot 2003, p. 16).

And it is not simply the circumstances of material poverty (e.g., malnutrition, dirty water, exposure to cold and infections, exposure to pollution and allergens, more common in disadvantaged neighbourhoods, lead ingestion in low-quality housing that hinders cognitive function and physical development of children) that are harmful to health, but the interaction between material disadvantages and their psychological and social implications. The social meaning of poverty, unemployment, marginalization and other types of social stigmas leads to psychosocial problems that are as much or more serious than material deprivations.

In this regard, several studies highlight the extent to which health-related behaviors are strongly influenced by social factors, such as income, education and employment (Stringhini et al. 2010; Braveman et al. 2011b). Marmot (2006, p. 3) analyzes the data that in the USA black men in deprived areas have 20 years' shorter life expectancy than richer white men. The main causes of this excess mortality are violent deaths, HIV / AIDS and cardiovascular diseases. In this case, the social environment affects health through psychosocial factors related to exposure to armed violence, sexual risk behaviors, drug use, etc. Often other risky behaviors such as tobacco and alcohol use, inadequate diets and lack of physical exercise (Cummins et al. 2006; Gordon-Larsen et al. 2006) are also socially conditioned. As noted by Marmot (2006, p. 3), the causes of the causes must be investigated. It is not by chance that people consume an excess of saturated fats and salt. Sometimes that is the nature of food available in their neighborhoods, culturally imposed and affordable.

The stress of living in poverty is also a psychosocial factor that has negative effects on mental and physical health (Braveman and Gottlieb 2014, p. 7), generating even greater risk of premature death. As a social being, the human being needs not only good material conditions of life, but we also need, from early childhood, to feel valued and esteemed, to feel useful, to have friends and a certain control over valuable work. Without all this, people are more prone to depression, anxiety, despair, the use of drugs, aggressiveness, all of which in turn have an impact on physical health (Wilkinson and Marmot 2003, p. 9).

Moreover, health inequalities do not only affect situations of poverty, but also cross the entire social ladder. Hence, we can talk of a 'social gradient in health' that "runs from top to bottom of society" (Marmot 2006, p. 2). This stepwise gradient pattern was first noted in the United Kingdom. When analysing the data of the first Whitehall study of British civil servants, Marmot and colleagues observed that even among middle-class civil servants differences in the risk of suffering illnesses and/or premature death existed depending on the professional category. The lower the employment grade, the higher the risk of most diseases and causes of death (Marmot et al. 1978). Subsequent studies in several European countries (Shaw et al. 2006, pp.196–199) and in the USA. (Braveman and Gottlieb 2014) show similar results confirming the stepped gradation of health according to social class.

2. Early life experiences have a decisive impact on health (Wilkinson and Marmot 2003, pp. 14–15). Both observational research and intervention studies show that the foundations of adult health are established in the prenatal period and early childhood as a result of the interaction between biological development and social and environmental circumstances (Wadsworth and Butterworth 2006, pp. 31–53).

The consequences of poverty during pregnancy and childhood are devastating and last a lifetime. They affect long-term physical and cognitive development and even temperament and behaviour. And this as a result not only of material deprivations (eg. malnutrition), but also of psychosocial factors such as chronic stress (Evans and Schamberg 2009). When and for how long you experience stress is relevant to health. Overall, the effects of stress are manifested through subsequent chronic diseases, but in the case of experiences before 5 years of age these effects are intensified. And so the early-life socioeconomic disadvantage is associated with vulnerability to a range of adolescent and adult diseases, regardless of the socioeconomic status of the adolescent or adult in question (Braveman and Gottlieb 2014, p. 8).

Along these lines, resolution WHA 62.14 of 2009 emphasizes that "investing in comprehensive supports for early child development that are accessible to all children is a fundamental step in achieving health equity across the lifespan".

3. The level of education is another of the social conditioning factors of health. Based on the existing literature, Braveman and Gottlieb (2014, pp. 8–10) systematize the pathways through which education can influence many health outcomes. First, education increases knowledge and skills in health, illness, diet, exercise, smoking, etc. and consequently can contribute to the adoption of healthier lifestyles. Second, usually a higher educational attainment allows access to better jobs: with better working conditions and higher paid, which in turn favours health and well-being. Third, education can influence health through psychobiological processes, such as control beliefs (coping and problem solving, response to stressors, health-related behaviours); subjective social status (Demakakos et al. 2008), which is where one perceives oneself as fitting relative to others in the social hierarchy not only in terms of wealth, but also of prestige and influence; and social networks that provide social support, help mitigate stress, and transmit norms for healthy behaviours, etc.
4. The employment situation and the work environment are important factors that condition health. Job security increases health and well-being. On the contrary,

unemployment puts health at risk not only because of the economic problems it entails, but also because of its psychological consequences. Moreover, the repercussions of the lack of work on health affect not only the unemployed but also their families. In addition, unsecure and unsatisfactory jobs can be as damaging as unemployment. This has shown that long-term job insecurity generates chronic stress (Wilkinson and Marmot 2003, pp. 20–21; Bartley et al. 2006, pp. 78–96; Ballesteros 1992, pp. 137–143).

Likewise, the impact on health of working conditions (exposure to toxic materials, ergonomics, etc.) must be highlighted. Hence, the right to safety and health at work can be considered as a concretion or as a more specific manifestation of the right to health protection. But next to this, empirical studies reveal that the psychosocial environment in which work is developed, that is, the social organization of work, management styles, social relationships in the workplace, etc. are all equally important for health (Wilkinson and Marmot 2003, pp.18–19, Marmot et al. 2006, pp. 97–130).

5. Housing quality and conditions, including the circumstances of overcrowding in it, influence health. Also, as an additional factor, the place of residence and the housing environment characteristics are relevant. Indeed, economic, social-relational, service and physical aspects of the neighbourhood may be important for health. Factors such as concentred deprivation, de-industrialization and unemployment at the neighbourhood; social cohesion; health services, transport, retail outlets, lighting at night; pollution levels, presence of industrial and waste disposal sites, degree of urbanization, green spaces, proximity to main roads, can influence health. In addition, often these features of the neighbourhood overlap. More economically deprived areas are likely to have a worse social and physical environment and worse services (Stafford and McCarthy 2006, pp. 297–317).
6. The environmental conditions in which people live relate to social factors in a double sense. Because environmental deterioration is largely a result of human actions and because it is usually the most disadvantaged social groups and countries that suffer the worst consequences of environmental degradation. This finding is at the origin of the theoretical concern for environmental justice and the movements in favour of it that emerged in the 60s of the twentieth century in the USA in the context of the struggle for civil rights (Ruiz-Sanz 2016).
7. Gender and family relationships deserve special consideration as social conditioning factors of health.

As previously discussed, women have a longer life expectancy than men, but they have worse health. And this last is due, in part at least, to social factors. Valls-Llobet (2009, pp. 38 ff.) highlights two mainly. The first of these is the low valuation of women in the patriarchal culture that can influence even during foetal development and that causes women to have low self-esteem and a constant feeling of guilt, which is why they tend to be perfect, all of which generates a high mental stress. Secondly, the living and working conditions of women (accumulation of paid work and domestic work, excessive burden on them and lack of social support) have long-term consequences on their health manifested in the form of chronic diseases. Women experience pain and fatigue because they suffer chronic stress caused by excessive stress at work, double or triple working day and endless work as perennial caregivers of others.

8. Discrimination based on race/ethnicity, skin colour, religion, language, nationality, political or other affiliation, age, disability, sexual orientation or other characteristics associated with discrimination or marginalization is a factor that in itself and by itself can adversely affect health. It is true that discrimination and socio-economic disadvantages often overlap. But differences in experiences, for example among racial/ethnic groups, are not just socioeconomic. Racial discrimination could harm the health of individuals of all socioeconomic levels through psychobiologic pathways, i.e. chronic stress related to daily experiences with bias and discrimination, and/or to perceived discrimination, even without overtly discriminatory incidents (Williams and Mohammed 2009). Significantly, the black-white disparity in birth outcomes is largest among highly educated women (Braveman 2011).
9. Likewise, as previously mentioned, social and medical care services are also factors of great relevance for health, being of special importance that the latter be universal, accessible, effective and of quality.

From what has been said, it is clear that there are numerous and very varied social factors that affect health. Consequently, the effects of each given social factor are contingent depending on many other factors (Braveman and Gottlieb 2014, p. 6).

Thus there are protective social factors, such as social support, norms and attitudes that favour resilience, self-esteem, which can mitigate the harmful effects of adverse social conditions. These protective social factors have been found among Latin American immigrants in the United States (Franzini et al. 2001; Gallo et al. 2009).

On the other hand, social factors and genetic factors interact with each other. "Genetics [..] may play a role in an individual's vulnerability or resilience to socioeconomic adversity: different individuals' biological responses to the same socio-environmental trigger can vary markedly". At the same time, socioeconomic and other social factors play an important role in epigenetic processes that regulate whether genes are expressed or suppressed. They "can alter whether a deleterious (or protective) gene is expressed or suppressed" (Braveman and Gottlieb 2014, pp. 7–11).

3.5 Health in All Policies

SDH' approach has as its corollary the Principle of Health in All Policies (mainstreaming, comprehensive intersectoral approach).

The starting point is the conviction that "improvement of unfavourable social conditions is primarily a social policy issue" (WHA 62.14, 2009) that requires a comprehensive intersectoral approach, so that the promotion of health would not be the responsibility of the health sector alone, but we must act in all sectors and levels of government, because the policies of other sectors (child care, education, housing, employment, labour, urban planning, environment, etc.) can have an impact on health. It would also require cooperation and work across sectors; the commitment of all segments of society and in particular the collaboration of the private sector; and, on a global scale, the commitment of all members of the international community.

With regard to the content of the policies that should be adopted in a transversal and intersectoral manner to act on the social determinants of health and advance in the attainment of health equity, the following can be highlighted without the intention of exhaustiveness:

1. Eradication of hunger and poverty, guarantee food and nutrition security, as well as access to drinking water and sanitation.
2. Reduction of excessive social inequalities, understanding as such those that impede the capabilities of others.
3. Social welfare programs that address not only material needs, but also psychosocial problems.
4. Specific programs to eradicate child poverty.
5. In the field of educational policies, among others, reduce the levels of educational failure and introduce health education programs.
6. Employment policies and occupational health policies. In this last area, it is about establishing a 'virtuous circle': the improvement in working conditions will lead to a healthier work force, which in turn will increase productivity and thus the opportunity to improve the healthiness of workplaces, and so on (Wilkinson and Marmot 2003, 18–19).
7. Environmental, family and gender policies.
8. Guarantee universal access to health care and social services.
9. Promote equitable and sustainable economic growth or, what is the same, promote sustainable human development.

In this regard, the 9th Global Conference on Health Promotion focused on the reciprocal interdependence between the promotion of health and the Sustainable Development Goals. Thus the Shanghai Declaration proclaims not only that health and wellbeing are essential to achieve sustainable development, but also that health promotion must be carried out through action on all the SDGs and on all determinants of health.

As can be seen, this set of policies constitutes a very broad program of distributive justice, with a global scope, so that the merit of this approach lies, among other things, in highlighting the indivisibility between the various dimensions of social justice.

3.6 Conclusions

The approach of the so-called social determinants of health is placed within the framework of a holistic conception of health as a reality shaped by the interaction of multiple factors, so that the effects of a given factor are not inexorable, but contingent depending on many other factors. Thus, social factors interact with each other, potentiating or neutralizing each other and interacting with genetic factors. In addition, social factors exert their influence on individual attitudes and behaviors, both in a negative and positive sense. Thus, risk behaviors are often the result of the influence of the social environment. And, on the other hand, the focus of the social determinants of health relies on modifying unhealthy behaviors through public policies. However, this approach does not sufficiently emphasize the role of individual freedom, of the 'small spaces of freedom' (Valls-Llobet 2009, 104) that enable human beings to minimize, at times, the effects of adverse social conditions. And that same personal freedom explains that sometimes fail public policies that try to correct unhealthy personal habits. For this reason, compared to the vision of social factors as 'determinants' of health, I think it is more appropriate to speak of 'social conditioning factors' of health. In this regard, we must recognize that, together with the undeniable role played by favorable public policies, it is essential that the individuals themselves assume their share of responsibility in the care and promotion of individual and collective health.

The focus of the social determinants / conditioning factors of health and the principle of health in all policies imply a vision of social justice as an indivisible whole whose various components are interdependent, complementary and inseparable from each other. And that indivisibility occurs both in a negative sense (injustice in a given area leads to inequity in others), and in a positive sense (the demands of social justice -which include distribution and recognition- can only be satisfied properly if they are accomplished together). This approach to justice connects with the so-called indivisibility or integrity of human rights, according to which rights are interdependent and complementary to each other and can only be adequately carried out jointly. They cannot be 'rationed', because the human being needs all human rights simultaneously. All are essential for the realization of the human being in their social environment.

References

American Public Health Association (APHA). 2015, March. Better health through equity: case studies in reframing public health work. Washington, DC: http://www.apha.org/~/media/files/pdf/topics/equity/equity_stories.ashx. Accessed: 7 october 2023.

Ballesteros, Jesús. 1992. Los derechos de los nuevos pobres. In Ballesteros, Jesús (ed.), *Derechos humanos. Concepto, Fundamento, Sujetos,* 137–143. Madrid: Tecnos.

Ballesteros, Jesús. 2001. *Sobre el sentido del Derecho.* Madrid: Tecnos.

Bartley, Mel, Ferrie, Jane and Montgomery, Scott M. 2006. (2ª). Health and labour market disadvantage: unemployment, non-employment, and job insecurity. In Marmot, Michael and Wilkinson, Richard G., *Social determinants of health*, 78–96. Oxford: Oxford University Press.

Benjamin, Georges. 2015. Health Equity and Social Justice: A Health Improvement Tool. *Views from the field*, may 19.

Braveman, Paula. 2011. Black-white disparities in birth outcomes: Is racism-related stress a missing piece of the puzzle? In *Handbook of African American health: Social and behavioral interventions*, ed. A.J. Lemelle, W. Reed, and S. Taylor, 155–163. New York: Springer.

Braveman, Paula A., Kumanyika, Shiriki, Fielding, Jonathan, LaVeist, Thomas, Borrell, Luisa N., Manderscheid, Ron, and Troutman, Adewale. 2011a. Health disparities and health equity: the issue is justice. *American Journal of Public Health,* Supplement 1, 101(S1): 149–155.

Braveman, P., Egerter, S., and Barclay, C. 2011b. Princeton (NJ): Robert wood Johnson foundation. What shapes health-related behaviors? The role of social factors. Exploring the social determinants of health: issue brief no. 1.

Braveman, Paula, and Laura Gottlieb. 2014. The social determinants of health: it's time to consider the causes of the causes. Public health reports 129. *Suppl* 2: 19–31.

Commission on Social Determinants of Health. 2008. *Closing the gap in a generation: health equity through action on the social determinants of health. Final report of the Commission on Social Determinants of Health.* Geneva: World Health Organization.

Committee on Economic, Social and Cultural Rights. 2000. *The Right to the Highest Attainable Standard of Health.* General Comment No. 14. (E/C.12/2000/4).

Cummins, S., and S. Macintyre. 2006. Food environments and obesity-neighbourhood or nation? *International Journal of Epidemiology* 35: 100–104.

Demakakos, Panayotes, Nazroo, James, Breeze Elizabeth, and Marmot Michael. 2008. Socioeconomic status and health: the role of subjective social status. *Soc Sci Med* 67: 330-340.

Evans, Gary W., and Schamberg Michelle A. 2009. Childhood poverty, chronic stress, and adult working memory. *Proc Natl Acad Sci U S A.* 106: 6545–6549.

Franzini, L., J.C. Ribble, and A.M. Keddie. 2001. Understanding the Hispanic paradox. *Ethnicity and Disease* 11 (3): 496–518.

Fraser, Nancy. 2009. *Scales of justice.* New York: Columbia University Press.

Fraser, Nancy. 2003. Social justice in the age of identity politics: redistribution, recognition and participation. In Nancy Fraser and Axel Honneth, *Redistribution or Recognition? A Political-Philosophical Exchange.* London-New York: Verso.

Gallo, Linda C., Penedo, Frank J., Espinosa de los Monteros, Karla, and Arguelles, William. 2009. Resiliency in the face of disadvantage: do Hispanic cultural characteristics protect health outcomes? *Journal of Personality* 77 (6): 1707-1746.

Gordon-Larsen, P., M.C. Nelson, P. Page, and B.M. Popkin. 2006. Inequality in the built environment underlies key health disparities in physical activity and obesity. *Pediatrics* 117: 417–424.

Hamlin, Christopher. 2010. *Public health and social justice in the age of Chadwick: Britain, 1800–1854.* Cambridge (UK): Cambridge University Press.

Heidegger, Martin. 1977. Die Zeit des Weltbildes. In *Holzwege*, Gesamtausgabe, Band 5, 75–115. Frakfurt am Main: Vittorio Klostermann.

Henry J. Kaiser Family Foundation. 2009. Putting women's health care disparities on the map: examining racial and ethnic disparities at the state level. http://www.kff.org/minorityhealth/upload/7886.pdf. Accessed: 7 october 2023.

Izquierdo, María Jesús. 1998. *El malestar en la desigualdad.* Madrid: Cátedra.

Marmot, Michael G., G. Rose, M. Shipley, and P.J. Hamilton. 1978. Employment grade and coronary heart disease in British civil servants. *Journal of Epidemiology and Community Health* 32: 244–249.

Marmot, Michael. 2006 (2ª). Introduction. In Marmot, Michael and Wilkinson, Richard G., *Social determinants of health*, pp. 1–5. Oxford: Oxford University Press.

Marmot, Michael, Siegrist, Johannes and Theorell, Tores. 2006 (2ª). Health and the psychosocial environment at work. In Marmot, Michael and Wilkinson, Richard G., *Social determinants of health*, 97–130. Oxford: Oxford University Press.

Martínez Part, Salvador. 2016. Derecho a la salud: competencia pública/privada. In Fernández Ruiz-Gálvez, Encarnación/Garibo Peyró, Ana-Paz, *El futuro de los derechos humanos.* Valencia: Tirant lo blanc.

Nussbaum, Martha C. 2006. *Frontiers of justice: disability, nationality, species membership.* Cambridge, Mass: Belknap Press of Harvard University Press.

Nussbaum, Martha C. 2011. *Creating capabilities: the human development approach.* Cambridge, Mass: Belknap Press of Harvard University Press.

Peter, Fabienne. 2001. Health equity and social justice. *Journal of Applied Philosophy* 18 (2): 159–170.
Rawls, John. 1993. *Political liberalism*. New York: Columbia University Press.
Rosen, George. 2015. (revised expanded edition). *A history of public health*. Baltimore: Johns Hopkins University Press.
Ruiz-Sanz, Mario. 2016. La indefinición semántica de la expresión 'justicia ambiental' y sus comprensibles circunstancias estratégicas. *CEFD* 34: 270–293.
Sen, Amartya. 1992. *Inequality reexamined*. Oxford: Oxford University Press.
Sen, Amartya. 1993. Wellbeing and capability. In Martha Nussbaum and Amartya Sen (eds) *The quality of life*. Oxford: Clarendon Press.
Sen, Amartya. 1999. *Development as freedom*. New York: Oxford University Press.
Sen, Amartya. 2009. *The idea of justice*. London: Allen Lane.
Seoane, José Antonio. 2016. El derecho a una capacidad de salud segura. *Ius Et Scientia* 2 (2): 42–53.
Shaw, Mary, Dorling, Danny and Smith, George Davey. 2006 (2ª). Poverty, social exclusion and minorities. In Marmot, Michael and Wilkinson, Richard G., *Social determinants of health*, pp. 196–223. Oxford: Oxford University Press.
Stafford, Mai and McCarthy, Mark. 2006 (2ª). Neighbourhoods, housing, and health. In Marmot, Michael and Wilkinson, Richard G., *Social determinants of health*, pp. 297–317. Oxford: Oxford University Press.
Stringhini, S., S. Sabia, M. Shipley, E. Brunner, H. Nabi, M. Kivimaki, et al. 2010. Association of socioeconomic position with health behaviors and mortality. *JAMA* 303: 1159–1166.
Valls-Llobet, Carme. 2009. *Mujeres, salud y poder*. Madrid: Cátedra.
Valls-Llobet, Carme. 2018. *Medio ambiente y salud. Mujeres y hombres en un mundo de nuevos riesgos*. Madrid: Cátedra.
Venkatapuram, Sridhar. 2011. *Health justice. An argument from the capabilities approach*. London: Polity.
Venkatapuram, Sridhar. 2013. Health, vital goals, and central human capabilities. *Bioethics* 27 (5): 271–279.
Wadsworth, Michael and Butterworth, Suzie. 2006 (2ª). Early life. In Marmot, Michael and Wilkinson, Richard G., *Social determinants of health*, 31–53. Oxford: Oxford University Press.
Whitehead, Margaret. 1990. *The concepts and principles of equity and health*. Copenhagen: World Health Organization.
Wilkinson, Richard, and Michael Marmot, eds. 2003. 2nd. Social determinants of health. The solid facts: WHO.
Williams, David R., and Selina A. Mohammed. 2009. Discrimination and racial disparities in health: Evidence and needed research. *Journal of Behavioral Medicine* 32 (1): 20–47.
World Conference on Social Determinants of Health. 2011. *Rio Political Declaration on Social Determinants of Health*, Rio de Janeiro, Brazil, 21 October.
Zubiri, Xavier. 1963 (5ª). La nueva física. In *Naturaleza, Historia, Dios*. Madrid: Editora Nacional.

Chapter 4
Vulnerability: At the Source of Biolaw

Claudio Sartea

Abstract This work takes human vulnerability, in a philosophical perspective, as the starting point for tracing the development of biolaw as an interdisciplinary field of knowledge. The first part reflects on the category itself of vulnerability, analyzing the term and similar terms, verifying the legitimacy of a generalization of this element of humans, and illustrating the reasons why the accusation of naturalistic fallacy is not decisive for finding the foundations of justifications and the obligatoriness of biolegal rules. The second part creates a link between the anthropological perspective and biolegal theory and practice, starting from vulnerability, and developing a critical analysis of some applications already operating in current positive regulations. In the context of a biolaw that sees itself as a protector of human rights related to the corporeity of every human being, these reflections provide a non-contingent anthropological reason that, applied to different situations, justifies existing rules or allows a reasoned and proactive criticism of them.

Keywords Corporeity · Vulnerability · Biolaw · Anthropological foundation of legal rules

4.1 Introduction

Can weakness be a form of strength? Are our limits, needs, or overall fragility a sign of our failure or of our greatness and peculiar beauty? Martha Nussbaum may be right when she states that "part of the peculiar beauty of human excellence just is its vulnerability. The tenderness of a plant is not the dazzling hardness of a gem. There seem to be two (perhaps incompatible) kinds of value here. Nor, perhaps, is the beauty of a true human love the same as that of the love of two immortal gods, only shorter. The liquid sky that covers these people and circumscribes their

C. Sartea (✉)
University of Perugia, Perugia, Italy
e-mail: claudio.sartea@unipg.it

© The Editor(s) (if applicable) and The Author(s), under exclusive license to Springer Nature Switzerland AG 2024

J.-A. Seoane and O. Vergara (eds.), *The Discourse of Biorights*, The International Library of Bioethics 109, https://doi.org/10.1007/978-3-031-66804-3_4

possibilities also lends to their environment a quick, gleaming splendor that would not, we suspect, be the climate of heaven" (Nussbaum 1984, p. 2).

Continuing along these lines, we could say much more about the relationships between gods and men, immortals and mortals, heaven and earth, but we would be crossing the borders of philosophy and entering the even more mysterious domain of theology. This work however, framed within the world of mortals, will move in a different direction, taking human vulnerability, in a philosophical and anthropological perspective, as the starting point for tracing the development of biolaw as an interdisciplinary field of knowledge.

The first part reflects on the category itself of vulnerability, analyzing the term and similar terms, verifying the legitimacy of a generalization of this element of humans, and illustrating the reasons why the accusation of naturalistic fallacy is not decisive for finding the foundations of justifications and the obligatoriness of biolegal rules (and of legal norms in general). The second part creates a link between the philosophical perspective and biolegal theory and practice, starting from vulnerability, and develops a critical analysis of some applications already operating in current positive regulations.

According to the Italian philosopher Sergio Cotta (Cotta 1991, *passim*, Cotta 2015, pp. 127), the best justification for legal rules is that they promote coexistence as an essential modality of human beings. Legal rules exist and oblige because that coexistence is necessary for the survival of human beings: they guarantee its possibility. When the rule of law does not coincide with the mere exercise of power, it needs a foundation that makes it reasonable and justifies its claim to obedience even in the absence of sanctions.

The specificity of biolegal relationships is that, as they affect the manifestations of our 'bios', they expressly involve a dimension of vulnerability typical of human beings. It is by being animal (even before being social and rational) that human beings show their vulnerability. Together, materiality, corporeity, penetrability and vulnerability constitute a series of inescapable cognitive sequences for discovering and understanding human beings. Of these aspects of our being, and of the relations that depend on it, biolaw must concentrate its normative attention on that of vulnerability.

In the context of a biolaw that conceives itself as a protector of human rights related to the corporeity of every human being, these reflections try to provide a non-contingent anthropological reason that, applied to different situations, justifies existing rules or allows a reasoned and proactive criticism.

4.2 Human Beings Are Vulnerable

Compared to the category of fragility, which can also legitimately be used for an philosophical reading of biolaw (D'Agostino 2011, pp. 119–126; Sartea 2012, *passim*), that of vulnerability is even richer and more interesting. As has been observed by

Alfredo Marcos, "the vulnerability of human beings [is] due to their biological condition as animals" (Marcos 2012, p. 95; my translation). Compared to fragility, vulnerability better describes and represents the vital situation of human beings. Crystal is also fragile, but the image to which the term 'vulnerable' alludes metaphorically is necessarily connected to two related factors unrelated to crystals. For, if vulnerability is equivalent to the ability to be traversed (the term derives from *vulnus*, meaning 'wound', and *habilis* meaning 'aptitude' or 'predisposition', in this case to receive a wound), every vulnerable being as such must per force be a living being, and secondly be completely covered and surrounded by a surface which is penetrable under certain conditions and by certain bodies. This surface signifies and functions as protection, containment and to a certain extent (at least at the existential level) identity, because it contains the material bases of the organism's vitality. For example, the sap of a plant cannot flow out without causing the plant to die (and therefore the vital core of the plant needs to be covered by a cortex, a peel, or some other protective surface); the blood of an animal in order to circulate effectively not only needs vessels like veins and arteries, but also needs to remain enclosed in them, just as these vessels in turn need to be protected from external elements by the skin, hair and fat that fully cover the animal's body to avoid the risk of fatal hemorrhaging. The *vulnus* is the gash in this protective surface, the interruption of its continuity necessary for life, the penetration that causes a discontinuity (which may or may not be traumatic), an opening in the protective tissue or of vital valves normally closed to protect the intimate homeostatic balance of the living being.

Vulnerability thus means life (albeit perhaps wounded life), and the ability of being penetrated from the outside. That which is only fragile, and not also vulnerable, breaks when it is stressed by external forces. It does not allow itself to be traversed. Just as fragility is associated with breakage, vulnerability is associated with penetration, which may or may not be of a violent nature and may even be necessary. If we consider such typical processes of living animals as breathing, nourishment and reproduction, we can see that each of them requires vulnerability as here defined. Each requires the presence of porosity or organs of passage from the outside to the inside. Without exception, all these processes emphasize the structural dependence of living beings on the environment in which they are located, to live both as individuals and as a species. If there were no accesses, if living organisms were impenetrable and invulnerable (i.e., completely covered by a surface that cannot be traversed in any way, and which is therefore insulating, or without biological inputs), they could not breathe, exchange nutrients or hydrating substances with the outside, or activate the reproductive processes. They would ultimately find themselves in a situation incompatible with life, both as individuals and as a species.

That there is no substantial difference between vulnerability and penetrability, with respect to living organisms, is also confirmed by the fact that there can be violent reproductive acts (in rational beings for example, these are clearly vulnerabilities of the body or the will), significant food problems (such as poisoning from toxic substances taken by mistake by a human or non-human animal, or—more basically—indigestion, or the decision not to eat or to obstruct breathing). But if this is the case, it is even clearer that, far from being a limit, a defect, a handicap, a conditioning, or however else we want to define it in negative terms, vulnerability is rather the condition itself (or at least one of the main conditions)[1] of our vitality. It is a commonplace in physiology that the organic maturation and fullness of the individual coincide with his, her or its environmental interaction (for a classic text, see Eccles 1979). Signs of good health and the promise of development are certainly not found in biological self-references nor in the closure of the organism, but rather in its ability to interact effectively with the external environment. From this point of view, dependence is therefore not a symptom of contingent immaturity or structural imperfection, but rather its opposite (Musio 2006). Just as solitude and isolation are not indices of autarchy, but rather of a critical situation for living beings that can even become a cause of death.

With the above observations I have tried to show, on the phenomenological and biological levels, that: (a) vulnerability is a richer and more expressive conceptual category to describe the human condition than fragility; (b) vulnerability and penetrability converge in describing the natural opening of the living individual to the outside world, an opening characterized by ambivalence; (c) the interaction between external and internal is a condition of the vitality of the individual; (d) the dependence among living beings and of living beings with their environment, which derives from this interaction, is not a limitation of individuals but rather a vital necessity, a fundamental need.

4.3 *Excursus*: Vulnerability According to Jorge Luís Borges

What we have observed about the vital functions of the organism can also be extended to the psychic development of rational living beings: knowledge is also willingness to let oneself be penetrated from the outside, just as, even more so, is every desiring and volitive activity. For a long time, and thanks above all to the phenomenology of the first half of the last century,[2] Western philosophy has undertaken the collective effort required by the advancement beyond Cartesian dualism. With evocative, intense words, Emmanuel Lévinas, a thinker who is certainly sensitive to these suggestions, places us in the new scenario when, for example, he stresses that "the *psyche* or animation is the way a relationship between uneven terms, without any common time, arrives at a relationship [...]. Animation is not better expressed by the metaphor of inhabitation, the presence of a pilot in the helm of his boat, a vital principle immediately assimilated with a directive principle, or the virility of a *logos* and a command. Animation can be understood as an exposure to the other, the passivity of the for-the-other in vulnerability, which refers to maternity, which sensibility

[1] Moreover, it is the classical concept of intuition that defines the body of every living being as *principium individuationis* at least if one understands it in the Aristotelian-Thomist sense of a *materia signata quantitate*.

[2] Take for example the contribution to Edmund Husserl's phenomenological thinking by scholars like Merleau-Ponty (1958).

signifies" (Lévinas 1981, pp. 70–1). On sensibility, Lévinas adds: "Sensibility [...] is a pre-original not resting on oneself, the restlessness of being persecuted—Where to be? How to be? It is a writhing in the tight dimensions of pain, the unsuspected dimensions of the hither side. It is being torn up from oneself, being less than nothing, a rejection into the negative, behind nothingness; it is maternity, gestation of the other in the same. Is not the restlessness of someone persecuted but a modification of maternity, the groaning of the wounded entrails by those it will bear or has borne. In maternity, what signifies is a responsibility for others, to the point of substitution for others and suffering both from the effect of persecution and from the persecuting itself in which the persecutor sinks. Maternity, which is bearing par excellence, bears even responsibility for the persecuting by the persecutor" (Lévinas 1981, pp. 75–6).

In some pre-ontological and therefore prerational manner, our existence is linked to motherhood as a constitutive dependence of the absolutely vulnerable on the womb that protects and nourishes it, conditioning our own possibility of coming into the world and then accompanying it without ceasing at least as unrepresentable, not communicable perception.

Indeed, even intellectual activity, which is the activity least bound to the senses (even in its most autonomous form, that of reflexivity), needs the opening of the external and internal senses to the outside world to become activated and to be constantly nourished. Even the way people talk (and therefore think and often react) is profoundly influenced by learning from those around us, just like the way we walk or style our hair. It is not necessary to question the innatist hypothesis to understand and accept that the universe of our concepts and our representations is indebted to the senses and to the relations with others for the vast majority of what it contains, starting from the words we use to describe it. Being an area that is—to a certain extent—prerational, art and literature can be of special help in exploring vulnerability with some hope of discursive success. After all, it is for geographic border situations like this that the very promising discipline *Law and Literature* has developed.

For our theme, I have in mind one of the central stories of a famous collection by Jorge Luís Borges, the one that gives the title to the anthology: *El Aleph*. The protagonist who finally manages to see the Aleph, that is, the imaginary place that constitutes the center of the universe, thus reports his experience: "I saw the Aleph from everywhere at once, saw the earth in the Aleph, and the Aleph once more in the earth and the earth in the Aleph, saw my face and my viscera, saw your face, and I felt dizzy, and I wept, because my eyes had seen that secret, hypothetical object whose name has been usurped by men but which no man has ever truly looked upon: the inconceivable universe".[3] It should be noted that, in order to obtain this prodigious vision because it is universal but concise, and therefore most desired, Borges's protagonist must place himself in a position of special vulnerability, which he does almost without being aware of it, until he comes to himself again and understands,

[3] "Vi el Aleph, desde todos los puntos, vi en el Aleph la tierra, y en la tierra otra vez el Aleph y en el Aleph la tierra, vi mi cara y mis vísceras, vi tu cara, y sentí vértigo y lloré, porque mis ojos habían visto ese objeto secreto y conjetural, cuyo nombre usurpan los hombres, pero que ningún hombre ha mirado: el inconcebible universo" (Borges 2006, p. 241).

after the fact, the risk he had accepted: "Suddenly I realized the danger I was in; I had allowed myself to be locked underground by a madman, after first drinking down a snifter of poison".[4] (In fact, the Aleph's observation point is located in the dark basement of the house of a little-known host, who, we should add, offered his guest a strong drink, which may have been a poison).

For our purposes, there is an even more suggestive (and brilliant) story in the same collection of Borges's works: *La escritura del dios*. Here, the protagonist is incarcerated, and consequently has all the time he wants to meditate on the destiny of the universe and the function of language: "I reflected that even in the languages of humans there is no proposition that does not imply the entire universe; to say 'the jaguar' is to say all the jaguars that engendered it, the deer and turtles it has devoured, the grass that fed the deer, the earth that was mother to the grass, the sky that gave light to the earth".[5]

Sergio Cotta also perceived the profound philosophical significance of Borges's words: "This is the phenomenological sense of being-with: being together in the vital interconnectedness of the different entities that constitute it—in this case, human beings" (Cotta 1991, p. 69; my translation). But this "vital interconnectedness", of which Borges speaks poetically and Cotta philosophically, essentially depends on what we have described above as an aptitude to letting ourselves be penetrated (not only cognitively, but more generally: I would say *existentially*) by the world, events, vital processes, by physical, chemical, biological, genetic and epigenetic relationships, which gradually forge our identity as real, historical and concrete living beings. Therefore, Marcos is right when he states that "We must try, as far as possible, to mitigate our vulnerability and protect ourselves from possible damage: but the aspiration to absolute invulnerability is somewhat absurd or contradictory for human beings" (Marcos 2015, p. 409; my translation. At this point, the author goes on to quote the myth of Achilles, immersed by his mother, Thetis, in the river of invulnerability but held by his heel by the caring, maternal hand, to avoid the risk of his drowning. Years later, the death of Achilles would come through that unique vulnerable heel, penetrated by Paris's poisoned arrow). In other words, trying to go beyond vulnerability would not only be risky or utopian, but explicitly anti-humanistic.

Here, in my opinion, lies the central objection to the transhumanist and post-humanist tendencies which, despite their differences in nuances, are all inspired by the Nietzschean idea of the man of today as a bridge to the man of tomorrow (Nietzsche 1964),[6] and entrust the task of empowering human beings (human enhancement)

[4] *Ivi*, p. 240: "Súbitamente comprendí mi peligro: me había dejado soterrar por un loco, luego de tomar un veneno".

[5] *Ivi*, p. 173: "Consideré que aun en los lenguajes humanos no hay proposición que no implique el universo entero; decir *el tigre* es decir los tigres que lo engendraron, los ciervos y tortugas que devoró, el pasto de que se alimentaron los ciervos, la tierra que fue madre del pasto, el cielo que dio luz a la tierra".

[6] "What is great about human beings is that they are a bridge and not a purpose: what is lovable about human beings is that they are a crossing over and a going under" (*Zarathustra's Prologue*, n. 4).

to biotechnologies and technoscience (see, for a reflection from the point of view of legal philosophy, Palazzani 2015 and 2017) to the point of being overtaken by a very different and far more pervasive “immanent transcendence” on the biological level than what Max Weber once wrote about. But if what we have considered thus far is true, this kind of perspective loses the very first thing that must be preserved and defended, mankind’s humanity (as Jonas claims, 1998). For beings who, as long as they live like human animals, receive and cannot not receive any kind of *vulnera* because of the necessary dialogue with the world that allows them to live, that is, positive penetrations, such as food, knowledge, vision, or negative one, such as bodily lesions, environmental germs, pollution (regarding this problem, see also the provocative essay by Sandel 2009).

4.4 Can Human Vulnerability Be Normative?

The above considerations take on an ethical and juridical importance if we apply them to the human animal, because the fundamental needs of this particular living being have normative relevance in themselves. To explain this, it is obviously necessary to address the implicit criticism in the so called ‘Law of Hume’ (the ‘Is-ought problem’: thus named for the first time and applied to the foundation of law by Moore 2013), according to which it would be forbidden (because logically unjustified) to go from being to having to be in order to lay the foundations for morality as well as for that sort of collective minimum moral that is human rights. In observance of this ‘law’, it would therefore not be permissible to transform into binding indications (in terms of the duties to which rights correspond) the needs of individuals, not even the most radical needs, because the one belongs to the level of being and the other to that of having to be.

This is not the place to discuss in detail the content of the ‘Law of Hume’, which has been the subject of many publications and re-elaborations (in Italy, probably the most accurate essay, even if a bit dated, is Carcaterra 1969). I will therefore limit my speech to some considerations more directly related to the legitimacy of considering the human condition of vulnerability as a basis for justifying duties towards it. This implies first of all the acceptance of a paradox, for we have said that vulnerability is a basic aspect of humans (as in general of all living things), and therefore cannot be overcome. But it is also a positive characteristic because being is positive, if we do not accept the alternative nihilist view.[7] But the duty to take

[7] On this point, I agree the work of two German thinkers: Hans Jonas (on the bioethics level: Jonas 1998), e Joseph Pieper (on the anthropological level: Pieper 2012): adherence to reality is also love, affirmation of its goodness as well as its necessity (inasmuch as it exists and is necessary for my existence). In any case, I recognize that it is a fundamental option. But I must also add that ideological premises are not necessary to take seriously the survival instinct and consider it a sufficiently reliable (because objective) guide for favoring existence over non-existence, which reflects the preferability of something with respect to nothingness. As is evident, this is an empirical and metaphysical use of the concept of nature.

action to meet the needs arising from it, particularly in special situations, leads to a different approach: no longer in positive terms of acceptance, but in oppositional and dialectical terms, as a call to do what is possible (and therefore due) to limit problems and promote respect for equality according to what is just. The explanation is not complicated. Among rational and therefore free beings, the dependency that arises from vulnerability can be a choice and not simply a destiny (on this see for example Kittay 1999). Thus, moral and juridical laws are conceivable that address, by means of rules and sanctions, the non-fulfillment of solidarity we owe to our fellow human beings.

What remains to verify is the actual content of the 'Law of Hume'. As has been well observed (D'Agostino 2006a, pp. 75–87), a minimal validity of this 'law' is undeniable. Otherwise, the very idea of normativity would be inconceivable, and ethics, law, political criticism would have no content. In other words, it is necessary to distinguish between being and having to be. For not everything that is must therefore also be, if we take the point of view of the person who must decide the action (especially if this person is a legislator aiming to indicate or prohibit conduct), or of the judge who must then evaluate it. But our attention is directed not to actions but to conditions or modes of being, and it is precisely from their structure that the binding effect derives, based on the implicit premise of the desirability of being. That is to say, since the recognition and protection/satisfaction of certain needs are necessary for the existence of certain living beings, and this existence is desirable and positive, then it is a right of those living beings to receive the necessary treatment, and it is a duty of the group to which they belong to grant it to them.

Consider, for example, the beings that, according to Jonas, represent the archetype of responsibility: newborns. If it is good that humanity as species exists, it is good that newborns exist. For them to exist, it is necessary to take care of them, and those responsible for this treatment are initially and generally the ones who generated them, and later the entire animal group involved in its own continuation, in our example, the human group. There is normativity but there is no naturalistic fallacy, and even if Jonas calls it a categorical imperative, from his Kantian perspective, it need not be considered in terms of a greater normative premise, as Höffe did for example (Höffe 1988). This author spoke of original intuitions, indemonstrable first principles of morality. Whatever conceptual configuration one wants to attribute to the starting point, the normative consequence derives linearly from it. I prefer to read it in metaphysical terms because in this way there is no need to perceive it extrinsically, like a pre-existing order or rule whose source and therefore whose legitimacy cannot be comprehended.

In the perspective I favor, the conditionality of conduct is not deduced from existence but from essence, which with the premise of the goodness of the existence of that essence, includes the merit of protection, the foundation of the obligation of satisfactory conduct, the justification of the penalty for its omission and even more so for the open violation of the rights in question (criminal law). To explain this, both Cotta and D'Agostino recall the theses presented by Edmund Husserl in *Logical Research*: "If we say 'A soldier should be brave', this does not mean that we or anyone else are wishing or willing, commanding or requiring this. One might rather suppose that a corresponding wishing and requiring would be generally justified, i.e. in relation to every soldier, though even this is not quite right, since it is surely not necessary that we should here be really evaluating a wish or a demand. 'A soldier should be brave' rather means that only a brave soldier is a 'good' soldier, which implies (since the predicates 'good' and 'bad' divide up the extension of the concept 'soldier') that a soldier who is not brave is a 'bad' soldier. Since this value-judgement holds, everyone is entitled to demand of a soldier that he should be brave, the same ground ensures that it is desirable, praiseworthy, etc., that he should be brave. The same holds in other instances. 'A man should practise neighbourly love', i.e. one who omits this is no longer a 'good' man, and therefore *eo ipso* is (in this respect) a 'bad' man" (Husserl 2001, pp. 23–24). As we can see, Husserl's intent is to release the duty of behavior from extrinsic deontological dependencies, and to place it inside the concept.

Within the essentialist perspective, where the discourse is transferred from logic to ontology, behavioral obligations are thus shown in terms of the ethical reverberation of an ontological matrix. I am convinced that in this perspective, much more than in the sophisticated scheme of Kant's, Rousseau's and nowadays Habermas's self-regulation (Habermas 1998), the problematic and paradoxical relationship between freedom and obedience can find a solution, which in legal discourse is reflected in the arduous, and entirely possible composition of rights and duties.

4.5 Biolaw in Action

Having overcome the objection of naturalistic fallacy, we can conclude this discussion of vulnerability as a source and guiding principle of theoretical biolaw (we can say 'biolaw in books', to evoke the distinction made for other purposes by Roscoe Pound—Pound 1010—and practical biolaw—'biolaw in action').[8] I will do so from two perspectives: philosophy of law and positive law.

5.1. From the perspective of philosophy of law, I consider vulnerability one of the concepts that most closely approximates the anthropological premise of juridical onto-phenomenology, that is, 'indigence'. This is a category introduced by Sergio Cotta in the 1970s but that, in my opinion, fifty years later continues to have a significant role in the anthropological reflection on law, and in current times to that part of the discipline identified as biolaw (for especially significant theoretical contributions in Italy on biolaw, see for example Palazzani 2002; Rodotà and Zatti 2008—the first chapters of the first volume are the most interesting from a philosophical perspective –; D'Agostino 2011; d'Avack 2015; Id. 2009). The anthropological extension I have elaborated on, which enlarges the scope of vulnerability to embrace humankind as its

---

[8] For an application to biolaw of the dichotomy applied by Pound to law in general, see Albert (2013).

constitutive and ineliminable condition, allows us to support it with Cotta's conceptual category, which obviously has a distinctly ontological character.[9] "Incompleteness, particularity and contingency can be gathered together in the unitary concept of the *finiteness* of being human [...]. The existential needs of security, cooperation and duration [which, as Cotta often repeats, are at the very origin of the need to structure human coexistence juridically], make us understand, with their undeniable reality, that finitude is perceived by humans as an *absence* or *defectiveness* of their being. Here lies the radical difference between humans on the one hand and animals and things on the other, which are also finite but not aware that their finiteness is defective. Consciousness of finiteness as a defect, drawn from experience and reflection, configures humans as indigent entities, in the literal sense of the word because they need something they lack. Indigence is the trait that marks the radical difference between the human and non-human level of being. It is therefore the first ontological characteristic of man" (Cotta 1991, p. 72; my translation). Vulnerability in human life, like indigence, or perhaps because it is a part of indigence, enters into self-consciousness and becomes not only a necessary stage of every individual's full self-understanding, but also the origin of the awareness of specific duties of care and therefore of the corresponding rights. I have tried here above to explain that vulnerability corresponds to openness toward the environment, in its ambivalent positive form (satisfaction of the vital needs of the individual and of the species, such as the exchange of oxygen and anhydride in breathing, or nutrition, or reproduction), and its negative one. Cotta also highlights the ambivalences inherent in the idea of relationship, which is both necessary and potentially harmful (Cotta 1991, 55), where this author speaks of *bellum omnium contra omnes* as of a possibility (which for the individualistic and sensational anthropology of Hobbes, is an unavoidable certainty), but where he also considers its reinterpretation beyond the "contrast of subjective truths", towards the composition in an "objective truth".

This process, which is generally valid for every human being, is further strengthened in those with special vulnerabilities, determined by age (newborn, child, or elderly), physical or mental health conditions, or specific disabilities or limitations. It is almost certainly due to this empowering effect that legislation to date has focused mainly on such specific situations of vulnerability. Although it is often overlooked, these situations share, as we shall see, a common anthropological background (according MacIntyre 1999), which is one of the reasons, by virtue of the principle of equality, for the ethical, moral and also legal obligation of the least vulnerable

[9] Here I am obviously not implying that Cotta's reference to phenomenology is the only possible reading today. For a more inclusive conceptual genealogy, in part because it includes contributions from other authors, see for example Patrão Neves (2006). It reaches the same conclusion: "The vulnerability principle exceeds the predominant logic of the claim of individual rights, and announces a logic of solicitude for the duties that concern the individual, highlighting the complementarity of a consolidated ethics of rights, founded on the freedom of the individual and developed through the strengthening of autonomy, and an urgent ethics of duties, founded on the responsibility of the other and developed with the strengthening of solidarity" (p. 172; my translation). For greater detail to the constitutive link between rights and duties in the semantics of human rights, see Sartea (2018).

to provide for the most vulnerable. This obligation does not compromise the principle of justice, but rather confirms it, as very appropriately observed D'Agostino (D'Agostino 2006b, 91). This author explicitly distances himself from certain positions of Martha Nussbaum: although she defends the dignity of the disabled person, she makes ambiguous distinctions that reveal in her position—as also in Rawls's and most of the others belonging to that North American philosophical thought (legal and political)—a preliminary, anti-metaphysical option full of disruptive consequences (see Nussbaum 2001, 47).

Our current times urge us to consider precisely this question.

5.2. This final section offers a survey of relevant legislation which begins with the UNESCO Universal Declaration on Bioethics and Human Rights (2005).[10] This is the first official regulatory document on international biolaw (although it clearly deals with 'soft law') to explicitly mention the vulnerability category[11] thus conferring it legal relevance.[12] The most central norm of this document for our discussion is found in Article 8, entitled *Respect for human vulnerability and personal integrity*: "In applying and advancing scientific knowledge, medical practice and associated technologies, human vulnerability should be taken into account. Individuals and groups of special vulnerability should be protected, and the personal integrity of such individuals respected". As the 2013 UNESCO Report on this Declaration explains, "the specific purpose of Article 8 is to address special vulnerabilities that occur, as a consequence of personal disability, environmental burdens or social injustice, in the contexts of healthcare, research and the application of emerging technologies in the biomedical sciences" (UNESCO Report 2013). The Report as a whole provides us with many valuable, international interpretations. It includes vulnerability among the anthropological categories that are crucial also for bioethics and human rights. It further indicates three macro areas calling for attention: "healthcare setting", "human participant research", "development and application of emerging technologies in the biomedical sciences". What is most significant for our purposes

[10] http://www.unesco.org/new/en/social-and-human-sciences/themes/bioethics/bioethics-and-human-rights/.

[11] It is the first, if we refer to the documents that have an express legal value, although it is preceded by other legal and ethical texts, such as the *US Belmont Report* (1978) which for many is considered one of the founding acts of bioethics as autonomous knowledge, the *International Ethical Guidelines for Biomedical Research Involving Human Subjects*, approved in its latest version in 2002 by the Council for International Organizations of Medical Sciences (CIOMS), as well as the latest edition (2013) of the Declaration of Helsinki, which specifically refers to vulnerability in articles 19 and 20. The *Barcelona Declaration*, issued in 1998, was drawn up following the project *Basic Ethical Principles in European Bioethics and Biolaw*, funded by the European Commission. The final report was written by the researchers and academics in the project, and therefore has no direct political and juridical value, although it has played an important role in the progressive emergence of vulnerability as an ethical-juridical principle and therefore of its insertion into the legal and political discussion: for a reconstruction, see the essay by two protagonists of the research, Kemp and Rendtorff (2008), 239–249. It should be noted that the title assigned by the group to the 2000 report was precisely: *Basic Ethical Principles in European Bioethics and Biolaw. Autonomy, Dignity, Integrity and Vulnerability*. It is explained even better in the previous study by the same author: Rendtorff (2002), 235–244.

[12] Those interested in a historical-evolutionary reconstruction can see Sartea (2017), 779–792.

in Article 8, where it focuses on situations of special vulnerability, is its consideration of this category as potentially extending to all human beings. The discussion here is similar to MacIntyre's where he explains that 'disability' (his use here of this term is analogous to our present use of the word 'vulnerability') is a question of degrees (MacIntyre 1999, p. 2[13]), since all living human beings are affected. Consequently, for MacIntyre, disability (i.e., vulnerability) strictly speaking should not be seen as a problem, a handicap, a limiting form of irregularity, but rather as a characteristic of living human beings, a structural condition. MacIntyre's position concurs with that of this paper.

The Report is very explicit in affirming the double value of the category, because it establishes 'human vulnerability' as a universal concept (the adjective 'human' in this sense is revealing), before referring to situations of 'special vulnerability' represented by individuals and groups in conditions of greater weakness and therefore in need of special protection.[14] The legitimacy of this universalistic extension of the concept is confirmed unequivocally by the following statement in the Report: "Vulnerability, in its first and more general sense, is an essential feature of human nature and may therefore boost awareness of a common destiny and responsibility. This Report seeks to elaborate the scope and content of Article 8 of the Declaration of 2005, focusing on special vulnerabilities and taking into account conditions that, more or less directly, impinge upon the capacity to live as free and autonomous individuals; and on the right to live in a world where significant inequalities in the capacity to meet everyone's basic needs are adequately addressed" (UNESCO Report 2013, *Introductory Remarks* by the President Semplici, p. 5).

The initial statement, according to which "vulnerability is an essential feature of human nature and may therefore boost awareness of a common destiny and responsibility", is a very effective synthesis of our philosophical discussion here above, including the link between vulnerability as human condition and vulnerability as source of rights and duties, and the related criticism of the 'Law of Hume'. As a constitutive dimension of 'human nature' (note that the document does not hesitate to resort to this philosophically very cumbersome term), vulnerability leads to the awareness and, more importantly, the responsibility of a common destiny. This is where originates the connection between vulnerabilities and sources of biolaw, already signaled in the title. It reflects a definitive acquisition also in the attitude of UNESCO, as is made clear by the following words taken from the same text:

[13] "So we are invited, when we do think of disability, to think of 'the disable' as 'them' and other than 'us', as a separate class, not as ourselves as we have been, sometimes are now and may well be in the future".

[14] It is this completely legitimate and even intuitive distinction that provoked criticism of the vulnerability principle, which sees it as being legislatively irrelevant and having weak anthropological roots. See for example Kottow (2012), pp. 25–44. But, aside from possible reactions to each of his critical arguments, it should be noted that Kottow's conclusion goes in the same direction advocated here: "Bioethics must overcome the phase of proclaming rights and start emphasizing its prescriptive role of obligations to care for those with specific problems that prevent them from caring for themselves" (p. 44, my translation). Previously, Kottow had already criticized the vulnerability principle: Kottow (2004), pp. 281–287.

"The human condition implies vulnerability. Every human being is exposed to the permanent risk of suffering 'wounds' to their physical and mental integrity. Vulnerability is an inescapable dimension of the life of individuals and the shaping of human relationships. To take into account human vulnerability acknowledges that we all may lack at some point the ability or the means to protect ourselves, our health and our well-being. We are all confronted with the possibility of disease, disability and environmental risks. At the same time, we live with the possibility that harm, even death, can be caused by other human beings" (UNESCO Report 2013, n. 6). As clarified immediately after these words, the main objective of Article 8 is to provide for the special vulnerabilities of some sections of the population, the so-called "social vulnerabilities" about which I will say something further on. Nonetheless, we cannot ignore the refusal on the part of the UN body to define any whatsoever perspective based on the clear distinction between 'us' (the healthy, the adults, the wealthy, the privileged), and 'them' (the sick, the children, the poor, the disadvantaged). The porosity of the boundaries (or, in MacIntyre's image, the circulation up and down the ladder of disability) makes it incorrect (and ultimately discriminatory) to admit a clear separation between groups, precisely because of the ontological nature of vulnerability, of its constitutive inherence in our common nature.[15] The identification of special vulnerable groups in Article 8 and in the whole 2013 Report that develops its applicative scope, must be considered a second level, understandable and tolerable only on the condition that the universal attribution of vulnerability, understood in a general sense, is preliminarily accepted.

Closely connected to this presentation of the problem is the other important distinction proposed in the Report: "Two fundamental categories are highlighted that are relevant to these special responsibilities and obligations: (a) special (temporary or permanent) disabilities, disease and limitations imposed by the stages of human life; b) social, political and environmental determinants: for example, culture, economy, relations of power, natural disasters" (UNESCO Report 2013, n. 12). The document is dedicated to the second group of situations, because they are the most relevant to institutional action, at least in the sense that here intervention to improve the situation in possible. "Many individuals, groups and populations nowadays become especially vulnerable because of factors created and implemented by other human beings, in many cases in blatant violation of fundamental human rights" (UNESCO Report 2013, n. 14). In this affirmation, special vulnerabilities are not a consequence of a "natural lottery" or of uncontrollable events, but the result of factors that, however complex, can be traced back to human will. It is therefore not only possible to identify responsibilities and demand restitution or compensation, but it is also conceivable to

[15] Of a different opinion is Solbakk (2011), pp. 89–101. He maintains that the main innovation of the 2005 UNESCO Declaration is that Article 8 "represents the first concrete step at the global level towards strengthening a dual-type of conception of vulnerability [that expressly frees vulnerability from its association with the human condition by introducing a special version on which would depend the very possibility of its effective protection]. In this way, at the same time it was possible to proclaim vulnerability as a universal principle, recognizing the need to develop a language of vulnerability capable of prescribing protection measures based on context" (p. 98, my translation).

intervene through institutions to stop the causes of vulnerability, or to diminish their negative effects.

As we can see, it is a matter of demanding justice, for which the Report identifies three directions. Although not exhaustive, they contain many operational indications of great interest at the national level. "Vulnerability in Healthcare Setting" (for example, access to healthcare, inequality of power in healthcare); "Vulnerability in Human Participant Research" (for example, equivocal donations—of antibiotics –, inappropriate research, or vulnerability as a result of lack of research, as in the case of 'orphan diseases'); "Vulnerability in the development and application of emerging technologies in the biomedical sciences" (for example stigmatization, unfair pressure, unconsented collection of genetic data).

In synthesis, there are numerous possible lines of intervention, just as there are numerous spaces in which the action of legal norms and institutions can significantly increase the quality of the response to the demand for justice that comes especially from situations of special vulnerability, whether voluntary or involuntary, controllable or fortuitous. Furthermore, from this point of view, founding the biolegal reflection on the anthropology of vulnerability is not only perfectly legitimate, but also promises important fruits first, in terms of an authentic understanding of the problems, and then in terms of efforts aimed at equality, and therefore of justice.

References

Albert, Marta. 2013. ¿Hacia un bioderecho universal? Bioderecho en acción y funzionalización del valor de la vida humana. *Cuadernos de Bioética* XXIV: 223–237.

Borges, Jorge Luis. 2004. *The Aleph and Other Stories* (1949). Translation by A. Hurley. London: Penguin Classics Paperback.

Carcaterra, Gaetano. 1969. *Il problema della fallacia naturalistica. La derivazione del dover essere dall'essere.* Milano: Giuffrè.

Cotta, Sergio. 1991. *Il diritto nell'esistenza. Linee di ontofenomenologia giuridica.* Milano: Giuffrè.

Cotta, Sergio. 2015. *Giustificazione e obbligatorietà delle norme.* Roma: Studium.

D'Agostino, Francesco. 2006a. *Lezioni di filosofia del diritto.* Torino: Giappichelli.

D'Agostino, Francesco. 2006b. *Parole di giustizia.* Torino: Giappichelli.

D'Agostino, Francesco. 2011. *Fragilità.* In Id. *Bioetica e biopolitica. Ventuno voci fondamentali.* Torino: Giappichelli.

d'Avack, Lorenzo. 2009. *Verso un antidestino. Biotecnologie e scelte di vita.* Torino: Giappichelli.

d'Avack, Lorenzo. 2015. *Il potere sul corpo. Limiti etici e giuridici.* Torino: Giappichelli.

Eccles, John. 1979. *The human mystery.* Berlin-Heidelberg: Springer Verlag.

Habermas, Jürgen. 1998. *Faktizität und Geltung. Beiträge zur Diskurstheorie des Rechts und des demokratischen Rechtsstaat* (1992). English translation by W. Rehg. *Between Facts and Norms. Contributions to a Discourse Theory of Law and Democracy.* Cambridge (MA): MIT Press.

Höffe, Ottfried. 1988. *Den Staat braucht selbst ein Volk von Teufeln. Philosophische Versuche zur Rechts- und Staatsethik.* Ditzingen: Reclam.

Husserl, Edmund. 2001. *Logische Untersuchungen. Erster Band: Prolegomena zur reinen Logik* (1900). English translation by J.N. Findlay. *The shorter logical Investigations.* London-New York (NJ): Routledge.

Jonas, Hans. 1998. *The Imperative of Responsibility: In Search of an Ethics for the Technological Age* (1979). Chicago (IL): University of Chicago Press.

Kemp, Peter and Dahl Rendtorff, Jacob. 2008. The Barcelona Declaration. Towards an Integrated Approach to Basic Ethical Principles. Syntesis Philosophica XLVI: 239–249.
Kittay, Eva. 1999. *Love's Labor: essays on women, equality, and dependency (Thinking Gender)*. London-New York: Routledge.
Kottow, Miguel. 2004. Vulnerability: What kind of principle is it? *Medicine, Health Care and Philosophy* VII: 281–287.
Kottow, Miguel. 2012. Vulnerabilidad entre derechos humanos y bioética. Relaciones tormentosas, conflictos insolutos. Revista de la Facultad de Derecho de la Pontificia Universidad Católica del Perú LIX: 25–44.
Lévinas, Emmanuel. 1981. *Otherwise than Being, or, Beyond Essence* (1974). The Hague-London: Nijhoff.
MacIntyre, Alasdair. 1999. Dependent animal rationals. Why Human Beings Need the Virtues. Chicago (IL): Carus Publishing Company.
Marcos, Alfredo. 2012. Dependientes y racionales: la familia humana. *Cuadernos de Bioética* XXIII: 83–95.
Marcos, Alfredo. 2015. Neuroética y vulnerabilidad humana en perspectiva filosófica. *Cuadernos de Bioética* XXVI: 393–414.
Merleau-Ponty, Maurice. 1958. *Phenomenology of Perception* (1945). English translation by C. Smith. New York-London: Routledge.
Moore, George E. 2013. *Principia Ethica (1903)*. Los Angeles (CA): Hardpress Publishing.
Musio, Antonio. 2006. *L'autonomia come dipendenza. L'io legislatore*. Milano: Vita e Pensiero.
Nietzsche, Friedrich Wilhelm. 1964. *Thus Spoke Zarathustra. A Book for All and None* (1888). English translation by R.J. Hollingdale. London: Penguin.
Nussbaum, Martha C. 1984. *The Fragility of Goodness. Luck and Ethics in Greek Tragedy and Philosophy*. New York (NJ): Cambridge University Press.
Nussbaum, Martha. 2001. Disabled Lives: Who Cares? *New York Review of Books* 48.
Nussbaum, Martha. 2000. The future of feminist liberalism. *Proceedings and Addresses of the American Philosophical Association* 74 (2): 47.
Palazzani, Laura. 2002. *Introduzione alla biogiuridica*. Torino: Giappichelli.
Palazzani, Laura. 2015. *Il potenziamento umano. Tecnoscienza, etica e diritto*. Torino: Giappichelli.
Palazzani, Laura. 2017. *Dalla bioetica alla tecnoetica: nuove sfide al diritto*. Torino: Giappichelli.
Patrâo Neves, Maria. 2006. Sentido da vulnerabilidade: característica, condiçâo, princípio. *Revista Brasileira de Bioética* II: 157-172.
Pieper, Joseph. 2012. *In Tune with the World. A Theory of Festivity* (1963). English translation by R. and C. Winston. South Bend (IN): St. Agustine's Press.
Pound, Roscoe. 1910. Law in books and law in action. *American Law Review* 44: 12–36.
Rendtorff, Jacob. 2002. Basic ethical principles in European bioethics and biolaw: Autonomy, dignity, integrity and vulnerability—Towards a foundation of bioethics and biolaw. *Medicine, Health Care and Philosophy* V: 235–244.
Rodotà, Stefano, and Zatti, Paolo (Eds.). 2008. *Trattato di Biodiritto*. Milano: Giuffrè.
Sandel, Michael J. 2009. *The Case against Perfection: Ethics in the Age of Genetic Engineering*. Cambridge (MA): Belknap HUP.
Sartea, Claudio. 2022. *Biodiritto. Fragilità e giustizia*. 2° ed. Torino: Giappichelli.
Sartea, Claudio. 2017. Da Oviedo a Parigi: la vulnerabilità prima e dopo l'autonomia. *Medicina e Morale* LXVI: 779–792.
Sartea, Claudio. 2018. *Diritti umani. Un'introduzione critica*. Torino: Giappichelli.
Solbakk, Jan Helge. 2011. Vulnerabilidad: ¿un principio fútil o útil en la ética de la asistencia sanitaria? *Revista Redbioética/UNESCO* II: 89–101.
UNESCO Report. 2013. http://unesdoc.unesco.org/images/0021/002194/219494E.pdf.

Chapter 5
The Issue of Bodily Rights Alienation

Noelia Martínez-Doallo

Abstract A widespread Western conception about the sanctity of the human body and its parts prevents from any morally acceptable disposition of these objects. However, this entails nothing but a dualistic conception of the human being as a composite of detachable parts—namely, body and mind. Understood as the antechamber of legal rights, moral rights perform an important—yet frequently overlooked—justifying function that permeates the political discourse. Although the connection among moral, political and legal discourses should be properly acknowledged, certain boundaries are to mediate among each scope for the sake of certainty and accuracy. Intermediate realities, as the so-called human rights, serve to connect the moral and legal domains, still they also blur the lines along which the discourse is deployed. Moral entities are essentially inalienable, to the extent that they demarcate the moral status of the subject. By contrast, legal rights are essentially negotiable and, thus, alienable. The controversial instance of bodily rights will serve to test the assertions above.

Keywords Bodily rights · Discourse of rights · Inalienability · Moral status

5.1 The Conceptual Problem About Bodily Rights and Personal Integrity

The term 'bodily rights' is an all-encompassing expression frequently used to include a number of basic human moral values with a physical dimension—namely, autonomy, privacy, dignity, well-being, etc., and conventionally considered to deserve a reinforced legal protection. Although the concept of bodily rights is frequently used rather loosely to cover the ambit of personal integrity in general, there is room for discussion about the delimitation of the bodily, mental and moral dimensions of the person (Douglas 2020, 378). Strictly speaking, the bodily or physical scope deals with

N. Martínez-Doallo (✉)
Universidade da Coruña, A Coruña, Spain
e-mail: noelia.doallo@udc.es

© The Editor(s) (if applicable) and The Author(s), under exclusive license to Springer Nature Switzerland AG 2024

J.-A. Seoane and O. Vergara (eds.), *The Discourse of Biorights*, The International Library of Bioethics 109, https://doi.org/10.1007/978-3-031-66804-3_5

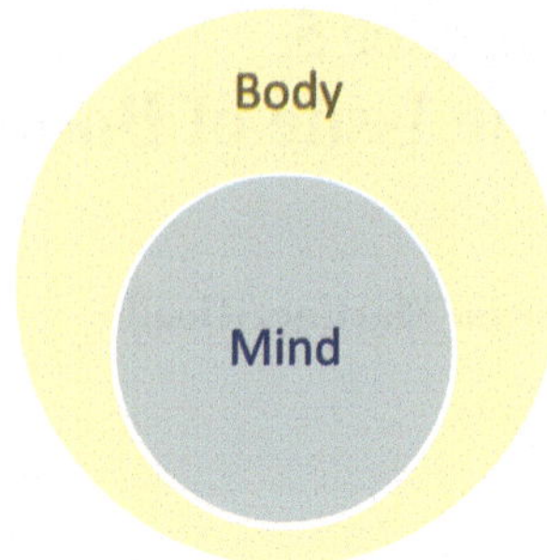

Fig. 5.1 The activity of the mind is essentially a bodily function

the corporeal boundaries of the human being, including the brain; whereas the mental or psychological scope refers to those emotional and intellectual processes leading to either deliberate or unintended actions and reactions derived from the information retrieved from individual and collective interactions. Despite the seeming straightforwardness of this distinction, physical and psychological scopes appear in fact deeply intertwined, for bodily exchanges with the natural and social environment provide individuals with certain stimuli that are captured through the senses, subsequently processed by the brain and assessed through the activity of the mind at various levels of profundity and complexity. It is within this assessment activity where the third element of human integrity comes into play, i.e., morality. Given that the brain is a bodily organ, both phases can be scientifically described as part of the activity of the human body in a broad sense, which leads to conclude that the mental sphere shares substantial room with the corporeal ambit, regardless of whether the mind can (interactionism) or cannot (epiphenomenalism) influence the body (Hergenhahn 2009, 18) (Fig. 5.1).

Still, the foregoing description by no means should be seen as resembling the Cartesian duality matter-mind (Descartes and Williams 1996, 57–72), for I define the mind as a type of matter. From the rejection of dualistic premises and determinism, I will make the case for a three-fold explanation in which morality—whether understood as a genuine human capability or the distinctive activity of human soul—fulfils a central role in the definition of human agency. Surely, the moral scope is the most uncertain element of personal integrity, often identified with the intellectual functions of the mind and, consequently, confused with the mental or psychological ambit. However, I suspect that it must be something different, beyond the physical bounds of the human body, while consubstantial to it. The fact remains that, from both individual and collective intellectual mind processes, human beings explain and refashion their existence and the settings in which they cohabitate. The conclusions obtained from such mental processes eventually become an important part of individuals' personal identity, since it is from the reflection around them that humans define, redefine and adopt the values and principles that will lead their individual and communal lives and make up their lifestyles within the respective milieu and tradition. The moral dimension rarely is the result of individual intellect alone, but rather a cultural construction. Nevertheless, individual contributions do count as genuine,

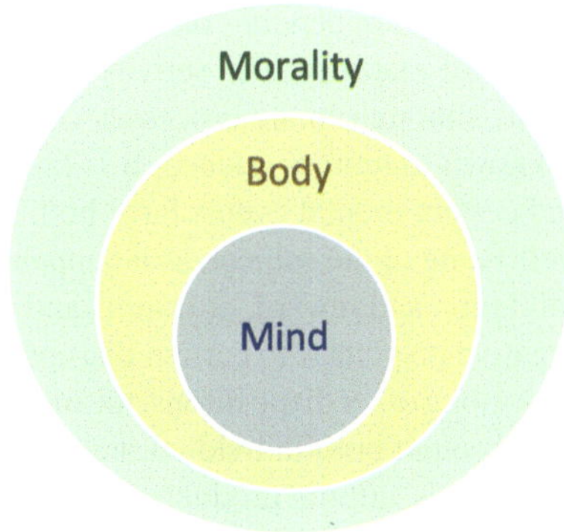

Fig. 5.2 Trinitarian personal integrity: body, mind and morality

potentially distinct elements of extant partially or completely shared moral systems under continuous revision and transformation. Even when the common morality of the pre-existing cultural tradition is seriously challenged and reformed, a certain substrate unavoidably remains. This approach to the conceptual problem about the definition of personal integrity not only broaches enduring philosophical discussions on the mind–body problem, but also as to the very essence of the human being and the composition of reality overall. Among the various sources of disagreement, dualistic conceptions of the person emerge as an important boundary to the understanding of intermediate entities placed at the intersection of the subjective and objective dimensions of human reality (Fig. 5.2).

Many instances show how humans tend to clumsily define reality from the schemes of dualism, a clear example comes from negative definitions, that is, that habitual practice of defining something through what the item under examination is not. By determining things through their opposites, human knowledge restricts itself to dualistic categories, losing perspective of important intermediate realities and processes. The widespread—though not unanimous—understanding of the person as a dual entity composed of body and mind illustrates this to perfection. I would rather suggest to adopt an approach able to encompass all possible sides of reality from the margins of a reasonable epistemological disagreement for, in further steps, anticipating guidelines to be adopted when a certain existential facet instantiates. Conceivably, there is a layered reality that goes along a continuum, whose constitutive tiers sometimes overlap and evolve over time. Be that as it may, a dualistic stance is excessively reductionist and only enables the comprehension of opposite ends of myriad existing realities and, therefore, it appears as an inadequate methodological approach.

Appling the previous premises to personal integrity, it seems possible to surmise that the body functions as an interface with the outer reality. The existence of such body and its parts is empirically demonstrable and quantifiable and, for this reason, constitutes a tangible proof of worldly existence. Besides, to have a body is a condition sine qua non for agency. Together with a body, persons characteristically have certain intellectual capabilities affording both inward and outward reflection, to a greater or lesser extent depending on the concrete individual, their phase of development and degree of maturity. The activity of the brain is also empirically measurable up to a point, although many processes concerning its formation and development remain unknown to human science. It is fair to say that there is a bodily scope of the mind and certain mental events have both positive and negative effects over the physical well-being of the subject, as it happens to occur with satisfaction derived from social validation and reward, or trauma and other forms of emotional distress coming from negative responses to certain disrupting events.

Among other dispositions, the mind collects, reacts to and learns from experiences. It is through both individual mental activity and collective exchange that cohabitation affords cultural products as language. Probably, available representations of individual perception emerge due to an urge to show, convey and share the perceived outer world and the conclusions obtained from it with congeners, which manifests human sociability and interdependent individuality, for it is the sum of individualities what conforms society and its many cultural outputs. Still, this commonality by no means prevents disagreement and paradigm disruption. Individual moral dimensions arise from the interaction of individuals' inner and outer worlds and, although proactively construed by them, it ultimately is the cultural upshot of a certain exchange, given the undeniable social human nature, even if it admits degrees. Many other factors also condition these processes, so that the foregoing explanation merely outlines the basic framework of individual bodily and moral cohabitation. Unfortunately, the description herein provided is only partial, approximate and necessarily reductionist, being possible to anticipate that many aspects of personal (co)existence have been unintentionally left aside.

Thus, personal integrity is not merely twofold but tentatively triple, since a differentiated moral dimension can be extracted from the interaction between the body and the mind, carried out through the human capabilities for reasonability and agency, being possible to reunify all these elements in the person, insofar as an inseparable substance. As it also happens to be with bodily and mental functions, morality represents an interpersonal capability, indeed the most special and distinctive human ability for—although not without controversy—it is precisely moral agency what apparently distinguishes human decision making and action from the activity of other species. This latter assumption is what shapes human dignity or, in other words, it is the either current or potential ability to act morally what confers dignity to the human being and, consequently, full moral status, i.e., moral personhood and responsibility. For the sake of coherence, the full moral status should be extended to any non-human being that exhibits readiness to moral agency. This attempt to unveil the moral human nature shows that it is within the moral dimension, the most characteristic realm of the 'ought,' where human values and principles are forged; whereas the physical and the mental scopes essentially lie in the 'be.' It is simply not true that 'ought' and 'be' are separated realities, for reality is both multifold and simultaneous. The need for conceptual isolation does nothing but to demonstrate the limits of human cognition and epistemological apprehension, yet there is no reason to think of it as the way in which natural substances exist.

Given all the above, to talk about bodily autonomy, bodily privacy, bodily dignity, etc. constitutes a rough simplification, for the exercise of either autonomy, privacy and human agency straightforwardly refers to the personal moral scope, that is, the sphere wherein persons give themselves guidelines for appropriate action and, at least, approximate descriptions as to the necessary conditions for agency and personal flourishing. Therefore, the term 'bodily rights' appears as excessively reductionist and incomplete when assessed from the holistic approach to the person herein presented. Still, since it is the consensus term used by both the relevant literature and jurisprudence, I will use it henceforth to refer to the problem of alienation of those legal rights devoted to ensuring not only physical but also moral integrity of persons. Before that, however, I consider necessary to disentangle an ulterior confusion among the different scopes wherein the discourse of rights happens—namely, the moral, political and legal domains, respectively, because the meaning of concepts and the positions of the parties involved may be relevantly different in each case.

5.2 The Transition from the Moral to the Legal Discourse

For the reasons above, I suggest a definition of personal integrity that considers those bodily, mental and moral traits defining the essence of the person. It is well known that the scope of morality is fundamentally practical for action is the context of morality, being only through action that the person confronts the requisites of moral agency, and it is within the collective discussion about morality where moral concepts arise and settle. Guidelines for moral action indicate how to behave both inwards and outwards. As to moral action towards oneself, there may be different levels of stringency or laxity according to the stance adopted, yet any moral obligation towards oneself rests upon the consideration of the full moral status of agents themselves. In the contemporary discourse, more emphasis is placed on how to behave towards our fellow beings. Many reasons explain this focus on the outward behaviour in the present-day Western moral discourse—inter alia, secularity and the decline of religious approaches, the triumph of anthropocentrism and libertarianism, the influence of capitalism and liberal democracies, and increasingly individualistic mind-sets as a result.

Among the various factors prompting looser moral standards towards oneself, I would highlight the growth and expansion of the discourse of rights, which has been equally prolific in the moral, political and legal landscapes, perhaps due to the strong emotional meaning the concept of rights brings along, since once a moral entitlement really turns into positive law, not only the titleholder has a power to bring action before the institutionalised justice, but also its enforcement justifies the use of physical force and coercion by the legitimate authority. Ironically enough, it was the triumph—and posterior distortion—of natural law conceptions about rights what triggered the consideration of rights as the most effective means for the protection of individual positions, even above an alternatively possible 'discourse of duties' that would have potentially been more conceptually rigorous and protective. The fact is that the popularisation of the discourse of rights brings about a certain discursive logic.

In the sense just pointed out, it appears as inconsistent to quotidian logic to speak of 'rights against ourselves,' for rights are assumed to essentially involve the idea of opposition or dispute among parties. Nonetheless, whereas to talk about legal duties to ourselves is fairly absurd, it is not so to speak of such duties at the moral level. This happens because whilst legal norms refer—or should refer—to minimum requirements for peaceful cohabitation, moral norms address the whole scope of moral agency, thus encompassing a wider area of human behaviour including both inward and outward actions. The widespread absence of these concepts in the current discourse somehow shows the pervasive influence of the legal language of rights.

Although, in order to avoid force and coercion as much as possible, the legal protection granted through legal rights should constitute a matter of minimum requirements devoted to creating the conditions for tolerable social coexistence, this does not prevent fellow beings from performing beyond their legal duties, and it may occur that sometimes they will even be morally required to do so. Inasmuch as this qualitative behaviour constitutes a moral duty, such acts are not supererogatory but they fall within the scope of subjects' moral duties that could well surpass the legal exigencies. In the absence of such moral duties, paying attention to others' interests and acting accordingly may lead to supererogation, sanctity and heroism, which cannot be labelled as obligatory in any conceivable sense. In any case, the moral dimension provides the rationale and foundation for the eventual positivisation of certain conducts that might give rise to correlative legal rights. Therefore, the ultimate reason for the legal institutionalisation of individual rights resides in the moral scope, in which various cultural upshots interplay with human experience to produce norms of conduct intended towards the exercise of moral agency to the greatest possible extent under the given circumstances and considering all interests at stake in the concrete case.

Moral arguments naturally interact with and permeate the political debate. It is precisely in the heart of the political discussion wherein many moral conceptions become part of the institutionalised discourse adopted by the legitimate authority, eventually becoming black letter law as a result of the corresponding law-making process. Thus, resembling the three-fold division of personal integrity, the discussion about due behaviour might be classified in three ambits—namely, moral, political and legal. The legal framework provides information about the minimum conditions of human behaviour within the given jurisdiction, as resulting from a well-established political debate with the proper formal and material guaranties. The moral discourse, in turn, supplies the foundations in which the above-mentioned legal positions substantiate and that have been sufficiently endorsed through appropriate political exchange (Fig. 5.3).

Despite the foregoing, the distinction between these three realms is not straightforward and a variety of moral, political and legal arguments is used at once in practice to uphold a myriad of different viewpoints and, above all, seek the support and acceptance of the community at various levels. This panorama really complicates the disentanglement of these scopes, their respective features and corresponding

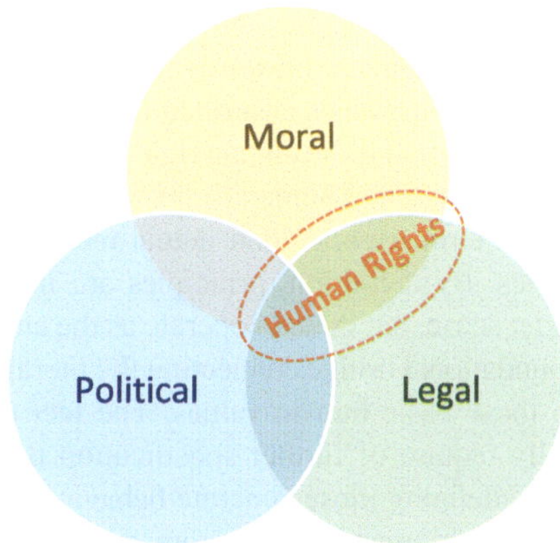

Fig. 5.3 Position of the human rights discussion in the moral, political and legal domains

language, which has frequently led to confuse either moral and legal entitlements with mere wishes lacking of sufficient basis. In addition, certain legal norms display a hybrid character for they incorporate justificatory elements proper to the moral discourse. Although it is a good legal practice to facilitate the interpretation of certain, especially open norms through means of explanatory legal provisions encompassing definitions, the issue raised herein refers to something rather different. Concretely, the so-called human, fundamental and constitutional rights—that, in other respects, are substantially similar yet formally different—could be categorised as a sort of hybrid legal norms in that they incorporate elements that are characteristic of both moral and political discourses. I will only focus herein on the intersection between the legal and the moral, yet the explanation requires of an additional conceptual distinction, viz., the classification of norms in rules and principles.

5.3 Human Rights Norms: Human Rights Legal Principles and Rules

Deeply inspired by Robert Alexy's works, I have adopted the classification of the norm in rules and principles. For the sake of concision, I will omit here an in-depth analysis about this conceptual distinction, yet it is worthwhile to roughly outline the aforesaid classification to build upon it afterwards. Principles require the realisation of their content to the greatest extent possible considering the legal and factual possibilities at hand. In Alexyan terms, principles are 'optimisation requirements' characterised by their fulfilment in various degrees in view of the circumstances of the case. Whereas opposing principles and rules determine the scope of legal possibilities, valid rules can only be observed or unobserved for they always relate to what is factually and legally possible. Consequently, the difference between rules and principles is not gradual but qualitative (Alexy 2010, 47–8).

In essence, either human, fundamental and constitutional rights establish commands directed towards lawmakers to create legal systems in keeping with the basic human values enshrined through such human rights legal principles. An analysis of most of these human rights provisions comprised in both Western constitutions and international human rights law documents reveal that, despite the deliberate use of the term 'rights,' their actual meaning and practical functioning is that of principles. By definition, principles are ill-suited to establish subjective rights in the strict sense, but they do operate as the antechamber of such rights, understood as the foundational bridge connecting the moral discourse with the legal protection granted to those basic human values. The fact that human rights provisions characteristically require of further specification through the establishment of domestic legal rules defining those concrete behaviours that subjects must adopt and follow under certain circumstances, customarily supplemented with legal actions that discharge in titleholders' will the motion of their enforcement, supports their classification as principles.

Human rights legal principles typically confer on individuals an enforceable claim to have their human rights interests legally protected by the authority. To this purpose, constitutional legal orders grant individuals the possibility to lodge writs of protection with the corresponding domestic constitutional court. Besides, at the international level, citizens of Council of Europe's member States have resort to the European Court of Human Rights to have the decisions issued by the respective domestic judicial bodies reviewed, which could be seen as a further, ultimate, international application for human rights revision. Nonetheless, these instances of legal recourse and protection in the hands of individuals are not horizontal, but they refer to the commitment national authorities have to respect citizens' human rights positions in the performance of their functions, at the risk of losing their international legitimacy otherwise.

Strictly speaking, subjective rights invariably involve horizontal relationships derived from detailed norms of conduct imposing correlative duties on other individuals through the formulation of legal rules. According to the correlativity doctrine, rights necessarily imply duties, even if not all duties imply rights. Yet, what is most characteristic of subjective rights is the enclosed power of titleholders to bring legal action before the competent authority, in case of inobservance of the correlative obligation. Still, this ascertainment does not prevent certain subjective rights from having a reinforced groundwork by virtue of the foundational principle supporting those legal positions of the parties comprised in the rule. This way, human rights legal principles provide reinforced foundations for the subsequent construction of an itemised legal order through rules. These principles necessarily describe the relevant behaviours in considerably broad terms that, especially at the international level, serves to ensure the respect for sovereignty and reasonable disagreement with regard to the specification of their content. Besides, directly exercisable claims of subjects derived from human rights legal principles are specifically intended to control that those basic human values enshrined in them are observed by the legislature, the executive or the judiciary when exercising their competencies and, in this sense, are nothing but mechanisms for monitoring the activity of state authorities.

So, does to hold the argument above equate to deny the very existence of human rights? Certainly not. Human rights do exist, at least formally, within constitutional legal orders and, which is more, they enjoy a reinforced standing. The conceptual problem herein pointed out comes from the laxity with which the legal category of rights is used. An example will shed light on this issue: can informed consent to medical intervention be classified as a human right? The answer is not straightforward. It is clear that informed consent is a subjective right of patients, actually a bundle of subjective rights to receive certain medical information and be respected in their decisions concerning the avenues of alternative medical treatment at hand, including non-intervention. These rights are, of course, correlative to medical professionals' duties to act accordingly. Norms establishing these subjective legal positions are rules that specify certain principles of human rights—namely, respect for private life encompassing, inter alia, personal integrity, autonomy, self-determination, and free decision making. Thus, those norms establishing the behaviour that medical professionals must follow when dealing with their patients are human rights legal rules with a disjunctive structure: they are observed or they are not. In turn, privacy and personal integrity typically adopt the form of principles requiring of further specification through the aforementioned rules of conduct, and function as optimisation requirements addressed to state authorities to pursuit the realisation of their content to the greatest possible extent in light of the extant factual and legal circumstances. Thence, informed consent is a subjective right of patients and the expression of their human rights to privacy and personal integrity.

Once human rights norms classified, it is time to consider whether and to what extent such sub-categories display the traits conventionally attributed to human rights—namely, universality, absolute character and inalienability. Nonetheless, the focus herein will be on inalienability and the case of bodily rights.

5.4 The Inalienability of Human Rights

Any definition of inalienability as a feature of human rights requires to properly distinguish it from the other two anticipated traits ascribed to human rights: absolute character and universality (Laporta 1987, 42). Whereas the absolute character of human rights prevents any third party, specifically state authorities, from taking the human rights of subjects; inalienability excludes titleholders' power or competence to consent or bargain a transgression of their human rights. Thus, such characterisation of human rights might be accused of actually granting a paternalistic protection that prioritises certain human values in detriment of others—particularly, human freedom. Likewise, inalienability substantially differs from universality because the criteria used for the adscription of human rights have nothing to do with the competence or incompetence of titleholders to give up their entitlements. Nonetheless, it could be maintained that in light of the universal attribution of these rights to all human beings without exception—and regardless of their degree of actual capability—it is necessary to prevent titleholders from alienating such important human values and goods, for such unconditional means of protection is precisely what justifies the imposition of correlative duties and the restriction of others' freedom. In that sense, human rights inalienability would not only entail unconditional correlative duties, but also immunities to ourselves (Thompson 1990, 59; Laporta 1987, 44). Ultimately, the issue of human rights inalienability can be reconducted to a moral question about the unwaiverability of human rights' contents (Laporta 1987, 43).

In the strict sense, human rights inalienability refers to the incompetence of titleholders to give up their corresponding legal positions, for their consent is consider to be invalid to produce any changes either in their own positions and those of their counterparties (McConnell 2000, ix). Therefore, correlative duties will invariably remain in full effect, in spite of titleholders' acts or statements alienating their human rights. Extrapolating Hohfeldian fundamental legal conceptions to the case of human rights (Hohfeld 1913, 20), the feature of inalienability would not entail an immunity to ourselves, but an incompetence to grant privileges for breaching correlative duties, in sharp contradiction with the postulates of the known as will or choice conception of rights. In this sense, to accept the inalienability of human rights brings out the denial of titleholders' consent as a valid contractual element for the construction and definition of human rights' legal positions. On the other hand, to support the alienation of human rights presupposes titleholders' capability for decision making and consent, which somehow runs up against the universal ownership of human rights, for not all human beings have these capabilities.

Nonetheless, a crucial question has gone unnoticed thus far: the hybrid nature of human rights, understood these latter as both partially moral and legal entities. To overlook this structural composition easily leads to multiple misunderstandings and unfortunate conclusions. The moral nature of human rights hampers a straightforward implementation of legal categories in their definition, in fact the very use of the word 'rights' to refer to such moral entities is in itself misleading, especially considering that, as to the legal side of their formulation, they mostly adopt the form of principles and these, as already explained, cannot lead to the establishment of subjective rights as such, but rules are needed to do that. Indeed, inalienability is a feature of human rights insofar as moral entities, a trait that is partially transferred to their legal formulation through the category of human rights legal principles. However, understood as optimisation requirements, principles need of further specification to become operative elements of the legal order and, for this purpose, the articulation of legal rules is the habitual avenue deployed by Western legal orders. Whilst human rights legal principles inherit the features of moral human rights, this is not the case of legal rules, due to a fundamental question of compatibility underlying the concept of subjective rights. The fact remains that, when concretised through legal rules, human rights legal principles naturally tend to adopt the form of subjective rights and it is so how they enter fully in the legal domain.

The legal category of subjective rights has its own complexity for it encompasses a variety of subjective legal positions—namely, rights correlative to duties, and powers correlative to liabilities—of the parties involved in the legal relationship, which presupposes the presence of both norms of conduct and norms of competence. Resorting to Kelsenian terms, norms of conduct establish the content of duties that frequently—yet not necessarily—correlate to 'reflex rights,' whereas norms of competence may grant legal action to the titleholder of these reflex rights, thus instituting 'subjective rights in the technical sense.' It is precisely through this two-fold structure that Western legal orders habitually create subjective rights (Kelsen 1984, 539–546). Subjective rights constitute the characteristic mechanism operated by liberal legal orders to allow the participation of subjects in the state will and the construction of the legal order through the drive of individual norms (Kelsen 1961, 89). In this sense, subjective rights are by no means inalienable, but essentially negotiable tools of titleholders and, as cultural products, they obviously reflect the Western liberal model.

If this is so, then: to what extent is it possible to speak of inalienable human rights? and how do the previously noted conceptual interrelations work in practice? An example will allow to better understand the scheme I have in mind. Consider the human right to privacy as enshrined in Article 8 ECHR, and subsequently interpreted in the ECtHR's case law as:

> [A] broad term encompassing, inter alia, aspects of an individual's physical, psychological and social identity such as the right to personal autonomy and personal development, the right to establish and develop relationships with other human beings and the right to respect for both the decisions to have and not to have a child (*Evans v. the UK*, para. 71; *E.B. v. France,* para. 43; *V.C. v. Slovakia,* para. 138).

The transcribed definition clearly shows that, at least in the Council of Europe's framework, privacy comprises elements of personal integrity as outlined in the first section of this piece of writing. A glance over the ECHR and its jurisprudence is enough to verify the necessity of further specification of the ECHR's provisions for being applied in practice. This has been so, for instance, as to application of Article 8 ECHR to the case of informed consent for surgical intervention. Considering the conceptual premises previously introduced, the principle of moral integrity included in the notion of private life is inalienable, meaning that it cannot be negotiated by titleholders, as for it represents a legal command directed towards state authorities and the foundation of further entitlements derived from it.

By contrast, when moral integrity and privacy crystallise in the known as patients' right to informed consent, the matter becomes substantially different because the very content of such entitlement consists in allowing the transaction of the parties involved in the medical relationship. In this sense, patients must receive the relevant medical information and discuss with the medical professionals involved about the available avenues for medical intervention. This previous informational phase prepares the way for an ulterior decisional phase, in which patients are entitled to take a decision about the concrete means of medical treatment or intervention to adopt, free from coercion, manipulation or duress. The singular feature of informed consent is that, despite the transactional nature of such patients' entitlements, the decision-making process is materially impossible to alienate since, even when patients delegate their decisions to a third party, they are deciding that others will decide yet deciding anyway. By contrast, the right to receive the medical information is fully alienable, which has even been described as a right of patients 'not to know,' in line with the second sentence of

Article 10.2 of the Convention on Human Rights and Biomedicine (Andorno 2013, 128). However, for the sake of consistency with the conceptual scheme presented above, I prefer to conceive that withdrawal to receive the medical information as the exercise of a power to alienate the right.

5.5 Avenues for Bodily Rights Alienation

From the foregoing account, the question arises of whether it is adequate to maintain the alienation of bodily rights—understood these latter as human rights legal rules—and, if so, to what extent such alienation is compatible with those human rights legal principles in which they originate. To answer the first question, two avenues for rights alienation have been distinguished in the literature—namely, to waive a right without losing its ownership and to relinquish it completely. A rights waiver affords titleholders to retain the ownership of their rights, leaving room to their recovery and eventual exercise (Van De Veer 1980, 165–76; Laporta 1987, 44). Contrariwise, the relinquishment of a right involves the complete loss of its ownership as is irrevocable. From this classification, some commentators have argued the acceptability of rights waiver, while rejecting their relinquishment. Accordingly, the exercise of the right could be alienated, whereas its ownership would fall outside titleholders' reach (Feinberg 1980, 242–6).

A closer look at this assessment criterion shows that two further classifications underlie to it—viz., a distinction between the content of the right, that is, the protected good and the right protecting it, and the entitlement to a good and its exercise. Thus, following the criterion above, whilst right and entitlement are inadmissibly alienable, content and exercise may be alienable. In practice, it may conceivably occur that the waiver of a certain good necessarily entails the relinquishment of the right to that good as a whole, particularly when the alienated good is materially unrecoverable, as the human right to life illustrates, since persons cannot waive their lives without losing as a result their corresponding entitlements, being nonsense to claim the right to life of those who have voluntarily chosen to die. Thus, in such cases, the alienation of the right is outrightly unacceptable according to the explanation just presented.

Still, to define alienability in terms of revocability and proceed straightaway to make the acceptability of the first dependent upon the presence of the second seems to be a methodologically questionable practice, for the revocability of an alienating act simply informs on some of the consequences derived from the waiver, yet it says nothing about the weight of the reasons leading to the very waiver. If only the object of the right—i.e., the protected good—can be justifiably alienated, then the exercise of the right in question is admittedly alienable, whilst the ownership must invariably remain intact. Unfortunately, this assessment criterion casts serious doubts for, in fact, the alienation of rights constitutes the exercise of an autonomous human right, that is, the right to private life as defined above. In this sense, the notion of self-determination included in the right to private life brings out a certain paradox: the free and informed decision not to undergo a life-saving medical intervention that leads to lose both the good and the right to life must be considered unacceptable, yet the very reason for asserting this does not come from the alleged inalienability of human rights, but from the denial of their absolute character, since it entails nothing but an external boundary to the exercise of the right by its titleholder.

The transfer constitutes another avenue for rights alienation. A right transfer prompts a bilateral change affecting the positions not only of transferring titleholders and recipients, but also of duty-bearers, which presupposes the presence of norms of competence establishing the procedure to follow for carrying out valid rights' transfers. Similarly to waiver and relinquishment, a right transfer equates to authorise an act that would be otherwise forbidden. An example of transfer can be found in the informational phase of informed consent, when patients appoint a third person of their trust for receiving the medical information, thus being medical professionals required to inform that third person from then on. Given that rights transfers are in principle revocable through titleholders' mere declaration of will or parties' agreement, they fulfil the criterion of acceptability introduced at the beginning of this section. However, it is worth noting that the possibility to transfer human rights is most probably limited to certain expressions of the right to private life, as the case of informed consent so exemplifies.

The absence of exercise of a right, by contrast, cannot be considered an instance of rights alienation, since it does not authorise the inobservance of third parties' correlative duties, and the titleholder retains the ownership (McConnell 2000, 11). Therefore, to refrain from exercising a right and its alienation constitute different attitudes of the titleholder with different implications. To speak of 'mandatory inalienable rights,' however, would entail the conflation of non-abstention and inalienability. Whereas an inalienable right could be 'unexercised' yet neither waived nor transferred, an allegedly mandatory inalienable right would imply that the titleholder is unable to either waive or transfer it while obliged to exercise it. In addition, to assert the existence of this kind of rights would bring about the recognition of 'duties to ourselves,' meaning that such rights are more than inalienable. In the literature, the case has been made that the right to vaccination against certain diseases could be defined as a mandatory right, in the sense that it involves a 'half-liberty' to get vaccinated (Feinberg 1980, 157).

Forfeiture has also been pointed out as a possible, yet indirect, pathway to rights alienation. In this convoluted modality, titleholders would intentionally jeopardise their rights with the purpose of taking advantage of the legal consequences accorded by the law for the commission of certain unlawful actions. An example of this would be to infringe certain criminal law norms in order to be detained with the sole intention of avoiding to stay in the street overnight (Meyers 1985, 2 and 9). Apart from the residual and exceptional nature of this alienation track, it is actually questionable to regard forfeiture as an avenue for rights alienation, since the change produced on titleholders' positions does not come from the result of their acts, but it is a mere consequence of them which, in turn, fully depends on the existence of a legal norm linking a concrete punishment to the performance of a certain behaviour. Therefore, the relevant decision does not lie with the titleholder, but with the corresponding legal authority. What is more, the forfeiture of the right falls outside of the scope of titleholders' will, being only by means of mere coincidence that the legal consequence collapses with the effect that a certain titleholder wants to attain.

Thus, at least two arguments advise the conceptual separation of alienation and forfeiture. First, the explanation as to the interruption of the right is different in each case. When titleholders alienate their rights, it is their consent what justifies the suspension of the correlative duty; whereas in the case of forfeiture, it is the wrongdoing performed by the titleholder what prompts the application of a legal norm establishing such forfeiture. Second, although connected to the foregoing argument, the source of the will producing the loss is different in each case. As to alienation, titleholders' free and deliberate consent prompts the change in the relevant subjective positions of the parties involved; whilst in the case of forfeiture, it is required a previous legislative process defining the behaviour as unlawful and linking it to the forfeiture of a certain right of the wrongdoer (McConnell 2000, 13–4). The paradox pointed out above reappears when upholding forfeiture as a means for rights alienation, since it is only through the application of the law that a right is forfeit, which is tantamount to confuse inalienability with absolute character.

It might be thought that titleholders' consent is neither sufficient nor necessary to alienate a bodily right. It is insufficient because, by definition, to support inalienability as a feature of all human rights will prevent the titleholder's disposal of the right. Moreover, it is unnecessary for both forfeiture and suspension of correlative duties due to stronger moral considerations are enough to justify the inobservance of the right in question (McConnell 2000, 20). Nevertheless, these arguments entail once again a confusion between inalienability and absolute character, given that to resort to stronger moral reasons to justify the suspension of the right and, therefore, its correlative duties has nothing to do with titleholders' relation with their entitlements, but it equates to reject an understanding of rights as totally unconditional entitlements, that is, to deny their absolute character, on the premise that there must be limits in place to strike a fair balance among all interests at stake, including the legitimate interests of the community.

If titleholders' consent justifies an act that otherwise would equate to an infringement of their rights, then such authorisation could be translated into the exercise of a power to void correlative duties and create new subjective positions, whose object would be forbidden without titleholders' act of will (Lomasky 1987, 211; Simmons 1979, 76; Fletcher 1996, 109). However, it seems possible to bring into question whether titleholders' authorisations are sufficient to justify the inobservance of the correlative duty, and to what extent such recognition is coherent with human rights legal principles as enshrined in the national and international legal texts on the matter. Although the attendance of the fully competent titleholder's consent guarantees a wide range of values covered under the principle of respect for private life, to only consider the latter appears as simply not enough since other morally relevant interests might also come into play. In fact, it is not infrequent to find legal barriers to the fully suspension of legal duties derived from certain rights alienation, as ex officio prosecution of consented bodily injuries exemplifies. In such cases, there is a collision between the principle of respect for autonomy and the principle of justice in a broad sense, serving this latter to the communitarian interests of society at large.

Furthermore, even if inalienability is considered to be a feature of rights, it does not mean that titleholders' consent is completely irrelevant to ascertain the compensation of harms since, as the principle *volenti non fit injuria* says, to one who has consented no wrong can be done (Feinberg 1986a, b a, 115–7; Feinberg 1986a, b b, 173–7; McConnell 2000, 43–4).

5.6 Conclusions

The discussion on human rights alienability is fraught with conceptual misunderstandings. Not only inalienability is frequently mixed-up with the so-called absolute character of human rights, but it is not even clear if the discussion is held in—and thus settled in the terms of—the moral, legal, political or, most likely, in their intersection. Indeed, it is both confusing and inconvenient to rely too much on conceptual categories and distinctions, because they can easily darken intermediate realities and blur the whole picture. The lack of a consensus definition of personal moral integrity provides a good example of this sort of conceptual uncertainties.

The human body and its parts are rightly considered to deserve the highest legal protection since, at the moral level, the ascertainment of the full moral status of the human being obliges everybody to behave towards each other, as also towards ourselves in keeping with the various requisites and limits derived from the principle of respect for human dignity. Still, to translate the foregoing into legal language necessarily asks for adjustments. From the classification of the norm in rules and principles, I have suggested that whereas human rights legal principles inherit most—if not all—traits of the purely moral discourse, human rights legal rules require of further adaptation. Concretely, the habitual practice of specifying human rights legal principles through the establishment of subjective rights through legal rules necessarily derives in granting subjects the control over the legal relationship and, thus, letting the aspects of their exercise and enforcement at titleholders' convenience, which means essentially alienable legal positions. However, as Kelsen said, subjective rights are a mere legislative technique. Alternatively, the establishment of duties without correlative rights or the imposition of justified limits to the exercise of those rights would help to preserve the exigencies coming from the moral domain, yet that would shift the discussion to the alleged absolute character of human rights.

References

Alexy, Robert. 2010. *A Theory of Constitutional Rights*. Trans. J. Rivers. Oxford: Oxford University Press.

Andorno, Roberto. 2013. *Principles of International Biolaw*. Bruxelles: Bruylant.

Descartes, René, and Williams, Bernard (intro). 1996. *Descartes: Meditations on First Philosophy: With Selections from the Objections and Replies*. Trans. and ed. J. Cottingham. Cambridge: Cambridge University Press.

Douglas, T. 2020. From bodily rights to personal rights. In *The Cambridge Handbook of New Human Rights: Recognition, Novelty, Rhetoric*, ed. A. Von Arnauld, K. Von der Decken, and M. Susi, 378–384. Cambridge: Cambridge University Press.

Feinberg, Joel. 1986a. *Harm to Others*. The Moral Limits of the Criminal Law, volume 1. New York: Oxford University Press.

Feinberg, Joel. 1986b. *Harm to Self*. The Moral Limits of the Criminal Law, volume 3. New York: Oxford University Press.

Feinberg, Joel. 1980. *Rights, justice, and the bounds of liberty: essays in social philosophy*. Princeton, NJ: Princeton University Press.

Fletcher, George P. 1996. *Basic concepts of legal thought*. New York: Oxford University Press.

Hergenhahn, Baldwin R. 2009. *An introduction to the history of psychology*, 6th ed. Belmont, CA: Cengage Learning.

Hohfeld, Wesley N. 1913. Some fundamental legal conceptions as applied in judicial reasoning I. *Yale Law Journal* 23 (1): 16–59.

Kelsen, Hans. 1961. *General theory of law and state*. New York: Russell & Russell.

Kelsen, Hans. 1984. *Hauptprobleme der Staatsrechtslehre entwickelt aus der Lehre vom Rechtssatze*. Aalen: Scientia Verlag.

Laporta, Francisco J. 1987. Sobre el concepto de los derechos humanos. *Doxa* 4: 23–46.

Lomasky, Loren E. 1987. *Persons, rights and the moral community*. New York: Oxford University Press.

Meyers, Diana T. 1985. *Inalienable rights: a defense*. New York: Columbia University Press.

McConnell, Terrance. 2000. *Inalienable rights: the limits of consent in medicine and the law*. Oxford: Oxford University Press.

Simmons, Alan J. 1979. *Moral principles and political obligations*. Princeton: Princeton University Press.

Thompson, Judith J. 1990. *The realm of rights*. Cambridge, MA: Harvard University Press.

Van De Veer, Donald. 1980. Are human rights alienable? *Philosophical Studies* 37(2): 165–76.

Chapter 6
Rethinking with Onora O'Neill the Kantian Concept of Autonomy in Biolaw

María Jesús Vázquez Lobeiras

Abstract The concept of autonomy plays a significant role in Bioethics as well as in Biolaw, the Kantian conception of autonomy being an unavoidable element in the debate. Some of the most relevant contributions in this discussion stem from Onora O'Neill's work. Prof. O'Neill promotes an anti-individualist interpretation of autonomy and, in order to increase its ethical efficiency, suggests reconsidering the meaning of autonomy as closely linked to trust. This chapter tries to show how intertwined information, autonomy and trust are at a time when medical technologies and care need to be interpreted and disclosed in order to be properly understood.

Keywords Autonomy · Biolaw · Kant · O´Neill · Trust

6.1 Introduction

Onora O'Neill, in one of her writings, considers that the trajectory of the Kantian concept of autonomy can be compared to that of a pop star, at least in comparison with other concepts that Kant uses for the development of his ethical thought (cf. O'Neil 2004: 14). The author does not further clarify this metaphor. It seems to suggest that the Kantian concept of autonomy enjoys an extraordinary popularity, which perhaps does not correspond to its real importance in the argumentative contexts in which it appears. Onora O'Neill herself has devoted outstanding works to clarifying it and analysing its scope, particularly in relation to the problem of informed consent. Informed consent and the ethical and legal principle of autonomy are closely linked, since the former is usually considered a genuine expression of the latter. Let us take as a reference the main Spanish legal text concerning this matter: Law 41/2002, of November 14, basic regulation of patient´s autonomy and of their rights and

M. J. Vázquez Lobeiras (✉)
Universidad de Santiago de Compostela, Santiago de Compostela, España
e-mail: mxv.lobeiras@usc.es

© The Editor(s) (if applicable) and The Author(s), under exclusive license to Springer Nature Switzerland AG 2024

J.-A. Seoane and O. Vergara (eds.), *The Discourse of Biorights*, The International Library of Bioethics 109, https://doi.org/10.1007/978-3-031-66804-3_6

obligations regarding clinical information and documentation (BOE number 274 of 15,711/ 2002).

Considering informed consent to be one of the main expressions of autonomy, although not the only one, in what follows we will analyse it from the perspective of Onora O'Neill. Kant's texts will be consulted once again in order to clarify what the eminent thinker of Königsberg understands by autonomy and to what extent his concept of application can be applied in the field of biolaw.

It is possible that O'Neill's metaphor will be confirmed and that the constant invocations of the Kantian concept of autonomy have something in common with the career of a pop star, but a star to whom the following happens: due to their great fame, they always appear in the list of guests at major concerts—in this case, at major discussions—around bioethical and bio-legal issues; but the fact is that they do not share the style or harmonise with the performers who usually perform concerts—in this case, the discussions—of these issues. There is some research, however, such as that of Sheila A. M. Mclean (2010), which invites us to consider a facet of Kant's thought that is normally forgotten in bioethical and bio-legal discussions, but which, however, can be considered as an essential element of Kantian thought on autonomy that, moreover, could shed light on these discussions. This is the Kantian notion of *Selbstdenken* (thinking for oneself), that speaks of autonomy in the sense of the ability to judge and make decisions independently, and also, as the Königsberg thinker points out in prominent passages of his work, to think consistently with oneself (Cf. Kant, Log AA 09: 57; KU AA 05: 295 and Anth AA 07: 200 and 228–229).[1] The Kantian concept of autonomy (*Autonomie, Selbstgesetzgebung*) is a central part of Kant's thought on ethics, but it has, at the same time, an undeniable metaphysical dimension (cf. Gracia Guillén 2012; Vázquez Lobeiras 2017), because on it is based the existence of an intelligible world (the moral world) that transcends the world (physical-natural world). The Kantian notion of autonomous thought (*Selbstdenken*), which can be linked to an important aspect of autonomy as this concept is posed in the bioethical and biolegal debate, is located in a different dimension that, although its ethical implications cannot be identified with the notion of moral autonomy and even less with autonomy in a metaphysical sense, but rather appears linked to what we could call the culture of enlightened rationality (cf. Vázquez Lobeiras 2018). It should be remembered that, in this sense, there is at least one passage from Kant that directly evokes the situation of dependency, or, on the contrary, of autonomy, in which a person can find him- or herself in front of the doctors. It is found at the beginning of the brief writing of 1784, *An Answer to the Question: what is Enlightenment?*: "It is so comfortable to be immature. If I have a book that reasons for me, a pastor who acts as my conscience, a physician who determines my diet for me, etc., then I need not make any effort myself" (WA, AA 08: 35).[2] Autonomy in the bioethical and biolegal field has been applied to issues as the goal of a long road that has allowed us to move from paternalism, existing since Hippocratic times,

[1] Kant's works are cited according to the conventions of the Kant-Studien and with the English text of the translations indicated in the final references.

[2] Quoted from Mary C. Smith's English translation.

to the current situation: "Medical ethics have ultimately transcended the 'closed shop' ideology of Hippocrates, largely eschewed the dominance of paternalism and now flourishes (or not) in the spotlight of autonomy" (McLean 2010: 6). Current legislation is aimed at curbing paternalistic inertia in the exercise of the medical profession and tries to guarantee autonomy in the sense of the coming of age of the human being to which the passage from Kant alludes. However, as this suggests, perhaps one cannot speak of autonomy without considering the type of 'effort' that corresponds to the supposedly autonomous subject. As McLean points out:

> Nonetheless, even when people are legally presumed to be autonomous, the conundrum of how to facilitate their exercise of that autonomy from a traditional position of relative weakness has become pressing and is arguably particularly urgent in modern healthcare. As medicine´s capacities expand, and become ever more esoteric, the gap in the knowledge between doctor and patient becomes ever greater, even given the massive expansion in the availability of information, for example from the internet. In order to facilitate or protect the capacity of an autonomous person to make an autonomous choice—one that reflect his or her own values—it is necessary to develop standards that can ensure meaningful patient participation in healthcare decisions (McLean 2010: 3).

6.2 Informed Consent and Other Facets of Autonomy in the Biolegal Field

The bioethical and biolegal debate has paid special attention to the problem of informed consent, described as "the most discussed topic in western medical ethics and research ethics" (Manson and O'Neill 2007: 1), but the notion of autonomy is not exhausted in this matter.[3] It can be related at least to three clearly differentiated areas of problems: informed consent, advance directives and the availability of information about the public health system.

If we take these three problematic areas together, the first evidence is that this concept is applied in a relational context and that, among the many popular and philosophical connotations of the notion of autonomy, the first to emerge is that of 'independence': the independence of one of the poles with respect to the other in this relational context. How should this relational context be understood? Is it an interpersonal relationship, like, for example, the doctor-patient relationship, or is it rather the relationship of a person with a structure as complex and anonymous as the health system? The difficulties in posing the matter in terms of interpersonal relationship are obvious.

[3] The bioethical and biolegal debate concerning the principle of autonomy has been raging at least since the publication of Beauchamp & Childress' *Principles of biomedical ethics* (1984). O'Neill draws attention to the fact that Beauchamp & Childress themselves have acknowledged, in the 1994 edition, that the principle of autonomy is sometimes of greater importance than, e.g., the principle of beneficence (cf. O'Neill 2002: 35). Although the discussions on informed consent and the principle of autonomy are mutually reinforcing, the other aspects of autonomy that emerge in the Spanish legal regulation are also relevant.

In the case of informed consent, on one side of the relationship we find the person, an entity with traits such as freedom, will, capacity to receive information. On the other side, the weight does not fall on the personal character of the individual involved in the relationship, which clearly appears veiled, but on the material (we could say the object) that is supplied in this side, namely, in the first instance, 'information'. The depersonalisation of this second side is such that it could be said that the only 'person' who plays a role in informed consent is the patient, who is in a position to give or withhold consent. On the other side, only with some effort can you glimpse the figure of a health professional to whom the consent is granted. Rather, what appears is the image of an indefinite and impersonal structure that, with the appropriate mechanisms (this includes the figure of the doctor) carries out the action of transferring information about medical procedures. It is really very difficult to maintain the idea that informed consent occurs in the context of an interpersonal relationship. In grammatical terms, we would say that it is not so much a relationship between two subjects (one who informs and another who receives the information, assesses it, and decides to give or deny their consent) but rather between a subject (the patient) and a direct object (the information, which is received). In the case of advance directives, the transcendent character of the person is clearly emphasised, from the point of view of his or her will, which must be respected even when it can no longer be exercised. The relational key is also present: on one side is that person endowed with will who declares their intentions in advance in matters concerning the end of their life, or at least the end of their volitional life. On the other hand, there is a depersonalised entity (the health system) that stands as the depository of the abovementioned intentions. Finally, in the case of the right to receive information about the health system, the emphasis is put on the notion of 'right'—which also corresponds to the notion of person as a subject of rights—and on the notion of 'information', which, if applicable to a right, must also correspond to a basic need. But the notion of information projects us towards the other pole, namely, that of the origin of that information. The relational context is, therefore, again evident. And also on this occasion we find the figure of a person who establishes a relationship with an abstract and depersonalised entity.

The meaning of the notion of autonomy in the biolegal field seems to oscillate between two poles: on the one hand, it refers to the expression of the will of a subject (especially in the case of informed consent and advance directives) and on the other, to the capacity of a subject to receive and evaluate information (also in the case of informed consent, and also concerning the right to receive information about the health system). In a first approximation we have reinterpreted the notion of autonomy as 'independence'. Now we are in a position to add that it is not about independence in an interpersonal relationship (independence of one person from another), but rather the independence of the person (from every person), with respect to a social structure such as the health system, which has become very complex both from the point of view of medical knowledge and of its application. It is not only that the knowledge of the medical professional is increasingly sophisticated, but also that the application of this knowledge is mediated in an increasingly intensive way by highly complex technological means. The difficulties of this situation mainly concern information, which is an essential element of autonomy in the biolegal field.

But, if the main purpose of the health system is to preserve health, it is worth asking whether the preservation of autonomy contributes in any way to a better fulfilment of the main purpose, or what relationship the preservation of autonomy has with it. There is the paradox that the health system could perfectly fulfil its main purpose by completely skipping the requirement to preserve the autonomy of patients. Why then has the issue of autonomy become so important? Onora O'Neill's analysis can be very useful for clarifying this question, with the particularity that this author has managed to think, on a Kantian background, "beyond autonomy" (Manson and O'Neill 2007: 69) considerably qualifying the importance that in recent decades has been given to this concept in the bioethical and biolegal discussion.

6.3 Onora O'Neill on the Problem of Autonomy

The analyses performed by Onora O'Neill on the concept of autonomy are directed with great determination against the important role assigned to information, particularly in the regulation of informed consent:

> we have noted how the—orthodox and ubiquitous—'autonomy'-based justifications for informed consent assume that information is to be thought of as a material of decision making and that individual decision-making ought to be respected. Information is what we need in order to decide, detaches that content from the full demands of successful communicative transactions (Manson and O'Neill 2007: 48).

According to O'Neill, informed consent is justified by the need to preserve the autonomy of the patient and this is usually based on the fact that the patient has sufficient information about the medical procedures to which they are going to be subjected, as well as about the available alternatives. Current standards, typified by O'Neill as "the conduit/container model" (Manson and O'Neill 2007: 68), which: "focuses on *disclosure for decision-making*" (Manson and O'Neill 2007: 69), are characterised by the fact that "the relevant information flows to—*is disclosed to*— those who have to decide or choose" (Manson and O'Neill 2007: 69). Faced with this model, the author develops an alternative, called "agency model, as we focus not only on the content, but also on the speech acts" (Manson and O'Neill 2007: 68–69). In this alternative model, information continues to be a key element, and in this sense, it does not supplant the autonomy model, but rather complements it. But as a consequence of the change in focus, not only information,[4] but also autonomy, lose their pre-eminent place as justifications for the need for informed consent, so that: "respect for individual autonomy will *not* be the sole, nor perhaps the main, basis for justifying medical and research practice" (Manson and O'Neill 2007: 71).

---

[4] The overemphasis on information also leads to excessive formalism of procedures: 'In effect, explicit and specific consent requirements insist on formalistic, uniform and, strictly speaking, impossible procedures and rules, rather than seeking feasible, proportionate and normatively justified requirements' (Manson and O'Neill 2007: 11).

O'Neill's revision of the concept of autonomy takes into account Kant's point of view in different ways. On the one hand, she considers it to be a kind of unavoidable toll at the beginning of any discussion about the problem that, however, has little to do with the concept of autonomy, which, according to the author, is most common in the bioethical and biolegal debate. On the other hand, she vindicates certain components of the Kantian concept of autonomy linked to the notion of trust, which she herself claims as a firmer pillar than that of autonomy to establish the ethical foundation of informed consent: "Autonomy is usually identified with individual independence [...] its ethical credentials are not self-evident [...] Trust is surely more important" (O'Neill 2002: *Preface*, ix).

According to Onora O'Neill, in the discussion three[5] different concepts of autonomy are invoked and confused; what she calls "principled autonomy" (Manson and O'Neill 2007: 17), with Kantian roots, can, according to the author, "be set aside" (ibid.), since: "Kant used the term autonomy to refer not to a characteristic of individuals, but to the formal properties of principles of action that can serve for all, and in particular to the combination of law-like form and universal scope" (Manson and O'Neill 2007: 17).

Autonomy, understood as a characteristic of individuals, with the connotation of individual independence alluded to in the previous section is, according to O'Neill, the most common perception in the bioethical discussion:

> Contemporary work on autonomy is quite different. It views autonomy as a property of individuals, and specifically as a form of individual Independence [...] It is easy to see why those who see autonomy as a matter of individual independence link it so closely to informed consent: informed consent procedures protect individual choice, and with it individual independence, hence individual autonomy (Manson and O'Neill 2007: 18-19).

Individual autonomy can, in turn, be understood in two different ways, either as "a matter of *mere* choice" (Manson and O'Neill 2007: 19), or "as some form of rational or reflective choosing" (Manson and O'Neill 2007: 19).

In relation to the concept of autonomy, O'Neill's conclusions relevant to the thread that we are following here are two: (a) that the Kantian concept of autonomy as 'principled autonomy' is dispensable in the bioethical and biolegal discussion and (b) that, in general, the principle of autonomy, understood most of the time under the scarcely Kantian meaning of individual autonomy, has been given excessive importance in the bioethical and biolegal discussion, linked to the problem of informed consent:

> Across the last forty years informed consent requirements in biomedical practice have grown enormously [...]. The reason most commonly given for the expansion [...] is that they are needed to secure respect for individual autonomy [...]. We entirely accept that seeking and giving informed consent displays a minimal form of individual autonomy. Those who consent to some action choose that it be done, and might have refused. But the fact that a consent to action is chosen shows very little about reasons for requiring consent for all medical and research interventions. That some act is chosen is, after all, neither necessary nor sufficient to justify doing it (Manson and O'Neill 2007: 185).

[5] However, many more meanings of autonomy could be identified (O´Neill 2002: 22).

But Onora O'Neill, while making these criticisms, reestablishes the Kantian concept of autonomy from a completely different point of view, linked to his proposal to overcome the 'conduit-container model' in favour of the 'agency model', which places the accent, not on the information that acted as a guarantor of the patient's autonomy, but on the communicative dimension of the act of supplying the information: "We may think that 'autonomous decision-making' can only be respected if full, explicit, information is disclosed [...] an approach to informed consent that takes norms for adequate communication seriously has a lot of advantages" (O'Neill 2007: 95). The requirement of 'adequate communication' results in the re-personalisation of the relational pole that we considered as depersonalised. The situation would not be that of a vulnerable person (the patient), facing a system legally obliged to provide certain information, but rather we would be facing effective and effectively interpersonal acts of communication. The Kantian notion of autonomy implies reciprocity: "Principled autonomy is expressed in actions whose principle *could be adopted by all others*" (O´Neill 2002: 85). In fact, as we will see in the next section, it is directly linked to the notion of a community of rational subjects, and with it to the very possibility of an ethical community. Reciprocity is, in turn, the key to the notion of trust that O'Neill wants to convert into the new foundation of informed consent:

> I shall argue that Kant´s distinctive conception of autonomy is quite different from the ethically inadequate conception of individual autonomy so commonly ascribed to him; that the links between Kantian autonomy and practical reason are strong and powerful and that its ethical implications underpin the importance of trust (O'Neill 2002: 74).

In this way: "autonomy is seen as a precondition of genuine trust" (O'Neill 2002: 19). Informed consent, for its part, is seen as an act that seals mutual trust between the patient and the doctor and not as an act that seals autonomy. While the emphasis on individual autonomy generally contributes to generating tension and mistrust between doctor and patient, autonomy in the Kantian sense, or 'principled autonomy', fosters trust. From this point of view, both coercion and deception are reprehensible:

> Whereas individual autonomy is constantly in tension with relations of trust, principled autonomy provides a basis for relations of trust.
>
> Relations of trust require us to reject deception as they require us to reject coercion [...] So it is of a great significance to establish a fundamental human obligation to reject deception. This obligation provides the ethical basis for trustworthy action (O'Neill 2002: 97).

Consequently, the medical professional has to face medical practice and the legal act of informed consent under the moral obligation, not only not to exercise coercion, not to harm physically or morally, etc., but also not to disappoint the patient: "If we are committed to principled autonomy, we must also be committed to rejecting principles of destruction, injury, coercion and deception, and to supporting others´ survival and capacities to act." (O'Neill 2002: 145).

In what follows we will try to go more deeply into Onora O'Neill's point of view by examining some of the fundamental concepts linked to the notion of autonomy in the Kantian sources.

6.4 Rethinking Kant on Autonomy

Onora O´Neill justifies her point of view on Kantian autonomy as 'principled autonomy' on the basis of a cursory analysis of the principle of autonomy expressed in the following way in the *Groundwork of the Metaphysics of Morals*: "To choose only in such a way that the maxims of your choice are also included as universal law in the same volition" (GMS, AA 04: 440).[6] The formula works, according to the author, as "a test that shows which principles of action *could* be chosen by all, that is to say, which principles are capable of universalization, or *fit to be universal laws*" (O´Neill 2002: 84). But if the author's objective is to underpin the reciprocity implied in the notion of trust, perhaps it would be convenient to broaden the exposition with some of the notions that accompany this formulation of the principle of autonomy. Particularly noteworthy is the notion of the kingdom of ends (*Reich der Zwecke*). From these analyses, a notion that we would call 'rational reciprocity' can be easily derived. However, the question of whether this rational reciprocity is enough to underpin trust, as Onora O'Neill claims, remains open for debate. In any case, the author makes it clear that the notion of trust that she uses has nothing to do with the blind trust typical of traditional paternalism, nor with any kind of emotional or sentimental trust, but rather that it is "reasonable trust" (O'Neill 2002: 18), understood as: "The only trust that is well placed is given by those who understand what is proposed, and who are in a position to refuse or choose in the light of that understanding" (O'Neill 2002: 18).

The notion of a 'kingdom of ends' (*Reich der Zwecke*) appears in the *Groundwork of the Metaphysics of Morals* in line with the formulation of the so-called principle of autonomy, to which reference has been made previously and which Kant presents as the great novelty of his moral thought: "It was seen that the human being is bound to laws by his duty, but it never occurred to them that he is subject only to laws given by himself but still universal" (GMS, AA 04: 432). The Kantian notion of autonomy is condensed in this idea of obedience to an 'own' and 'universal' legislation. The expression 'man' (*der Mensch*) obviously refers to the human being in general and not to the specific individual. An individualistic reading of the Kantian phrase is hardly possible since the idea of legislation for a single individual who creates it and submits to it seems absurd: the notion of self-legislation (*Selbstgesetzgebung*), frequent in Kant's text, does not correspond to any form of autarky or autocracy. The notion of a 'proper' legislation means that it has its source in the human being himself, specifically in his rational dimension and, as Kant explicitly points out, this legislation is 'universal':

> This lawgiving must, however, be found in every rational being himself and be able to arise from his will, the principle of which is, accordingly: to do no action on any other maxim than one such that it would be consistent with it to be a universal law. (GMS, AA 04: 434).

---

[6] The *Groundwork of the Metaphysics of Morals* is quoted according to Jonathan Bennett's translation.

The human being finds themselves, in relation to the law, in a double position: they are a legislator (or rather, they are a co-legislator, together with the other rational beings) and at the same time they are subject to the law. The key for autonomy is found in the idea that the source of the law is the rational nature inherent to the human being, and not any other instance, in which case we would be talking about heteronomy (GMS, AA 04: 433). 'Universality' and 'rationality' are correlative terms. 'Rationality' refers to the fact that action is determined solely by reason and not by other dimensions of the human psyche, but reason entails universality. Kant expresses this idea by resorting to the notion of 'end': "Now, what serves the will as the objective ground of its self-determination is an end, and this, if it is given by reason alone, must hold equally for all rational beings." (GMS, AA 04: 427). Practical rationality is a rationality of ends; a 'rational end' is both an 'objective end' (which Kant opposes to 'subjective ends')[7] and is also an 'end in itself' (which Kant opposes to 'means').

Both in the case of autonomy and heteronomy, the situation is one of submission to the law. Autonomy, therefore, is not preserved by independence from the law, but by the fact that the human being submits to the law that they give themselves. But legislation is co-legislation at the same time and this is the idea that Kant wants to emphasise by introducing the notion of a 'kingdom of ends':

> The concept of every rational being as one who must regard himself as giving universal law through all the maxims of his will, so as to appraise himself and his actions from this point of view, leads to a very fruitful concept dependent upon it, namely that of a kingdom of ends.
>
> By a kingdom I understand a systematic union of various rational beings through common laws. Now since laws determine ends in terms of their universal validity, if we abstract from the personal differences of rational beings as well as from all the content of their private ends we shall be able to think of a whole of all ends in systematic connection (a whole both of rational beings as ends in themselves and of the ends of his own that each may set himself), that is, a kingdom of ends, which is possible in accordance with the above principles. […]
>
> A rational being belongs as a member to the kingdom of ends when he gives universal laws in it but is also himself subject to these laws. He belongs to it as sovereign when, as lawgiving, he is not subject to the will of any other.
>
> A rational being must always regard himself as lawgiving in a kingdom of ends possible through freedom of the will, whether as a member or as sovereign. […]
>
> Reason accordingly refers every maxim of the will as giving universal law to every other will and also to every action toward oneself (GMS, AA 04: 433-434).

The Kantian 'kingdom of ends' is made up of all rational beings (it includes, therefore, the hypothesis of non-human rational beings). In this Kingdom, which represents the legislation of reason, everyone is both chief and member. Autonomy is preserved by the status of chiefs, but the status of members makes co-participation

---

[7] In Vázquez Lobeiras (2017) can be found an analysis of various concept pairs that Kant uses to determine his concept of autonomy, in particular will (*Wille*)/discretion (*Willkür*), but also objective ends (*objecktive Zwecke*)/subjective ends (*subjektive Zwecke*), motive (*Triebfeder*)/Motive (*Bewegungsgrund*). On the possibility of reconstructing a Kantian concept of 'personal autonomy', different from 'moral autonomy', linked to the prudential dimension of practical rationality, which can be very useful in the field of bioethics and biolaw cf. Taylor (2005)

explicit at the same time: the idea that this rational legislation is always co-legislation and therefore entails reciprocity. In short, as Onora O'Neill has been able to see, reciprocity is an essential ingredient of the Kantian notion of autonomy, which places it light years away from any form of autonomy with an individualistic orientation.

Translating these analyses to the level of the doctor-patient relationship, we could say that preserving autonomy is equivalent to accepting the patient's word in a situation of rational dialogue with the doctor and not only of reflective balance regarding an information that is provided in a mechanical and bureaucratic manner. Autonomy, now redefined as rational reciprocity,[8] would require emphasising mutual recognition between doctor and patient as members of a rational community: "For too long it was assumed that respect was needed only from patient to doctor. Respect for patient autonomy, on the other hand, requires that doctors also trust patients to make their own decisions and respect them once taken" (McLean 2010: 34). The doctor's obligation cannot be reduced to 'informing', but must be extended to 'arguing', questioning the patient in his/her rational dimension and trusting his/her decisions. At the same time, in view of the difficulties that medical information currently entails, due to specialisation and the increasing use of technology, the patient must be able to trust that the doctor will apply the highest degree of both scientific and ethical rationality in their actions. From the perspective of the Kantian notion of moral autonomy, the emphasis goes neither to the whims nor to the particular worldviews of an individual, but rather to the reciprocity and the recognition that rational beings owe each other as such.

At the beginning of this paper reference was made to another facet of Kantian thought on autonomy, linked in this case not to the self-legislative capacity of moral reason (*Selbstgesetzgebung*), but to the capacity to think for oneself *(Selbstdenken)*. It was pointed out, with reference to certain well-known passages whose detailed commentary has been omitted on this occasion,[9] that this Kantian notion entails the requirement "to think oneself into the position of someone else" (Log AA 09: 57).[10] Also in this case, reciprocity appears in Kant as an unavoidable element of rationality: the ability to think autonomously (by oneself) is in no way equivalent to solipsism, but rather entails reciprocity: the consideration that rationality is a common patrimony, universally shared, and that can only be realised in an equally common, reciprocal exercise.

[8] McLean speaks of 'relational autonomy' (McLean 2010: 22) as opposed to 'individualistic autonomy' (McLean 2010: 33).

[9] Cf. Kant, Log AA 09: 57; KU AA 05: 295 y Anth AA 07: 200 y 228–229. On the relevance of these passages as another dimension of the Kantian notion of autonomy that can be applied in the field of biolaw, cf. Vázquez Lobeiras (2018).

[10] Quoted according to the translation by Thomas Kingsmill Abbott.

References

Beauchamp, Tom L., and James F. Childress. 2009. *Principles of biomedical ethics*. New York: Oxford University Press.

Gracia Guillén. Diego. 2012. The many faces of autonomy. *Theor Med Bioeth* 33: 57–64.

Kant, Immanuel. 1900ss. *Gesammelte Schriften*. Berlin–Göttingen: Walter de Gruyter (Vols. 1–22, Preussische Akademie der Wissenschaften, vol. 23, Deutsche Akademie der Wissenschaften zu Berlin, after vol. 24, Akademie der Wissenschaften von der Berlin-Brandenburgischen Akademie der Wissenschaften zu Göttingen).

Kant, Immanuel. 1992. *Lectures on Logic*. Translated and edited by M. Yong. Cambridge: University Press.

Kant, Immanuel. 1998. *Groundwork of the Metaphysics of Morals*. Translated and edited by M. Gregor with an Introduction by Ch. M. Korsgaard. Cambridge: Cambridge University Press.

Kant, Immanuel. 2008. *An Answer to the Question: what is Enlightenment?* In *Toward Perpetual Peace and Other Writings on Politics, Peace, and History*. Edited by Pauline Kleingeld. Translated by David L. Colclasure. Yale: Yale University Press.

Manson, Neil, and Onora O'Neill. 2007. *Rethinking informed consent in bioethics*. Cambridge: Cambridge University Press.

McLean, Sheila A. M. 2010. *Autonomy, Consent and the Law*. London–New York: Routledge-Cavendish.

O'Neill, Onora. 1989. *Constructions of Reason. Explorations of Kant´s Practical Philosophy*. Cambridge: Cambridge University Press.

O'Neill, Onora. 2002. *Autonomy and trust in bioethics*. Cambridge: Cambridge University Press.

O'Neill, Onora. 2004. Self-legislation, autonomy and the form of law, en Nagl-Docekal, H. & Langthaler, R., en *Recht—Geschichte—Religion. Die Bedeutung Kants für die Gegenwart*. Berlin: Akademie Verlag, pp. 13–26.

Taylor, Robert S. 2005. Kantian personal autonomy. *Political Theory* 33–5: 602–628.

Torre Díaz, Javier de la; Junquera de Estéfani, Rafael; Aparicio Rodríguez, Luis Cayetano; González Morán, Luis (compiladores). 2010. *Normas básicas de Bioderecho*. Madrid: Dykinson–UNED–Univ. de Comillas.

Vázquez Lobeiras, María Jesús. 2017. Kant como interlocutor en el ámbito de la bioética y la biojurídica: el problema de la autonomía. *Estudos kantianos. Revista do centro de pesquisas e estudos kantianos Valerio Rohden* 5-1: 187-206.

Vázquez Lobeiras, María Jesús. 2018. El problema de los bioderechos a la luz del pensamiento de Immanuel Kant. In *Los rostros de la razón: Immanuel Kant desde Hispanoamérica*. Vol. II: *Filosofía moral, política y del derecho*. Ed. G. Leyva, A. Peláez, P. Stepanenko, 247–264. México: Anthropos-UAM.

Chapter 7
Autonomy and Advance Care Planning in Liquid Times of Brain Activity: The Sound of Silence

Joaquim Gomes

Abstract Autonomy is a *fashionable and fresh concept* because it has recently generated a permanent and vigorous debate. This discussion is simultaneously bright, imparting meaning to human dignity, and briefly, because it suddenly appears and vanishes from the free will discourse. The post-contemporary construction of autonomy is relevant to understand the role of advance care planning as a strategic puzzle to prepare and shape our final stage of life in a decent society. Analytical autonomy, with its anatomy and structure, dimensions, modalities, variants, and measurability, gives us the tools to evaluate the autonomous agent. Personal autonomy enabled by neurotechnology may create a new insider trading mechanism, disclosing some relevant and innovative answers to the knowledge of ongoing free will, and bridging the gap between the autonomous agent and the hidden agent. This essay aims to explore this path of autonomy, encountering situations involving mental or cognitive disabilities or unconsciousness not as an insuperable obstacle, but as a challenge. The border between the conscious and the unconscious takes us into a grey zone where language develops other meanings and significance, where communication is oscillatory or even non-existent. However "the vision that was planted in my brain, Still remains, Within the sound of silence".

Keywords Advance care planning · Autonomy · Life plans · Mental capacity · Neurotechnology

7.1 Introduction

The exercise of patient's autonomy in the health care relationships has come a long way until established minimally founded on ethical and legal values and norms. However, understanding the meaning of personal autonomy of the patient has not

J. Gomes (✉)
Judge of Court of Appeal of Porto, Member of Portuguese Data Protection Authority, Porto, Portugal
e-mail: j.correia.gomes@udc.es

© The Editor(s) (if applicable) and The Author(s), under exclusive license to Springer Nature Switzerland AG 2024

J.-A. Seoane and O. Vergara (eds.), *The Discourse of Biorights*, The International Library of Bioethics 109, https://doi.org/10.1007/978-3-031-66804-3_7

followed a linear path. Besides, patient's autonomy has been focusing on the immediate clinical events, expressed by the doctrine of informed consent, without being considered or without reaching the future foreseeable or unforeseeable health events. This has only started through advance directives (advance decisions and/or health care proxy). Lately, however, there has been a need to plan the future of health care. This requires a dialogue process that enables health professionals to understand the patient's will and to make their wishes clear, especially on a context in which their mental capacity begins to irreversibly deteriorate. In these cases, it is particularly acute to know when that moment arrives, sometimes instantaneously, sometimes in a development procedure, with moments of lucidity and others of reverie.

The purpose of this paper is to determine the foundations of autonomy and its meaning in these liquid times of uncertainty (Bauman 2007), establishing a method to measure autonomy and simultaneously elaborating a key-concept of mental capacity, the gateway of autonomy. Considering this design, we have the right conditions to understand the meaning of advance care planning until the moment we have the mental capacity to determine the puzzle of our lives, in these moments of the brave new world of the brain.

7.2 Autonomy: The Foundation of an Idea

7.2.1 Origins and Terminology: A Political Idea (Political Autonomy)

The etymology of the word autonomy lies in the Greek (αὐτονομία), through the composition of two words: *auto* and *nomos*, meaning "by oneself" and "norm" or "law" respectively, but with the literal meaning of "self-norm" or "self-legislation". Its etymology allows us to know its grammatical origin, signalling its meaning and sense, but it does not provide its content. Incidentally, there has been some misunderstanding about its scope, although it may have multiple meanings: political people status; capacity or quality of a person; characteristics or state of a mechanism, to name a few. Regarding its meaning, both moral and legal, it often appears as a synonym for self-determination or associated with independence or freedom. Its substance is practically unknown. The purpose is to determine the ideation of the moral meaning of autonomy and its evolution over time, even if we make the leap between antiquity and Enlightenment modernity, a time when everything or almost everything was questioned and reflected upon (Schneewind 2005, pp. 514–515).

Autonomy appears as the political expression of each city-state or communities at the level of their territorial organisation, best expressed in their external relations (*autópolis*), but encompassing other autonomies, such as fiscal (*autotelés*) and judicial (*autódikos*). The autonomy and freedom (*eleuthería*) of each territory (*khóra*) would be the maximum expression of its political integrity and sovereignty. In practice, however, autonomy ended up being a concession by the most influential or powerful city-states in relation to the others, allowing each of them to establish their own rules of coexistence (Ostwald 1982, pp. 7–12). Meanwhile, and in the context of Hellenic literature, it has been recognized that the word autonomy (αὐτονομία)—an example of which is Sophocles' Antigone –, was used as a metaphor for political autonomy, to describe a personal characteristic of those who challenged the powers of the polis, or else, as it happened in the Hippocratic Treatise, as an antinomy of despotism. But it was also taken as a "principle of life", as invoked by the Stoics from their "philosophy of life", stating that only sensible people could live according to their choices (Cooper 2003, p. 5). Autonomy has been confused or equated with autarky, which has its origins in the Greek autarkeia (αὐτάρκεια)—and is often associated with freedom and independence (Fischer 2017, p. 431). The previous expresses "self-rule" at an internal level, with the exercise of powers or faculties, as well their direction, while the latter means "self-sufficiency" in relation to external influence, assuming a convinced isolationism (May 2008).

7.2.2 The Enlightenment: A Moral Idea (Moral Autonomy)

The philosophical basis of the Enlightenment lies in the social contract and natural law, the former being the justification for human beings to live in a community and the latter being the support for structuring their actions. As a result, monarchical power, as a divine emanation, lost its legitimacy and religious determinism gave way to free will, with the foundation of modern constitutionalism lying in the autonomy of the political sphere and sovereignty, as well as the liberal dimension of contractualism. In this respect, a moral theory of autonomy and an utilitarian theory of freedom were developed, apparently disparate, but converging in the idea of the secularisation of morality and the limitation of interference by the state and society.

The Enlightenment concept of moral autonomy was essentially developed by Immanuel Kant. Autonomy is the ability to establish rational universal laws, that lies in the rational way in which duties of conduct are expressed, enabling everyone to act in accordance with their will, respecting others, but without them interfering in their choices. Thus, a person is autonomous if their personal interests correspond to their will and if this is expressed in accordance with their reason. The principle of autonomy means that every rational being must consider themselves as a universal legislator for all the maxims of their will in order to, from this point of view, to judge themselves and their actions (Kant 2011, p. 75). Consequently, autonomy is the foundation of the dignity of the human nature and of all rational nature, in the context of a *mundus intelligibis*, with the autonomy of the will emerging as the "supreme principle of morality" (Kant 2011, pp. 100–108). The Kantian perspective of moral autonomy is not only the foundational framework of the modern and rationalist human being, but also the moral zeniths of social contractualism.

The utilitarian perspective of liberty played a major role in John Stuart Mill's philosophy. His concern to find limits to society's power over individuals was evident in the dilemma between liberty and authority. Although autonomy was not a lexical reference for him, he found liberty to be the insurmountable barrier to despotism. The primordial or utilitarian function of liberty, both at a civil and social level, would not only go through the classic vision of protection against the tyranny of political rulers, but would go further, realizing the nature and establishing limits to the power that can legitimately be exercised by society over the individual. (Mill 2015, p. 5). According to this approach, liberty turns out to be an essential prerequisite for life in society and for maximizing happiness, the limit of which would lie in what Stuart Mill conceived as the "harm principle", *i.e.*, the exercise of individual freedom could not cause harm to others, damaging their freedom.

7.2.3 The Hierarchical Construction: An Individual Idea (Isolated Autonomy)

The recent positions on autonomy bring an idea of justice, based on the ideal of an autonomous and rational person, free from influence and able to control their will and actions. For this, it is necessary to establish an integral process of reflection and decision-making, in an environment free from external pressures and influences. Therefore, we need a method, structure, or process, which guides and prioritizes everything that can converge in the will, connecting and filtering preferences, desires and wishes. Consequently, without exhausting the different positions that line up in this methodology for individual autonomy, this paper will just give an account of two hierarchical theories of autonomy, one institutional and the other procedural (Christman 2007).

The institutional hierarchical theory is undoubtedly best supported by Harry Frankfurt's doctrine (Frankfurt 1971). For this purpose, it starts from the person not only as the singularity of the "people", but essentially from the "will structure of the person". Through this structure it is possible to distinguish persons from other creatures, introducing a structural decision-making mechanism, made up of two hierarchical levels: (i) the "first-order desires" (desires of the first order), which are simple aspirations to do or not to do, to do this or that; (ii) the "second-order desires" (desires of the second order), which imply a capacity for reflection and self-evaluation, in which one decides to do or not to do according to what one had previously desired at the first level. Thus, for the agent to have a free will, there must be an identity between these primary desires and the actual desires, excluding any interference in this decision-making process.

The hierarchical procedural theory developed by Gerald Dworkin (1997, pp. 48, 103–109) led him to associate autonomy with the idea of agency, as the capacity to act critically on one's own behalf and with responsibility. To this end, he began by considering an agent to be anyone who is active or acts for a cause, while a moral agent would be anyone who lives autonomously, tracing and developing their actions in accordance with the norms they establish. His hierarchical system emerged from a procedure with two levels: (i) the "first-order preferences, desires and wishes", in which there are (ii) "second-orders reflections", through the critical capacity to accept or change these preferences, desires or wills. Autonomy appears as agency, corresponding to a person's ability to act on their own, reflecting on their decisions beforehand, weighing up their conditions and constraints.

7.3 Reinventing Autonomy

7.3.1 The Construction of Bioethics: A Decision-Making Process (Deliberative Autonomy)

Autonomy is a key concept in bioethics. It was triggered by the Belmont Report of 1976, which in turn had been catalysed by the *Tuskegee Syphilis Study* (1932–1972). This report establishes three basic ethical principles for medical research: (1) Respect for persons; (2) Beneficence; (3) Justice. Autonomy was a print value of the first one with this declaration: "Respect for persons incorporates at least two ethical convictions: first, that individuals should be treated as autonomous agents, and second, that persons with diminished autonomy are entitled to protection" (B. 1).

The bioethics literature reformulates and introduces other principles, namely: "(1) *respect for autonomy* (a norm of respecting and supporting autonomous decisions), (2) *nonmaleficience* (a norm of avoiding the causation of harm), (3) *beneficence* (a group of norms pertaining to relieving, lessening, or providing benefits and balancing benefits against risks and costs); (iv) *justice* (a group of norms for fairly distributing benefits, risks, and costs)" (Beauchamp, Childress 2013, p. 13). These principles are not hierarchic, and demand balancing.

Autonomy has three-conditions: (i) intentionality, which means a representation of the events required by actions, excluding accidental decisions or actions; sometimes its eligible a plan; (ii) understanding, which means that autonomous actions need a substantial level of comprehension, although not a full one; (iii) no control of influences that determine actions, which implies that a person is free of external (*e.g.*, manipulation) or internal domination (*e.g.*, mental disability) (Beauchamp, Childress 2013, pp. 104–105). The essential focus of this theory is the autonomous choice and not the autonomous general governance. In the bioethics, the goal of autonomy is the implementation or compliance of informed consent, with a decision-making process that respects the three conditions enumerated above: intentionality, understanding and no control.

Otherwise, a new bioethics literature made some critics to the autonomous choice theory, because it fails to correctly identify nonautonomous actions and choices, it gives a false account for differentiating autonomous or nonautonomous actions and choices, and it does not fully justify the moral demand to respect autonomy (Walker 2009). This way, the theory of procedural autonomy emphasizes a mapping-process decision (Pugh 2020, pp. 15–16). This method incorporates two dimensions and four elements. The decisional dimension enables autonomous decisions to be made, with two pillars: a cognitive element (the agent's beliefs and understanding) jointly with a reflective element (the reflection or motivating desire). The practical dimension has also two supports, one as negative freedom (the absence of incapacitating forces that prevent the agent from acting), and the other as positive freedom (abilities or capacities for action). Considering this process and a rational test, this theory offers an autonomous decision-making and underpins a standard for the disclosure of information of a free and rational consent.

7.3.2 The Feminist Construction: A Relational Idea (Relational Autonomy)

The structuring autonomy, through a hierarchical model of the autonomous agent, is based on a rational, individualistic, and abstract model. In other words, it is built on a superman or superwoman, immune to all interference and pressures, who ignores everyone, disregards all social relationships and all situations of dependence. Consequently, this autonomous and individual super-agent would only be possible if they would liv in an alien or avatar world—in this sense, autonomy is simply a myth (Fineman 2004, pp. 20–22). The Feminist theories of autonomy developed a strong criticism of this individualist model of autonomy, which ignores the human frailty and generates dependencies. This study will only mention three possible readings of these theories: a strong substantive theory, a global substantive theory and a comprehensive theory.

The strong substantive theory establishes a different kind of autonomy, breaking out the bureaucratic and selfish meshes of individualism (Nedelsky 1989). Instead, it suggests a language based on the value of autonomy, while recognizing the demands of human capacities, maintaining that a person is not only an individual creation, but also a social creation. Autonomy is not an isolation, but rather a relationship, especially with those who can support and come to one's aid. This theory does not imply that people assume themselves to be passive or subordinate beings, but it simply recognizes that personal autonomy is compatible with interdependence. The existence of a strictly individual and isolationist autonomy is illusory.

The global substantive theory emphasizes that autonomy is essentially a socio-relational phenomenon (Oshana 1998). Accordingly, although autonomy is an individual manifestation, it develops itself in a social context. In this confluence, values, desires, and convictions are acquired, as well as choices and actions. However, this approach establishes four conditions: (i) a critical reflection; (ii) an independent procedure, although it may not be neutral, but without any coercion or manipulation; (iii) the access to a level of relevant and appropriate options; and iv) one's own social relationship. All of this will allow for social autonomy, which is strongly undermined when there are relationships of subordination, subservience, economic, psychological or any other dependency that implies control over choices or options.

A comprehensive feminist theory of autonomy is based on a multidimensional understanding of autonomy (Mackenzie 2014). There is no single concept of autonomy, but rather different dimensions, which appear to be interdependent, suggesting a relational comprehension of them. One of these dimensions is self-determination (i), which is related to the external conditions, whether social or political, that interfere with or provide both freedom and the opportunity for the agent to evaluate their environment. The other dimension is self-governance (ii), centered on internal conditions, such as the skills and capacities needed for each person to make choices and decisions, to understand relevant information, to make a judgement about the situation and communicate it. The third and final dimension is self-authorization (iii), that refers to the exercised control over one's life and body, implying the existence of normative authority, which unfolds in various valences, such as responsibility, attitudes of self-evaluation and social recognition.

In summary, one can say that these critical feminist visions of isolationist autonomy pave the way for overcoming an atomistic view of the individual by bringing them into the social reality and their environment, assuming a globalizing view of the individual, and accentuating their relational nature. These theories re-found autonomy.

7.3.3 The Contemporary Construction: An Idea of Recognition (Personal Autonomy)

Autonomy is not only an expanding concept, but also a particular characteristic of people. Given its historical roots in a political model of self-governance or self-determination, there could be a temptation to transpose it to the personal sphere, which would be a clamorous mistake because, from the outset, self-representation would be omitted (Baumann 2000, p. 10). One could also easily fall into autarky, *i.e.*, self-sufficiency, which characterizes the binary models of (in)capacity—one either has capacity or not—and therefore many people would be left without an adequate legal response. The correct answer, however, involves a human rights discourse, in a clear language of rights, recognizing autonomy as a political, moral and legal reality, which cannot be the privilege (the right) of some and the disadvantage (no right) of others.

The legal recognition of autonomy, as a value and a principle, is a proper model that operates in personal relationships, both intersubjective (horizontal) and citizens/state (vertical), but also in the specific social micro relations (atomistic). In a decent society, one that does not humiliate people, autonomy is the cornerstone of respect and trust between those who are situated in the micro relationship of healthcare, generating rights and duties. Thus, whenever necessary and appropriate and in order to deal with the dependence or vulnerability of the person concerned, this potential autonomous agent should be leveraged through a support structure for their empowerment, prioritizing the sustainability of this condition of autonomy, as a structuring element of citizenship status (Anderson, Honneth 2005, pp. 144–145). In fact, this urgency is a requirement for people with a complete, permanent and irreversible lack of discernment or in end-of-life situations, in which human rights and human dignity are often forgotten and a certain "ethic of life" ends up being an "immoral suffering" (Bielefeldt 2017, p. 49).

7.3.4 The Post-Contemporary Construction: An Idea of Empowerment (Capability Autonomy)

Autonomy is a *carrefour concept* which can be better understood by following the contributions of a multidimensional theory of autonomy (Killmister 2018). Autonomy can only exist if there is the capacity to exercise it, both in the present and in the future, personally or through support measures, including representation. Taking this approach, this essay follows the contributions of the capability approach centred on human rights, as a way of achieving well-being, which is better understood through capabilities (Sen 1992, 2004; Nussbaum 2006 2011). Accordingly, one can establish a specific index of basic capabilities, refined by the secure functionings approach as a response to disadvantages (Wolff, De-Shalit 2007, pp. 36–62).

Through this theoretical approach it is possible to achieve three essential purposes: (1) differentiating a person rather than wrapping them up in reductive packages (*e.g.*, disability versus ability), once one has their own singularities, not only personal, but also social, cultural and environmental; (2) having a flexible and multi-purpose intervention framework, whether legal, judicial or even informal; (3) implementing the infrastructures of a support system in concrete rather than in abstract. This leads to an inventory of needs, both at an individual and social level, (i) combining them with the human functions of that specific person (ii) and which, in practice, need to be enabled, (iii) and ensuring and maximizing their autonomy when they are in a vulnerable situation. A person will have the capacity to do and be itself if those secure functionalities that are necessary, adequate, and appropriate for them to pursue their free will and their legitimate interests are established and developed.

7.4 A Analytical Framework of Autonomy

7.4.1 Anatomy

Autonomy, like Janus, has two faces, one negative and one positive. Negative autonomy refuses the interference from outside powers or any kind of supremacies that aim at controlling or determining a person's behaviour, choices or interests.

Differently, positive autonomy seeks to ensure that everyone has the necessary conditions to develop their own judgements and reasons, exercising their power of action over themselves or others accordingly to their free will.

Autonomy has an immense elasticity and is not univocal, because the human being is complex and has no standard, contrary to what the concept of the *bonus pater familiae* entailed—the *bonus mater familiae* was always missing. It would be reductive to find a single modality of autonomy, which often happens when using self-determination strictly connecting or instead of autonomy. In this regard, following the aforementioned and bearing in mind its historical significance and contemporary understanding, one can list the following modalities: (a) self-governance (internal conditions); (b) self-determination (external conditions); (c) self-validation or self-authorization (responsibility, self-assessment and social recognition); (d) self-representation, either direct (through the self), or indirect (through a proxy or agent); (e) self-prospective (planning), with the meaning of developing strategies for future times or situations when one has a decreasing or even absent autonomy, including a plan management of one's assets, health care and life itself.

Autonomy is not a unitary concept, although one can establish its negative and positive dimensions in order to delimit its meaning and realize its value and relevance as a principle, as mentioned before. Therefore, in order to better understand its content, the following developments can be highlighted: (a) *informational autonomy*, which has a cognitive function (i), of knowing the personal and social situation, a hermeneutic function (ii), of interpreting that reality, as well as an expository function (iii), of clarifying itself in the social context, providing elements and data; (b) *reflective autonomy*, which is based on their needs, choices and the analysis of both; (c) *functional autonomy*, which combines their capacities, attributions and personal performance; (d) *decision-making autonomy*, which unfolds the evaluation, weighing up, usefulness and meaning of their decisions (i) and in the actual making of that deliberation (ii); (e) *communicative autonomy*, which consists of "making common" the elements, data and reasons for the assessment and/or resolution process, using their own instruments, whether personal (visual, gestural, audio), mechanical (written, digital) or any other that makes it possible to establish a link between the sender and the receiver.

7.4.2 Measurability

Assessments of autonomy and empowerment are an essential tool for setting up the infrastructure of any support system sustained by a language of rights, precluding the implementation of substitution systems, which destroys legal capacity and leads to a "civil death". Consequently, in these evaluation measures, one can distinguish three phases. The *identification phase* (a) looks for the self-definition of values, beliefs, and objectives (i), as well as the self-organization through preparation, ordering and planning (ii). The *concretization phase* (b) seeks self-executions, through internal and external fulfilment (i), and self-unification, through personal and social integration (ii). Finally, the *reconsideration phase* (c) aims at achieving a self-reconstitution of the past and the present (i), permitting self-rethinking about future options (ii). In turn, through empowerment measures ones estimates a person's concrete capacities (internal level), as well as the contingent and adverse circumstances of their environment (external level), gauging the existing and necessary means or instruments (level of goods and resources).

7.5 Plans and Planning Care: A Puzzle of Life

7.5.1 The Ethical Foundations of Care

The word "care" has its origins in the Latin word *cura*, which according to the Stoic perspective corresponded to the process of being truly human, through solicitude, with the meaning of providing well-being to others, consciously or out of devotion (Reich 2004, pp. 103–104). However, "care" is also essential to the human condition, whether by emphasizing an understanding of one's virtues or through relationships of interaction and dependence.

The contemporary feminist approach of care underscores the moral experience of dependence and rethinks the ontological relations of human beings focusing on the most vulnerable. Care is understood as the connection with others in the most different ways, a channel to listen voices (communication) and practicing acts (performing) (Gilligan 2003, p. 2). This proposition changes the paradigm of the health care relationships. The intend and the objective of health care is not only a deontological or technological medical approach, but essentially a human vulnerability approach, with a straight connection with one's free will, wishes and interests.

A relational care perspective was now brought to the concept of autonomy as an alternative to the individualistic approach of the liberal theory (Engster 2021). Humans are relational beings, with cultural, social, economic and historical relationships, through which they develop their capabilities to be autonomous agents or instead decrease their competences to be potentially subordinated. A self-confident base of life with secure attachments is a significant factor to reflect their choices, desires and interests, because they "retain a capacity for autonomy". According to this perspective "Sensitive and responsive care supports the development of the secure attachments that constitute autonomous selves", and "they need at the very least to be protected from abusive, neglectful, and other harmful forms of care and provided opportunities to develop the basic capabilities most people enjoy in a given society. In order for individuals to be able to exercise autonomy, they likewise need to receive the care supportive of secure attachments".

7.5.2 The Philosophical Foundations of Life Plans

Strategic life plans date back to antiquity, both for the fate of property, carried out in writing, and for establishing the values of life (*e.g.*, virtue), carried out orally, through the *techne dialektike* by attempts and through dialogue, in private or in public, between at least two participants, through questions and answers (Dreche 2015). Life plans regain their interest in philosophical literature in the course of 1900. The person as a human being has a trajectory of life, with their own values and interests, sometimes with a plan, sometimes without it. However, one's personality always reveals the "plans and purposes of my life" (Royce 1908, p. 167). More recently it can be found the following prominent theories of life plans. According to the rational theory, planning means projecting the future, organizing, and structuring our existence according to our ideals, ensuring a "harmoniously satisfying interests" and pursuing the "fulfilling desires without interferences" (Rawls 1999, p. 80). To the lifestyle theory strategic life-planning express "the substantial content of the reflexively organized trajectory of the self", based on the "self's biography" and the existence of a personal "life-plan calendars", handled by the lifespan (Giddens 1991, p. 85). The intentional theory implies a "rational reflection" coordinating present and future activities, not in isolation, but with other persons, and can even be a "shared intention" (Bratman 1999, pp. 165–166). The rational choices and objectives theory is concerned with both life plans and short-term plans, aimed at satisfying a "higher goal" or even a "basic goal" (Baron 1985, pp. 52–53). However, according to coherent plan of life, the existence of a plan is not so much to emphasize the moment of death, but rather to establish the right perspective for "choosing how to live one's present life" (Finnis 2011, pp. 103–104).

7.5.3 Advance Care Planning: A New Challenge?

Advance care planning (ACP) emerged at the beginning of the new millennium as a communication strategy in the relationship between doctor and patient, which may involve the patient's relatives, to enable control of medical treatment in a terminal life situation (Sabatino 2010). Its philosophy expresses personal autonomy and informed consent (Singer et al. 1996). It was generated in an evolutionary way, after a certain inertia and disappointment with the implementation of advance directives that appeared in the 1970s. The implementation of advance directives in the USA was considered a "authentic failure" (Fagerlin, Scheneider 2004), and there was also a strong criticism at the European level (Andorno et al. 2009, pp. 209–210). Both find similar critics: (i) the vagueness and ambiguity of the prior instructions, because the future clinical situation was unknown; (ii) the resistance of medical professionals, who are losing their medical authority.

The various stratagems that have emerged in the meantime regarding the improvement of advance directives have also enhanced advance care planning, creating a symbiosis between them. There are essentially two kinds: (a) *medical orders*, such Do-Not-Resuscitate (DNR) or Provider Orders for Life Sustaining Treatments (POLST) and similar; (b) *demanding an individual tailor information*, for example Life Support Preferences Questionnaire (LSPQ), and Making Your Wishes Known: Planning Your Medical Future. ACP may also be implemented in mental health, establishing an effective communication in Psychiatric Advance Directives, which began as a proposal for the patient to refuse coercive measures or compulsory hospitalization (Szasz 1982, 2003; Appelbaum 2004).

The US Uniform Law Commissioners—later known as the Uniform Law Commission (ULC)—recognized the necessity of uniformization of law but also increased a flexible support of health models protection. Thus, in 1982 it passed the Model Health-Care Consent Act, supplemented in 1985 by the Uniform Rights of the Terminally Ill Act (URTIA), revised in 1989 and reformulated in 1993 by the Uniform Health-Care Decisions Act (UHCDA). More recently, in July 2023, it passed the New Uniform Health-Care Decisions Act (Kohn 2023).

In a report entitled *Taking Care—Ethical Caregiving in Our Aging Society* adopted in 2005, and facing the growing inevitability of a "mass geriatric society", the President's Council on Bioethics rethought the ACP trajectory by suggesting its use for the propose of long-term care of old age or chronic illness. In these cases, it has been considered appropriate to distinguish "care planning", as a process of discussion and reflection to achieve the objectives outlined, from "care plans", which is the written document that records the outcome of this process of conversation (Jenni Burt et al. 2014). In these circumstances, not only treatment options are at stake, but also housing and care preferences, especially in cases of long-term physical and mental decline. Nonetheless, the communication strategy remains. Prudent planning at long term cases allows the person concerned to prepare for crisis and emergency situations together with their relatives and may defuse future conflict situations. Accordingly, ACP can have a healthcare nature as well as an assistance characteristic and can even include estate planning.

ACP was first conceived as a *complementary process* to advance directives, and then emerged as a *propaedeutic process* for its realization and/or the appointment of a health care proxy. At a third stage, it could also emerge as *specific planning* for mental health care. At a fourth stage, it has the potential to provide a *global planning* of care of personal interest, in health care or assistance, as well as property interest. Essentially, ACP is a support and protection measure centered on the person concerned, but involving others who can accompany or interfere in the reflection and decision-making process. ACP has an enormous potential to formulate life plans and to express prospective autonomy.

7.6 The Brave New World of the Brain

7.6.1 Legal Capacity Versus Mental Capacity

Legal capacity and mental capacity are different concepts. Legal capacity is a legal mechanism for any person to be the subject of legal relations (*legal status*), exercising their rights and fulfilling their duties (*capacity for exercise*). Mental capacity reveals the ability of decision-making, which involves the understanding of received information, considering the benefits and harms of decision-making or decision-refraining, as well as the ability to communicate one's decisions to others (ComRPD 2014, § 13). Mental capacity is an emerging mixed concept, with legal, bioethical, medical and philosophical resonances. However, it will be better understood as an expression of personal autonomy in a relational context and through a multidisciplinary reading (Owen et al. 2009).

A bioethical approach comes from the US President's Commission report *Making Health Care Decisions*, who pointed the following elements of capacity: (1) the existence of a set of values and objectives (authenticity); (2) the ability to understand and transmit information (communication); (3) the ability to rationalize and deliberate on one's choices, comparing the impacts of the results of alternatives on personal objectives and life plans (rationality) (President's Commission 1982, p. 57). Others stressed the diversity of personal capacities to decide, because one may have capacity for one specific subject but not for another, and therefore proposed an assessment of specific capacity (Etchells et al. 1996). In the context of informed consent, the importance should focus on the ability to understand relevant information regarding a treatment decision in three variations: consequences, alternatives and refuses.

The medical approach influenced by the psychiatric point of view is strictly based on cognitive ability tests (Appelbaum and Grisso 1988). These involved reasoning, perception, memory, verbal and mathematics abilities that raised general subjects or had specific targets and presented the following points: (1) the ability to communicate the choice; (2) the understanding of the relevant information; (3) the assessment of the clinical consequences of the situation; (4) the rational formulation of treatment choices. On the same occasion and keeping the medical-psychiatric reference, the *MacArthur Treatment Competence Study* aimed at providing a specific and differentiated response to each situation in which effective decision-making by hospitalized people, with and without mental disorders, was required. The following assumption of mental capacity were considered: (1) the ability to make a choice; (2) to understand the relevant information; (3) to acknowledge the nature of their own situation; (4) and to rationalize information.

A consistent philosophical perspective can be found in the multidimensional autonomy theory (Mackenzie and Rogers 2013). This position stands that a primarily cognitive point of view it is not enough, because it ignores some "demanding autonomy conditions", relating to freedom circumstances, competence states and authenticity, reflecting the different dimensions of autonomy (*e.g.*, self-governance, self-determination). The topics for evaluating capacity of an autonomous agent are the connection with diachronic and synchronic elements, which reflects coherence and consistency, responsibility to others, and sentimental attitudes towards oneself. Diachronic approaches examine the values, beliefs and commitments of human agency throughout times, within the "broader context of the person's history", meanwhile a synchronic approach gives the prominence in the present situation.

A functional perspective of mental capacity has emerged in recent times, based on the subsequent molds: (1) mental capacity is not static, but fluctuates, and there can be moments of lucidity or reverie; (2) mental capacity cannot be established solely through clinical diagnosis; (3) assessment must be centered on a specific task and a particular moment; 4) the degree of aptitude differs according to the type of case and the demands of the situation in question (Gergel and Owen 2015). The functional capacity test is an important tool to assess an effective decision-making ability (Webb et al. 2020). This test is an instrument for supported decision making, with the following elements: (1) the ability to understand information; (2) to retain information long enough to be able to make a decision; (3) to appreciate the relevance of the information and to use and weigh that information as part of the process of decision-making; (4) to communicate their decision; (5) to identify the tools to ability and support decision-making.

Mental capacity is differentiated from an objective and subjective point of view. On the one hand, one can have objectively better skills for decision-making on specific matters comparing to others (*e.g.*, property business ≠ securities business ≠ agriculture ≠ pisciculture). On the other hand, personal abilities are subjectively variable, as it is the case of persons with bipolar disorder, Alzheimer's or in dementia situations, all depending on the circumstances in which they find themselves and express their will. Mental capacity is a prerequisite for personal autonomy with its specific relational context, which does not mean manipulation and can be strengthened through empowerment measures, such as the decision-making support model on the human right to legal capacity (12 CRPD). Reasonable accommodation develops a central role to a complete and real social participation and promote equality of opportunities and non-discrimination (5 CRPD).

7.6.2 Neurotechnology: A Post-Contemporary Challenge to Mental Capacity

The object of neuro-philosophy is more about a mind-brain problem than a mind-body problem (Walter 2009, p. 87). The mind-brain relation is essential to explain when one is an autonomous agent to make a free will deliberation, sometimes with certainty, sometimes with more doubts. A decision-making process does not develop encapsulated and a deliberation is not an isolationist act, a *autarkeia* performance. The natural autonomy is a basic demand for an autonomous agent, who essentially requests a troika of interrogations: (i) when are we able to choose? (ii) when does self-decision exist? (iii) when are these decisions intelligibly?

The contemporary human brain is a kind of 'personal hard disk' containing private memories or images and neural data that can be accessed, changed or even deleted, but also collected, stored and analysed. The development of a "human Brain/Cloud Interface" is paving the way to a matrix-style of live for the post-contemporary days. Neurotechnology, nanomedicine, artificial intelligence and computational science are powerful instruments that read the mind, mapping the conscience or nonconscious brain, connecting the human brain to a digital network or to a vast cloud-computing complexes system. Besides, they may also improve cognitive capacities, medical benefits in biopsychic or mental impairments, enhancing human brain and mental capacity.

Neuroanatomy is a nuclear arena that identifies the structure and organization of the nervous system and the relations with the general central functions of the brain with the unities of nervous cells (neurons). Understanding the brain may propitiate some answers about mental dilemmas, but it will not solve them. The Stephen Hawking human singularity is a case study on using technology not only for mobility, but also to communicate, when one has an amyotrophic lateral sclerosis (ALS) with a progressive degenerations of brain motor neurons which interferes with muscles control of the body, but not with their cognitive mind. With a technologic support (reasonable accommodation), they could develop effective strategies to personal care, speaking, writing and expressing their autonomy and plan is life.

The *Report of the International Bioethics Committee of UNESCO (IBC), on the Ethical Issues of Neurotechnology* gives some important conceptual tools. Neurotechnology "is the field of devices and procedures used to access, monitor, investigate, assess, manipulate, and/or emulate the structure and function of the neural systems of animals or human beings". These include technical and computational tools that measure and analyse chemical and electrical signals in the nervous system (i), and technical tools that interact with the nervous system to change its activity (ii). Neuroimaging or brain imaging are techniques used to either directly or indirectly access the structure and function of the central nervous system. These techniques include electroencephalography (EEG), magnetoencephalography (MEG), positron emission tomography (PET). Neurodevices can replace parts of the body and stimulate or inhibit functions of the brain, such implanted deep brain stimulators (DBS), which may be utilized for Parkinson's disease, essential tremor, dystonia, epilepsy and obsessive-compulsive disorder. Brain Computer Interfaces (BCIs) it's a type of neurotechnology that makes it possible translate the brain processes underlying thought and action. These techniques may detect awareness and establishing forms of communication that until now were unthinkable (Owen 2012), but also developing mental capacity. A neural code of language allows to discover several cognitive faculties, which are distinct from grammatical constructions, but are nonetheless a specific language (Murphy 2021, pp. 135–137).

7.7 Conclusion

The post-contemporary discourse of rights is essential for a human ethos, taking new forms of constructive hypotheses and renovated concepts. This also potentially introduces multiple notions or legal mechanisms, with several channels, yet more humane, because humans are deeply complex (*e.g.*, the human right to legal capacity, the decision-making support model, the reasonable accommodation). In this regard, mental capacity is dynamic and nonbinary. This paper sought to establish a connection based on prospective autonomy and the self, in times where mental capacity is deeply in a grey zone, building some jus-philosophical hypotheses to achieve a new legal capacity status. Life plans and advance care planning are an excellent "legal laboratory" for designing a new architectural judicial framework and for establishing the meaning of personal autonomy in the past, present and future. This would give a supported decision-making model for mental capacity, reinforced by neurotechnology as an instrument for reasonable accommodation, and would discover the "sound of silence" of the brave new world of the brain.

References

Anderson, Joel and Honneth, Axel. 2005. Autonomy, Vulnerability, Recognition, and Justice, in Christman, John and Anderson, Joel, *Autonomy and the Challenges to liberalism—New Essays*, Cambridge: CUP. 2005, pp. 127–145

Andorno, Roberto, et al. 2009. Advance health care directives: towards a coordinated European policy? *European Journal of Health Law* 16 (2009): 207–227.

Baron, Jonathan. 1985. *Rationality and intelligence.* Cambridge: Cambridge University Press.

Bauman, Zygmunt. 2007. *Liquid times: living in an age of uncertainty.* Cambridge: Polity.

Baumann, Peter. 2000. *Die Autonomie der Person*, Paderborn: mentis.

Beauchamp, Tom L. and Childress, James F. 2013. *Principles of Biomedical Ethics*, Oxford: Oxford University Press (7th Edition).

Behavioral Research. 1979. *The Belmont Report—Ethical Principles and Guidelines forthe Protection of Human Subjects of Research.*

Bielefeldt, Heiner. 2017. Menschenwürde und Autonomie am Lebensende—perspektiven der internationalen Menschenrecht, in Welsh, Caroline *et al* (Hg.), *Autonomie und Menschenrechte am Lebensende Grundlagen, Erfahrungen, Reflexionen aus der Praxis*, Bielefeld: transcript, pp. 45–66.

Bratman, Michael E. 1999. *Faces of intention: selected essays on intention agency.* Cambridge: Cambridge University Press.

Burt, Jenni et al. 2014. Care plans and care planning in long-term conditions: a conceptual model, in *Primary Health Care Research & Development*, no. 15, pp. 142–354.

Christman, John. 2007. Autonomy, history, and the subject of justice. *Social Theory and Practice* 33 (1): 1–26.

ComRPD General comment no. 1. 2104. Article 12: Equal recognition before the law

Cooper, John M. 2003. Stoic Autonomy, in Paul, Ellen Frankel *et al* (Edited by), *Autonomy*, Cambridge: CUP.

Dreche, Iovan. 2015. Dialectical strategic planning in Aristotle. *Symposion: Theoretical and Applied Inquiries in Philosophy and Social Sciences* 2(3): 287–309.

Dworkin, Gerald. 1997. *The theory and practice of autonomy.* Cambridge: CUP.

Engster, Daniel. 2021. Care ethics and liberal freedom, in Bhandary, Asha and Baehr, Amy R. (eds.), *Caring For Liberalism: Dependency and Liberal Political Theory*, New York: Routledge, pp. 97–119.
Etchells, Edward, Sharpe, Gilbert, Elliott, Carl, and Singer, Peter. 1996. Bioethics for Clinicians: 3. Capacity. *Canadian Medical Association Journal* 155(6): 657–661.
Fagerlin, Angela, and Carl E. Scheneider. 2004. Enough: the failure of the living will. *The Hasting Center Report* 34 (2): 30–42.
Fineman, Martha Albertson. 2004. *The Autonomy Myth: A theory of dependency*, New York.
Finnis, John. 2011. *2011*, 103–104. Natural Law and Natural Rights, Oxford: Oxford University Press.
Fischer, Karsten. 2017. Das Paradox der Autonomie und seine Entfaltungen Eine Urgeschichte politischer Liberalität, in Bumke, C. und Röthel A. (Hrsg), *Autonomie im Recht—Gegenwartsdebatten über einem rechtlichen Grundbegiff*, Tübingen: Mohr Siebeck, pp. 411–434.
Frankfurt, Harry. 1971. Freedom of the will and the concept of person. *The Journal of Philosophy* LXVIII(1): 5–20.
Gergel, Tania, and Gareth Owen. 2015. Fluctuating capacity and advance decision-making in Bipolar affective disorder—self-binding directives and self-determination. *International Journal of Law and Psychiatry* 40: 92–101.
Giddens, Anthony. 1991. *Modernity and self-identity: self and society in the late modern age.* Stanford: Stanford University Press.
Gilligan, Carol. 2003. *Ina different voice: psychological theory and women's development.* Cambridge: HUP.
Kant, Immanuel. 2011. *Groundwork of the Metaphysics of Moral, Cambridge: CUP, translation from 1786. Grundlegung zur Metaphysik der Sitten*, Riga: J. F.Hartknoch.
Killmister, Suzy. 2018. *Taking the measure of autonomy: a four-dimensional theory of self-governance.* New York: Routledge.
Kohn, Nina A. 2023. The new uniform health-care decisions act: an overview. *Bifocal—Journal of the ABA Commission on Law and Aging* 45(1): 6–7.
Mackenzie, Catriona, and Wendy Rogers. 2013. Autonomy, vulnerability and capacity: a philosophical appraisal of the mental capacity act. *International Journal of Law in Context* 9 (1): 37–52.
Mackenzie, Catriona. 2014. Three dimensions of autonomy: a relational analysis, in Veltman, Andrea; Piper, Mark (Edit.), *Autonomy, Oppression, and Gender*, Oxford: OUP, pp. 15–41.
May, Thomas. 2008. The concept of autonomy in bioethics—an unwarranted fall from grace. In *Taylor, James Stacey, Personal Autonomy—New Essays on Personal Autonomy and Its Role in Contemporay Moral Philosophy*, 299–309. Cambridge: CUP.
Mill, John Stuart. 2015. On Liberty (1st edition 1859). *On Liberty, Utilitarianism and Other Essays*, Oxford: OUP.
Murphy, Elliot. 2021. *The oscillatory nature of language*, 135–137. Cambridge: Cambridge University Press.
Nedelsky, Jennifer. 1989. Reconceiving autonomy: sources, thoughts and possibilities. *Yale Journal of Law & Feminism* I (1): 7–36.
Nussbaum, Martha. 2006. *Frontiers of Justice: Disability, Nationality, Species Membership*, Cambridge: HUP; *Creating Capabilities*. 2011, Cambridge: HUP.
Oshana, Marina. 1998. Personal autonomy and society. *Journal of Social Philosophy* XIX(1): 81–102.
Ostwald, Martin. 1982. *AUTONOMIA: its genesis and early history*, 1982. USA: Scholars Press.
Owen, Adrian M. 2012. When thoughts become actions: Neuroimaging in non-responsive patients, in Richmond, Sarah *et al*, *I Know What You're Thinking: Brain Imaging and Mental Privacy*, Oxford: Oxford University Press, pp. 73–87.
Owen, Gareth S., et al. 2009. Mental capacity and decisional autonomy: an interdisciplinary challenge. *Inquiry* 52 (1): 79–107.

Pugh, Jonathan. 2020. *Autonomy, rationality and contemporary bioethics*. Oxford: Oxford University Press.
Rawls, John. 1999. *A theory of justice*. Cambridge: Harvard University Press.
Reich, Warren T. 2004, Care, post, Stephen G. (Edited by), *Encyclopedia of Bioethics*, Vol. I, New York: Thomson/Gale, pp. 349–361.
Royce, Josiah. 1908. *The philosophy of loyalty*. New York: The MacMillan Company.
Sabatino, Charles P. 2010. The evolution of health care advance planning law and policy. *The Milbank Quarterly* 88 (2): 211–239.
Schneewind, J.B. 2005. *The invention of autonomy—a history of modern moral philosophy*. Cambridge: Cambridge University Press.
Sen, Amartya. 1992. *Inequality Re-examined*. Oxford: Claredon; Elements of a theory of human rights. *Philosophy & Public Affairs* XXXII(4), 2004: 315-356.
Singer, Peter, et al. 1996. Bioethics for clinicians: 6. Advance care planning. *Canadian Medical Association Journal* 155(12): 1689-1692.
The National Commission for the Protection of Human Subjects of Biomedical and.
Walker, Rebecca L. 2009. Medical ethics needs a new view of autonomy. *Journal of Medicine and Philosophy* 33 (6): 594–608.
Walter, Henrik. 2009. *Neurophilosophy of free will: from libertarian illusions to a concept of natural autonomy*. Cambridge: MIT Press.
Webb, Paul et al. 2020. Key components of supporting and assessing decision making ability. *International Journal of Law and Psychiatry* 72(2). https://doi.org/10.1016/j.ijlp.2020.101613.
Wolff, Jonathan, and Avner De-Shalit. 2007. *Disadvantage*. Oxford: OUP.

Chapter 8
Artificial Intelligence and Neurorights: Lessons Learned for a Future Global Regulation

Daniel García San José

Abstract This paper starts from the idea that there is a relationship between neurorights and artificial intelligence wider than explored until now, like the two sides of the same coin, with pros and cons. It is assumed at theoretical level the need for a global regulation of the complex ways such relationship expresses, even though the principal international actors seem reluctant to do it. The exam of previous efforts to manage with controversial bio juridical issues in past (by way of an international treaty and nonbinding codes of conduct, or thanks to judicial activism by international tribunals of human rights), might not to be useful for a proper normative choice, if it is not recognized that the best response by the world community to this matter must face three challenges: how to produce it upon a democratic basis, according to informing principles on a collective consensual basis, and it being ready to be socially accepted without the help of coercion.

Keywords Neurorights and human dignity · Artificial intelligence and ethical issues · Global governance of neurotechnology · Common concern of humankind

8.1 Introduction

Research questions in this contribution are the following: first of all, what is the role of Artificial Intelligence (AI) in neurotechnology? In other words, what is the real shape of the link between these two challenges we are facing now? Many authors warn about the convenience of cautiousness when addressing the role of AI in some specific human activities (Farisco et al. 2020, p. 2413). In this early research question we focus on clarifying the ways AI interferes in human brain activities in several ways: decoding thoughts from neural activity, enhancing cognitive abilities and controlling our will and action, thanks to brain-computer interfaces (BCI) and other devices.

D. García San José (✉)
University of Seville, Seville, Spain
e-mail: dagarcia@us.es

© The Editor(s) (if applicable) and The Author(s), under exclusive license to Springer Nature Switzerland AG 2024

J.-A. Seoane and O. Vergara (eds.), *The Discourse of Biorights*, The International Library of Bioethics 109, https://doi.org/10.1007/978-3-031-66804-3_8

Second research question, closely related to the first one is the following: considering the speed of its progression, which are the ethical priorities for neurotechnologies and AI? For instance, what are the ethical concerns on an unstoppable process of human and AI interaction? (Miller 2019, p. 1) In a scenario that Elon Musk in his company *Neuralink* has called "AI symbiosis" (Regalado 2020), is human dignity and human rights jeopardized with new advances in neurotechnologies? In this context, is an amendment to the UN Charter of Human Rights to include the so-called "neurorights" the most urgent action to be taken to neutralize these risks? Such an amendment can be even more controversial considering that there is not yet international consensus on what constitutes neurorights (Yuste et al. 2021, p. 161). Could we even defend the idea that we should address the question as a common concern for humankind, given that what it is at stake is the human brain, which makes us significant and unique as species? Finally, the third set of research question is complementing previous ones: how can we promote innovation and, at the same time, protect neurorights by ensuring ethical development of AI-human brain symbiosis? In other words, what challenges do we face at global, national and corporate governance of the use of AI in neurotechnologies? Is it enough the adoption of a kind of tecno-oath (similar to Hippocrates oath in Medicine)? Is the adoption of a new specific international convention on neurorights the most suitable option? Can we be imaginative enough to consider other possible options? In the following pages we try to provide answers to these questions.

8.2 The Symbiosis of AI and Neurotechnologies

The scenario we are facing at present as regards Artificial Intelligence (AI) and neurotechnologies is not new. As a matter of fact, it seems familiar to us: scientific advances and technological innovation appearing in our societies and provoking us a bitter-sweet taste, considering their promises of better times for us and frightening us because of their risks and potentially bad effects in our lives and social relationships. Our parents and grandparents faced similar challenges decades ago with the discovery of nuclear energy or with the generalized research on human embryos, just to quote a couple of significant examples. Now it is neurotechnology the object of our attention and there is long way already done, hand by hand, by AI and neuroscience, in particular, Psychiatry (Monteith 2022, pp. 709–721) (Rainery and Erden 2020, pp. 2439–2454). As the Committee on Bioethics of the Council of Europe has asserted in its Strategic Action Plan on Human Rights and Technologies in Biomedicine (2020–2025):

"Technological developments in the field of biomedicine create new possibilities for intervention in individual behavior. For instance, certain technologies raise the prospect of increased understanding, monitoring, and control of the human brain, while other developments allow for the permanent health monitoring of individuals. These developments raise novel questions relating to autonomy, privacy, and even freedom of thought.... In the light of these developments, the third pillar of the

Strategic Action Plan addresses concerns for physical and mental integrity. Guaranteeing respect for a person's integrity in the sphere of biomedicine is one of the central tenets of the Oviedo Convention. This is understood as the ability of individuals to exercise control over what happens to them with regard to, inter alia, their body, their mental state, and the related personal data." (Committee on Bioethics of the Council of Europe 2019, pp. 21–22).

Why should I be particularly worried this time with the symbiosis of AI and neurotechnologies? It is well known in the field of clinical trials, that what can be done with lab animals, sooner or later could be done with humans. Some experts in neuroscience, like Yuste, Genser and Herrmann, have alerted how nowadays it is possible to control lab animals actions with Brain-computer interface (BCI): firstly, it is recorded in their brain while they are performing any action. Secondly, it stimulates the same part of the animals' brain, according to data recorded. Thus, such action is repeated on and on. In a case, for instance, of mice eating, under this process, these mice will eat again, even though they lack any desire of eating again. (Yuste et al. 2021, p. 156). So, the key point here is that, for the very first time in History, we are close to intervening in the very essence of what "human being" means. As it has been affirmed by experts (García-López et al. 2021, p. 1) the convergence of AI technology with data from brain activity, while is accelerating our understanding of the mental processes underpinning human behavior, it directly jeopardize human dignity, as these technologies relate to the heart of human personhood and identity. Jotterand and Bosco have expressed the same fears of these neurotechnologies combined with AI endangering our existence as bio-psycho-social beings. In their own words: "AI and neurotechnologies may be used to alter, control and manipulate human ontology (nature), expressions of personal identity and even disregard the right to mental privacy and mental integrity. In other words, human beings are, at the same time, the agents using the technology to control and shape their surroundings but also potentially objects of control and manipulation (physical, psychological, emotional and intellectual)." (Jotterand and Bosco 2022, p. 2).

The BCI can be invasive (a device inside the brain) or non-invasive (some kind of helmet or cup covering the head or attached to the skull; there are also more and more developed magnetic scanners which have been proved at labs that they are able to read the mind. In any case, BCI software needs to be updated periodically, as the apps we consume in our devices. Furthermore, even the hardware implanted inside the brain would need to be replaced as long as new versions of brain implants are launched into the market. So, apart from the ways in which safeguards at the hardware and software level are established (Kelmeyer 2021, p. 83), another question not yet solved as regards these neurotools is whether individuals can be completely free to dispose of their bodies and mental integrity as they wish, even if, once implemented the neurotechnology, it might be impossible to "go back" (Inglese and Lavazza 2021, p. 5). Apart from BCIs, authors warn against other devices like deep brain stimulators (DBS) which "have the potential to disrupt users' narratives, strange them from actions and emotions they should feel ownership over, and make their sense of self more precarious." (Goering et al. 2021, p. 1) There are also authors who wonder whether AI may become part of the person (self-learning algorithms in a symbiosis with neurotechnologies) and in that case, what will be the key ethical and legal implications of it (Bublitz 2022, pp. 1–22).

8.3 Ethical Priorities for Neurotechnologies and AI

The shadows of the scenario presented above must be completed with the lights that AI and neurotechnologies brings up, at least, for a small part of us. Accessing to neuro-data is a blooming future business for a minority group of citizens, not for the vast majority of us. The right to the privacy of someone's thought is at stake; not only at the level of defending mental privacy, but specially preventing people from being mentally manipulated. Once a BCI allows reading –as it is a reality nowadays- lab animals' brain activity, the door is open to enter into the subconscious, conditioning these lab animals' behavior. Consider those employers able to make their employees not to feel tired at work, no matter how hard tasks they are forced to carry on. Think about those dictators having at hand the final instrument of mental control of their subjugated populations: hardly ever could they sleep calmer! Imagine those generals proud of their fearless army, never questioning any order received because they have assumed that the *ius in bello,* that is, the limits in the conduct of hostilities at war, is not valid any longer. The list of nightmares like these briefly presented is endless.

In 2017, under the sponsor of Columbia University, a set of ethical rules were proposed concerning the increasing development of neurotechnologies. Among these ethical proposals, two at least are outstanding: on the one hand, complementing the current legal framework for protecting human rights with the so called "neurorights"; on the other hand, assuming a code of conduct (a "technocratic oath") to be voluntarily assumed by any juridical and physical person implementing neurotechnologies, in a similar way, *mutatis mutandis* to the Hippocratic Oath done by doctors. Neurorights can be defined (Ienca 2021, p. 1) as "the ethical, legal, social or natural principles of freedom or entitlement related to a person's cerebral and mental domain; that is, the fundamental normative rules for the protection and preservation of the human brain and mind." Many authors convene in signaling, in a non-exhaustive list, the following five neurorights (Yuste et al. 2021, p. 160):

- the *right to identity*, considered like the ability to control both one's physical and mental integrity;
- the *right to agency*, or the freedom of thought and free will to choose one's own actions;
- the *right to mental privacy*; that is, the ability to keep one's thoughts protected against disclosure;
- the *right to fair access to mental augmentation*, or the ability to ensure that the benefits of improvements to sensory and mental capacity through neurotechnology are fairly distributed in the society; and
- the *right to protection from algorithmic bias*; that is, the ability to ensure neurotechnologies do not insert prejudices, such as race or gender.

Some open questions on these neurorights divide authors. Particularly controversial is the question whether such neurorights are to be considered as brand new human rights or as evolutionary interpretations of existing rights. Some authors (Yuste et al. 2021, pp. 159 and 161) defend the first option. In their opinion, neurotechnology addresses two novel ethical challenges which are not presented by other forms of technology: mental privacy and human agency. Consequently, even though there are existing international instruments protecting privacy, they do it in very generic terms, often subject to interpretation whereas the ramifications of neurotechnology would require specificity. This is also the opinion of other authors (Lavazza and Giorgi 2023, p. 10) (Wajnerman 2021, p. 1), who defend the need for a particular protection of mental privacy as a neuroright, given that it is different to other forms of privacy due to its relation to relevant aspects of personal identity. Other authors consider neurorights as a needed measure to be complemented with others like new methods of identifying and preventing bias and the adoption of public guidelines for safe and equitable distribution of neurotechnological devices. (Goering et al. 2021, p. 1).

Considering that most national and international instruments of human rights already protect freedom, consent, equality, integrity, privacy and information, some authors find out more convenient –in line with the second option- to prepare justice operators to adequately interpret constitutional rights considering the challenges presented by neurotechnologies (Borbón and Borbón 2021, p. 3) (Hertz 2023, p. 5). There are also authors supporting the second option as more suitable to avoid a risk of rights inflation which "dilutes the core idea of human rights and distracts from the central goal of human rights instruments which is to protect a set of truly fundamental human interests and not everything that would be desirable or advantageous in an ideal world." (Ienca 2021, p. 8) (Bublitz 2022, p. 7).

This seems to me to be the prevailing position of scholars at the end of the day, as it results from a recently published interdisciplinary study (Ligthart et al. 2023, p. 13). As it was concluded in that study "there are substantial differences in how neurorights are understood by scholars. Since these notions can be conceptualized differently in terms of their philosophical and ethical foundation, it is debatable to what extent it is desirable and necessary to translate and condense them into specific legal rights at the international level as well as integrate them into the existing human rights system."

Be as it may, I think this question needs to be addressed from another angle. Are these neurorights enough action for global neurotechnology governance? Are they even the most suitable way of preserving human dignity from these neurotechnologies? I honestly disagree with those who would answer "yes" to both questions. Let's see the first one. As I defended in a contribution on the risks of AI in human embryonic research (García San José 2021, pp. 255–276), a comparative reading of the main texts issued on ethical principles for AI, evidences the lack of agreement regarding whether AI systems pose a threat only to human rights or also to human dignity. The consideration of human dignity only in relation to people born seems evident in the main texts adopted in recent years on the ethical dimension of artificial intelligence (García San José 2022a, pp. 513–516). By way of example, in Recommendation CM/Rec (2020) 1 of the Committee of Ministers to Member States of the Council of Europe on the impacts of algorithmic systems on human rights, on April 8, 2020 (Available at https://rm.coe.int/09000016809e1154 Accessed March 1, 2022), there is not a single mention of dignity in connection with the risks of artificial intelligence.

The references to human dignity and human rights throughout the UNESCO Recommendation on the ethics of AI, approved on November 21, 2021, in its preamble, in its section II [Aims and objectives, art. 8.c)] but above all, in section III.1 [Values, article 13 in connection with article 16], they give the false impression that both the rights and freedoms of the person are protected, as well as the dignity of being human. However, the definition of human dignity used in this instrument is very restrictive, since it refers only to the dignity of a human person already born. The UNESCO Recommendation has opted for a restrictive concept of human dignity, in such a way that it protects the dignity of the person but not of the human being against the risks of AI. In doing so, the UNESCO Recommendation on the Ethics of AI distances itself from the Convention on Human Rights and Biomedicine, which distinguishes between "person" (each individual) and "human being" (comprehensive term for human life in all its forms) in its preamble (paragraph 10) and in its first article, which does not use the term "human beings" as a synonym for "persons", but rather "human being" as a synonym for "human species".

All references are made in said text to fundamental rights and freedoms. Given this finding, we can ask why the risks of neurotechnologies on a human person already born by AI systems should be avoided and not do the same with respect to a human person in formation; that is, a person not yet born? It is a question that deserves an answer from the Law, essentially, because in the current state of scientific and technological advances, nothing prevents us from thinking that in the near future it will be decided to apply neurotechnologies (especially brain implants) in unborn fetuses with the same intention –or even a worse one- than the one pursued when doing the same in adult individuals. Here one has to recall the sentence of the Court of Justice of the European Union, of October 18, 2011, in case C-34/10 Oliver Brustle against Greenpeace ev, especially, considering its paragraphs 33 and 34, read in the light of paragraph 96 of the conclusions of the General Advocate, of March 10, 2011 in the case, when it expressly stated that "human dignity is a principle that must be applied not only to the existing human person, to the born child, but also to the human body from the first stage of its development, that is, of fertilization." (García San José 2022a, p. 519).

With these evidences, we want to highlight that the approach followed by many experts, such as Rafael Yuste and Sara Goering (Yuste and Goering 2017, pp. 161–162) among others (Ligthart, Sjors et al. 2023, pp. 1–21), defending the need to protect neurorights -of which people are holders-, means ignoring the growing and real threats that systems of AI, in interaction with neurotechnologies, pose for the human being as a human species and its intrinsic dignity. Even though, accepting the need to protect neurorights (together with the human dignity from neurotechnologies risks), I would still have to disagree on the convenience of new instruments for protecting such neurorights, coinciding with the majority of authors. It has not been necessary in the recent past when advances in science challenge the existing legal framework protecting human rights.

The experience of monitoring bodies, especially if they are of judicial nature, is illustrative in this regard. See, for instance the experience of the European Court of Human Rights interpreting the European Convention on Human Rights as a living instrument (according to present day threats). Such a teleological approach is globally accepted (not restricted to the European area). Thus, the Article 31 of the Vienna Convention on the Law of Treaties settles down a general rule of interpretation, when it says: "1. A treaty shall be interpreted in good faith in accordance with the ordinary meaning to be given to the terms of the treaty in their context and *in the light of its object and purpose.*" (Emphasis added). The teleological interpretation in international instruments protecting human rights has been useful in the past and it still has a role to play in protecting neurorights. See, for instance, the experience of the European system for the protection of human rights.

Unlike other international instruments for the protection of human rights in which there is an express mention of the environment, in the system of the European Convention no right to the environment appears. This gap is explained by the year of its writing, 1950, at a historical moment prior to the awareness and concern for the global protection of the environment in contemporary International Law, from the United Nations Conference on the Human Environment of 1972. However, thanks to an evolutionary interpretation of the Convention, developed by the European Court, expanding the content of the rights already guaranteed and updating their content as moral values and conceptions have evolved in democratic societies, this deficiency has been corrected. In this way, one can speak of a rich jurisprudence, which spans three decades, on the protection of the right to the environment in the European human rights protection system, without it having been necessary to elaborate an additional ad hoc protocol with said right (García San José 2022c, pp. 113–115).

I fully agree with the authors (Ligthart et al. 2023, p. 12), who consider that the notion of "mental integrity"—protected as part of private life under Article 8 ECHR—embraces the ability to control our own mental states. So, the right to mental integrity could comprise the right to mental self-determination and the right to cognitive liberty. They remark how, up to date, the European Court has accepted "private life" to cover a right to mental integrity (judgment of 12 October 2006, case of Mayeka and Kaniki Mitunga v. Belgium, para. 83), a generic right to self-determination (judgment of 27 August 2015, case of Parrillo v. Italy, para. 153), as well as a specified right to informational self-determination (judgment of 27 June 2017, case of Satakunnan Markkinapörssi Oy and Satamedia Oy v. Finland, para. 137).

Be as it may, I still maintain that the proposal of these neurorights is not enough for a global neurotechnology governance. I will develop this statement in the following paragraphs.

8.4 The Challenges of AI and Neurotechnologies Governance

History recalls that four legal answers are possible facing new scientific discoveries: (a) the incentives of such activities throughout governmental financial support and their legal protection with patent law; (b) the refusal of authorities to regulate it, according to the well-known liberal principle of "laissez faire, laissez passer"; (c) the option of legal regulation, controlling and banning an activity or a part of it as it happened after the crack in 1929 which followed the economic growth in the XIX Century; (d) the most usual answer in past: the interdiction of a particular idea or discovery. (Martyn 2001, p. 375).

At this point, the complexity surrounding the governance of AI and neurotechnologies seems to be largely motivated by two factors: firstly, the dialectical tension between ethical and economic constraints in play; on the other hand, the distorting presence of different subjects and international actors: States, international organizations, for-profit companies, private individuals with very unequal social and economic status involved in neurotechnologies, non-governmental organizations, etc. In this complex context, it is to be welcome efforts made by the institutionalized community of states since 2021 [see, the Report of the Special Rapporteur on freedom of religion or belief, Ahmed Shaheed, on *Respecting, Protecting and Fulfilling the Right to Freedom of Thought*, to the 76th session of the General Assembly of United Nations (Doc. A/76/380); OECD Recommendation on Responsible Innovation in Neurotechnology, adopted by the OECD Council on 11 December 2019; the 2021 Report of the International Bioethics Committee of UNESCO on *Ethical Issues on Neurotechnology* (SHS/BIO/IBC28/2021/3Rev.); the *Strategic Action Plan on Human Rights and Technologies in Biomedicine (2020–2025)*, already mentioned, adopted by the Committee on Bioethics of the Council of Europe at its 16th meeting (19–21 November 2019); or the Declaration of the Interamerican Juridical Committee on Neuroscience, Neurotechnologies and Human Rights: *New Legal Challenges for the Americas* (CJI/DEC. 01 –XCIX-0/21, August 11, 2021) (Ligthart et al. 2023: p.2).

Even with these efforts, it is necessary to provide a center of gravity to print a systemic order of all possible considerations in this matter, prioritizing and relativizing them. Firstly, regulation should be international because if our desire is to establish an effective global governance of neurotechnologies, we cannot accept the existence of territorial sanctuaries where it can carry out abhorrent practices that can deploy legal effects in other States. An ethical basis in any attempt of global governance for AI and neurotechnologies is also necessary, if we want that such regulation is effectively accomplished even by reluctant States, by companies which have shown their rejection, and even, by the same individuals whose rights protection is pursued. As it has been posed by Inglese and Lavazza, what should be our attitude towards "post humanist people ''? That is, those who wish to make strong use of neurotechnologies, or even, hybridize with them? (Inglese and Lavazza 2021, p. 1).

Let's imagine a first scenario of self-regulation by companies and operators of AI and neurotechnologies (in a wide sense of the concept of "operator"). The voluntary codes of conduct and social responsibility of companies is not new. In 1999 the General Secretary of the United Nations launched at Davos (Switzerland) the *Global Compact* initiative. It was directly addressed to big firms operating around the world in order to persuade them to adhere to a set of non-binding principles related to labor conditions, protection of fundamental rights and environment. There was no punishment for infraction of the code of conduct any firm freely accepted, being the only "punishment" the public shame of being openly identified as a "liar" for having promised something which later was discovered to be untrue. The review of the sum of academic articles defending and attacking such an initiative would prevent us from finishing these pages. It is enough to mention here that what was thought to be an instrument for the "mobilization of shame", not very, has seemed to be the "immobility of shamelessness".

How can be guaranteed that such code of ethical conduct on neurotechnologies and AI be respected by all operators in this field? As regards human cloning, Dr. Antinori became notorious for his will of cloning human beings on a ship in the high sea, in international waters out of any State jurisdiction. Will be able to convince millionaires like Elon Musk not to carry on with his plans of facilitating the appearance of super human beings with enhanced cognitive functions thanks to BCIs?

Paradoxically, at present, consent is given very easily to internet companies for the commercialization of users' data at convenience. It is contrary to what happens in the context of human trials where volunteer's' consent to the use of information resulting from that trial never is presumed. It must be an explicit consent where it is in extent said for which purpose and by whom, the information resulting from such a trial is allowed. Consequently, we could also think of technological possibilities to protect us against potential abuse of neurotechnologies. This is the case of block chain technology which could protect neurodata. Thus, it has been defended by authors like Inglese and Lavazza that all manufacturers should produce and place on sale only neurotools that incorporate devices capable of signaling and blocking unauthorized interference on the users' mental integrity. (Inglese and Lavazza 2021, p. 5). In this line, these authors have also proposed to apply an analogy between the human body and the brain's outcomes in order to prevent neural-data from getting into the wrong hands: "brain data should not be given away for any reason, just as organs cannot be sold" (Inglese and Lavazza 2021, p. 5). It is not free of controversy if neurodata can be assimilated to the human brain. To solve this dispute, some authors, like Wajnerman, have argued that the neurodata of individuals are analogous to neurocognitive properties of their brain. Neurodata are a 'medium independent' property that can be characterized as natural semantic personal information about their brains and that brains not only instantiate this property but also has an exclusive ontological relationship with these individuals: this information constitutes a domain that is unique to their neurocognitive architecture. (Wajnerman 2021, p. 1).

Other authors prefer to focus on the own potential of AI to self-control under some tecno-principles as a sufficient way of facing challenges posed by neurotechnologies. Thus, it is argued that when constructing AI algorithms, the overarching goals of society should be taken into account in a way that self-governing AI systems, for instance, should align to goals and practices of human values. (Paraman and Anamala, 2023, p. 602). This general principle can be disclosed in five normative commandments (Gervais 2023, p. 401) which clearly might have a significant role to play when interacting with neurotechnologies: firstly, all AI machines should be programmed with a kill switch to deactivate the machine temporarily or permanently. Secondly, human-defined ethical behavior rules should be embedded in AI Code. This means that human programmers could and should be held liable, in appropriate cases, if and when it can be shown that they were negligent in not considering relevant ethical issues, which would be measured against ethical norms applicable in the programmer's field of activity. Thirdly, ethical rules should apply to humans responsible for AI machine's learning, including data sets that will be used to inform the machines' decision-making process. Fourthly, the use and/or degree of autonomy of AI in certain areas should be prohibited or severely limited where the risks clearly outweigh benefits by imposing serious penalties on humans who design, market or use those systems. Lastly, in cases where no person (human or legal) can fairly be held liable due to the absence of (proximate) cause, an insurance scheme mandated by law should be created to compensate for harms.

It is evident that, as with other sensitive issues such as human cloning or climate change (García San José 2022b, pp. 1–23), the possibility of human thoughts being decoded and manipulated using technology has ceased to be a matter of internal interest of States according to Article 2.7 of the United Nations Charter. The regulation of the risks of AI and neurotechnologies must be universal in scope, assuming appropriate principles and values for all states of the International Community as a whole. (García San José 2022a, pp. 626–528). Without such an international approach any normative effort will be useless since it will always be possible to find a place where those who act illegally can find impunity. It is also evident that the international community needs a new paradigm of security, shifting from the security of States to the security of people. This new paradigm of security for the 21st Century centered on people means "protecting fundamental freedoms, freedoms that are the essence of life. It means protecting people from critical (severe) and pervasive (widespread) threats and situations. It means using processes that build on people's strengths and aspirations. It means creating political, social, environmental, economic, military and cultural systems that together give people the building blocks of survival, livelihood and dignity." *Human Security Now*, Report of the Commission on Human Security, New York, 2003, p. 4.

I agree with authors who propose democratic and inclusive summits to establish globally-coordinated ethical and social guidelines for neurotechnological development and application. (Goering et al. 2021, p. 1) These summits should be interdisciplinary, counting on the experience of those who have been working for years on neuroethics (Farisco et al. 2022, p. 4) In order to achieve Ethical principles common to all peoples and cultures represented in the Organization of the United Nations, there are only three possible approaches: the cultural imperialism and value absolutism, the value relativism, and the transculturalism and value reciprocity, respectively (Gbadegesin 2009, p. 30). The first approach consists of defending and retaining Western values and imposing them on other cultures for universal application as principles and rules. The second one is to reject the universal validity of Western values and recognize a plurality of values as the basis for principles and rules in different cultures. In other words, no common morality is needed. The third approach which seems more suitable than the previous ones is to look out for common foundational values which transcends cultures and which could be used to formulate general ethical principles for AI and neurotechnologies. This seems to me the best basis of regulatory intervention demanded by most authors (Ienca et al. 2022, 20).

International regulation in this matter must be based on general principles –the result of as universal a consensus as possible- that would be the starting point of an international corpus iuris of variable geometry based on the political and cultural singularities of each State that participates in the international community represented by the United Nations Organization. Based on our experience in relation to global governance of human embryonic research, we think of the following guiding principles that, without being exhaustive, it is possible to identify at an international level (García San José 2022a, p. 530):

- principle of human dignity in its broadest sense, as we defend in relation to bioethical issues, and of the protection of the different legal rights implied by the primacy of the human being, as a person and as a species, in AI and neurotechnologies.
- Principle that brain-computer interfaces (BCIs) applied to human beings born or in embryonic formation (whatever their origin) should only be authorized taking into account respect for the precautionary principle to prevent risks to life and health.
- Principle of voluntary, free and informed participation of the subjects, guaranteeing their right to privacy and granting special protection to neurorights of the most vulnerable persons, like teenagers, particularly against algorithmic bias. (Muñoz and Marinaro 2022, pp. 1–2).
- Principle of the prohibition of profit and free use for economic purposes of neurodata, which are closely linked to the brain (the main organ of the human body). This is so, regardless of the protection by means of patents, of the discoveries made under the freedom of investigation on AI and neurotechnologies.
- Principle of justice and beneficence, in particular, with regard to the improvement of cognitive abilities and protection of health. Science is to be considered as a public good of general interest for the benefit of all humanity, which must be contrasted with other informative principles in the presence, such as the legitimate legal protection of research results in AI and neurotechnologies with the purpose of their commercialization.

Once we have identified the general principles in this area, the task ahead of us is to find out the best way of implementing them. I firmly believe in establishing an ad hoc High Commissioner of the United Nations for AI and neurotechnologies, like the preferable option in this regard.

The High Level Panel on Digital Cooperation, established by the United Nations Secretary-General in July 2018 to propose cooperation to address challenges in the digital age, assumed that any AI regime should meet the following four objectives: coordination: To coordinate and catalyze AI-related efforts within the framework of existing international treaties and organizations (both specialized agencies and subsidiary bodies); comprehensive coverage: to fill existing gaps in international governance, such as the use of AI-enabled surveillance technologies, cyber warfare, and the use of AI in decision-making; cooperation over competition: that is, fostering international cooperation and collaboration between AI groups in projects for the public good; and collective benefit: to ensure the benevolent and responsible development of AI technologies and the equitable sharing of benefits.

In light of these objectives, extrapolating to the field of Artificial Intelligence and neurotechnologies the Report of the Secretary General of the United Nations entitled Intergenerational solidarity and the needs of future generations (Doc. A/68/322, of August 15, 2013), I believe that the establishment within the United Nations of a high commissioner for responsible use of AI in connection with neurotechnologies can be defended. This high commissioner would promote the global objectives of development and application of AI and neurotechnologies in accordance with the purposes and principles of the United Nations Charter; in particular, respect for human dignity and the protection of fundamental human rights.

The figure of said United Nations High Commissioner would promote the integration of ethical issues in the decisions that could be made by all the actors involved (Governments, companies and individuals) in the life cycle of artificial intelligence systems and neurotechnologies. At the same time, it would carry out a task of promoting the values that promote scientific and technological advances in an institutionalized context of international cooperation and not confrontation, for the benefit of all humanity.

To date, the most notable attempt to analyze the risks of AI for privacy has been made by the Office of the United Nations High Commissioner for Human Rights, in its report *The right to privacy in the digital age* (Doc. A/HRC/48/31) of September 13, 2021. The option of the high commissioner for responsible use of artificial intelligence systems and neurotechnologies seems the most appropriate, for the same reasons as those expressed by the Secretary General in his aforementioned 2013 report (Doc. A/68/322) regarding a similar figure for future generations: not only would this high commissioner act as a defender of responsible AI and neurotechnologies, through contacts with Member States and other interested parties, as well as among United Nations entities and specialized agencies, but would also count with the specific support of a related office, in a similar way to the other existing high commissioners: the high commissioner for refugees and the high commissioner for human rights.

In this way, the office attached to the High Commissioner for the Responsible Use of AI Systems and Neurotechnologies, would conduct research and promote expertise on good practices in the design, planning, development, implementation and monitoring of these AI systems and neurotechnologies in accordance with the principles and values of the Charter at the international, regional, national and subnational levels, and disseminate such knowledge and experience as deemed appropriate. To all of the above, it should be added that this high commissioner and his related office would provide advice, upon request by the United Nations or any of its entities, specialized agencies or affiliated organizations, on compliance with intergovernmental commitments adopted within the framework of responsible use of said systems and neurotechnologies.

8.5 Concluding Remarks

In these pages we have presented some features of the complex role of Artificial Intelligence (AI) in neurotechnology. In particular, we have commented on the way AI interferes in human brain activities thanks to devices like brain-computer interfaces (BCI) and deep brain stimulators (DBS). Like in previous epochs of History, the arrival of scientific advances and technological innovation appear to provoke in our societies a dual feeling of comfort, considering their promises of better times, and of frightening because they jeopardize our lives and social relationships. Specifically, we have addressed the way in which the so-called "AI-brain symbiosis" put at risk human dignity and human rights and how this challenge could be faced. Doctrine seems divided as regards the convenience of proclaiming new "neurorights" for several reasons. We have defended that the main problem of this proposition is not the risk of inflation of instruments of human rights but the fact that they do not protect human dignity of human beings like species. Although AI-brain symbiosis can be applied both to adults and to unborn people, the neurorights proposed from academia only seek to protect the first group of people. In any case, the proposal of neurorights seems not to be sufficient for efficient global neurotechnology governance. Departing from past experience facing similar challenges (like the human cloning research) we have explored some proposals from experts to face this task. A scenario of self-regulation by companies and operators of AI and neurotechnologies (the adoption of a kind of tecno-oath similar to Hippocrates oath in Medicine), does not seem convenient to us considering its weakness. The possibility of human thoughts being decoded and manipulated using technology has ceased to be a matter of internal interest of States according to Article 2.7 of the United Nations Charter. Consequently, any regulation of the risks of AI and neurotechnologies must be universal in scope and juridically binding, assuming appropriate principles and values derived from consensus of States integrating the International Community. Once we have identified the general principles in this area, the task ahead of us is to find out the best way of implementing them. At this regards, I have defended like the preferable option the establishment of an ad hoc High Commissioner of United Nations for AI and neurotechnologies.

Accession to brain thoughts, memories included, concern our identity. Opening the door to entering into the subconscious, into the lab where our ideas are created, affects human dignity. It would be possible to manipulate our hidden desires and deep fears: generating or deleting them at the convenience of those controlling neurotechnologies. No faith; no religions; no morality; no red lines in our behavior. It will be a "collective world electronic mind" of human brains on line, all together, marching at the same path. Never in past dictators' dreams came out to such an extent. The neural-gedom is knocking on the front door. Don't let it come in.

References

Borbón, Diego and Borbón, Luisa 2021. A critical perspective on neurorights: comments regarding ethics and law. *Frontiers on Human Neuroscience* 15: 703121. 1–4. https://https://doi.org/10.3389/fnhum.2021.703121.

Bublitz, Jan Christoph. 2022. Might artificial intelligence become part of the person, and what are the key ethical and legal implications? *AI & SOCIETY*. https://doi.org/10.1007/s00146-022-01584-y.

Farisco, Michele, et al. 2020. Towards establishing criteria for the ethical analysis of artificial intelligence. *Science and Engineering Ethics* 2020 (26): 2413–2425. https://doi.org/10.1007/s11948-020-00238-w.

Farisco, Michele, et al. 2022. On the contribution of neuroethics to the ethics and regulation of artificial intelligence. *Neuroethics* 15: 4. https://doi.org/10.1007/s12152-022-09484-0.

García San José, Daniel. 2021. Implicaciones jurídicas y bioéticas de la inteligencia artificial (IA). Especial consideración al marco normativo internacional. *Cuadernos de derecho Transnacional* 13: 255-276.

García San José, Daniel. 2022a. El Derecho internacional frente a los riesgos de la inteligencia artificial (IA) en la investigación embrionaria humana. *Cuadernos de derecho transnacional* 14: 512-532.

García San José, Daniel. 2022b. La humanidad como catalizadora de obligaciones omnium et erga omnes en la lucha contra el cambio climático. *Revista electrónica de estudios internacionales* 43: 1-23.

García San José, Daniel. 2022c. Treinta años de protección del derecho al medio ambiente por el Tribunal Europeo de Derechos Humanos: balance crítico de una jurisprudencia con luces y sombras. *Anuario Mexicano de Derecho Internacional* XXII: 109–150.

García-López Eric, Muñoz José and Andorno Roberto 2021 Editorial: Neurorights and Mental Freedom: Emerging Challenges to Debates on Human Dignity and Neurotechnologies. *Frontiers on Human Neuroscience* 15: 823570. 1–3. https://https://doi.org/10.3389/fnhum.2021.823570.

Gbadegesin, Segun. 2009. Culture and bioethics", in A companion to Bioethics, Kuhse, Helga and Singer, Peter (eds.) 2nd edition, pp. 24-35. Oxford. Wiley-Blackwell.

Gervais, Daniel. 2023. Towards an effective transnational regulation of AI. *AI & SOCIETY.* 38: 391–410. https://doi.org/10.1007/s00146-021-01310-0.

Goering, Sara, et al. 2021. Recommendations for responsible development and application of neurotechnologies. *Neuroethics* 14: 365–386. https://doi.org/10.1007/s12152-021-09468-6.

Hertz, Nora. 2023. Neurorights: do we need new human rights? A reconsideration of the right to freedom of thought. *Neuroethics* 16: 5. https://doi.org/10.1007/s12152-022-09511-0.

Ienca, Marcello. 2021. On neurorights. *Frontiers on Human Neuroscience* 15: 701258. 1–11. https://https://doi.org/10.3389/fnhum.2021.701258.

Ienca, Marcello et al. 2022. Towards a governance framework for brain data. *Neuroethics* 15: 20. https://doi.org/10.1007/s12152-022-09498-8.

Inglese, Silvia and Lavazza, Andrea. 2021. What should we do with people who cannot or do not want to be protected from neurotechnological threats? *Frontiers on Human Neuroscience* 15: 703092.1–6. https://https://doi.org/10.3389/fnhum.2021.703092.

Jotterand, Fabrice, and Clara Bosco. 2022. Artificial intelligence in medicine: a sword of damocles? *Journal of Medical Systems* 46: 1–5. https://doi.org/10.1007/s10916-021-01796-7.

Kellmeyer, Philipp. 2021. Big brain data: on the responsible use of brain data from clinical and consumer-directed neurotechnological devices. *Neuroethics* 14: 83–98. https://doi.org/10.1007/s12152-018-9371-x.

Lavazza, Andrea, and Rodolfo Giorgi. 2023. Philosophical foundation of the right to mental integrity in the age of neurotechnologies. *Neuroethics* 16: 10. https://doi.org/10.1007/s12152-023-09517-2.

Ligthart, Sjors et al. 2023. Minding rights: mapping ethical and legal foundations of 'Neurorights' Cambridge Quarterly of Healthcare Ethics, pp. 1–21. https://https://doi.org/10.1017/S0963180123000245.

Martyn, Susan. 2001. Human cloning: the role of law. *University of Toledo Law Review.* 32: 375–386.

Miller, Anthony. 2019. The intrinsically linked future for human and artificial intelligence interaction. *Journal of Big Data.* 6: 38. https://doi.org/10.1186/s40537-019-0202-7.

Monteith, Scott. 2022. Expectations for artificial intelligence (AI) in psychiatry. *Current Psychiatry Reports.* 24: 709–721. https://doi.org/10.1007/s11920-022-01378-5.

Muñoz, José, and José Ángel Marinaro. 2022. Algorithmic biases: caring about teens' neurorights. *AI & SOCIETY*. https://doi.org/10.1007/s00146-022-01516-w.

Paraman, Pradeep, and Sanmugam Anamala. 2023. Ethical artificial intelligence framework for a good AI society: principles, opportunities and perils. *AI & SOCIETY* 38: 595–611. https://doi.org/10.1007/s00146-022-01458-3.

Rainey, Stephen, and Yasemin Erden. 2020. Correcting the brain? The convergence of neuroscience, neurotechnology, psychiatry, and artificial intelligence. *Science and Engineering Ethics* 26: 2439–2454. https://doi.org/10.1007/s11948-020-00240-2.

Regalado, Antonio. 2020. Elon Musk's Neuralink is neuroscience theater. MIT Technology Review. At https://technologyreview.com/2020/08/30/1007786/elon-musks-neuralink-demo-update-neuroscience-theater/ (visited 18.07.2023).

Wajnerman Paz, Abel. 2022. Is your neural data part of your mind? Exploring the conceptual basis of mental privacy. *Minds and Machines* 32: 395–415. https://doi.org/10.1007/s11023-021-09574-7.

Yuste, Rafael, Jared Genser, and Stephanie Herrmann. 2021. It's time for neurorights. *Horizons* 18: 154–164.

Yuste, Rafael, and Sara Goering. 2017. Four ethical priorities for neurotechnologies and AI. *Nature* 551: 159–163.

Chapter 9
Protecting My Mind: Cognitive Liberty, Commons, and Neurorights

Paolo Sommaggio

Abstract Neurotechnology represents both an extraordinary opportunity for our intellectual capacities and a risk for the security, privacy, autonomy, and integrity of our minds and cognitive acts. Therefore, it is very important to find legal protection for the mind and its contents, that is, to recognize as an individual and social value the integrity of cognitive processes linked, or not, to the subjectivity of the individual. Suppose this issue has traditionally been addressed through recourse to categories such as individual private property, a new perspective that can allow the mind (and its products) to be recognized as having a peculiar "status": is the one of the Commons. In this essay, I question the elements of these Commons: Mental Integrity and Cognitive Liberty.

Keywords Neurotechnology · Mental states · Commons · Mental integrity · Cognitive liberty

9.1 Introduction

As is well known, neuroscience consists of those "disciplines that carry out scientific research on the nervous system to understand the biological basis of behavior" (Committee 2009). In recent years, however, technological progress has helped neuroscience to evolve as an extraordinary opportunity for our intellectual capacities, as a risk to the security, privacy, autonomy, and integrity of our minds (Sommaggio 2015). Indeed, despite their undoubted usefulness in the fields of medicine, education, entertainment, and work, neurotechnologies are poorly regulated to date.

Often, when one thinks of what might happen to our mental sphere due to these new (neuro)technologies, one thinks of all those behaviors that can cause direct physical or psychological harm. In such cases, what is often frightening is the possibility that something or someone could interact directly with the contents of our encephalon,

P. Sommaggio (✉)
University of Padova, Padova, Italy
e-mail: paolo.sommaggio@unipd.it

© The Editor(s) (if applicable) and The Author(s), under exclusive license to Springer Nature Switzerland AG 2024

J.-A. Seoane and O. Vergara (eds.), *The Discourse of Biorights*, The International Library of Bioethics 109, https://doi.org/10.1007/978-3-031-66804-3_9

invading and undermining the most intimate sphere of the human being: the brain and what is inside it (Craig 2016; Fuselli 2020; Douglas and Forsberg 2021).

The main concern, therefore, seems to be related to the possibility of being subjected to new modes of individual or social interference (if not control) (Roskies 2002). It is not only a matter of preventing unwanted behavior but also, for example, of preventing its occurrence by directly controlling the brain of the individuals (Sommaggio 2014, 2016).

To protect the safety and integrity of our mind, it, therefore, essential to start discussing some special recognition and legal protection for the mind both in terms of physical and biological aspects and in terms of its contents—i.e., to recognize as an individual and social value the integrity of mental processes, especially those related to the structuring of the individual's personality. Since the law already deals with human subjectivity—using categories such as individual rights—and ensuring health protection—understood as psycho-physical well-being—the study of such issues should begin by asking which of the existing legal institutions is already suitable to represent the relationship between the individual and their mind.

This work, therefore, aims to study the possibility of setting up the protection of the mind and its contents, not so much as the property of the individual but as a guarantee of physical and mental freedom—also through the concept of non-interference. In other words, this article will deal with Cognitive Liberty (Sommaggio et al. 2017; Sommaggio and Mazzocca 2020). Indeed, as will be shown in the following sections, cognitive liberty could help protect the freedom of subjects from any possible form of interference in their minds, and, at the same time, it could guarantee everyone's freedom to self-determine their inner sphere.

9.2 Neurotechnologies and Their Risks

There are many neurotechnologies currently available. For the sake of exposition, I divide them into four groups: brain imaging, brain stimulation, brain alteration, and brain-computer connection. This order of exposure, moreover, is not random: it follows the progressive intrusiveness of these technologies. They range from the least invasive—brain imaging—to the most invasive—i.e., devices capable of establishing a direct connection between brain and computer via electrodes or wireless (Simeral et al. 2021).

The first group of neuro-technologies is therefore formed by the so-called brain imaging techniques. This heterogeneous group includes technologies such as electroencephalography (EEG), functional magnetic resonance imaging (fMRI), or positron emission tomography (PET). These technologies share the same characteristics: they all provide structural or functional information about the brain by constructing visual artifacts (images). All of them, moreover, also share a certain degree of legal uncertainty regarding privacy and the protection of so-called "brain data" (Farah 2010). However, the reason why one should not underestimate these technologies is their impact, as they make certain information appear more authoritative and credible (Weisberg et al. 2008). The risk, indeed, is the stigmatization and probable discrimination of all those individuals who present brain images that can be considered indicative of deviant behaviors (Morse 2011a, b, Glannon 2011).

The second group of devices designed to affect the human brain would, instead, seem designed to offer (electrical or magnetic) impulses that can stimulate the brain from the outside. These are devices such as transcranial magnetic stimulation (TMS) or deep brain stimulation (DBS). The problem with this kind of stimulation lies in their potential capacity to alter the personality—and even the identity—of a person. It should be noted, indeed, how many clinical trials show different degrees and types of alterations depending on the modalities, intensity, and brain areas involved in the stimulation. Consider for instance DBS: recent studies show mood and personality changes such as, for instance, states of arousal, euphoria, or impulsiveness in individuals receiving such treatment (Jotterand—Giordano 2008).

The third group of neuro-technologies is designed to alter the subject's reactions and consists mainly of the so-called psychoactive drugs. The latter are substances known for their ability to induce changes in the personality of individuals. Drugs such as Methylphenidate Hydrochloride (Ritalin), Modafinil (Provigil), Donepezil (Aricept), Fluoxetine (Prozac), or Amphetamine (Adderall) are now commonly used to treat pathological conditions such as attention deficit disorder (ADD), narcolepsy, Alzheimer's disease, dementia, or depression. The question is: what could they cause to individuals not suffering from such diseases? Just consider, for example, the oxytocin hormone (Baumgartner 2008): recent studies have shown how it can lower the perception of risk (by decreasing the so-called suspiciousness), thus exposing those to whom it is administered to possible fraud and deception (Kosfeld 2005).

Finally, the last category of neurotechnologies, brain-computer interface, includes all those technologies that can rightly be considered the most invasive of our cerebral intimacy. These technologies are systems based on a connection between a computer and a brain in which the computer "acquires brain signals, analyzes them, and translates them into commands that are relayed to an output device to carry out a desired action" (Shih et al. 2012: 268). Consequently, the overall purpose of such a computer-brain system is to detect and quantify brain activity characteristics that indicate the user's intentions (Clausen 2010).

Of course, the main benefit that is aimed from usage of these technologies is the restoration of certain abilities that may have been lost through illness or accident. Nevertheless, one must always consider the degree of invasiveness involved in such technologies. In addition, there is always the risk of potential physical and psychological damage for the users of brain-computer interface technologies. Some authors, for instance, have pointed out how such technologies could lead to potentially serious damage from their intense use. Other authors emphasized how computer-brain interfaces could easily be used to "access" patients' brains without their consent. Consequently, several risk–benefit ratios should be calculated when dealing with this type of neurotechnology (Glannon 2014).

The idea behind neurotechnologies is that the benefits a patient could obtain from such devices and treatments must outweigh the potential risks, and when this is achieved, user safety is considered to be safeguarded (Clausen 2009).[1]

One of the most significant fears related to these technologies recently appeared in a study presented by researchers at Columbia University. This research shows how specific groups of neurons, known as neuronal ensembles, would play a causal role in human behavior. Specifically, the researchers identified specific neuronal ensembles in the mice while they were performing a visual task. Subsequently, they targeted the selected neurons (with single-cell precision), taking control of the mice's behavior. Later, one of the researchers, Yuste, claimed that the fact that one can provoke a sensory stimulus by activating specific neurons suggests that we might be getting closer to understanding what a perception or a thought is (Carrillo-Reid et al. 2019; Jennings et al. 2019).

Thus, it is clear that the studies, which are still at an early stage, have all the credentials to set out on the road to understanding the physiological basis of thought and behavior and to be able to control its magnitude and direction. A future scenario that requires an appropriate legal framework to avoid abuse, violence, and subornation.[2]

9.3 From Neurotechnology to Mental Integrity

From the brief analysis concerning neurotechnologies and the risks they may present, further considerations may arise. First, these are technologies that operate on the human brain and only (or almost only) on it. However, it is not only the human brain, in its physiological characteristics, at risk from these devices: even conscious thoughts, unconscious actions, and all that, more generally, constitute our subjectivity or identity may be at risk.

However, before proceeding further, a preliminary clarification is necessary: this work does not aim to investigate what mental states are or, more generally, exist in a person's mind. For my analysis, by mental states I mean the "representational content (i.e. an intentional object) and its conscious apprehension" (Klein 2015: 356). Of course, there are different types of intentional objects: ones that can be considered material objects—of which we would somehow be the authors—and the others that constitute our psychological continuity over time. Therefore, once this is clear, one might wonder what "legal goods" are being endangered by these neurotechnologies. First, one may observe how, given the technologies available today, it seems to be necessary to state a right to exclude any intrusion into one's own or others' mental

[1] Given their potential invasiveness, such devices are generally tested before they are approved and placed on the market. Testing and approval procedures are regulated in detail by national and international law and overseen by designated national agencies. Examples of these agencies are the Food and Drug Administration (FDA) for the United States, and the European Medicines Agency (EMA).

[2] Yuste stated in 2016 the need for ethical guidelines for developing new neuroscientific technologies (Goering and Yuste 2016).

states, and thus protect so-called "mental integrity" (Nisco 2012).[3] The problem is to understand what is meant by mental integrity. Are there, in fact, any kind of "mental assets"?

The attempts to elaborate a cultural context providing a legal framework for these issues are closely related to the progressive replacement of traditional legal sources by new neuroscientific paradigms. This approach, also called "reductive neurolaw", would effectively conceptually reduce legal institutions to mere coercive instruments—the contents of which would be formed by the new neuroscientific standards. Traditional law, indeed, would not be able to maintain the right order in society. Thus, the new neuro-law should be solely in the domain of scientists (or neuroscientists). From a (neuro)scientific point of view, then, law would come to be seen as:

> the source of social order—to produce social order is the function or purpose or end of law. [...] The subtle but fundamental difference can be put thus: law is order, versus law maintains order (Tamanaha 2007: 5).

According to neuroscientific standards—which would thus become the subject of this new neuro-law—the mental states of individuals should be considered as material objects owned by people. In other words, the brain (and its contents) is considered a material object at the disposal of individuals following the ownership model—so much so that it is referred to as "mind's ownership" (Campbell 2002). This terminology, however, is not very convincing, given the questionable use of the legal category of "private property". And, of course, it is since Descartes' time that, in a sense, the intentional objects of the mind are reduced to objects at the disposal of the individual. Indeed, as Descartes wrote:

> when I consider the mind, that is, myself in so far as I am only a thinking thing, I cannot distinguish any parts within me; rather, I understand myself to be mani- firstly one complete thing. Although the entire mind seems to be united to the entire body, nevertheless, were a foot or an arm or any other bodily part to be amputated, I know that nothing has been taken away from the mind on that account (Descartes 1998: 101).

The legal relationship with this particular object—i.e., the mind—has, therefore, traditionally been conceived along the lines of the legal relationships of the *ius commune*. These last are traditionally characterized by the will and their connection with material objects. And among them, the most exemplary legal relationship is precisely the property right. In other words, according to this conception, the brain and its contents would be nothing more than a *res* with which the individual enters into a relationship comparable to property rights. The problem is to determine who should be the owner of this *res*.

Problems such as the one just mentioned always admit at least two possible solutions: those who favor the ownership of the individual and those who argue that the people's minds should belong to the community. Those who favor individual

---

[3] This expression is contained, for example, in the Charter of Fundamental Rights of the European Union, which, in Article 3, recognizes that "Everyone has the right to respect for his or her physical and mental integrity".

property adhere to a Lockean perspective. According to the well-known English philosopher, indeed, every individual possesses a property right over their life—and thus, by extension, over their body (including their brain).[4] John Locke, therefore, may well be counted among the first exponents of an individualistic conception, whose most radical version today takes the side of the individual's full ownership of their body-object. In a nutshell, it is about a kind of liberal-individualist version of the body/brain paradigm, understood as something that the individual, through their will, disposes of for all intents and purposes as if they owned it (Del Bò 2002a; Del Bò 2002b). The supporters of this individualist position generally make no secret of being inspired by Lockean natural law's cultural heritage. Consider, for example, Robert Nozick's conception in which one can find the self-ownership concept directly derived from John Locke's works (Nozick 1974).

However, regarding the problem of who should be considered the owner of human brain data, there is at least another direction of reasoning: which can be defined as the community one. In this regard, one can consider Rousseau as the first theorist of this conception. Exactly like Locke, indeed, he argued that the human body (including the brain) can be considered a *res*. However, according to the well-known Genevan philosopher, the will that decides whether and how to dispose of a human's biological component should not be that of the individual but that of the general will, i.e., the collectivity. In his works, he attempted to frame human subjectivity in.

> a form of association that may defend and protect with the whole force of the community the person and property of every associate, and by means of which each, joining together with all, may nevertheless obey only himself, and remain as free as before (Rousseau 2002: 163).

Indeed, according to Rousseau, each of us should "put in common his person and all his power under the supreme direction of the general will" (*Ibidem*: 164). These words assume, then, that only the community is the concrete source of the right to dispose of the object-body of every community member, whether they want it or not.

The gap between the individualist and communitarian conceptions of the ownership of the human mind thus appears, now as then, to be surmountable only by resolving the question as to who is the most suitable subject to dispose of the human mind and the data derived from it: the individual or the community. Both can be considered the owners of the body and, therefore, by analogical extension, of the integrity of the mind (*rectius* of mental states).

9.4 Objectification and Availability of Mental States

The assumption for which we conceive of the brain and mental states as objects (*res*) has a long-standing tradition. Such an assumption implies that the human being is regarded as an expression of a dualistic principle: on the one hand, the *bios*, the

[4] On this point, John Locke himself is very clear when he states that "every man has a property in his own person: this nobody has any right to but himself." (Locke 2003: 111).

material substratum of man—in short, their physical body –, and on the other hand, what makes him human, namely his spirit, his consciousness, or his mind and what it yields—i.e., what I have proposed to call mental states. On closer inspection, one can observe how this cultural assumption is easily understood through the study of Hans Jonas' teaching. In his famous work on Gnosticism, the German philosopher argues for a kind of actualization in the contemporary world of the body/soul dichotomy in the new body/brain-activity dichotomy. On the one hand, the physiological sphere of the individual, and on the other, their mental sphere.

The original dualism is between, on the one hand, God and the world and, on the other hand, man and the world—which constitutes the main metaphysical implication of the Gnostic experience –and is laid at the foundation of the modern human conception by Jonas. Men especially would relate to their bodies in the following way:

> Men especially would relate to their bodies in the following way: As a part of this sum, as an instance of nature, man is only a reed, liable to be crushed at any moment by the forces of an immense and blind universe in which his existence is but a particular blind accident, no less blind than would be the accident of his destruction. As a thinking reed, however, he is no part of the sum, not belonging to it, but radically different, incommensurable: for the *res extensa* does not think, so Descartes had taught, and nature is nothing but res extensa—body, matter, external magnitude (Jonas 2001: 322).

It is this cultural background that, according to Jonas, branches into two alternatives that, while attempting to resolve duality in favor of one of the two elements of the relationship, presupposes it. Materialism and idealism would be, in fact, the contemporary speculative outcomes of this separation. The materialistic perspective (with which the contemporary neurotechnological mindset appears to be permeated) continues to logically presuppose a transcendent dualism, for only through the fact of having (without admitting it) in the background the "other world" of duality can it afford in its field to disregard the evidence of the spirit and to interpret reality, so far as it has to do with pure materiality (Jonas 1999: 172).

It might seem that the dualist premise concerns only the proponents of a rigid materialist perspective. But this is not the case, as even proponents of the existence of a non-material reality (be it soul, mind, or whatever) accept the co-presence of two realities.

Therefore, as sciences with a deterministic status, neurosciences consider the human reducible to at least two realities: physical and nonphysical. But, as anticipated, there is also another premise. It would probably lead us very far in our topic. I outline it, therefore, only in its essential features. +

Previously, in response to the query regarding what is the thing that bounds an individual to their brain and mind, I mentioned a relationship analogous to the right of ownership. In other words, to argue that a person is "master of his own thoughts", it is necessary to consider once again the relationship that binds individuals to their belongings: private property. In this sense, both individualist and collectivist conceptions postulate the dominance of the will in the property right: sometimes that of the individual, sometimes that of the community. In each case, people have always considered their ownership of the human body a privilege of the will. This is where the problem arises: jurists inspired by the work of neuroscientists claim that free will (i.e., one of the concepts that can most closely approximate the will as continental jurists know it) would not exist. Thus, possessing no capacity for self-determination, humans would behave as 'machines' determined by their biological configuration and, for these reasons, should not be held morally responsible for their actions.

This point is particularly persuasive, for example, for authors like Green and Cohen. These last, indeed, were among the first jurists to argue that according to neuroscience, "no one person is more or less responsible than any other for actions" and that we "are all part of a deterministic system that someday, in theory, we will completely understand" (Greene and Cohen 2004: 1780).

For these reasons, they believe a radical rethinking of traditional Western legal systems by neuroscientific findings is inevitable. According to them, the concept of free will will be abandoned in the near future, leading to reconsideration of criminal liability and contractual autonomy. As, indeed, they write:

> Free will as we ordinarily understand it is an illusion generated by our cognitive architecture. Retributivism notions of criminal responsibility ultimately depend on this illusion, and, if we are lucky, they will give way to consequentialist ones, thus radically transforming our approach to criminal justice. At this time, the law deals firmly but mercifully with individuals whose behavior is the product of forces that are ultimately beyond their control. Some day, the law may treat all convicted criminals this way. That is humanely» (Greene and Cohen 2004: 1784).

Other authors, however, take a very different view. Among them, for example, it is possible to mention Stephen Morse. The latter not only recognizes limited usefulness to introducing neuroscience results into the content of legal rules but does not even consider them to be able to revolutionize legal systems shortly. His perspective would thus be a "compatibilist" perspective between traditional legal concepts and neuroscientific discovery results—that is, between a free will and a determinist perspective (Morse 2013).

Indeed, cultural and psychological premises would already be implicitly present in Western legal systems. It would be these common-sense assumptions—so-called folk psychology—that would underlie the anthropological model on which law is based. (Morse 2007). According to Morse, then, the law is based on common-sense psychology, neuroscientific findings will not drastically revolutionize it. Every legal system, in fact,

> presupposes a "folk-psychological" view of the person and behavior. This psychological theory explains behavior in part by mental states such as desires, beliefs, intentions, willings, and plans. Biological and other psychological and sociological variables also play a causal role, but folk psychology considers mental states fundamental to a full causal explanation and understanding of human action. Lawyers, philosophers, and scientists argue about the definitions of mental states and theories of action, but that does not undermine the general claim that mental states are fundamental. Indeed, the arguments and evidence that disputants use to convince others presuppose the folk psychological view of the person. Brains do not convince each other, people do. Folk psychology presupposes only that human action will at least be rationalizable by mental state explanations or will be responsive to reasons—including incentives—under the right conditions (Morse 2011a, b: 598-599).

However, whether adhering to Greene and Cohen's theses or following Morse's less alarming perspective, it remains open to consideration that there is an underlying logical problem in the neuroscientific findings. Neuroscientists believe both that mental states are assimilable to a property of the individual—i.e., a disposition of their will—and that free will constitutes a cognitive illusion. In other words, we face a contradiction: either self-ownership is supported by free will, or if free will does not exist, one cannot speak of self-ownership. Thus, we can say that the only possibility is to consider one's brain from a sort of "common-ownership" perspective. Such a possibility, however, would risk shifting the problem to an anti-liberal social mechanism and, perhaps, unacceptable even to scientists.

Thus, the only possible solution seems to be reconsidering the relationship between the person and the deep self as one of fruition of an object that cannot be considered entirely one's own.

9.5 Concluding Remarks

This paper examined the risks to which current neurotechnologies expose our mental states on both the physical and cognitive levels. The mind (and its contents) was presented as an asset to be protected, and the debate over "who is entitled to this asset" was subsequently analyzed. I later pointed out how most scholars and jurists treat the problem of mind ownership precisely using the legal category of private property—with obvious problems of conceptualization. Starting with analyzing conceptual problems related to the supposed ownership of the mind, I delved into some of its best-known explanatory approaches, examining forms of entitlement other than private property referable to the mind and its product. Finally, I sketched the hypothesis that mental integrity could be treated as a common good (like other commons) designed to establish a network of safeguards against risks arising from the criminal, erroneous, or invasive use of neurotechnology. Therefore, all that remains is to outline the possible future lines of research development regarding this new way of considering the integrity of the mind and its products.

First, one should start to consider the relationship between individuals and their minds (and their products) in terms of prerogatives of freedom and not in terms of object entitlement. Thus, one should set the focus of studies not on the object (mind) but on the person who might suffer harm due to the lack of or distorted enjoyment of that "object". Therefore, let us consider mental integrity a common good and simultaneously configure it as a personal prerogative of an individual, not a property right. Thus, a concept is needed that can become an integral part of those "rights that impose obligations on governments and other citizens to refrain from interfering with the rights bearer" (Blank 2016: 52).

In this regard, to ensure this strong protection from undue interference, one can look at the concept of cognitive liberty, which may become the most suitable defense tool.[5] Of course, nowadays, in the international debate, the concept of Cognitive Liberty refers more to an inhibition-type demand: protect the mental sphere of any individual from potential abuse by third parties such as the police force, medical institution, or private company that could read, alter, or modify the minds of individuals, without prior conscious and informed consent (Boire 2004; Sommaggio 2017; Sommaggio and Mazzocca 2020). However, one should also consider cognitive liberty's positive aspects, represented by the freedom to independently modify one's mental integrity through neurotechnological devices (Maslen et al. 2014).

Desirably, then, legal recognition of the conceptual tool of cognitive liberty can not only lead to the complete legal legitimacy of the possibility of modifying one's mental sphere but can also lead to the configuration of a new fundamental human right: the right to the management of one's mental sphere free from interference, whether framed as a new property right, a new common good, or a new right of the person (Blitz 2016).

Chile has gone in this direction. In recent years, this country has amended its Constitution to introduce closer protection of people's rights from the unknown threats posed by neurotechnology. In addition, through ordinary legislation, the Chilean parliament has established several neuro-rights for its citizens (Ienca 2021; Yuste et al. 2021). Such neuro-rights include the rights to personal identity, free will, mental privacy, equal access to cognitive enhancement technologies, and protection against algorithmic biases (prejudices). Indeed, the Chilean neuro-protection project includes an innovative interpretation of mental privacy: it provides access control to neural data and information about cognitive processes and states that can be obtained by analyzing them. Among other things, the choice is entirely novel: the Chilean legislature proposes to treat neural data (which comes from an individual's brain) as a special kind of information that is intimately related to who we are and that defines our identity; therefore, it will have to be treated in the same way as organic tissue of human origin. By treating neuro-data as an organ, the law prohibits Chileans from being forced to surrender brain data, and, crucially, its collection will require explicit authorization. Another implication of this legal analogy is that brain data cannot be sold but can be donated for charitable purposes.

Admittedly, this is legislation largely in advance of the technical possibilities of neurotechnology. However, this is the time to begin developing models of legal protection before the risks become terrible realities.

Chile encourages the world to take a stand on neuro-rights and is one of the first and most important regulatory interventions globally. And I hope many other countries will follow suit.

---

[5] A negative formulation of the concept of cognitive freedom has already been applied, for example, in *Sell v. United States*. In order to articulate some legal limits on the use of neurotechnology, the court, in that case, set the following four requirements: (1) there must be a public interest; (2) drugs administered ought to return the individual to a normal condition and not cause unwanted effects; (3) the defendant cannot be subjected to alternative health treatments that can provide the same results; and (4) the drug should be administered following best medical practices and according to the person's health condition.

References

Baumgartner, Thomas, Markus Heinrichs, Aline Vonlanthen, Urs Fischbacher, and Ernst Fehr. 2008. Oxytocin shapes the neural circuitry of trust and trust adaptation in humans. *Neuron* 58 (4): 639–650.

Blank, Robert H. 2016. *Cognitive enhancement: social and public policy issues*. London: Palgrave Macmillan.

Blitz, Marc J. 2016. A constitutional right to use thought-enhancing technology. In *Cognitive enhancement: ethical and policy implications in international perspectives*, ed. Fabrice Jotterand and Veljko Dubljevic, 302–306. New York: Oxford University Press.

Boire, Robert G. 2004. Neurocops: the politics of prohibition and the future of enforcing social policy from inside the body. *Journal of Law and Health* 19 (2): 234–258.

Campbell, John. 2002. The ownership of thoughts. *Philosophy, Psychiatry, & Psychology* 9 (1): 35–39.

Carrillo-Reid, Luis, Shuting Han, Weijian Yang, Alejandro Akrouh, and Rafael Yuste. 2019. Controlling visually guided behavior by holographic recalling of cortical ensembles. *Cell* 178: 447–457.

Clausen, Jens. 2009. Man, machine and in between. *Nature* 457: 1080–1081.

Clausen, Jens. 2010. Ethical brain stimulation—neuroethics of deep brain stimulation in research and clinical practice. *European Journal Neuroscience* 32 (7): 1152–1162.

Committee on Opportunities in Neuroscience for Future Army Applications, Board on Army Science and Technology, Division on Engineering and Physical Sciences, National Research Council of the National Academies. 2009. *Opportunities in neuroscience for future army applications*. Washington, D.C.: The National Academies Press.

Craig, Jared N. 2016. Incarceration, direct brain intervention, and the right to mental integrity—a reply to Thomas Douglas. *Neuroethics* 9 (2): 107–118.

Del Bò, Corrado. 2002[a]. Proprietà di sé e giustizia distributiva: un conflitto necessario? Il Politico LXVII, 1: 137-149.

Del Bò, Corrado. 2002b. La tesi della proprietà di sé: linee generali del dibattito in corso. *Filosofia e Questioni Pubbliche* VII (3): 127-134.

Descartes, René. 1998. *Discourse on method and meditations on first philosophy*. Indianapolis and Cambridge: Hackett Publishing Company.

Douglas, Thomas and Lisa Forsberg. 2021. Three rationales for a legal right to mental integrity. In *Neurolaw: advances in neuroscience, justice & security*, ed. Sjors Ligthart, Dave van Toor, Tijs Kooijmans, Thomas Douglas, and Gerben Meynen, 179–201. London: Palgrave Macmillan.

Etheridge, Ari U., and John R. Chamberlain. 2006. Application of sell vs United States. *Journal of the American Academy of Psychiatry and the Law* 34 (2): 248–250.

Farah, Martha J., M. Elizabeth Smith, Cyrena Gawuga, Dennis Lindsell, and Dean Foster. 2010. Brain imaging and brain privacy: a realistic concern? *Journal of Cognitive Neuroscience* 21 (1): 119–127.

Fuselli, Stefano. 2020. Mental integrity protection in the neuro-era. Legal challenges and philosophical background. *BioLaw Journal* 1: 413–429.

Glannon, Walter. 2011. What neuroscience can (and Cannot) tell us about criminal responsibility. In *Law and Neuroscience. Current Legal Issues*, ed. Michael Freeman, pp. 13–28. New York: Oxford University Press.

Glannon, Walter. 2014. Ethical issues with brain-computer interfaces. Frontiers in Systems Neuroscience 8, https://doi.org/10.3389/fnsys.2014.00136. Accessed 2 August 2023.

Goering, Sara and Rafael Yuste. 2016. On the necessity of ethical guidelines for novel neurotechnologies. *Cell* 3: 882–885.

Greene, Joshua, and Jonathan Cohen. 2004. For the law, neuroscience changes nothing and everything. *Philosophical Transactions of the Royal Society b: Biological Sciences* 359: 1775–1785.

Ienca, Marcello. 2021. On neuroright. Frontiers on Human Neuroscience 15, https://doi.org/10.3389/fnhum.2021.701258. Accessed 2 August 2023.

Jennings, Joshua H., Christina K. Kim, James H. Marshel, Misha Raffiee, Li., Ye, Sean Quirin, Sally Pak, Charu Ramakrishnan, and Karl Deisseroth. 2019. Interacting neural ensembles in the orbitofrontal cortex for social and feeding behavior. *Nature* 565: 645–649.

Jonas, Hans. *1999, Organismo e libertà. Verso una biologia filosofica. Torino: Einaudi.*

Jonas, Hans. 2001. *The gnostic religion: the message of the alien god and the beginnings of Christianity*. Boston: Beacon Press.

Jotterand, Fabrice, and James Giordano. 2008. Transcranial magnetic stimulation, deep brain stimulation, and personal identity: Ethical questions, and neuroethical approaches for medical practice. *International Review of Psychiatry* 23 (5): 476–485.

Klein, Stanley B. 2015. The feeling of personal ownership of one's mental state: a conceptual argument and empirical evidence for an essential, but underappreciated, mechanism of mind. *Psychology of Consciousness: Theory, Research, and Practice* 2 (4): 355–376.

Kosfeld, Michael, Markus Heinrichs, Paul J. Zak, Urs Fischbacher, and Ernst Fehr. 2005. Oxytocin increases trust in humans. *Nature* 435: 673–676.

Locke, John. 2003. *Two treatises of government and a letter concerning toleration*. New Haven and London: Yale University Press.

Maslen, Hannah, Thomas Douglas, Roi Cohen Kadosh, Neil Levy, and Julian Savulescu. 2014. The regulation of cognitive enhancement devices: Extending the medical model. *Journal of Law and the Biosciences* 1 (1): 68–93.

Morse, Stephen J. 2007. The non-problem of free will in forensic psychiatry and psychology. *Behavioural Sciences & the Law* 25: 203–220.

Morse, Stephen J. 2011. Lost in Translation? An Essay on Law and Neuroscience. In *Law and Neuroscience. Current Legal Issues*, ed. Michael Freeman, pp. 529–562. New York: Oxford University Press.

Morse, Stephen J. 2011b. The status of neurolaw: a plea for current modesty and future cautious optimism. *Journal of Psychiatry & Law* 39: 595–626.

Morse, Stephen J. 2013. Compatibilist criminal law. In *The future of punishment*, ed. Thomas A. Nadelhoffe, 107–132. Oxford: Oxford University Press.

Nisco, Attilio. 2012. *La tutela penale della integrità psichica*. Torino: Giappichelli.

Nozick, Robert. 1974. *Anarchy*. State and Utopia, New York: Basic Books.

Roskies, Adina. 2002. Neuroethics for the New Millennium. *Neuron* 35: 21–23.

Rousseau, Jean-Jacques. 2002. *The social contract and the first and second discourses*. New Haven and London: Yale University Press.

Shih, Jerry J., Dean J. Krusienski, and Jonathan R. Wolpawc. 2012. Brain-computer interfaces in medicine. *Mayo Clinic Proceedings* 87 (3): 268–279.

Simeral, John D., Thomas Hosman, Jad Saab, Sharlene N. Flesher, Marco Vilela, Brian Franco, Jessica N. Kelemen, David M. Brandman, John G. Ciancibello, Paymon G. Rezaii, Emad N. Eskandar, David M. Rosler, Krishna V. Shenoy, Jaimie M. Henderson, Arto V. Nurmikko, and Leigh R. Hochberg. 2021. Home use of a percutaneous wireless intracortical brain-computer interface by individuals with tetraplegia. *IEEE Transactions on Biomedical Engineering* 68 (7): 2313–2325.

Sommaggio, Paolo and Marco Mazzocca. 2020. Cognitive Liberty and Human Rights. In *Neuroscience and Law. Complicated Crossings and New Perspectives*, ed. Antonio D'Aloia and Maria Chiara Errigo, pp. 95–111. Berlin: Springer.

Sommaggio, Paolo, Marco Mazzocca, Alessio Gerola, and Fulvio Ferro. 2017. Cognitive liberty. A first step towards a human neuro-rights declaration. *BioLaw Journal* 3: 27–45.

Sommaggio, Paolo. 2014. Neurocivilizzazione. *Etica & Politica* XVI: 130-168.

Sommaggio, Paolo. 2015. Scenari di neurocivilizzazione. *BioLaw Journal* 3: 137–149.

Sommaggio, Paolo. 2016. Neuro-civilization: A New Form of Social Enhancement. *ATINER'S Conference Paper Series*, SOS2016–2106: pp. 3–18.

Tamanaha, Brian Z. 2007. How an instrumental view of law corrodes the rule of law. *DePaul Law Review* 56: 1–52.

Skolnick, Weisberg Deena, Frank C. Keil, Joshua Goodstein, Elizabeth Rawson, and Jeremy R. Gray. 2008. The seductive allure of neuroscience explanations. *Journal of Cognitive Neuroscience* 20 (3): 470–477.

Yuste, Rafael, Jared Genser, and Stephanie Herrmann. 2021. It's time for neurorights. New human rights for the Age of Neurotechnology. *Horizons* 18: 154–164.

Chapter 10
From Therapy to Enhancement: Ethical and Legal Issues About Neurotechnologies in the EU Framework of Human Rights

Silvia Salardi

Abstract Neurotechnologies represent a new frontier in effectively treating diseases and disorders that affect the human brain. Moreover, they are already used outside the medical field for enhancing purposes, amongst others. The use of these technologies is as promising as complex. In the medical field, issues concern different aspects: unwanted relevant side-effects, access to all patients, research funding and publication of results, devices ethically designed by default, privacy issues etc. Outside the medical field, there is an increasing marketing of non-invasive neurotechnologies directly to consumers for enhancing purposes. This use lacks a minimum basic consensus at the ethical level and has not a precise legal foundation in the European system. Therefore, it raises specific ethical and legal concerns that force a reflection on how to protect users from manipulation, abuses, and misuses. The current essay will discuss both ethical and legal issues concerning medical and non-medical applications of neurotechnology framing the discussion within the European value-based vision on technological innovation where fundamental freedoms and rights represent the common shared standards of social coexistence.

Keywords Neurotechnologies · Enhancement · Human rights · Medicine

10.1 Introduction

In the book titled *The Age of Rights* (original title *L'età dei diritti,* Bobbio 1997, p. 263), published in its first edition in 1990, the Italian philosopher and politician Norberto Bobbio examines the distinctive characteristics of a contemporary form of power, which requires, in his view, a strengthened defense of the human being: the power of science and technology. The increase of knowledge in the second half

S. Salardi (✉)
University of Milano-Bicocca, Milan, Italy
e-mail: silvia.salardi@unimib.it

© The Editor(s) (if applicable) and The Author(s), under exclusive license to Springer Nature Switzerland AG 2024

J.-A. Seoane and O. Vergara (eds.), *The Discourse of Biorights*, The International Library of Bioethics 109, https://doi.org/10.1007/978-3-031-66804-3_10

of the twentieth century has indeed accelerated the possibility of human dominance over nature and over human beings (Jonas 1984). As there is an inverse relationship between power and freedom, because when one increases the other decreases, and vice versa, human rights have been called into question to counterbalance this effect. They are indeed a way of marking out a protected area, fulfilling the double function of promoting freedom, as they are grounded in the idea of autonomy and self-realization, and of protecting individual from threats and risks. Thus, in the time since, new human rights were elaborated extending the existing list. Consider, for instance, the right to data protection,[1] the right to non-discrimination based on the genetic make-up (Article 21 of the European Charter of Fundamental Rights), the right to a sound environment (Article 37 of the European Charter of Fundamental Rights), and so forth.

Today, the debate about rights is a continuing one as rights play a key role in legal and moral arguments about emerging technologies like neurotechnology. In this field, the tension between power and freedom is exacerbated by the relevance of the good at stake: the individual mind.

I will use the paradigm of the tension between power and freedom as an instrument of ethical and legal assessment in the following analysis. As a metatheoretical paradigm, this tension depicts a doctrine that justifies the interference with individual freedom if and only if this is to preserve an essential collective good like health or if there is individual informed consent. As a normative paradigm, this tension expresses the need for a system of procedural and substantial guarantees protecting the weakest link of the relationship, that is, the individual in her different social roles as patient, consumer, and final user.

In the current reflection, the meaning of power is not identified just with public power as was the case in the early stages of liberalism. Rather, this notion includes private powers, specifically economic and technological powers (big tech companies). As a matter of fact, all these powers share the ability, described by Bertrand Russell (Russell 1938) in his definition of power as integrated by Wrong, "to produce intended and foreseen effects on others." (Wrong 1995, p. 2).

The effects produced by private powers (in)directly affect the area of individual freedom in two possible directions. On the one hand, thanks to private funding and investment in the research of neurotechnology, private actors are the major contributors to the well-being of some categories of users like patients. On the other hand, through monopoly or oligopoly of data management, they can maintain control of and influence on consumers' attitudes and behaviors. In this scenario, they may put some essential aspects of individual life at risk as I will discuss later.

This risk zone includes agency, privacy, identity, and personality. Indeed, neurotechnology allows deep interference with and manipulation of all the mentioned aspects, and those who control the technology have a great power to interfere with identity and personality. In what follows, I will discuss the various problematic implications of the asymmetric relationship between power and freedom in the current

[1] In the European context, the Council of Europe addressed this issue in 1981 with the Convention 108.

social order. I will take into account the use of neurotechnology in the medical field as well as outside of it.

10.2 Definitions, Applications, and Risk Class

In order to put the further discussion in context, it is worthwhile to define the notion of neurotechnology and to briefly describe its characteristics, applications, and risk classification. The 2019 OECD's *Recommendation of the Council on Responsible Innovation in Neurotechnology*[2] defines neurotechnology as "devices and procedures used to access, monitor, investigate, assess, manipulate, and/or emulate the structure and function of the neural systems of natural persons." (OECD 2019, p. 6) This broad definition catches the main characteristics of a range of technologies as described in what follows.

Among the first developed neurotechnology for brain reading activity there is neuroimaging. Neuroimaging is still in use in diagnostics "to detect abnormalities in the brain of neurological patients such as lesions, tumours, or indicators of epileptic episodes." (Ienca 2021, p. 15) A relevant step forward was made when neurotechnology was developed to "create a direct communication channel with digital computers." (Ienca 2021, p. 15). This is the field of brain-computer interfaces (BCIs). Today, there are four BCIs reading brain signals from different locations. A technical distinction, albeit ethically controversial as later discussed, is between non-invasive and invasive neurotechnology. The distinction relies indeed on a technical feature, that is, non-invasive neurotechnology does not require a surgical intervention, whereas invasive neurotechnology requires surgery to implant a chip or array into the cortex. (Karanasiou 2021, p. 763). According to Eric Smalley, "electroencephalography (EEG) electrodes record aggregate signals […] from the surface of the scalp; electrocorticography (ECoG) electrodes record the local field potentials of hundreds to thousands neurons from the surface of the cerebral cortex; intracortical electrodes record signals of individual neurons, or action potentials, from below the surface of the cortex, and deep brain recording electrodes monitor action potentials of individual neurons from a deep brain structure or nucleus, beneath the cortex." (Smalley 2019, p. 979).

Non-invasive neurotechnology also includes a range of neurostimulation techniques ranging from transcranial electrical stimulation (TES), transcranial magnetic stimulation (TMS) to transcranial direct current stimulation (tDCS), which both "involve the activation or inhibition of brain activity." (Di Nuzzo et al. 2018, p. 336).

Neurotechnology has shown important results in the clinical field to treat mental disorders not responsive to pharmacological treatments and to treat persons

[2] Available at https://www.oecd.org/science/recommendation-on-responsible-innovation-in-neurotechnology.htm#:~:text=Promote%20international%20deliberation%2C%20engagement%2C%20and,neurotechnologies%20for%20health%2Drelated%20applications.

with severe neuromuscular disorders to recover functions like communication and mobility.

Non-invasive neurotechnology is also applied outside of the clinical context as it is wearable, portable, scalable, and potentially ubiquitous (*pervasive neurotechnology*) (Ienca et al. 2018). The direct-to-consumer market of pervasive neurotechnology is growing rapidly[3] as I will discuss later. Consider, for instance, wearable tech like EEG (Neurosky, Emotiv, Mindwave) and tDCS like Thync.

As for the risk classification, there are differences between the USA and the European Union.

In the USA, FDA approval is not necessary when no claim for medical use is provided (Waltz 2019, p. 987).

Both invasive and non-invasive neurotechnologies are classified according to the level of the risk posed by the device. There are indeed identified risks. For invasive neurotechnologies like DBS, there may be, amongst others, surgical complications or worsening of mental or emotional status as reported by the American Association of Neurological Surgeons.[4] For non-invasive neurotechnologies like TMS, the FDA mentions seizure, thermal injury, and hearing loss, to name a few.[5]

In 2019, upon request, the FDA has moved TMS from class III (premarket approval) to class II (special controls) when it is used for neurological and psychiatric disorders and conditions.[6]

In the EU, the final version of the reclassification (Regulation EU 2022/2347) became effective at the end of 2022 and included all non-medical NIBS products in class III of the Annex XVI of the Regulation (EU) 23,017/745 on medical devices. This means that specific safety and clinical performance conditions must be met and summarized by the manufacturers as stated by Article 32 of the mentioned Regulation. In addition, manufacturers of class III custom-made implantable devices shall be subject to the conformity assessment as specified in Chapter I of Annex IX. This EU decision has been strongly criticized by the European Society for Brain Stimulation (ESBS).[7] According to the EBSB's Manifesto "This reclassification has a major impact on our field, not only for manufacturers, but also for researchers, clinicians and patients and we judge this reclassification a mistake. First, the evidential basis for this change is a flawed assessment of the safety literature. Second, the consultation

---

[3] *The Market for Neurotechnology: 2022–2026. A Market Research Report from Neurotech Reports* available at https://www.neurotechreports.com/pages/execsum.html

See also the *Market Report on Pervasive Neurotechnology: a Groundbreaking Analysis of 10′000 + Patent Filings Transforming Medicine, Health, Entertainment and Business*, available at https://sharpbrains.com/pervasive-neurotechnology

[4] See https://www.aans.org/en/Patients/Neurosurgical-Conditions-and-Treatments/Deep-Brain-Stimulation

[5] See the Federal Register at this link https://www.federalregister.gov/documents/2019/03/14/2019-04709/medical-devices-neurological-devices-classification-of-the-transcranial-magnetic-stimulation-system#:~:text=The%20Food%20and%20Drug%20Administration%20(FDA%20or%20we)%20is%20classifying,class%20II%20(special%20controls).

[6] Ibid.

[7] See position at this link https://www.brainstimjrnl.com/article/S1935-861X(23)01698-4/fulltext.

process has occurred without input from specialists or stakeholders professionally active in the field of NIBS."[8]

The previous, non-exhaustive, description of the relevant characteristics, applications, and risk classification of neurotechnology offers us a glimpse into the technical complexity that characterizes this field. This technical complexity may exacerbate the tension between power and freedom as referred to earlier, as it often hides profound ethical problems and conceptual confusion that may not be easily identified. I will try to sketch some of these problems in the following analysis.

10.3 Neurotechnology for Clinical Use: Some Major Open Ethical Challenges

Applications of neurotechnology in the medical field is ethically and legally justified by its basic objective, which is to promote mental health and ameliorate disease conditions. Moreover, the medical field represents a well-regulated area, where the tension between power (of the physician) and freedom (of the patient) has been eased by providing a strict regulation of the duties and rights of health professionals and patients. Key aspect of this regulation is the correct communication process between the physician and the patient (Borsellino 2018). This process allows the patient to express an informed consent. In the informative model of the physician–patient relationship (Emanuel and Emanuel 1992), patient's autonomy is respected and is not influenced by any outside opinions from the physicians that may lead her to a choice she does not want.

This is the general framework for any discussion about novel technologies in the medical field.

In Western countries, and in Europe in particular, the current discussion about neurotechnology occurs within this paradigm governed by a framework of regulations and liability rules. In Italy, for instance, the informative model has been clearly incorporated in Act n. 219/2017 on informed consent and advance directives. Although the debate on neurotechnology takes place within this strictly regulated framework, this kind of technology requires however additional ethical and legal attention due to potential harmful effects on the good at stake: the individual mind. Indeed, some clinical applications may alter a range of mental states critical to thought, personality, and behavior. This has been documented, for instance, with DBS for advanced Parkinson disease (Glannon 2022, p. 876). In such situations, the main concern is about the patient's autonomy, "specifically regarding his capacity to consent to continuation or discontinuation of DBS and thus the ability to change his mind." (Glannon 2022, p. 879) Despite the difficulty of this situation, the well-regulated communication process offers a guidance to manage it. As was observed, "[m]edical professionals and patients together need to consider the effects of DBS on the brain and mind. In

[8] See the Manifesto at the following link https://www.brain-stimulation.eu/manifesto-eu-reclassification-of-nibs/.

the end, though, it is the competent patient who has to decide whether the tradeoffs in any given treatment would be acceptable and whether he or she should have or continue to have it." (Glannon 2022, p. 882).

As is evidenced by the previous considerations, the physician–patient relationship offers the adequate environment to grant both the maximization of beneficial effects and the minimization of harmful and unwanted relevant side-effects of neurotechnological applications.

This risk/benefit evaluation is of the utmost importance considering that the European Union is facing a severe mental health crisis as documented by the 2023 *Communication of the Commission to the European Parliament, the Council, the European Economic and Social Committee and the Committee of the Regions on a comprehensive approach to mental health.*[9] This Communication inaugurates a new EU strategic approach to mental health based on "three guiding principles that should apply to every EU citizen: (i) to have access to adequate and effective prevention; (ii) to have access to high quality and affordable mental healthcare and treatment; (iii) to be able to reintegrate society after recovery." (European Commission 2023, p. 2).

Neurotechnology may contribute to implementing the second principle because recent developments show that non-invasive brain stimulation like TMS and tDCS (Maier et al. 2023, p. 1) is a promising and innovative therapy for mental diseases like depression, anxiety, and schizophrenia. However, despite this potential for symptom relief and improved well-being, these treatments have not been made available to all EU patients yet. Thus, equal access to safe and effective neurotechnological treatments should be a priority for the new strategic approach to mental health. In order to succeed in this direction, the strategic approach should consider overcoming the differences in health insurances among the different EU countries. Accordingly, availability of treatments should be granted by private as well as by public health insurance. When treatments are based on non-invasive stimulation and are portable, possibility of home-use should be also considered as a viable option to overcome logistical problems that patients living far away from hospitals may experience.

The medical use of neurotechnology also raises privacy issues. In fact, during treatments brain data are usually collected. These data have not been clearly defined yet (Ebers 2020). The European General Data Protection Regulation does not directly mention them. It explicitly refers solely to biometric and genetic data (Ebers 2020). In addition, a clear data management policy covering informed consent is still lacking, and questions concerning incidental findings as well as the possibility of exercising the right not to know have not been sufficiently examined so far.

All the mentioned critical issues concern both the development and use of neurotechnology for inpatient and outpatient settings, including home-use. To effectively tackle the different problems and "ensure that no one is left behind" (European Commission 2023, p. 2) and "citizens have equal access to prevention and mental health services across the EU", it is important that all relevant stakeholders are

[9] The Communication is available at this link https://eur-lex.europa.eu/legal-content/EN/TXT/?uri=CELEX%3A52023DC0298.

included in the discussion, that is, "patients, their families, and patients' organizations, healthcare organizations and healthcare professionals […], health insurers […], scientists and researchers […], industry […], ethicists and lawyers, international organizations […] and regulatory institutions at the level of the European Union" (Maier 2023, p. 5).

The participatory approach may facilitate solutions to promote the beneficial clinical use of neurotechnology and to limit abuses and misinterpretations. Moreover, involvement of different stakeholders may contribute to better study designs, to reducing unrealistic patients' expectations, to designing technology following ethical standards, and in general to seriously working on safety and effectiveness of neurotechnological treatments.

10.4 The Direct Marketing of Neurotechnology: Cognitive Enhancement as the Critical Frontier

Unlike the medical use of neurotechnology, the direct-to-consumers (DTCs) neurotechnologies are not covered by an all-embracing framework of regulation granting supervision and scrutiny. They seem to float in an open space, with relevant grey legal zones.

This situation raises many ethical, social, and governance questions (Pfotenhauer 2021, p. 661) that cannot be effectively tackled by industry self-regulation alone. This because the use of DTCs neurotechnology poses relevant questions concerning individual and collective responsibility, and industry would give priority to its own interests. The categories of individuality, diversity, plurality, and of *governance of the self* have to be reconsidered to avoid surreptitious erosion that put the *fullness of the person* into question (Rodotà 2012a, b, p. 373). In fact, as Kirchschlaeger observes "[w]earables change humans. Increasingly, humans are triggered to find themselves not in themselves but rather in the numbers, results, assessments, and comparisons (with other carriers of wearables) collected, structured, interpreted, and communicated in the form of imperatives by wearables." (Kirchschlaeger 2021, p. 295). Thus, the acceptability and justifiability of the direct marketing of these devices depends on their compatibility with human rights, specifically on the possibility to ease the tension between power and freedom in favor of the latter. In other words, as Bublitz puts it, "the mere idea that the minds of citizens are a legitimate target for governmental intrusions is, by itself, unsettling" (Bublitz 2016, p. 100), and this consideration also extends to intrusions by private powers. As observed, industry and tech companies alone cannot grant collective and public interest as they usually offer guarantees compatible with their own interests. Accordingly, their call for ethics may result in an illusion. Indeed, the problem of *ethics washing* is well-known. The notion refers to "the practice of implementing superficial ethics mechanisms or principles in response to public pressure while purposefully side-tapping more fundamental issues." (Pfotenhauer 2021, p. 663).

Therefore, a serious reflection on the DTCs is unavoidable, as the direct market of non-invasive neurotechnological devices is indeed growing. As mentioned earlier, the current available applications are non-invasive, wearable, and portable. These characteristics have facilitated their public acceptance through a subtle and inadvertent embedding in the social fabric. Moreover, the ethical acceptability of neurotechnology used for enhancement has not been fully, clearly, and publicly discussed. Most of the users of DTCs have no idea about the implications of enhancement both for the individual and the society. But a serious discussion about DTCs implies a critical analysis of human enhancement.

Therefore, in order to properly understand the challenges of DTCs, the discussion has to be framed within the human enhancement debate (Salardi 2024, 2023, 2018).

The first institutional European *Human Enhancement Study* was published in 2009 by the European Parliament Science and Technology Options Assessment (STOA). The Study defines human enhancement (HE) "as a modification aimed at improving individual human performance and brought about by science-based or technology-based interventions in the human body." (STOA 2009, p. 17) The Study recognizes that this is a highly contested issue and outlines possible strategies for HE in Europe. The mentioned Study proposes setting up a European body for the development of a normative framework that should have guided the formulation of EU policies on HE. In the time since, no progress in this specific direction has been made. The topic remains at the center of a heated ethical debate where a minimum shared consensus on the ethical justifiability of such practices and interventions is still lacking. Legally, there is no explicitly established right to enhancement (Salardi 2018). In the European context, there is the right to freely construct one's personality which mutually involves the right to individual autonomy and self-determination, all enshrined in the constitutional texture: for instance, in Italy in Article 2 of the Constitution. As Stefano Rodotà has deftly illuminated "self-determination is [...] identified with the life plan pursued by the person concerned [...] for it is governed by the uninterrupted exercise of sovereignty, enabling the free construction of personality which we find enshrined at the outset of our own constitution as well as in others." (Rodotà 2012b, p. 1)

These rights are framed within a bundle of rights like the right to health, to physical and mental integrity, and to respect for dignity, amongst others, that are not necessarily grounding a right to enhancement. On the contrary, depending on the jurisprudential interpretation, all these rights may create an environment contrary to forms of enhancement that in principle can severely violate freedom and health of people. For instance, forms of enhancement considered disproportionate or unacceptably risky due to their invasive or irreversible nature, and in any case all enhancements that do not operate in accordance with the principles of proportionality and precaution.

Thus, the discussion about the societal limits needed to justify enhancement is a pressing issue. Despite the ethical and legal uncertainty surrounding the debate on HE, pharmaceutical and non-pharmaceutical enhancements have been marketed and used to cognitively enhance individuals for some decades now (Conrad 2007). The STOA's Study dedicated a paragraph to non-pharmaceutical enhancements where DBS and TMS were briefly mentioned, amongst others (STOA 2009, p. 30). Today, tech companies are increasingly investing in non-invasive neurotechnologies directly marketed to consumers, especially in the USA, where it suffices that a manufacturer does not claim that a device treat a medical condition to elude the FDA's control (Waltz 2019, p. 987). Indeed, as was clarified, "for emerging neurotech, traditional means of governance -including institutionalized research ethics, post hoc regulation and market mechanisms- are ill-equipped to capture the ways in which these technologies could reshape our societies, especially in terms of long-term consequences." (Pfotenhauer 2021, p. 661).

The sale of neurotechnological devices for do-it-yourself brain stimulation becomes easy and widespread through the Web. The growth of this market raises many ethical and legal concerns at the center of many institutional initiatives like UNESCO's recent conference on the Ethics of Neurotechnology dedicated to "Towards an Ethical Framework in the Protection and Promotion of Human Rights and Fundamental Freedoms" (July 13th, 2023).

In the commercial field, the tension between power of tech companies and freedom of users reaches its peak as the asymmetry of knowledge cannot be easily overcome (Zuboff 2019). Unlike the medical field, the use of neurotechnologies for enhancing purposes flies entirely under the radar of regulatory systems. No expert supervision can be granted, and the inexperienced user is alone in weighing benefits against risks. This problem has been recognized by a group of researchers, who published an open letter dating back to 2016 (Wurzman et al. 2016) and addressing tDCS. In this open letter, the authors explained some of the major problems of do-it-yourself tDCS: (1) stimulation affects more of the brain than a user may think; (2) stimulation interacts with ongoing brain activity, so what a user does during tDCS changes tDCS; (3) enhancement of some cognitive abilities may come at the cost of others; (3) changes in brain activity (intended or not) may last longer than a user may think; (4) small differences in tDCS parameters can have a big effect; (5) tDCS effects are highly variable across different people; (6) the risk/benefit ratio is different for treating diseases versus enhancing function.

In addition to the mentioned risks and problems, DTCs raise further ethical and legal questions. The abovementioned asymmetry of knowledge allows tech companies to easily exercise control over individuals as they collect and manage huge amounts of brain data. In so doing, they can manipulate individuals for economic or political purposes through targeted advertisements or behavioral nudges.

In this context, the vulnerability of the single individual is exacerbated by the illusion of autonomy, which is fed by the market's narrative. According to this narrative, adult individuals are autonomous beings able to choose what is best for them. Accordingly, it is up to the individual to decide whether she wants to enhance, for what reasons, and to what extent. In the free market, the individual finds the best solution for her own needs, and she can choose. This 'rhetoric of choice' (Cohen 1999, p. 1399) is a perilous narrative as it permits tech companies (private powers) to conveniently circumnavigate the problem of having to discuss how decisional autonomy is constructed and how they predetermine what is chosen (Salardi 2023). Individuals are not autonomous just because they reach adulthood. Rather, the construction of one's autonomy is a work in progress based on contingent information. This holds particularly true for complex technological advances. If information is misleading, then autonomy may "degenerate into the simple, stimulus–response behavior sought by direct marketers." (Cohen 1999, p. 1424).

Being aware of what autonomy requires to be truly exercised is the first step to empower individuals in a field where "there is no good way to ensure that the consumer can give truly 'informed' consent" (Jarchum 2019, p. 995), unless private powers are not urged to mobilize to seriously embrace ethics and responsibility in neurotechnological innovation: for instance, by ethically designing technology by default; by providing fair information about the potentiality of the devices; by avoiding misleading framing language in advertising the products. Language is indeed a potentially treacherous instrument when expressions and notions are not clearly defined. An example of framing language is the distinction between invasive and non-invasive neurotechnology. This is a distinction used by experts to describe a technical difference as discussed earlier in this essay. However, the distinction may not be clear to inexperienced users. As was stated "the use of the term non-invasive, especially when paired with a product marketed for non-clinical purposes, seems to imply trivial risks for the consumer" (Karanasiou 2021, p. 767), although this is not completely true. 'Non-invasive' means that no surgery is required. It does not mean that there is no influence on the brain physiology as the abovementioned open letter clearly explains. Thus, the expression 'non-invasive' provides an appearance of safety that is dangerously seductive and equally misleading for consumers, who may consent without really understanding what they are doing. This presumptive safety is potentially dangerous because it conceals the fact that marketed non-invasive neurotechnology has received a lower level of scrutiny.

In sum, direct-to-consumer marketing for enhancing purposes faces many open challenges that the individual alone cannot properly address. The existing gap between a minimum shared ethical consensus on what enhancements should be allowed or prohibited and the rapidly growing market of neurotechnology is one of the most pressing issues to be investigated.

10.5 Neurotechnologies and Human Rights: Some Prospective Remarks

In the European context, human rights offer the ethical and legal framework of reference to set priorities in the agenda-setting in technology. Human rights are the key instrument to ease the tension between power and freedom in favor of freedom. This because human rights function as the *laws of the weakest subjects* (Ferrajoli 2007, p. 59). Who are the weakest subjects in the neurotechnological realm? The answer to the question varies from case to case. In the medical field, the weakest subjects are the patients, who have their health and life at stake. In the free market, they are the consumers or final users, who are in an asymmetric position as regards knowledge and understanding of technology. All these actors can be protected through human rights. This is true for protection against public as well as private powers. In the EU, it is uncontroversial that human rights violations can be asserted against both public and private stakeholders (horizontal effect[10]) to adequately define the spheres of influence and responsibility. At the international level, the same protection may be more difficult to be achieved.

As for the medical field, the right to health, the right to autonomy and self-determination and in general the respect for dignity have been well incorporated in regulation of the physician–patient relationship. As observed earlier, this is grounded in the informative model.

In order to maximize the beneficial potential of neurotechnology, this model ought to be further supported and strengthened with reference to the coming challenges of mental health. In so doing, autonomy of the patient and responsibility of the health personnel can be reinforced to tackle new and unprecedented challenges posed by neurotechnology and by mental diseases. This can be done through an ad hoc regulation concerning brain data protection, by granting equal access to safe and effective neurotechnology, by providing trustworthy information, and by developing ad hoc rules covering informed consent issues.

As for DTCs, the EU institutions should engage in determining the societal limits of enhancing practices, specifically of cognitive enhancement while promoting at the same time beneficial use of innovative technologies. To this purpose, human rights offer a comprehensive framework of rights characterized by a logic of indivisibility, which contributes to drawing a clear line between admissible and inadmissible uses of neurotechnology. In so doing, they inspire regional and national legislation to enforce the respect for dignity, autonomy, integrity, and health of citizens. As human rights can be assessed against private actors, this means that they are subject to a growing public scrutiny, which may well be a useful driver for mobilization towards responsible innovation in the discussed technological field. In the debate about societal limits of enhancing practices and technology, matters of institutional concerns should be to grant health by providing effective and safe devices to consumers; to impose strict conditions on private powers to not impair the exercise of self-determination by consumers; to increasingly provide consumers with institutionally controlled and independent information channels like forums easily accessible by citizens and ad hoc informative campaigns with experts.

To overcome the information asymmetry is the essential starting point to ease the tension between power and freedom in favor of freedom. The right to freely construct one's personality offers a strong legal reference to seriously work on the duties of institutions to implement it.

Of course, this is not the panacea for the complex issues concerning neurotechnology. Nonetheless, it is the prerequisite to further work on elevating the cultural and moral standards of all the stakeholders involved in the use and commercialization of this promising technological innovation.

---

[10] See https://eur-lex.europa.eu/EN/legal-content/summary/the-direct-effect-of-european-union-law.html.

References

Bobbio, Norberto. 1997. *L'età dei diritti.* Torino: Einaudi.

Borsellino, Patrizia. 2018. *Bioetica tra 'morali' e diritto*, Milano: Raffaello Cortina.

Bublitz, Christoph. 2016. Moral enhancement and mental freedom. *Journal of Applied Philosophy* 33: 88–106.

Cohen, Julie. 1999. Examined lives: informational privacy and the subject as object. *Stan. Law. Rev.* 52: 1373–1438.

Conrad, Peter. 2007. *The Medicalization of Society. On transformation of Human Conditions into Treatable Disorders.* Baltimore: The John Hopkins University Press.

Di Nuzzo, C., R. Ferrucci, E. Gianoli, M. R. Reitano, D. Tedino, F. Ruggiero, and A. Priori. 2018. How Brain stimulation techniques can affect moral and social behaviour. *Journal of Cognitive Enhancement* 2: 335–347.

Ebers, Martin. 2020. Regulating AI and robotics: ethical and legal challenges. In *Algorithms and Law*, ed. Martin Ebers, 37–99. Cambridge: Cambridge University Press.

Emanuel, Ezekiel J., and Linda L. Emanuel. 1992. Four models of the physician-patient relationship. *JAMA* 267: 2221–2226.

European Commission. 2023. *Communication of the Commission to the European Parliament, the Council, the European Economic and Social Committee and the Committee of the Regions on a comprehensive approach to mental health*, COM/2023/ 298final.

Ferrajoli, Luigi. 2007. *Principia Juris.* Vol. II, Roma-Bari: Laterza.

Glannon, Walter. 2022. Stimulating brains, altering minds. In *Bioethics: An Anthology*, ed. Udo Schüklenk and Peter Singer, 876–882. New Jersey: Wiley Blackwell.

Ienca, Marcello, Pim Haselager, and Ezekiel J. Emanuel. 2018. Brain leaks and consumer neurotechnology. *Nature Biotechnology* 36: 805–810.

Ienca, Marcello. 2021. *Common Human Rights Challenges Raised by Different Applications of Neurotechnologies in the Biomedical Field*, Report commissioned by the Committee on Bioethics (DH-BIO) of the Council of Europe. Strasbourg: Council of Europe.

Jarchum, Irene. 2019. The ethics of neurotechnology. *Nature Biotechnology* 37: 993–996.

Jonas, Hans. 1984. *The Imperative of Responsibility. In Search of An Ethics for the Technological Age.* Chicago: The Chicago University Press.

Karanasiou, Argyro P. 2021. On being trans-human: commercial BCIs and the quest for autonomy. In *The Cambridge Handbook of the Law of Algorithms*, ed. Woodrow Barfield, 757–774. Cambridge: Cambridge University Press.

Kirchschlaeger, Peter. 2021. *Digital Transformation and Ethics.* Baden-Baden: Nomos.

Maier, M. J., Antal, A., Oliviero, A., Breuer, J., Ramasawmy, P., Baeken, C., Hölzle, K., Paulus, W., Rozynska, J., Ryan, D., Salardi, S., Tankisi, H., Vidalis, T., Zilio, F., and Northoff, G. (2023). STIMCODE Participative developed recommendations for non-invasive brain stimulation in the European Union. Fraunhofer-Publica. https://doi.org/10.24406/publica-1569.

OECD. 2019. *Recommendation of the Council on Responsible Innovation in Neurotechnology.* https://www.oecd.org/science/recommendation-on-responsible-innovation-in-neurotechnology.htm#:~:text=Promote%20international%20deliberation%2C%20engagement%2C%20and,neurotechnologies%20for%20health%2Drelated%20applications.

Pfotenhauer, S. M., N. Frahm, D. Winickoff, D. Benrimoh, J. Illes, and G. Marchant. 2021. Mobilizing the private sector for responsible innovation in neurotechnology. *Nature Biotechnology* 39: 661–670.

Rodotà, Stefano. 2012a. *Il diritto di avere diritti.* Roma-Napoli: Laterza.

Rodotà, Sefano. 2012b. Editorial. *Salute e Società* 3: 1–4.

Russell, Bertrand. 1938. *Power: a new social analysis.* London: Allen and Unwin.

Salardi, Silvia. 2018. The 'Project of Moral Bioenhancement' in the European legal system. Ethically controversial and legally highly questionable. *Rivista di Filosofia del Diritto – Journal of Philosophy of Law* VII(2): 241-260.

Salardi, Silvia. 2023. *Intelligenza artificiale e semantica del cambiamento: Una lettura critica.* Torino: Giappichelli.
Salardi, Silvia. 2024. *Neurotecnologie tra potere e libertà. Medicina, etica, discriminazioni di genere.* Milano: Wolters Kluwer.
Smalley, Eric. 2019. The business of brain-computer interfaces. *Nature Biotechnology* 37: 978–982.
STOA. 2009. *Human enhancement study.* Brussels: European Parliament.
Waltz, Emily. 2019. The brain hackers. *Nature Biotechnology* 37: 983–987.
Wrong, Dennis. 1995. *Power: its forms, bases, and uses*, 2nd ed. New York: Routledge.
Wurzman, R., R. H. Hamilton, A. Pascual-Leone, and M. D. Fox. 2016. An open letter concerning do-it-yourself users of transcranial direct current stimulation. *Annals of Neurology* 80: 1–4.
Zuboff, Shoshana. 2019. *The age of surveillance capitalism: the fight for a human future at the new frontier of power*. London: Profile Books Ltd.

Chapter 11
Gestational Surrogacy, Private Life and the European Court of Human Rights Case Law

Alfonso Ballesteros

Abstract This chapter analyses the surrogate motherhood case law of the European Court of Human Rights. A case law that focuses on the protection of everyone's right to respect for private and family life (art. 8 ECHR). Usually the case decision is about the States' refusal to recognise a birth certificate from a foreign country that has allowed a surrogacy agreement. Court's decision does not recognize a right to become a father or a mother. And it does not usually declare the right to respect for family or private life of the intended parents has been violated. The decision often states that the right to private life of the children has been violated. Children's identity and inheritance rights should be protected and the State condemn. This case law leads to protecting children but it leaves little room for the States to oppose surrogacy, whitening the practice.

Keywords Gestational surrogacy · Surrogate motherhood · Private life · Family life

11.1 Introduction

How Law should tackle the issue of gestational surrogacy has been a subject of discussion in the political, social, and academic arena for more than a decade. This phenomenon is fundamentally determined by its international nature and therefore by the presence of both multiple legal systems and differing views on parenthood, family and morality.

In this chapter, I address case law on surrogate motherhood, which is very much connected with article 8 of the European Convention of Human Rights (in what follows, ECHR) and two interrelated rights: respect to family life and private life. The Court does not recognize the alleged right of couples or separate individuals to

---

A. Ballesteros (✉)
University Miguel Hernández, Elche, Spain
e-mail: aballesteros@umh.es

© The Editor(s) (if applicable) and The Author(s), under exclusive license to Springer Nature Switzerland AG 2024

J.-A. Seoane and O. Vergara (eds.), *The Discourse of Biorights*, The International Library of Bioethics 109, https://doi.org/10.1007/978-3-031-66804-3_11

have children at any cost. This case law also leaves the States with little practical means to oppose gestational surrogacy, despite they are not enforcing it to legalize it in their territory (Puppinck 2018 p. 45). At the same time, although case law usually recognizes the importance of children's identity, the very practice of surrogacy leads to neglect an essential part of the identity of the children (especially that of knowing the biological or genetic mother and the gestational mother), and also ignores the right to be raised by their biological parents (when it is possible).

The right of private life is usually the right at stake in this case law. But the meaning of private life cannot be mistaken with the notion of privacy. The right to private life is wider and includes the right to develop relationships with other persons and the outside world. In the case law we are going to present, the right to private life of the children is about the right to be recognized as children of the intended parents when there is a biological link with one of them.

11.2 European Court of Human Rights Case Law on Surrogate Motherhood

The ECHR case law on surrogate motherhood is on the rise. The problem generally arises in the following way: those who want to be parents, the so-called intended parents reach a gestational surrogacy agreement in a country where it is allowed. It is when they come back to their country of origin that the problem of registration arises on the birth certificate in the national birth register. Thereupon, national and European case law has started to emerge to resolve cases that have arisen. The ECHR has decided on the birth of children via agreements in the ambit of surrogacy in cases against France, Italy, Iceland, Denmark and Norway. Among them, *Mennesson v. France* and *Labassee v. France* (both 26 June 2014), *Foulon et Bouvet v. France* (21 July 2016), *Paradiso and Campanelli v. Italy* (27 January 2015 and GC 24 January 2017), *Valdís Fjölnisdóttir and Others v. Iceland* (18 May 2021), *A.M. v. Norway* (24 June 2022) and *K.K. and Others v. Denmark* (6 December 2022) stand out. In all these cases, the right the claimants (the intended parents or the intended parents and the children) claim that it has been violated is their right to respect for private and family life, included in Article 8 of the European Convention, and sometimes concurrent with other rights.

The ECHR case law allows in theory a margin of appreciation in the hands of States and declares to allow a free space that reflects the plurality of statutory answers to this problem. This might solve the problem of the variety of statutory regulation of the States of the Convention. In 2017 surrogacy was expressly prohibited in fifteen of the thirty-five States parties of the Convention. In ten others there were no regulations on gestational surrogacy, and the question was prohibited under general provisions, not tolerated or legally uncertain. And only seven States allowed surrogacy. Of the total of thirty-five States only in thirteen was possible for the intended parents to obtain legal recognition of the parent–child relationship (*Paradiso and Campanelli v. Italy* [GC], p. 81).

11.3 Mennesson v. France and Labassee v. France

The cases of *Mennesson v. France* and *Labassee v. France* are very similar and the procedure of them was followed simultaneously. The *Foulon et Bouvet v. France* case is alike and follow this case law. For this reason, I will focus on the first case. In the Mennesson case, the first and second applicants are husband and wife unable to have children of their own, because the wife is infertile. They made unsuccessful attempts using in vitro fertilization (IVF) and finally, using gametes of the husband and an egg of a third party, made a contract in California with a surrogate mother who had a much higher income than them and declared that it was an act of solidarity on her part. The surrogate mother gave birth to twins in 2000 (*Mennesson v. France*, pp. 7–10).

We will fail to understand the reason for the appeal if we do not pay attention to the aforementioned article 8. It hereby recognizes the right to respect for private and family life without illegitimate interference. The article is set out in two paragraphs. The first states: "Everyone has the right to respect for his private and family life, his home and his correspondence". The second highlights that this right can be restricted in some cases and it compiles the situations in which the State can interfere in the private and family life of an individual. These cases refer to when there is a provision by law, with a legitimate purpose and if it is essential in a democratic society. In the interpretation of the second paragraph, it is suggested that the State has a "margin of appreciation", and a certain degree of discretion when applying the article. However, this margin is not always the same: it is greater if it is assumed that there is no European consensus on the matter, but it narrows when the interest of the children is at stake.

In the Mennesson case, the French Government refused to record the particulars of the US birth certificates in the French register of births, marriages and deaths. The reason given by the authorities was that this would have given effect to a surrogacy agreement, which was formally forbidden and constituted a punishable offense if performed in France. French law states that the human body cannot become a commercial instrument and the child be reduced to the object of a contract (*Mennesson v. France*, p. 60).

The ECHR considers that the refusal of the French State to legally recognize the intended parents as parents of the children is an "interference" to family and private life. The ECHR points out this was its approach in other cases referred to the legal recognition of an adoption established in foreign countries (*Wagner and J.M.W.L. v. Luxembourg*, p. 123 y *Negrepointis-Giannisis v. Greece*, p. 58). In these cases, there has been interference regarding "family life" and also "private life". Such interference will be in breach of article 8 unless it can be justified (*Mennesson v. France*, pp. 48–49). With this line of reasoning the Court allows similarities between adoption and surrogacy by giving them equal treatment. However, French authorities justify the distinction between adoption and a surrogacy agreement, because the latter agreement is null and void and affects the inalienability of the human body (*Mennesson v. France*, p. 56). In particular, the government gives three reasons for neglecting legal recognition of the surrogacy arrangement (and therefore, justifying the "interference", that is, refusing to register the civil-status of the children):

1. Proscribing any possibility of trafficking in human bodies.
2. Guaranteeing respect for the principle that the human body and a person's civil status were inalienable.
3. And protecting the child's best interests (*Mennesson v. France*, p. 72).

With the second reason the state recurs to the "principle of inalienability" of a person's civil status, but this was subject to numerous practical arrangements. Transsexuals, for example, could obtain a change of sex stated on their birth certificate in French law. With respect the first and third reason France has recognized "intended" parents as one woman who carried the embryo of another couple and it was recognized legal mother with her couple (*Mennesson v. France*, p. 66).

However, the Court sets the focus somewhere else. According to the Court, the issue is about a decision which deprived children of their civil-status. Those children were born as the result of a surrogacy agreement lawfully performed abroad and the documents that probed their legal relationship with their parents, including their biological father, were not accepted by French authorities (*Mennesson v. France*, p. 63). French authorities did not recognize the parenthood of the biological father, which was also the intended father. The French authorities justified it by arguing that "it seem[ed] preferable to place both parents on the same level of legal recognition" (*Mennesson v. France*, p. 72). The Court considers the case child's best interests in a radically opposed manner to the French authorities. And as the child's best interest is affected, this has the effect of restricting the States's margin of appreciation (*Mennesson v. France*, p. 63).

Another important element of judgment, that will be followed in similar case law is the distinction the ECHR makes between the intended parents' right to respect their family and private life and the rights of the children (*Mennesson v. France*, p. 86). The Court considers there is family life between applicants and children. However, the French government's *interference in family life is justified* because it strikes a fair balance between the interests of the applicants and those of the State (*Mennesson v. France*, p. 94). Here the Court asserts: "They were all four able [intended parents and the twins] to settle in France shortly after the birth of the third and fourth applicants, [they] are in a position to live there together in conditions broadly comparable of those of other families" (*Mennesson v. France*, p. 92). However, *children's private life interference is not justified* based on identity problems and inheritance rights for the following reasons:

1. Everyone should be able to establish details of their identity as individual human beings, which includes the legal parent–child relationship. The applicants are

considered parents of the children in the US, but not in France, and a contradiction of that nature undermines the children's identity within French society (*Mennesson v. France*, p. 96).
2. The children face a worrying uncertainty as to the possibility of obtaining recognition of French nationality although the biological father is French (*Mennesson v. France*, p. 97).
3. The consequences for their inheritance rights as the death duties will be calculated in the same way as for a third party, that is, less favourable (*Mennesson v. France*, p. 98).

Concerning private life, it can be said that the ECHR recognizes the effects of surrogacy in favour of children. In practice means recognizing the freedom to recur to surrogacy by the intended parents when one of them has biological ties with the children.

11.4 Paradiso and Campanelli v. Italy [GC]

Let us move on to the *Paradiso and Campanelli v. Italy* (Grand Chamber, 4 January 2017, no. 25358/12), a case which came about as a result of the following events. An Italian married couple went to Russia where surrogacy was legal and they came to an agreement. The woman took her husband's seminal fluid to Russia (or she said she did), the egg was from a third party and the resulting embryos were implanted in the woman hired to that effect and a child was born. On their return to Italy, the Russian birth certificate was refused. Furthermore, and this is crucial, a test carried out on the husband promptly evidenced that there was no biological relationship between him and the minor. The minor was then withdrawn from the care of the commissioning parents and assigned to foster parents. The intended parents then appealed at the domestic level in Italy and the Italian courts turned down all the appeals made by the commissioning parents to get the child back. Then applicants recurred to the ECHR and they alleged that the measures taken by the Italian government concerning the child were incompatible with their right to private and family life.

The Chamber of the ECHR declared that Article 8 of the Convention had been violated, but this decision was appealed by the Italian government to the Grand Chamber which overturned the previous ruling and considered that there had not been a violation of this article.

This case differs from *Mennesson and Labassee* where the issue at the heart of the cases was the refusal to register the particulars of a birth certificate drawn up abroad (*Mennesson v. France*, p. 132). Unlike these cases, the Paradiso case is not about registration of a foreign birth certificate, but the active measures taken by the Italian authorities to withdrawn the minor from the care of the intended parents. Therefore, the legal question at the heart of this case are: (1) if article 8 is applicable, (2) if the measure taken by the authorities amounts to an interference in the applicant's right to respect their family or personal life and (3) and if so, whether the impugned measures were legitimate and according with the Convention or not (article 8.2).

The Grand Chamber's answer to this case can be summarized as follows. First, the Grand Chamber declared there is no family life between the intended parents and the child. Even though the Court allows the existence of a de facto family life between an adult or adults and children in the absence of biological ties. In this case, there is no "family life" because of the short duration of the relationship and the uncertainty of the ties from a legal perspective (*Mennesson v. France*, p. 157). However, the Grand Chamber considers that there is an interference in the private life of the intended parents, but it is an allowed interference by the exceptions in article 8.2 of the Convention.

The Paradiso case, as there is no biological tie between the child and the applicants, is linked with *A.M. v. Norway* case where there was no biological tie between the child and the intended mother who was the applicant. The importance of the biological ties between children and the commissioning parents can be seen from the rulings handed down on this matter. And this objective measure of parenthood is linked with the important conclusion of *Paradiso and Campanelli v. Italy* [GC] recognizing that the Convention does not identify a right to become a parent (*Paradiso and Campanelli v. Italy* [GC], *Conclusion*).

The Concurring Opinion by Judge Dedov provides interesting insides in this respect. He considers that when there is a biological link between intended parents and children this is a sufficient reason to allow the recognition of the intended parents. However, this is not the case in *Paradiso and Campanelli v. Italy*. Following this idea, Judge Dedov points out that this recognition of those parents that are linked by biological ties should be counterbalanced by an individual penalty to prevent the practice in the future (*Paradiso and Campanelli v. Italy* [GC], Concurring opinion). I would say this point is essential as it emphasizes more clearly the distinction between parents' and children's private life. The Court might protect children born by gestational surrogacy and at the same time discourage surrogacy in the future by penalizing parents.

The Charter of Fundamental Rights of the European Union (article 3) allows the prohibition of making the human body as such a source of gain. This is the case of surrogacy when it is the result of a contract. However, to understand the phenomenon one must understand the way it is justify. Judge Dedov points out that gestational surrogacy can be defended based on concepts such as "market economy (…) and solidarity". As regards the "solidarity" rationale, Judge Dedov states that solidarity cannot be within the domain of surrogacy because "solidarity is intended to help those whose life is at stake, but not those who *merely desire* to enjoy a fully private or family life" (*Paradiso and Campanelli v. Italy*. Concurring Opinion, emphasis added) and he goes on to say that "in the absence of an emergency, surrogacy cannot be considered a proper way to facilitate social solidarity" (*Paradiso and Campanelli v. Italy*, Concurring Opinion). It is not an act of solidarity or altruism, but a sacrifice (Vergara 2022, p. 932). Furthermore, women are not generally prepared to carry out this task for nothing in exchange. As a result, people turn to a developing country for these services, to an "incubator country" where the necessity of some women allows for agreements to be reached very cheaply (Bellver Capella 2015, p. 9, Albert Márquez 2018, p. 144). The ECHR has recognized this particular practice in the *Foulon et Bouvet v. France*. This mass production of children raises even more ethical problems concerning to the children and women.

11.5 A.M. v. Norway

Case *A.M. v. Norway*, no. 30254/18 is constituted by the following facts. A Norwegian couple that lives together (since 2002) try to conceive naturally and made attempts at in vitro fertilization and finally made attempts to become parents through surrogacy helped by a company based in the US (2010). However, the relationship deteriorated and the man moved out (2012). Nonetheless, the couple remained in contact about the surrogacy agreement and they made arrangements with the clinic and the gestational mother. Afterward, the man (E.B.) started to leave with another woman. Finally, the child was born in 2014 with E.B. sperm and a third-party woman gametes. After more than a year of making the child live 24 h with each one of the intended parents, and after requirements of the social services indicating that the twenty-four hour-arrangement was not in child's best interest, E.B. decided not to allow the applicant (the woman) to be with the child again. E.B. was the biological and therefore the legal father according to Norwegian law. These events made the woman apply for the recognition of her maternity of the child or, in the alternative, adoption. The Norwegian Government did not accept her claims as surrogate motherhood is illegal in Norway.

The Court stresses that the State did not act to remove the child from the applicant (as happened in the Paradisso case), but the origin of the dispute is E.B.'s decision to keep the child and stop his contact with the applicant. The ECHR determined that there was no de facto family life between the applicant and the child as they spent approximately eight months together, similar to the Paradiso case. Moreover, unlike the applicants in Paradiso and Campanelli, she did not live with the biological father of the child (*A.M. v. Norway*, p. 106). The Court also concluded that there had been no violation of the right to the private life of the intended mother.

It is essential in this case that the applicant could not adopt the child without the legal father's consent. The Norwegian legislation did not allow recognition of the applicant's parenthood as adoption will require consent from the person holding parental responsibilities, e.g., E.B. (*A.M. v. Norway* p. 129). Therefore, no right has been violated in this case (*A.M. v. Norway* p. 131).

This case has a concurring and a dissenting opinion that allow to understand the case and the general phenomenon of surrogacy more deeply. In his concurring opinion Judge O'Leary writes: "It is entirely legitimate, under the Convention, for a State to seek to deter its nationals from having recourse to methods of assisted reproduction outside the national territory which are prohibited under its own territory" (*A.M. v. Norway*, p. 12). But when the alleged interferences are against the child's rights by the lack of formal recognition of his or her family ties (e.g. *Mennesson, Labasee,*

Foulon and Bouvet v. France) this will narrow the margin of appreciation enjoyed by States. But this is not the case in this judgment. The concurring opinion clarifies why this case law did not benefit the applicant:

1. The recognition of *the child's* family ties and rights was not before the Court. The child was not one of the applicants, as the woman had no legal basis to represent the child's interests before the courts. In the Mennesson case the children were also the applicants, and this is the reason why the Court decision was positive for the applicant.
2. In the other cases the "family" remained a stable unit and the intended parent was supported by the legally recognized biological parent. However, in this case, the applicant wanted to adopt the child despite the absence of consent by the biological and legal father.

The concurring opinion by Judge O'Leary concludes by reminding us how the children can become the victims of well-intentioned but desperate, and at times conflictual parental projects (*A.M. v. Norway*, Concurring opinion).

In her dissenting opinion, Judge Jelic considers that there is family life in this case. Moreover, judge argues that there is a short of individual right to become a parent by any means if one cannot become parent by biological means. Knowing the peculiar circumstances of the case, this right should even be recognized against the will of the biological and legal father and against the need for a stable family for the child (who had a stepmother and stepbrother by that moment).

The judge considers that the intended mother has a right to be a mother by alternative means. This is the reason why being biologically unable to be a mother is so important for Judge Jelic. The judge writes: "the Court should have taken notice of the applicant's inability to have a child of her own and *the need* to find alternative channels if she *wanted* to become a mother" (*A.M. v. Norway*, p. 32, emphasis added). The judge even says that the Court decision penalises individuals biologically unable to procreate. The judge considers that it is a form of discrimination (art. 14).

According to the dissenting opinion, rejecting a valid foreign birth certificate is not justified as all "kinds of family" are equally good and eligible: "Contrary to traditional understandings of family life, there are ever more different constellations of motherhood in the twenty-first century, ranging from genetic mothers (providing the fertilized ova), birth/gestational mothers, adoptive mothers and intended mothers. In that regard, it seems over simplistic to limit Norwegian law to recognizing only the birth mother as the legal mother" (*A.M. v. Norway*, p. 34).

The judge also argues that every child has the right to know his "identity", and unknowing it could cause severe emotional damage. This identity includes not only biological parents but also intended parents. However, the surrogate mother is of little importance as she did not live with the child. The Judge points out "the lack of any ties between X [the child] and his recognized biological mother [the American surrogate mother]" as they did not live together (*A.M. v. Norway*, p. 37). Judge seems to ignore that the child "lived" not with his gestational mother, but *inside* her for nine months.

Another element of discussion is the purpose of raising the child together. This could make the applicant holder of a right to see the child. In this respect, in a very wide understanding of "raising the child together", Judge Jelic considers that social practices legitimate widening what the term means. The judge seems to understand "together" not in the literal sense, but in a very wide way:

"The notion of 'raising a child together' in the authorities' understanding is remote from the reality of family life and family constellations in the twenty-first century. A multitude of couples raise their children together, ranging from separated or divorced couples to families whose parents, commute or simply decide to live apart while maintaining their romantic relationship [...] There is thus no evidence that the concept of raising a child together implies the existence of shared family home" (*A.M. v. Norway*, p. 40).

If we opt to ignore the meaning of "separate" and "together" as the dissenting opinion, still the dissenting judge seems to forget the effects of this wide understanding of raising a child together, how weak was this arrangement in the case (the social services were called to intervene) and especially the child interest as the child did not have a home of his own, neither a family. Can we say a child can have two simultaneous families with no damage to his identity and development? Can we say being divorced or living together is irrelevant and equally good for children? Judge O'Leary seems to ignore that the notion of family cannot be endlessly expanded just because certain behaviours become popular.

11.6 K.K. and Others v. Denmark

The last case on surrogacy follows the previous case law but it gives even more implicit recognition to gestational surrogacy. The facts are the following. A Danish couple arranged for a surrogacy in Ukraine and twins were born. The husband was the biological father of the children and was recognized as the legal father in Denmark. The wife was not recognized as the mother as the Ukranian birth certificate had no effect in this country. However, children obtained Danish nationality because of their family ties to their father. Danish authorities refuse to grant the first applicant (the intended mother) adoption of the children since the surrogate mother has been paid to consent to renouncing her rights as mother. In this case, as in the French cases (*Mennesson, Labassee and Foulon et Bouvet*) children were also applicants, something essential for a favorable decision.

Following the French cases the ECHR considered there was a violation of the children's private life, but not that of the mother, and neither family life of any of the applicants. There was family life, but this life did not appear to encounter any obstacles or practical difficulties, as the authorities recognized shared custody of wife and husband. However, refusing the intended mother to adopt the children is considered a violation of the private life of the children. The reason is not the protection of the identity of the children, but the possibility of those children to inherit *as* the offspring of the intended mother and not just of the father. Otherwise, the children would not be her heirs by a legal parent–child relationship.

This case shows how far has gone the ECHR to recognize the effects of surrogacy, reducing a lot of States' margin of appreciation. As in previous judgments, the Court declares a violation of the private life of the children, which is a way to legalize surrogacy in its effects. This case is singularly clear as the children had no other advantages in being recognized as the offspring of the intended mother by adoption other than a different treatment as heirs. Moreover, the Court condemns Denmark to pay 5,000 euros in respect of non-pecuniary damage to each of the second and third applicants (the children). This shows that surrogacy is not only blessed in its effects but strongly defended by penalties like this. Something that is not new in ECHR case law: in the *Foulon and Bouvet v. France* case children were awarded for moral damages with 5,000 euros each and *Foulon and Bouvet* were each awarded with 15,000 euros for costs and expenses.

As it could be argued that, in the *K.K. and Others v. Denmark* is desirable to recognize the intended mother as the legal mother of the children, this recognition could be counterbalanced as we said above. Per example, taking an individual penalty to the parents (as suggested by Judge Dedov in the Paradiso case). Even worse, not only no counterbalance is considered, but it is recognized the non-pecuniary damage to the children. In short, ECHR encourages the freedom to subscribe surrogacy agreements in foreign countries and reduces a lot the margin of States to decide less favourably on surrogacy cases.

11.7 Some Assumptions Behind Gestational Surrogacy and the Problem of Children's Identity

Michael Sandel quite rightly points out that eugenics and genetic engineering are a triumph of will over giftedness and of mastery over reverence (Sandel 2007, p. 39). The same could be said about surrogacy, which establishes the same assumption about the child, as something to be mastered and not appearing as a gift. Gifts are something we receive, that are not due. We do not deserve them. But this case law implicitly recognizes the possibility of gestational surrogacy as something that gives birth, in practice, to a new right, a right to have children. Natural birth or adoption can be seen in the realm of giftedness, but surrogacy, even the so-called altruist surrogacy, are about mastery and as we have seen the Court gives them equal treatment.

The woman who engenders the child is not the child's legal mother, and so a different type of maternity to biological motherhood is imposed on him, which is something that goes against the best interests of the child (Bellver Capella 2015, p. 12). Some questions can be asked about the necessary protection of natural motherhood. Are there no ties between a mother and a child during pregnancy? Is not unfair to be born in a foreign country and be taken from the hands of one's natural mother to satisfy someone else's desire to become a parent independently of any natural bounds? Can be nature completely ignored in this respect?

In any case, the future child will not be aware of who are his biological and gestational mothers. This can seriously affect the child who is in a situation of uncertainty as regards his identity (Balaguer 2017, p. 177). The child can demand to find out the information on the third party that relates to biology (medical records, health), but he cannot know their identity (López Moratalla 2018, p. 56). As for the issue of personal identity, the ECHR deemed this important to allow a woman to donate embryos produced with her genetic material to science. According to the ECHR, Article 8 was applicable as the embryos in question contained the applicant's genetic material and accordingly represented a constituent part of her identity (*Parrillo v. Italy* [GC]). If embryos are part of the identity of a woman, how cannot be the biological and gestational woman part of the identity of the children? The practice of gestational surrogacy neglects the importance of identity. If child identity, as part of their private life, was one of the reasons to condemn European countries that refused to inscribe children born by gestational surrogacy, identity should also count in biological terms. However, if identity is not something real and objective, then *the will* of the intended parents to keep and raise the children is what matters. The biological ties are insufficient if the adult does not want to be part of the life of the children as it occurs with the gestational mother and the biological mother.

In traditional surrogacy, the child has two mothers: the biological birth mother (egg and gestation) and the legal mother. In gestational surrogacy, in the best-case scenario, the child will have three mothers: the birth mother and the genetic or biological mother if the latter coincides with the intended mother (which is unusual), or three mothers if we distinguish between the genetic mother, the birth mother and the intended mother. Paternity is more uncertain as is shown by the Paradiso case. There can be various fathers: the third party that sells his gametes and the intended father. In a way, there is a total of five "progenitors". Can we say blessing this kind of arrangement is compatible with the respect of child-identity? If we take a real case, such as *A.M. v. Norway*, the child had six parents between social, legal and intended. By the age 17 months, the child born by surrogacy had had:

1. One biological father (E.B.).
2. One genetic mother (an anonymous third party).
3. One gestational surrogate mother (K.J.).
4. A first "social" mother or intended mother (the applicant).
5. One "legal father" (J.J.), the husband of the surrogate mother K.J. It was the legal father until the recognition of the biological father E.B.
6. A second "social" mother (H.), who, as E.B. partner and the biological mother of his second child also cared for the child (X). (*A.M. v. Norway*, pp. 3–5).

This variety and complexity that has developed in the realm of procreation cannot be understood without technology. Thus: in vivo fertilization, in vitro fertilization, prenatal medical tests, abortion, sterilization, frozen embryos, embryos used in science or gestational surrogacy. These techniques reveal the possibilities to manipulate, destroy, freeze or scientific use of life, which brings with it materialism and the demise of all things sacred just as Martin Heidegger has stated: "the essence of materialism does not consist in the assertion that everything is simply matter but rather in a metaphysical determination according to which *every being appears as the material of labour*. [...] The essence of materialism is concealed in *the essence of technology*" (Heidegger 2000, p. 96, emphasis added).

Without losing sight of what has just been said, Bellver Capella has detected a dual assumption in gestational surrogacy. The first is that the will of the individual to satisfy his/her desire to be a father or mother is dominant (1). The second is that the "renting" of a woman's womb is, in theory, an action that does not harm her dignity or her freedom (2) (Bellver Capella 2015, p. 7). It is worth pausing here to elaborate on these assumptions.

The first one refers to the fact that the will of the individual to satisfy his/her desire to be a father or mother is dominant (1). Of course, this assumption has to do with privacy as an autarchic desire and of course with the aforementioned technical possibilities, but its justification originates in personism. In its most radical form, personism deems that only the autonomous adult is a person, but the more accepted version contends that only someone who has been born is a person. This version is the one that is usually reflected in Western legal systems. Given the lack of recognition of personality in unborn children, having children via any procedure or not having them even after having conceived them are among the "reproductive" rights of the adult.

On this point, some cases that have reached the Court of Strasbourg directly or *indirectly* recognize the dominant nature of the rights of autonomous (and wealthy) adults. The "personalistic" and individualistic nature of these alleged rights can be seen therein. We encounter the conflict between the adults (parents) having rights with about the provisions for their unborn children, in one sense or another. Thus, there have been disputes between progenitors over whether to abort or not (*Boso v. Italy*) or whether to destroy or implant their children frozen at an embryonic stage (*Evans v. The United Kingdom*). Some of the appellants go so far as to appeal to the right of property of Article 1 for their children in an embryonic phase, although they have not been successful (*Parrillo v. Italy*). In any case, although the ECHR does not consider unborn children to be objects, it does not recognize them as persons either, nor does it recognize them as having rights (*Vo v. France*), disregarding the principle of *summa divisio iuris* between the holders of rights and those things which are the object of such rights.

The second assumption highlighted by Bellver Capella is that the "renting" of a woman's womb is, in theory, an action that does not harm her dignity or her freedom (2). The body is something that can be used by the individual, but the activities and practices of the body remain far from the realm of the soul, the soul remains identical. The body is considered not as a personal body, but as something that develops certain functions, such as the reproductive one. In the area of procreation, assisted reproduction techniques lead to the reduce or erase the connection with the body of others involved in the process, especially in the case of heterologous insemination (moreover, in these cases, the donor of the gametes is anonymous) and this lack of connection also stands in the case of gestational surrogacy, given that no relationship is established, apart from the bare and necessary minimum, with the birth mother.

The practice of surrogacy easily leads to the conclusion that the body is owned in a very peculiar sense. Certain acts, like carrying a baby lose their intrinsic meaning and become just a means to an end. The will or the soul are not necessarily linked with the tasks that the body accomplishes, or not affected by them. It reminds the assertion by Descartes that reduces the human being to present self-awareness, separating itself from the body: "the Soul by which I am what I am, is *entirely distinct* from the body" (Descartes 2006, p. 29).

As regards sexuality, Han writes that capitalism "puts everything on display as merchandise and renders it hyper-visible" (Han, 2013, *passim*). Paraphrasing and criticizing Agamben, Han mentions a "public use of sexuality". Interestingly, Han insists on the fact that the fragmentary image of the human body is pornographic, the body loses all unity and with it, its profound and sacred nature. Any part of the body which is isolated from the rest would be pornography, and we can add, that precisely because it destroys the unity of the personal body.

As regards procreation, similarly, it can be said that the manner of procreation postulated by capitalism is an unnatural reproduction, using techniques that divide the reproductive function into the smallest number of parts. This is not a visual fragmentation like with pornography, but a functional one. Thus, the term "womb for rent" itself does not only represent the obvious commodification of the woman but something that goes hand in hand, the fragmentation of her body which ceases to be a personal, unified body as if one could rent out only a womb (Albert Márquez 2008, p. 131).

In such a way these gestational surrogacy services could be called a "public use of procreation". This public use has to do with assisted human reproduction techniques and also gestational surrogacy which relies on these techniques to become a reality. The public nature of it does not mean it is accessible to everyone in this context. Rather, it means it has been removed from the private arena, from the unprofitable domain of gift, and it is taking place on the market, sometimes at large scale, with plentiful financial returns. Think, for example, about the man who is a seller of gametes and who already has 150 children (The New York Times, Sept. 5, 2011).

Modern technology enables the provision of the service (Bellver Capella 2015, p. 4) of gestational surrogacy without requiring sexual intercourse, going deeper into the rationale of separation. Given all this, the human body is becoming more and more superfluous for procreation and sexuality: completely artificial forms of human generation are being sought (gametes or artificial wombs) (López Moratalla 2018, p. 55), in the same way that the market already offers completely artificial forms of sexuality in the form of sexuality with robots (Foundation for Responsible Robotics 2017).

Some Final Considerations

We consider it necessary to advocate the universal prohibition of gestational surrogacy as other authors have done. The desire to be a father or a mother, however commendable it may be, can only become a genuine right at the expense of the rights of the children who acquire the status of commodities and property of the parents which is what some appellants have dared to profess before the ECHR. It is not even possible as a full-blown negative right where the State relinquishes jurisdiction because if it is recognized as a freedom, it passes over the incompatibility of commercial and personal relations. The person cannot be treated as something that belongs to the market and it is precisely this which marks a clear limit to the freedom of being parents. The ECHR case law on gestational surrogacy protects children's private life at the expense of whitening gestational surrogacy. It is reasonable to recognize parenthood that is linked by biological ties with the child, but this should be counterbalanced by an individual penalty to prevent the practice in the future. I would say this point is essential as it emphasizes more clearly the distinction between parents's and children's private life. The Court might protect children born by gestational surrogacy and at the same time discourage surrogacy in the future by penalizing parents.

European Court of Human Rights Cases

Boso v. Italy judgment of 5 September 2002 (no. 50490/99).
Vo v. France [GC] judgment 8 July 2003 (no. 53924/00).
Evans v. the United Kingdom [GC] judgment of 7 March 2006 (no. 6339/05).
Wagner and J.M.W.L. judgment of 28 June 2007 (no. 76240/01).
Negrepointis-Giannisis v. Greece judgment of 3 May 2011 (no. 56759/08,).
Mennesson v. France judgment of 26 June 2014 (no. 65192/11), *Labassee v. France* (no. 65941/11).
Parrillo v. Italy [GC] judgment of 27 August 2015 (no. 46470/11).
Foulon and Bovet v. France judgment of 14 July 2016 (no. 10410/14).
Paradiso and Campanelli v. Italy [GC] judgment of 24 January 2017 (no. 25358/12).
A.M. v. Norway judgment of 18 June 2022 (no. 30254/18).
K.K. and Others v. Denmark of 6 December 2022 (no. 32185/20).

References

Albert Márquez, Marta. 2018. La maternidad altruista y la maternidad subrogada, In *La maternidad subrogada. Qué es y cuáles son sus consecuencias*, ed. Nicolás Jouve de la Barreda, 115–145. Madrid: Sekotia.

Balaguer, María Luisa. 2017. *Hij@s del mercado. La maternidad subrogada en un Estado Social*. Madrid: Professor-Universitat de Valéncia.

Bellver Capella, Vicente. 2015. ¿Nuevas tecnologías? Viejas explotaciones: el caso de la maternidad subrogada internacional. *SCIO. Revista de Filosofía* 11: 19–52

Foundation for Responsible Robotics. 2017. Our Sexual Future with Robots. A Foundation for Responsible Robotics Consultation Report, prepared by Sharkey, Noel, Aimee van Wynsberghe, Scott Robbins and Eleanor Hancock.

López Moratalla, Natalia. 2018. *Mater semper certa est*. El vínculo madre-hijo durante la gestación. In *La maternidad subrogada. Qué es y cuáles son sus consecuencias*, ed. Nicolás Jouve de la Barreda, 49–83. Madrid: Sekotia.

Puppinck, Grégor. 2018. Mi deseo es ley. Los derechos del hombre sin naturaleza, Madrid, Encuentro. Trad. Fernando Montesinos y Miguel Montes.

Sandel, Michael J. 2007. The Case against Perfection Ethics in the Age of Genetic Engineering Harvard University Press.

Vergara, Óscar. 2022. El relato de la gestación subrogada: una contribución narrativa al debate ético y jurídico sobre su eventual institucionalización. *Oñati Socio-Legal Series* 12 (4): 908–944.

Chapter 12
Gestational Surrogacy as a New Right: A Narrative Approach

Oscar Vergara

Abstract As Jhering pinpoints, the birth of a new right is always painful and as with human birth, it involves a certain amount of violence. It is fair to say that the birth of the recognition of the right to gestational surrogacy is not without its complications. Although the practice has been technically possible since the late seventies, only a minority of States have granted legal recognition. It has been argued that gestational surrogacy constitutes a prior right which States must institutionalize. We will challenge this idea and then we will approach the issue from the perspective of narrative bioethics. It is this perspective, conceived in a certain way, which can not only shed more light but also push the boundaries to a greater extent than two of the most relevant methodologies in biomedical ethics, principlism and casuistry.

Keywords Gestational surrogacy · Narrative ethics · Human rights · Principlism · Casuistry · Virtue ethics

This paper is part of the research project "New Human Rights: Legal Theory and Political Praxis" (PID2019-111115 GB-100), funded by the Ministry of Science, Innovation and Universities (2020–2023).

So, as Jhering pointed out, the birth of a new right is always painful and as with human birth, it involves a certain amount of violence (Jhering 1947, p. 19). It is fair to say that the birth of the recognition of the right to gestational surrogacy (GS) is not without its complications. According to the Spanish Bioethics Committee (hereinafter SBC 2017), GS is "when a woman agrees to gestate and give birth to a baby for another person or persons who will become the child's legal parent(s) after birth" (SBC 2017, p. 6). This practice entails that the firmly rooted, traditional legal principle *mater semper certa est* be challenged. At least for the time being, not all States are prepared to do so.

There has been a deluge of publications on GS and the issue has been examined from many different perspectives but this does not mean that there is nothing left to

O. Vergara (✉)
University of A Coruña, A Coruña, Spain
e-mail: oscar.vergara@udc.es

© The Author(s) 2024

J.-A. Seoane and O. Vergara (eds.), *The Discourse of Biorights*, The International Library of Bioethics 109, https://doi.org/10.1007/978-3-031-66804-3_12

be said. There are several reasons for this. First, this practice can be approached from multiple viewpoints. Second, the GS debate is continuously being enhanced through new opinions and contributions both from individuals and institutions. Third, the lack of universal consensus on its moral validity or invalidity renders this continuing dialogue worthwhile. Finally, its legal treatment is far from permanent given that legislative, judicial or administrative acts are constantly being created, entailing amendments to the different legal systems that constitute international legal order. These acts then influence each other in the way of a kind of soft law.

It has been said that the discourse around new rights is situated within a context of linguistic relativization which obeys the performative role of those pressure groups whose aim is to institutionalize them (Ollero 2012, p. 59). This has been particularly evident with regard to GS (Jouve 2017, p. 154; Serrano 2017, p. 220; Sabaté 2017, pp. 1367, 1379; Puleo 2017, pp. 165, 168; Balaguer 2017, pp. 75, 191). If this is the case, we believe that the narrative approach adopted here can serve to shed some new light on the matter. However, first of all, the most imperative point of all those relating to the institutionalization of GS needs to be addressed. That this purported right already exists prior to the law, which would mean that failing to recognize it would be unjust.

In 2019, in Spain, the political party Citizens (*Ciudadanos)* presented a draft law to legalize and regulate GS (hereinafter DLCit). At this moment in time, the initiative has expired given that the term of office during which it was presented has also come to an end, but there is no reason why the initiative could not be presented again in the future.

12.1 GS as a Prior Right

For J.A. Robertson, one of the first authors to defend GS academically, procreative autonomy includes the right to what is termed "collaborative reproduction". That is to say, to solicit the assistance of third parties through human Assisted Reproductive Technology (ART). In his view, it is a fundamental right which cannot consequently be unduly restricted by the State. It can only be regulated for the purpose of reconciling diverse interests. The mere existence of risk does not justify its comprehensive prohibition, given that these risks are not exclusive to this form of reproduction (Robertson 1983, pp. 32–33).

Alexy (2000) identifies five features a claim must fulfill in order to be considered a human right which must be recognized institutionally by the State: universality, moral validity, fundamentality, priority and abstraction. However, not one can be validated in the case of GS.

(a) *Universality* refers to the fact that we are dealing with rights that apply to all human beings, without limit or exception (Alexy 2000, p. 24). They are rights for all against all. However, it is evident that this alleged right to GS is not possessed by virtue of a universal condition, but it is fully contingent, as is the gestation contract. In this case, they are rights for some against some others.

(b) *Moral validity* means that human rights are moral rights, the implication being that they are based on a moral norm which can be substantiated with regard to all that is involved in rational reasoning (Alexy 2000, p. 26). In other words, an illusion, a decision or an ideology cannot be institutionalized. According to Alexy, the following are able to be morally substantiated: (1) rights of the liberal tradition; (2) protective rights; (3) political rights; (4) social rights; (5) procedural rights. GS could be considered to be included in (1) and (4) but Alexy is referring to, in the first case, negative rights which involve the abstention of others, and in the second case, to rights which protect minimum subsistence. But GS requires the services of a third party (the surrogate mother) and it has nothing to do with minimum subsistence. Indeed, procreating with the assistance of a third party is a rather high aspiration.

(c) *Fundamentality* makes reference to the fact that human rights protect fundamental interests and needs (Alexy 2000, p. 28). According to Alexy, an interest or need is fundamental when its violation or non-satisfaction lead either to death or to a serious health condition, or else if the core of autonomy is affected. Evidently, not allowing GS only affects a concrete manifestation of the possible content of autonomy, but not autonomy as such, given that the subject is still free to pact any other content that is not against the law, morality or public order. The easier it is to justify a right, the more fundamental it is, such as the right to life. This is not the case, however, in the highly controversial GS. Moreover, and as explained further on, from the perspective of the surrogate mother, her autonomy can even be compromised in certain circumstances.

(d) *Priority* as regards positive law means that compliance with human rights is a necessary condition of the legitimacy of positive law. Thus, if this law violates human rights, its content becomes invalid and in the most serious cases, it can even lose its legal status (Alexy 2000, pp. 29–30). It does not seem possible to claim that a positive law which does not admit GS should be an invalid law, as has been sustained by the European Court of Human Rights (ECHR) in the cases of Mennesson v. France (n.° 65,192/11) and Labassee v. France (n.° 65,941/11), settled concurrently in the ruling of 26 June 2014, and in the case of Paradiso and Campanelli v. Italy (25,358/12), in its rulings of 24 January 2017 (Grand Chamber) and 27 January 2015 (2nd Section), by explicitly accepting the discretion of the States.

(e) *Abstraction* is the fifth property of human rights and it makes reference to the recipients, the modality and the restriction of the right. GS, however, is an extremely specific right, in all cases: for the recipient (the surrogate mother); for the modality (a specific service, bearing a child for a third party); and for the restriction (perfectly defined in its content). As Susi (2020) points out, the element of abstraction (and this also applies to the element of universality) decreases in the claim of each new human right, up to the point in which a demand, because of its low level of abstraction (or universality) ceases to be a human right.

In line with this conclusion, the International Conference on Population and Development held in Cairo from 5 to 13 September 1994 makes no reference to GS in the whole chapter of its report dedicated to "reproductive rights". The IV United Nations Conference on Women held in Beijing from 4 to 15 September 1995 and focusing on the "empowerment" of women from the perspective of "gender equality" do not seem to refer to GS either. Article 95 of the Beijing Declaration and Platform for Action, agreed at this conference, declares that "the human rights of women include the right to take control of and decide freely and responsibly about their sexual health, which includes their sexual and reproductive health". The problem with GS is that it involves having control over the sexual and reproductive health of a third party.

Finally, the European Parliament, in its resolution of 17 December 2015 on the annual report on human rights and democracy in the world (2014) and the European Union policy [2015/2229(INI)] make the following declaration asserting that GS is contrary to the dignity of women "given that their bodies and their reproductive functions are used as a commodity". They thus advocate the prohibition of this practice, which particularly affects vulnerable women in developing countries whose reproductive functions are exploited, whereby "a request is made to review this prohibition as a matter of urgency within the framework of the instruments of human rights".

12.2 A Principlist Approach to the Problem

In view of the observations of the previous section, there is nothing to indicate that we are dealing with a prior right which must consequently be institutionalized. However, neither does this mean that it should not be institutionalized if it can be demonstrated that GS is not ethically wrong in any of its forms. In order to evaluate this question, the two most relevant methodologies in biomedical ethics will be considered, principlism (in this section) and casuistry (Sect. 12.3). If the results are inconclusive, a narrative approach will be examined (Sect. 12.4).

12.2.1 Applicability of the Principles to GS. Difficulties

R. Ber indicates that with GS, not only do doctors have to attend to the strictly medical and psychological aspects, but they also have to bear in mind the fulfillment of the four basic principles of autonomy, beneficence, non-maleficence and justice (Ber 2000, p. 154). As is generally known, the principlist approach (its main exponents are Beauchamp and Childress) is in fact based on the formulation of the four aforementioned general principles. In medical practice, there is a broad consensus around these principles which form part of its common morality (Beauchamp and Childress 2019).

GS is not referenced by these authors in their prominent book and it is true that reaching any kind of unequivocal conclusion about the moral validity of GS is no easy task taking their work as a basis, mainly for the following reasons.

(1st) The principles are based on medical praxis and not on a single theory and so they tend to conflict. This would also appear to be the case for GS (Morales 2019, p. 453). In favor, the principles of autonomy (there is a free pact) and beneficence (all of the parties supposedly benefit from this type of contract in the end) may be relied upon. However, these principles conflict with those of non-maleficence (the risks associated with ART, the breaking of the bond between the surrogate mother and the new-born, among others) and justice (the surrogate mother is used as a commodity and these women are generally from a background of limited social and financial resources). Establishing which principle takes precedence is a matter of values, which boils down to deep moral convictions that are beyond the scope of the principles.

(2nd) As Ber states (2000), the functionality of the principles is complicated by the many legal relationships which are affected by this practice and are compatible with the conflict of interests. First of all, there are at least two mothers (the surrogate mother and the intended mother), and there can even be a third, the genetic mother when she is neither of the previous two. Secondly, the genetic mother's attending physician does not normally need to be (and perhaps should not be) the same person as the surrogate mother's attending physician. Finally, the biological father will not necessarily be the intended father. All in all, this means that there can be up to 5 parents involved in GS. This concurrence of parents begs the question of whether doctors who apply ART to the surrogate mother are beneficent to the same extent with her or whether they are especially beneficent with the intended parents (by proxy). Is the autonomy of the surrogate mother, usually a woman of limited resources, respected or is the autonomy of the (usually affluent) intended parents respected? Is it just with the surrogate mother when taking a baby she has carried or is it just with the intended parents when handing over the baby, especially when the surrogate mother regrets her decision? Finally, is it proportionate or not to compromise the health of the surrogate mother in order to satisfy the desire of the intended parents?

(3rd) The principles are abstract and they need defining. For this purpose, Beauchamp and Childress, following Richardson, make use of what the latter terms specification. This basically consists of restricting the scope of the principles through clauses which establish the what, the where, the when, the why and the how, by which means, by whom and for whom (Richardson 1990, p. 295). For Beauchamp and Childress, specification is the procedure through which the vagueness of the principles is reduced and through which more specific content can be created to be able to guide action (Beauchamp and Childress 2019, p. 17).

12.2.2 The Specification of Principles. Difficulties

(a) Let us first examine *the principle of autonomy*. As regards the informed consent of the surrogate mother, the question arises as to the extent to which she can be informed to be able to give her consent to bear a child without knowing what her feelings will be when the baby is born. This could be overcome by specifying the principle of autonomy in such a way that the woman's consent can only be considered valid if she has previously given birth, as provided for in DLCit, for instance.

However, another problem arises which is more difficult to resolve. Even if the surrogate mother is well informed, the next issue is the extent to which a woman is free when she is generally in a situation of poverty or marginalization, as exposed in the aforementioned report from the European Parliament. In order to avoid this situation, would it be possible to specify the principle in such a way that the consent be valid *provided that the act is an altruistic one*? This is the case in UK law and in the aforementioned DLCit, to give but two examples. Nevertheless, the doubt would remain as to whether this would truly guarantee respect for the dignity of the surrogate mother. This is a key point, as it is evident that nobody who upholds the moral validity of GS will at the same time concede that this practice undermines the dignity of women, given that it would be inconsistent with all that moral argumentation represents. Forming an opinion on the basis of the principle of autonomy demands this fundamental assessment which principlism as such is unable to resolve.

(b) *The principle of non-maleficence* is also compromised from the perspective of the surrogate mother. The physical and psychological risks of pregnancy are evident and even if the pregnancy runs smoothly, the surrogate mother is likely to be affected in some way, even if it is only for the breaking of the bond established between her and the foetus. Viewed from this perspective, commercial GS would be more easily admitted as it would provide monetary compensation for the detriment to the woman's health and it would empower poor women by providing them with resources (Purdy). It could also avoid the perpetuation of the traditional gender norms which conclude that a woman's natural destiny is to be a mother (Roach Anleu 1990). This specification conflicts with that of a). Furthermore, this specification would have to address the significant objection to the economic exploitation of women (Albert 2018; Nuño Gómez 2016; Puleo 2017), which brings us right back to the previous issue of dignity.

(c) As regards *the principle of beneficence*, there is a contract from which everybody supposedly benefits: the intended parents, the ART clinic, the GS agency and the surrogate mother. The surrogate mother? There is indeed financial gain in the case of commercial GS, when it is permitted, but this modality of GS is debatable, as has just been pointed out in (a) and (b). As far as altruistic GS is concerned, the benefit to the surrogate mother consists of *being allowed to do the intended parents a favor*. This benefit seems somewhat paradoxical, especially when the law prohibits this practice within the family circle (as proposed in DLCit). As noted by M.Albert, this is why the DLCit has euphemistically converted the (contractual) duty of the surrogate mother into her *right*, given that the aforementioned draft law introduces an article denominated "rights of women" in which the "right" of the surrogate mother is proclaimed to carry to term and give birth to the child of the intended parents … (Albert 2018, pp. 119–120). However, it is still striking that precisely the most vulnerable party assumes the role of benefactor and the stronger party assumes the role of beneficiary (Albert 2018, p. 129). Ultimately, it does not seem realistic to claim that the surrogate mother benefits from this type of agreement, which leads us back to the matter of the legality or illegality of commercial GS, which in turn leads us back to the dignity of women.

One rather original specification in which it is claimed that all parties genuinely benefit is that of a proposal by R. Ber to use women in a chronic vegetative state as surrogate mothers (their consent would be sought via the same document used for organ donation). In this way, according to Ber, the four principles of autonomy, beneficence, non-maleficence and justice would be reconciled. As the proverb goes, cited by the author herself, "gain for one, loss for none" (Ber 2000, pp. 164–165).

(d) Finally, from the perspective of *the principle of justice*, GS a priori allows for a balanced distribution of resources in the sense that a woman who is able to bear children but does not want to can provide for a woman who wants to be a mother but is unable to conceive or carry her own child due to medical reasons. If this principle is to be specified, it must be assured that the two parties are in a situation of equality, which is why the demand is generally for altruistic GS, and that the process should not involve family members. However, the issue of the dignity of women once again needs to be resolved.

Ultimately, principlism would not appear to possess the necessary resources to decide on the underlying question. That is, it helps to regulate GS in such a way that none of the four principles on which it is based are directly affected. However, it does not contribute to the decision on whether or not GS should be comprehensively institutionalized. It is perfectly consistent with either the validity or the lack of validity of GS in much the same way as it is perfectly consistent with the validity or the lack of validity of euthanasia (Beauchamp and Childress 2019, p. 192).

12.3 A Casuistic Approach to the Issue

Jonsen and Toulmin (1988) are renowned for being the main exponents of casuistic methodology. Despite being considered an alternative method, casuistry is in fact an essential complement to principlism, because it is not possible to specify principles (determine the how, the when, etc.) unless it is done on the basis of cases (Vergara 2016, pp. 66–68). This decision-making system functions by establishing analogies between the case to be resolved and a paradigmatic case with a clear resolution. Jonsen has gathered the different elements of casuistic reasoning into three main categories, which he terms: morphology, taxonomy and kinetics (Jonsen 1991, pp. 295–307). There is no room to develop these elements here but a very brief summary of the procedure of casuistic analysis can be given. It consists firstly of describing all the relevant factual and legal elements of a case (all of the aforementioned statements on the subject of GS can serve as a basis for the purpose of the following remarks). Secondly, classifying them in the light of a paradigmatic case (it is essential to find a comparable case with a clear resolution). Thirdly, similarities and discrepancies are prudently determined in order to decide whether to apply a similar solution in relation to the degree of analogy. An examination of the different proposed taxonomies can be found below.

(a) GS is comparable to *adoption*. This is strictly the case when the intended parents or at least one of them draws upon legal procedure in accordance with provisions contained in the national legislations which authorize this alternative. However, GS as such presents a fundamental difference. On the one hand, adoption seeks the optimum solution for children who already exist, either because they have been born or at least conceived. On the other hand, the aim of GS is, as Ber states, to "plan a 'potential' child, creating a baby (as if it were a good) in an unconventional environment in which it is unclear who the real mother is" (Ber 2000, p. 162). The same could be said about the institution of family placement which aims to protect minors who are deprived of parental care. GS results in the creation of children who, if they find themselves deprived of parental care, it is due to the misconduct of parents who try to circumvent the national law that applies to them.
(b) GS is comparable to *organ donation by living donors* insofar as, when no money changes hands, both actions are outstanding demonstrations of solidarity. However, as V. Bellver has highlighted, there is no substantiated similarity between them which might require the same ethical assessment or equal legal treatment. In fact, there are six differentiating factors (Bellver 2017, pp. 235–236). First, the significant and lasting psychological and physical impact a baby has on the birth mother during pregnancy. Second, unlike donation, which is an isolated act, pregnancy is a nine-month process which requires the woman's complete involvement. Third, unlike donation, there is a latent conflict of interests between the intended parents who would like to control the pregnancy and the surrogate mother who would like to maintain the control of her own life. Fourth, while donation has no impact on third parties, the end result of GS is the birth of a new human life. In the case of altruistic GS, at least within a family circle or group of friends a dual relationship will be created, both biological and legal. Fifth, despite the broad consensus around the (positive) ethical assessment of donation as an altruistic act, there is considerable controversy around the ethical assessment of GS, which is perceived by many as an alienation of women. Sixth, the reason for donating an organ is to save the recipient's life or to radically improve their quality of life. The purpose of GS is to provide a child.
(c) It has been said that commercial GS is akin to *prostitution*, given that "access to the woman's body is gained by means of money" (Puleo 2017, p. 177; Balaguer 2017, pp. 176–177, 183, 190, 204). However, clearly the means of access are entirely different. One is sexual, the simple aim of which is organic pleasure.

The other is clinical, via ART, the aim of which is to provide a child to those for whom procreation is medically impossible. As L.M. Purdy says, prostitution is sex without procreation while GS is procreation without sex. For this reason, she considers this comparison to be more to do with emotional reasoning (Purdy 2017, p. 189).

(d) Analogies have also been established with other lucrative businesses, such as the following: *neocolonial extraction* of resources from poorer countries, given that surrogate mothers generally originate from the developing world (Puleo 2017, p. 180); *the buying and selling of organs*, in the sense that only persons with limited resources would appear to be willing to sell an organ (SBC 2017, p. 25); *the buying and selling of children*, insofar as a child can be procured for anyone that wants one in exchange for money (SBC 2017, p. 40); and *the use of women's bodies in advertising* (Balaguer 2017, pp. 176–177). Nevertheless, all of these comparisons are invalid in the case of altruistic GS. It can also be argued that the child brought into the world by a surrogate mother is not as a rule her child, at least from a genetic perspective, although this argument is rather debatable.

On balance, the arguments that can be presented in order to compare GS with other practices or organizations are not definitive, whether they be to claim its validity or for the purposes of moral censure. For this reason, the casuistic approach does not yield any decisive conclusions either.

12.4 The Narrative Approach

It is a good idea to begin by recognizing that it is not very clear what is actually meant by adopting a narrative approach, an element which distinguishes it from the previous, well demonstrated methodologies. Brody has this to say on the subject: those who represent narrative ethics "have divergent and unclear ideas as to just what the term (narrative) means and precisely how one does ethics with a narrative focus or a narrative turn" (Brody 2003, p. 174). According to Brody, narrative is not only a necessary complement to be refined in the application of principles, but it is also at the origin of the shaping of these principles. However, for historical reasons, narrative was marginalized with the shift to Modernity although there are precedents (to this marginalization) in Plato's approach. In contrast, the Aristotelian approach which aims to establish what it means to live a good life in the real world is open to a narrative analysis (Brody 2003, p. 188; Vergara, 2018).

In *Poetics*, Aristotle wrote that tragedy must include six elements: plot, character, thought, diction, music and spectacle (Aristotle 2011, 1450a). The first four of the six are general to any piece of narrative. What follows is an examination of these four elements in an attempt to establish whether any of them can shed new light on the subject under debate.

12.4.1 Language

As far as diction (λέξις) is concerned, significantly loaded rhetoric can be detected in the choice of language made by supporters and opponents of GS alike. Bear in mind expressions such as "wombs with legs", "ambulatory chalices", both of which make effective use of language. As stated by M. Albert on the subject of GS, terminology is far from neutral (Albert 2017, p. 178).

Jouve (2017, p. 154) reveals that there is a certain amount of abuse of language and a tendency to use euphemisms in an attempt to conceal the true meaning of the facts. This is evident in the following expressions: "wombs for hire", when in fact the entire person is hired and not just the womb; "maternity by substitution", because maternity is not substitutable, be it from a genetic or a biological perspective; or "gestational surrogacy", since motherhood goes beyond carrying a child and giving birth. For Serrano (2017, p. 220), in the bioethics debate and particularly in the context of GS, the use of "newspeak" has expanded in earnest alongside its correlative "neo-right" which Orwell describes in his famous novel *1984*. The purpose, according to Serrano, is to manipulate and prevent clear thinking and two conditions are exploited to great effect: sophistication and the avoidance of moral judgment. The aforementioned example is particularly striking in which M. Albert points out that DLCit transforms the onerous task of the surrogate mother into the "right to carry to term and give birth to the intended parents' child". For Balaguer, as regards GS, semantics is far from innocent as each denomination obeys an ideological undertone. In this sense, bear in mind that liberal discourse indeed prefers to speak of "gestation" and not "maternity" because a commercial difference is established between woman and uterus (Balaguer 2017, pp. 75, 191). Sabaté and Puleo speak along the same lines when they criticize the liberal language that conceals a practice which in fact goes against liberty and equality (Sabaté 2017, pp. 1367, 1379; Puleo 2017, pp. 165, 168).

This is obviously not to imply that linguistic resources are exclusively available to one side or the other of the GS debate because language can be loaded to appeal to either side. For instance, when terms such as "exploitation", "slavery", "buying children" or "women farms" are used by detractors (Serrano 2017, p. 224). This is also the case with the movement "we are not vessels"[1] which proclaims itself against the use of euphemisms but at the same time uses the term "vessel" which is a word loaded with rhetoric, also employed by other authors (Pateman 1995, p. 294; Puleo 2017, p. 172). Finally, the terms "reproduction farms" and "incubator" (Jouve 2017, p. 160) or "prostitution" (Pateman 1995, p. 295; Puleo 2017, p. 177) have been used.

12.4.2 Plot

For Aristotle, the plot or the storyline (μῦθος) is the most important element of tragedy and he considers it the purpose (Aristotle 2011, 1450a). Similarly to the previous ones, this element is to some extent of a formal nature. Chambers and

Montgomery state that there is no story without a plot. Each narrator adjusts the story to tell the narrative. However, they also affirm that the plot cannot be dissociated from opinion. Even if the narrator makes every effort to be objective, the fact remains that "in the very act of telling, (the narrator) is persuading listeners to take a particular position (the next element to be dealt with is thought), by shaping the telling of the events in a particular way" (Chambers and Montgomery 2002, pp. 79–80). In their view, plot is a rhetorical construction.

As such, a good story can sway hearts in favour of GS or turn hearts against it. For instance, the Spanish Association for Gestational Surrogacy included on its website the moving testimony of Marta, 31, wife of Antonio. In the first part, Marta explained how she lost the child she was expecting as a result of a series of medical errors which culminated in a hysterectomy leaving her incapable of bearing children. Inevitably, the case sparked the reader's empathy which avoided Marta the need to give any more details of the suffering she and her family endured. Having connected with the reader's emotions, Marta admited that for her it was very important that a citizens' legislative initiative should be launched in favor of GS. [2]

On the other hand, narratives which effectively raise antagonistic feelings against the practice of GS can also be found. By way of example, when the political party Citizens (*Ciudadanos*) launched its DLCit in 2017 (a pre-2019 attempt), a debate took place in the *El País* newspaper between professors M. Atienza and O. Salazar. The first stood in support of GS and the second rejected it. Atienza based his defense on three main points: that GS is not *in sensu stricto* forbidden, it is simply invalid; the woman is not used *merely* as a resource; and not acting in a supererogatory way is not the equivalent to bad moral behavior (Atienza 2017). He had previously expressed these views in a legal forum (Atienza 2015). A fortnight later, O. Salazar contributed another article in response which began as follows: "… I fear that he (Atienza) has not read the splendid novel *The Handmaid's Tale* by Margaret Atwood nor has he seen a single episode of the television adaptation (…)" (Salazar 2017a). Salazar goes on to complete his literary review, invoking the dignity of women and criticizing their secular submission to men, contentions that he develops in an article published around the same time in a legal journal (Salazar 2017b).

Salazar begins this article with the following quote from the aforementioned novel: "I resign my body freely, to the uses of others. They can do what they like with me. I am abject. I feel, for the first time, their true power" (Salazar 2017b, p. 79). *The Handmaid's Tale* is a work of science fiction which tells the story of how after a series of terrorist attacks, the USA becomes a theonomy called Gilead which creates a society model in which some women, the maids, are forced to conceive for and hand over their babies to their owners, the Commanders and their wives. Following Salazar's recommendation, I read the novel and although it did not have the suggested impact on me (the story is rather far-fetched), the truth is that this work has become an international bestseller, received a number of literary awards and subsequently been adapted not only to television (the series won several Emmy awards) but also to the cinema, the theatre and the radio (the BBC created a dramatized version). It is more than likely then that thanks to or because of this work of fiction, many readers, listeners or spectators of one or other of the versions have had their suspicions aroused about some or all of the forms of GS.

12.4.3 Thought

After plot, thought (διάνοια) is the next of Aristotle's significant elements. The Stagirite affirms that thought consists of having something meaningful and relevant to say. The following line from Atwood's novel seems interesting here, again spoken by the main character: "We are two-legged wombs, that's all: Sacred vessels, ambulatory chalices" (Atwood 2017, p. 196), which expresses the idea of the commodification of women, which through a small exercise of abstraction, leads us to the concept of human dignity. As far as Marta and Antonio's story is concerned, Marta states after describing the dramatic case: "The rest of the story, my family's suffering, my subsequent suffering, it goes without saying, you can just imagine it". There is a call for solidarity behind this line and since readers have empathized with their story to one extent or another they are invited to support the legislative initiative to regulate GS.

Certainly, the very fact that there are stories whose rhetoric or plot provokes pro-GS or anti-GS feelings indicates the existence of background reasons which justify either of the two options. Hence, academic debate revolves around this aspect and tends to avoid the other elements. Some of the reflections that a story could embody are the following: on the one hand, GS could constitute a (new) means for men to subordinate women (Pateman 1995, pp. 288–299); a commodification of children and the reproductive capabilities of women (Anderson 1990); a practice which violates the dignity of women and their right to integrity (Marrades 2017, pp. 220 ff.; Jouve 2018, pp. 19-20). On the other hand, GS could be a practice which, in specific circumstances, "empowers women" (Purdy 2007, p. 197); is a result of social evolution (Belinchón 2019, p. 191; Farnós 2019, p. 127); is a result of the procreative autonomy of women (Robertson 1983, p. 32; Farnós 2019, p. 137); in the altruistic sense, it can take place in an environment of trust (Beier 2015); or in the commercial sense, it allows women to overcome the traditional gender norms (Roach Anleu 1990).

Thus, both the use of language and the shaping of the plot are functions of the thought behind the story. The debate around thought takes us away from the narrative approach and leads us to the rational debate. Does this mean that the narrative approach has nothing to contribute to this debate, rendering it redundant? We cannot agree with this. It would be like throwing out the baby with the bathwater. A consideration of the fourth element will help us to grasp the specific contribution of the narrative approach.

12.4.4 Characters (Ἤθη)

Aristotle states that tragedy is the imitation of an action and for the sake of action, it generally imitates the persons who perform the acts as well (Aristotle 2011, 1450b). A little further on, he affirms that the character (*ἦθος*) is the one to reveal choice. This is why it is essential that narrative defines its characters. The moral judgment of their actions will depend not so much on the actions in themselves but more on the moral character that has prompted them. For this reason, supporters of GS construe this practice as one which responds to the altruism of the surrogate mother and the solidarity of society as a whole. The intended parents (Atwood's commanders) provide, if anything, the desire to become parents.

The justifying virtuality of this element is greater than in the case of language and plot, which are to some extent formal elements. Even if the rational debate is clearly not replaced, it is enriched with an enlightening new perspective in the same way that the parable of the good Samaritan is particularly illuminating with regard to the principle (a principle is a specific type of reason) that prescribes love thy neighbor. In this perspective, this principle is not about following rules, but about *being* a certain way. So, the decisive factor in Aristotle's ethics is not so much specific action but the *moral character*, which reveals an individual's core of moral truth and governes his/her acts.

For the Stagirite, a good act is a prudent act performed by a prudent individual (φρόνιμος) (Aristotle 2012, VI, 5, 1140a23–24). He also observes that the prudent individual is capable of adequate deliberation (καλῶς βουλεύσασθαι) about what is good, not in a partial sense (for health for instance) but to live a good life in general (1140a24–27). Individuals, however, can only deliberate adequately on the basis of virtue. It is noteworthy that the adverb καλῶς, asides from correctness, suggests the nuance of beauty, as the adjective καλός signifies, amongst other things, "beautiful", "noble", "honest" and "glorious". Therefore, a noble act, a good act is a beautiful act which is worthy of recognition.

In the rational debate on GS, the altruistic argument appears as one more reason in the set of arguments or reasons which contribute to sustaining the pretence of the moral validity of GS. However, when altruism is brought into play or substantiated in the form of narrative, the result is unsatisfactory.

Iolanda Anglés describes her personal experience of GS in her book *Gestational Surrogacy: A Glint of Hope*. Iolanda suffers from endometriosis which causes her infertility and when she resorts to in vitro fertilization, this option also turns out to be unviable. Throughout her book, she tells of the multiple tribulations she has been through until finally, a Californian woman accepts to carry a child for her and her partner using gametes from anonymous donors. Her story is one of hope as the couple overcomes adversity to fulfil their "dream". The book conveys this sense of hope all the way through, though there is no lack of heartbreak. She writes "It was really tough having to live forsaking such a visceral desire" (Anglés 2017, p. 73). In the face of such drama, any reader with a modicum of sensitivity can empathize with the author. However, the difficulty lies in plausibly characterizing the altruism of any of the parts of the contract. Iolanda writes: “For me, it was an incredible gesture which honored those women (…). There had to be an element of altruism” (Anglés 2017, p. 45). Further on, she states: “I came to the conclusion that it was more a case of altruism than of financial greed” (p. 105). As we can see, Iolanda writes, “there had to be”, “I came to the conclusion” ….: the altruism is assumed in the story as a presumption rather than something that was actually experienced and therefore suitable for storytelling.

The account of the personal misfortune of the main character allows us to clearly comprehend the drama of the situation and to empathize with her pain. On the contrary, the part of the story which describes the process of GS does not arouse such sympathies, nor does the altruism shine through, nor does it appear as beautiful as might be expected of such a virtuous story. This is not only because the surrogate mother is paid for her services but also because Iolanda herself frankly admits that the risks taken by the surrogate mother are wholly unacceptable. Her life is at risk, she acknowledges. She must undergo hyper stimulation of the ovaries, pregnancy and childbirth, which in this case, to make matters worse, is by Caesarean: “Irene was getting her stitches and I couldn’t help watching. It looked like they were mending a mattress” (p. 144). The author herself makes it clear that “what this girl was doing for us had more value for me than any amount of money in the world” (p. 124). Furthermore, she affirms that what the girl was doing, she herself the intended parent “would not have done, not even for all the money in the world” (p. 45). Further on, she says “So, would it not now be moral prejudices which would prevent me from becoming a mother” (p. 46).

The aim of this book is to vindicate the story behind GS, invoking the altruism storyline. However, this altruism does not succeed in transitioning from the realm of ideas to an embodiment by the specific characters involved in the story. When participating in a rational debate, if an argument is weak, another can be drawn upon, then another and then another until support can be provided for the position to a greater or a lesser extent. In narrative, telling one story after another has no sense or it would be an indication that the stories were not going anywhere. From a technical perspective, the language or the plot might be deficient and from an ethical perspective, the thought and the characterization. But it is characterization which is decisive to the story, and it is also especially illuminating for the rational debate.

Similarly, R. Westoby, in his book *Our Journey: One’s Couple’s Guide to U.S. Surrogacy* (2013), in which he describes the entire process that he and his partner, another gay man, had to go through to obtain their twins through GS, cannot avoid, despite the delicate sensitivity shown in many of his decisions regarding the pregnant woman, that she is perceived throughout the book as an instrument through which to satisfy their desire to become parents. For example, they draw a highly positive picture of her, highlighting the amazing and selflessness of her, but always in line with her ability and her efforts to carry out her service (pp. 25, 63, 89). It is not a minor detail that the surrogate woman (whom the author usually avoids calling mother) is an immigrant from the Philippines who has had to work hard to get ahead and raise her two children, whom she wants to give a good education, which is the very reason why she undergoes GS (p. 25).

For Westoby and his partner, the surrogate woman is after all an "oven" in which the egg of a carefully chosen donor and fertilized with their sperm is simply placed in order to "cook" it. In fact, they claim that they referred to her as their "Tummy Mummy," as the author also calls her in the text (pp. 8, 23, 59). In contrast, they seem to value more the contribution of the egg donor, with whom they have been in annual contact since the birth of the twins, just in case the latter ever want to know their genetic origins or there is a medical reason that makes it advisable to turn to her.

In short, characterization should not be achieved by means of a label, as might be the case when the surrogate mother is described as altruistic (this is one contention among others which, besides, needs to be proven). An individual is characterized through a chronicled series of acts, or in other words, a narrative. Narrative can sustain all manner of ideas, linguistic resources and storylines, but no matter how successfully these are employed, its impact will depend to a great extent on the concrete deeds which reflect the virtue (or lack of virtue) of the characters. GS does not appear to be a practice in which virtuous acts can be easily found.

Notes

1. http://nosomosvasijas.eu/ (we are not vessels) Last Access July. 17th 2024.
2. The website is no longer available, but the case has been reported, among other sites, in https://www.lavanguardia.com/vida/20140411/54404943370/la-gestacion-subrogada-una-necesidad-y-no-un-capricho-segun-sus-promotores.html Last Access July 17th 2024.

References

Albert, M. 2017. La explotación reproductiva de mujeres y el mito de la subrogación altruista: una mirada global al fenómeno de la gestación por sustitución (The reproductive exploitation of women and the myth of altruistic surrogacy: a global look at the phenomenon of gestation by substitution). *Cuadernos de Bioética* XVIII: 11–197.

Albert, M. 2018. La maternidad altruista y la maternidad subrogada (Altruistic maternity and surrogate pregnancy). In *La maternidad subrogada. Qué es y cuáles son sus consecuencias (Surrogate pregnancy. What are the consequences?*, ed. N. Jouve de la Barreda, 114–145. Madrid: Sekotia.

Anderson, E.S. 1990. Is women's labor a commodity? *Philosophy and Public Affairs* 19 (1): 71–92.

Alexy, R. 2000. La institucionalización de los derechos humanos en el Estado constitucional democrático (The institutionalization of human rights in the democratic constitutional State). *Derechos y Libertades (rights and Freedoms)* 8: 21–41.

Anglès, I. 2017. *Gestación subrogada, una estela de esperanza (Gestational Surrogacy: A Glint of Hope).* Wroklaw: Amazon Fulfillment.

Aristotle. 2011. *Poética (Poetics)*, 1778. Madrid: Bilingual version (Greek-Spanish) by Alonso Ordóñez das Seijas.

Aristotle. 1994. *Ética a Nicómaco (Nicomachean Ethics).* Bilingual edition (Greek-Spanish) by J. J. Marías. Madrid: CEPC.

Atienza, M. 2017. La gestación por sustitución (Gestation by Substitution). *El País*, 4 May 2017.

Atienza, M. 2015. Gestación por sustitución y prejuicios ideológicos (Gestation by substitution and ideological prejudice). *Notario del Siglo XXI – Revista* 63. https://www.elnotario.es/hemeroteca/revista-63/5373-gestacion-por-sustitucion-y-prejuicios-ideologicos Accesed, 5 Jul 2023.
Atwood, M. 2017. *El cuento de la criada (The Handmaid's Tale).* Barcelona: Salamandra.
Balaguer, M.L. 2017. *Hijos del mercado. La maternidad subrogada en un Estado social (Buying children. Surrogate pregnancy in a social state).* Madrid: Eds. Cátedra.
Beauchamp, T.L., and J.F. Childress. 2019. *Principles of Biomedical Ethics*, 8th ed. New York: Oxford University Press.
Beier, K. 2015. Surrogate motherhood: a trust-based approach. *Journal of Medicine and Philosophy* 40: 633–652.
Belinchón Romo, M.R. 2019. Gestación subrogada: especial referencia a la situación y a la voluntad de la mujer para prestar el consentimiento en el contrato de gestar para otro (Gestational surrogacy: a special reference to the situation and the will of women to agree to a contract to gestate for a third party). In *Gestación subrogada: principales cuestiones civiles, penales, registrales y médicas: su evolución y consideración (Gestational surrogacy: the main civil, penal, registration and medical issues: evolution and consideration) (1988–2019),* dirs. F. Lledó et alii, 167–193. Madrid: Dykinson.
Bellver, V. 2017. Tomarse en serio la maternidad subrogada altruista (Taking altruistic surrogate pregnancy seriously). *Cuadernos de Bioética* XXVIII: 229–243.
Ber, R. 2000. Ethical issues in gestational surrogacy. *Theoretical Medicine and Bioethics* 21: 153–169.
Brody, H. 2003. What Is narrative ethics? In *Stories of sickness*, 2nd ed., ed. H. Brody, 172–192. New York: Oxford University Press.
Chambers, T. and Hunter, K.M. 2002. Plot: Framing contingency and choice in bioethics. In *Stories matter. The role of narrative in medical ethics,* eds. R. Charon, and M. Montello, 77–84. New York: Routledge.
Farnós Amorós, E. 2019. Los acuerdos de gestación por sustitución: análisis a partir de una propuesta de regulación (Gestation by substitution agreements: ananalysis on the basis of a proposal for regulation). In *La gestación por sustitución (Gestation by substitution),* ed. A. Lucas Esteve, 119–142. Valencia: Tirant lo Blanch.
Jhering, R. von. 1947. *La lucha por el derecho (The Struggle for Law).* Trans. A.G. Posada. Buenos Aires: Atalaya.
Jonsen, A.R. 1991. Casuistry as methodology in clinical ethics. *Theoretical Medicine* 12: 295–307.
Jonsen, A.R., and S. Toulmin. 1988. *The abuse of casuistry. A history of moral reasoning.* Berkeley: University of California Press.
Jouve de la Barreda, N. 2018. El significado de la maternidad y la familia (The meaning of maternity and family). In *La maternidad subrogada. Qué es y cuáles son sus consecuencias (Surrogate pregnancy. What are the consequences?),* coord. N. Jouve de la Barreda (coord.), 11–47. Madrid: Sekotia.
Jouve de la Barreda, N. 2017. Perspectivas médicas de la maternidad subrogada (Medical perspectives of gestational maternity). *Cuadernos de Bioética* XXVIII: 153–162.
Marrades, A. 2017. La gestación subrogada en el marco de la Constitución española: Una cuestión de derechos (Gestational surrogacy within the framework of the Spanish Constitution: A matter of rights). *Estudios De Deusto* 65: 219–241.
Morales Benito, I. 2019. Gestación por sustitución y principialismo en bioética (Gestation by substitution and priciplism in bioethics. In *La gestación por sustitución (Gestation by substitution),* ed. A. Lucas Esteve, 445–466. Valencia: Tirant lo Blanch.
Nuño Gómez, L. 2016. Una nueva cláusula del Contrato Sexual: Vientres de alquiler (A new clause in the sexual contract: Wombs for hire). *Isegoría* 55: 683–700.
Ollero, A. 2012. Los nuevos derechos (New Rights). *Persona y Derecho* 66: 49–62.
Pateman, C. 1995. *El contrato sexual (The sexual contract).* Trans. by M.L. Femenías. Barcelona: Anthropos.

Puleo, A.H. 2017. Nuevas formas de desigualdad en un mundo globalizado. El alquiler de úteros como extractivismo (New forms of inequality in a globalized world. The hiring of wombs as extractivism). *Revista Europea De Derechos Fundamentales (European Journal on Fundamental Rights)* 29: 165–184.
Purdy, L.M. 2007. Surrogate mothering: Exploitation or empowerment? In *Issues in feminist bioethics*, 182–197. Cornell University Press.
Richardson, H.S. 1990. Specifying norms as a way to resolve concrete ethical problems. *Philosophy and Public Affairs*: 279–310.
Roach Anleu, S.L. 1990. Reinforcing gender norms: Commercial and altruistic surrogacy. *Acta Sociologica* 33: 63–74.
Robertson, J.A. 1983. Surrogate mothers: Not so novel after all. *The Hastings Center Report* 13 (5): 28–34.
Sabaté, F. 2017. Maternidades confrontadas. El uso político del lenguaje en los discursos sobre la maternidad subrogada (Confronted maternities. The political use of language in the discourse on surrogate pregnancy). *Géneros. Multidisciplinary Journal for Gender Studies* 6/2: 1361–1384.
Salazar, O. 2017a. Cedo mi cuerpo libremente para que lo usen los demás. Pueden hacer conmigo lo que quieran (I resign my body freely, to the uses of others. They can do what they like with me). *El País*, 22 May 2017.
Salazar, O. 2017b. La gestación por sustitución desde una perspectiva jurídica: Algunas reflexiones sobre el conflicto entre deseos y derechos (Gestation by substitution from a legal perspective: Some reflections on the conflict between desires and rights). *Revista De Derecho Político* 99: 79–120.
Serrano, J.M. 2017. Manipulación del lenguaje, maternidad subrogada y altruismo (Manipulation of language, gestational surrogacy and altruism). *Cuadernos de Bioética* XXVIII: 219–228.
Spanish Bioethics Committee (SBC). 2017. *Informe sobre los aspectos éticos y jurídicos de la maternidad subrogada (Report on the ethical and legal aspects of surrogate pregnancy)*. Bilbao, 16 May.
Susi, M. 2020. Novelty in human rights. The decrease in universality and abstractness thesis. In *The Cambridge handbook of new human rights*, eds. A. von Arnauld, K. von der Decken; M. Susi, 21–33. Cambridge: Cambridge University Press.
Vergara, O. 2018. The dramatic essence of narrative approach. *Theoretical Medicine and Bioethics* 39: 361–374.
Vergara, O. 2016. Principlism and normative systems. In *Bioethical decision making and argumentation*, eds. P. Serna, and J.A. Seoane, 57–71. Dordrecht: Springer.
Westoby, R. 2013. *Our journey: One's couple's guide to U.S. surrogacy*. CreateSpace.

Open Access This chapter is licensed under the terms of the Creative Commons Attribution 4.0 International License (http://creativecommons.org/licenses/by/4.0/), which permits use, sharing, adaptation, distribution and reproduction in any medium or format, as long as you give appropriate credit to the original author(s) and the source, provide a link to the Creative Commons license and indicate if changes were made.

The images or other third party material in this chapter are included in the chapter's Creative Commons license, unless indicated otherwise in a credit line to the material. If material is not included in the chapter's Creative Commons license and your intended use is not permitted by statutory regulation or exceeds the permitted use, you will need to obtain permission directly from the copyright holder.

Chapter 13
Ritual Circumcisions of Minors: Civil and Criminal Perspectives in Spanish Law

Agustín Motilla

Abstract For some time now, a millenary ritual act in religions as widespread as Judaism and Islam: the circumcision of infants has been questioned. Today's greater sensibility to the human rights of minors and respect for the autonomy of will have opened a debate that is as interesting as it is controversial. This study analyses the circumcision of minors from two points of view: from the perspective of the limits of parental authority to act for the benefit of children and to respect their personality rights; and from the perspective of possible criminal liability, considering circumcision as a crime of genital mutilation or common injury. The study of Spanish legislation and jurisprudence is the starting point for the proposals, *de iure condendo*, on possible modifications of the legal system in order to intensify the protection of minors in Spain.

Keywords Circumcision · Minor · Right to physical integrity · Sexual mutilation · Parental guardianship

13.1 Introduction

The circumcision of minors for non-therapeutic reasons has become a subject of controversy in society and it has inevitably transcended to the field of law. Scientific doctrine and the jurisprudence of the courts are considering whether this practice, age-old in certain cultures and traditions, violates the rights of unemancipated minors, particularly their physical integrity and their ideological and religious freedom.

The fundamental rights and freedom of individuals has become a cornerstone of political and social order in pluralist democratic regimes. By the same token, the protection and welfare of minors is a constitutional obligation of public authorities. The deliberation and further study of the rights of individuals under parental authority

A. Motilla (✉)
Universidad Carlos III, Getafe, Spain
e-mail: agustinmotilla@gmail.com

© The Editor(s) (if applicable) and The Author(s), under exclusive license to Springer Nature Switzerland AG 2024

J.-A. Seoane and O. Vergara (eds.), *The Discourse of Biorights*, The International Library of Bioethics 109, https://doi.org/10.1007/978-3-031-66804-3_13

or guardianship in doctrine and jurisprudence has cast doubt on an act which is an age-old ritual in some cultures.

In this paper, the scope of the study will be limited to the significance of the circumcision of minors in two religious traditions: Judaism and Islamism. In particular, for the religion of the Jewish people, where, as we shall now see, this act constitutes a religious requirement core to belonging to Yahweh's chosen people.

The Old Testament (Genesis, 17, 9-14; Leviticus, 12, 3) orders ritual circumcision on the eighth day of a newborn son's life: using a sharp knife, a protective shield and an article to retain the foreskin. The ceremony, called *Brit Milah*, is performed by the *Mohel* (a religious specialist affiliated to the Synagogue) while the child is held in the godfather's lap (Felix Ballesta 2000, pp. 189-192; Borghi 2019, pp. 2-4; Licastro 2019, pp. 37-38). After this, he receives his Jewish name. This description conveys the importance of this act for Hebrews, prescribed by Mosaic Law. It is a symbol of the covenant between God and the chosen people, and an identifying sign of belonging to the faith of Israel, thus separating believers from Gentiles or the uncircumcised.

In Islam (López Sidro 2012, pp. 1 ss.; Torres Fernández 2014, pp. 160 ss.), circumcision of minors is not so much a religious requirement as a tradition of Arabic or pre-Islamic origin. It is not mentioned in the Koran, although it is recommended in some of the *haddí* of the Prophet as an act of purification (Alshboul 2012, p. 13). Hence, the schools of Islam are divided between those who consider it obligatory (in Sunnism, Hanbali, Shafii and with Shiite Muslims) and those who consider it to be only a recommendation. Be that as it may, circumcision is widely practiced in the Islamic community. There is no specific age for it to be performed. It is usually carried out from the boy's birth until he is seven or eight, and always before puberty.

This age-old practice in two of the most widespread and long-standing religious traditions has been condemned by some as brutal and cruel. Doubts, which are stated in international human rights texts and adopted by legislations of pluralist democratic States, exist over the compatibility of circumcision with the principle of safeguarding the interests of minors. This principle must prevail above the powers inherent in parental authority. All this has been brought to light in contemporary doctrine, thus opening a fascinating and controversial debate highlighting the confrontation of the inherent rights of minors and of parents or guardians with ideological and religious freedom.

Nowadays, the circumcision of minors is a matter of public interest where multiple fundamental rights come into play. Parental rights in the religious and moral upbringing of their children, minors' rights both to physical integrity and to ideological freedom and freedom of conscience. These rights need to be deliberated and well balanced, addressing the following issues: the powers inherent in parental authority and the significance given to the superior principle of safeguarding the interests of minors, where public authorities play an important role in the comprehensive protection of children. This, in turn, is conditioned by the medical assessment of this surgical procedure which naturally determines its performance by medical professionals and in the public hospital network. Then, the criminal transcendence of the act must be added to this kaleidoscope of conflicting factors, since our legislature introduced the crime of female genital mutilation in 2003 adding a subparagraph to Article 149 of the Penal Code.

We will try to organise this paper by first tackling the conflicting fundamental rights and notably, those linked to the exercise of parental authority and its limits, in conformity with the provisions in the Spanish Constitution, the Civil Code and legislation on the legal status of minors. Particular attention will be paid to the significance of the expression "the minor's best interests" in our jurisprudence, which is a key factor to clarifying the timing and mechanisms of public authority intervention. Secondly, we will go on to address the potential criminalisation of male circumcision as an act punishable under Article 149.2 of the Penal Code and to pay attention to the factual circumstances of cases settled by the Spanish courts. The paper will be concluded with some remarks *de lege ferenda* around the potential legal regulation of the circumcision of unemancipated minors in Spain.

13.2 Parental Authority and the Inherent Rights of the Minor. The Best Interests of the Minor

13.2.1 Conflicting Rights. The Current Understanding of Parental Authority

As pointed out in the last section, the rite of circumcision of minors constitutes a so-called ceremony or act of worship which is essential for Jewish beliefs and traditional in the Islamic community. Its practice is covered as such in the right to ideological and religious freedom established in Articles 16.1 of the Spanish Constitution and 2.1.b of the Organic law 7/1980 of 5 July on religious freedom. Singularly, the Agreements with the Federation of Jewish Communities of Spain and the Islamic Commission of Spain in their respective Articles 6, establish duties derived from their tradition, their law and particularly their worship as functions pertaining to their religion. From the minors' perspective, and in accordance with Article 27.3 of the Spanish Constitution, public authorities shall ensure the right which helps parents so that their children may receive the religious and moral education which is in accordance with their own convictions. In this sense, it can be said that those parents who decide to have their son circumcised, just like those Christians who choose to have their child baptised, are exercising their right to religious education by including him in a community of beliefs on the basis of which his character might aim to be forged.

In any case, that the scope and the current content of parental authority is fundamentally different from the Roman view of the absolute right of *pater familias* of the life and death of a child must also be taken into account. The modern concept of underage status, especially on the basis of the Convention on the Rights of the Child, is characterised by the following criteria:

1st The minor naturally has certain fundamental rights, which he/she shall exercise through representatives while he/she is not capable of understanding them, or directly, when he/she is sufficiently mature.; 2nd It can be deduced that there is an evolutionary development to underage status, where in the latter stages, the minor shall be able to exercise his/her right, and so reinforce his/her freedom of choice, for the sake of the strengthening of personality development; 3rd The protection offered to him/her by parents or legal guardians, or public authorities (Article 39 of the Spanish Constitution determines the comprehensive protection of children by public authorities), as well as the duty of parents to provide assistance while they are minors must serve to promote the progressive acquisition of control over his/her life and decision-making and, at all times, under the pre-emptive principle of acting in the best interests of the minor.

These criteria have taken legal form in the Law which regulates *par excellence* the statute of minors: The Organic Law 1/1996, of 15 January, on the Legal Protection of Minors. Its explanatory memorandum reflects, in accordance with international texts, the desire to give greater prominence to minors in line with the important role they play in society: "The social and cultural transformations taking place in our society have brought about a change in the social *status* of the child". Consequently, the full "entitlement of minors to their rights and a progressive capacity to exercise them" is recognised, depending on the minor's different stages of maturity. This memorandum concludes that the Law aims to promote the autonomy of minors as individuals, which demands the need to balance protective systems with the minors' growing ability to participate in the decisions that affect them.

One reflection of these propositions is that the Organic Law, apart from recognising a series of fundamental rights for minors (ideological and religious freedom and freedom of conscience are among them (Article 6)), it prescribes their right to be heard within the family or in legal proceedings, in their own right or through a representative chosen by them "when they possess sufficient capacity of judgment" (Article 9.2). In the same vein, Article 154 of the Civil Code mandates that "if children possess sufficient capacity of judgment, they will always be heard before decisions affecting them are taken".

13.2.2 Limits to Parental Authority: Personality Rights.

There can be no doubt that the change in the understanding of the rights of minors, in the special guardianship set out in the regulation and in the development of their personality, substantially modifies the powers inherent in the exercise of parental authority, as was previously stated.

Article 162 of the Civil Code excludes legal representation of parents who have parental authority over their unemancipated minor children in "acts concerning personality rights". Although the precise delineation of what should be considered "personality rights" is tentative and open to interpretation from doctrine and jurisprudence, it is possible to define them as "those subjective rights whereby the holder's faculties of enjoyment and protection of the essential attributes and interests inherent in their person are recognized" (García Garnica 2004, p. 76). Nowadays, doctrine tends to assimilate them to those fundamental rights, included in our Constitution, which recognise enjoyment, and the corresponding public protection of interests inherent in the development of personality. These may be in their physical, tangible dimension (such as rights to life, to health or to physical integrity) or moral and spiritual (rights of personal portrayal, to honour, to privacy or to ideological and religious freedom).

Can the precept of the Civil Code be interpreted in the sense that at no time and under no circumstances will parents be able to represent the minor in cases of acts of an extremely personal nature as these actions are reserved to him/her? Obviously, the exercise of his/her rights will depend on whether the minor is mature enough. That is to say, whether he/she has the capacity to understand and want to fulfil those fundamental rights, regarding the carrying out of the intended specific act. If he/she possesses the critical skills and volitional aptitudes required, the parents' role is subject to the minor freely granting his/her consent. If the intended act could harm the minor's interests, the parents or the prosecution service will be able to take the case before a judge so that the minor be removed from danger or to avoid him/her coming to harm (Article 158.3º of the Civil Code).

That said, if the minor were not capable (it is assumed that there is an absence of discernment in children twelve years and under) the parents will have full exercise of rights on behalf of the minor, including personality rights, providing the intervention is beneficial for the minor, or at least not harmful. However, whenever possible and within those rights, the decision should be deferred until the minor (the holder of those rights) can give his/her consent.

13.2.3 The Minor's Consent in Surgical Procedures

Submitting a minor to surgical procedures offers us a practical example of this theoretical approximation to parent-child relationships and the limits of parental authority. This area includes the topic of this paper, male circumcision. Spanish legislation admits the general principle, established in the documents and agreements which refer to the rights of minors stemming from the international arena, of the patient's informed consent in any act in the field of health. Law 41/2002, of 14 November, which regulates patient autonomy, embodies this principle in its Article 3. Freedom over the choice of treatment is based on the right to respect for human personality, dignity and privacy. Only in emergency or life threatening cases where the patient's prior consent cannot be given, and the family is not present can the doctor provide the necessary care according to their conscience and professional expertise. In the case of minor children, Law 41/2002 states that those who have reached the age of sixteen have full autonomy in decision making. The minor decides, although the parents must be heard. Below this age, and providing the minor is sufficiently mature, treatments should not be imposed against his/her will, except on the physician's discretion in situations where the minor is at risk of loss of life or suffering irreparable damage. In these situations, the minor's representative will provide consent, once the patient has been heard (Article 9.4).[1] In this case, and in others where there is serious discordance between parents and child, the judge can intervene, deciding on the appropriate course of action based on the circumstances and always putting the minor's best interests first.

If the minor does not have the intellectual and volitional capabilities to take appropriate decisions or to comprehend the consequences of his/her actions, the parents or legal representatives will be the ones to grant consent for the surgical procedure, under certain conditions. It must be done in the minor's best interests (*ex* Article 154 of the Civil Code, as general criteria for the exercise of parental authority) and the minor must be heard if he/she possesses sufficient capacity of judgment[2] and always allowing for the possibility that the judge, at the behest of the doctor or the prosecution service, may authorise the surgical procedure should there be any doubt about the safeguarding of the minor's interests.

Why subject a minor to non-therapeutic surgical procedures? There is no doubt that being subjected to cosmetic surgery or organ donation can jeopardize one's health or even put one's life at undue risk. Whereby, parental consent will not be valid in these cases. Public authorities can exercise special protection of minors, subject to special guardianship, and they will intervene to prevent minors from being put in situations where they can come to physical harm. That said, only in certain exceptional cases, other legitimate interests can justify non-therapeutic interventions. One example is bone marrow harvesting in favour of a relative, as long as the health or life of the minor is not seriously jeopardised.

13.2.4 Circumcision and the Best Interests of the Minor. An Act Which Falls Within Parental Authority?

Under these premises, can circumcision be legitimised as a religious act in the interest of the minor?

As previously highlighted, the regulation of this matter in international agreements and Spanish Law is guided by the overriding principle of the best interests of the minor. *Favor filii* is built around the basis and the substantial purpose of parent-child relationships, present in every sentence handed down in court (Murcia Provincial Court ruling on 27 May 2004). If the concept of the best interests of the minor is undetermined, it will therefore have to be set case by case depending on the specific circumstances (in this way, the Supreme Court judgments of 5 March 1998 and of 23 February 1999). According to our jurisprudence, its definition must seek comprehensive protection, in such a way that it must "reject anything which might

[1] Article drawn up in accordance with the reformed law of 22 September 2015.

[2] "If children possess sufficient capacity of judgment, they must always be heard before decisions that affect them are taken" (Article 154.3°); the child may also recur to a judge should they believe the measures could harm them (*ex* Article 158.3° of the Civil Code). In health matters, Law 41/2002 imposes that a child who is above the age of 12 should give their opinion (Article 9.3.c).

contribute—or contributes—to causing the child emotional harm, injury or any kind of mental or emotional instability" (judgment of the Burgos Provincial Court of 26 February 1999). Ultimately, establishing what is good for the minor is in the hands of the judges. They make use of their discretionary powers to choose the solution they consider fair among several potential options (Rivero Hernández 2000a, b, pp. 272 ss.).

The best interests of the minor also shape the content of parental authority, which is regarded as a function, consisting of a set of rights and obligations which must be applied in the best interests of children and for the full development of their personality (Sentences of the Supreme Court of 24 April 2000 and of Las Palmas Provincial Court of 21 April 2003).

At this point, the question must be asked whether the carrying out of male circumcision as a surgical procedure negatively affects the minor, putting his health at risk. The answer to this question will be found in medical studies (Brusa 2004, pp. 273 ss.; López-Sidro 2012, pp. 8-9; Torres Fernández 2014, pp. 158-159; Licastro 2019, pp. 32-35).

In the past, the circumcision of male newborns became common in England and the United States as a preventive measure. Nowadays, and despite certain benefits of this surgery having been recognised,[3] its risks are also being emphasised (pain, trauma, psychological impact, post-operatory complications). To such an extent that reports from the WHO and paediatric associations do not recommend that circumcisions become standard practice unless they have a direct therapeutic purpose. In any case, it is acknowledged that in the case of newborns, the ease and simplicity of the operation means that there is almost no risk, when correctly carried out. This is not so in the case of young boys and adolescents, where it is recommended that the operation be carried out by a medical professional with appropriate instruments (Bioethics Committee, Italy 1998). Our jurisprudence shares the view that circumcision in newborns is relatively harmless. The ruling by Castellón Provincial Court of 21 September 2006(nº 355/2006)[4] specifies that this outpatient surgical procedure "when correctly carried out, does not affect the sensory-motor functionality as regards sexual intercourse or urination".

Summarising the doctrinal stances on the matter, it could be said that the reasons cited by some authors to advocate in favour of the proscription of circumcision of minors for ritual purposes are based on two types of conclusions:

> Circumcision is an irreversible act which affects the physical integrity of the minor. In this sense, it should be avoided as it undermines a fundamental right. As a personality right, it falls outside the exercise of parental authority. It will be the

[3] It has been described as an effective way to check the transmission of AIDS, to prevent cervical cancer in women (caused by a virus which nestles under the foreskin) or certain urinary infections.

[4] In similar terms, and with regard to Italian law, the Supreme Court's judgment of 24 November 2011 was handed down in relation to Jewish ritual circumcision. The legal reasoning of the judgment states that this act does not constitute a crime of injury because it does not cause an irreversible or permanent injury affecting the functional integrity or capacity of the minor (Borgui 2019, pp. 8–9; Licastro 2019, p. 50).

minor who makes the decision, when he is sufficiently mature (Márquez-García and García-Carvajal 2013, pp. 38–41; De Lora 2015, p. 76). In my opinion, this argument aims to dramatise an operation which, even if it does affect physical integrity, can only be described as low risk and not harmful in itself from a medical point of view (Briones Martínez 2016, pp. 21 ss.; Moreno 2011, p. 111), especially when carried out on newborns.

Circumcision on religious grounds is an act by which the parents integrate their child into a community of believers of a specific religion, which is particularly significant in the case of Judaism. Therefore, a decision that is only up to the minor is being made, in this case which religion to belong to. The minor has the right to exercise the right of religious freedom, which is a personality right which goes beyond the representative powers of the parents. The inherent powers of parental authority do not give them the right to take such a decision. Consequently, they will have to wait until the minor is mature enough and can decide whether or not to undergo this operation of religious significance (Rivero Hernández 2000a, b, pp. 284 ss.). Clearly, this "Rousseauian" take on the minor's upbringing would prevent parents from transmitting any type of value to their offspring. Let it not be forgotten that countless values originate from and are spread through religion. Furthermore, disallowing parents from deciding which specific faith their children will belong to does not provide a balance between the offspring's rights and the parents' rights to religious freedom and to education in keeping with their convictions (Article 27 of the Spanish Constitution). In a general sense, these convictions are not only confined to the choice of school but also to all aspects of the human and personal development of the minor (cultural, religious, moral, social) (Romero Coloma 2006, pp. 51 ss.; Moreno 2011, pp. 111 ss.; Torres Fernández 2014, p. 169). That is to say, everything that plays a part in the development and personal identity of the offspring. This is because, from the parents' point of view, the decision to circumcise integrates their son into a cultural community whose values seek to guide the minor throughout their whole life. Therefore, as a doctrinal sector indicates (Angeluci 2016, pp. 10 ss.; Robbers 2013, pp. 69–70; Silva Sánchez 2013, pp. 4–5; Torres Fernández 2014, p. 169), the integration of a child into the religious community is an important factor through which the act of belonging, canonically regulated in each faith, definitively plays in favour of the interests of the minor and justifies its appropriateness from the perspective of the rightful exercise of the powers of parental authority.

Despite concluding that the act of circumcision is decidedly harmless in nature, in the end, criminal jurisprudence has had to deal with alleged criminal cases on the matter. Nonetheless, other circumstantial factors of the operation (such as the knowledge and training of the person who carries out the procedure, the method, the instruments used, the aseptic conditions) which inflict harm and injury on the minor due to reckless behaviour result in criminal responsibility.

13.3 Criminal Responsibility in Acts of Circumcision for Religious Motives

13.3.1 The Criminal Approximation to Female Genital Mutilation

The criminal consequences of male circumcision were discussed following the international outcry against acts of female genital mutilation, which evidently had a repercussion in the decisions and recommendations made by supranational organizations for the protection of human rights. Equating the former with the latter, a sector of the doctrine called out for the punishment of circumcision as an irreversible form of genital mutilation carried out for non-therapeutic reasons. As with the feminine version, the mildest forms of which can resemble male circumcision, it involves the amputation of part of the male sexual organ with negative physical and psychological effects. In both cases, it should be punished as an offence of infliction of injury, although there should be a balance between the sentence and the extent of the injuries resulting from the operation when it is carried out on religious grounds (De Maglie 2012, pp. 81–84; Silva Sánchez 2013, pp. 1 ss.; Facchi 2014, p. 157; Torres Fernández 2014, p. 141; De Lora 2015, pp. 72 ss.). Other scholars argue that the differences between female genital mutilation in its most common forms and circumcision are qualitative if we pay attention to the effects and harm of the two. So, the criminal consequences should only extend to female mutilation which is, indeed, truly invasive (López Sidro 2012, p. 11; Angelucci 2016, pp. 1 ss.).

Broadly speaking, the legislations of the European States follow the guidelines of international human rights organisations. The criminalisation of female genital mutilation, be it through the modification of criminal laws to create an ad hoc offence or via the application of a type of criminal offence of the kind of injuries,[5] has not been extended to cases of male circumcision.

In Spain, Organic Law 11/2003, which covers specific measures in the domains of public safety, domestic violence and the social integration of foreigners, introduces a subparagraph to Article 149. In the first paragraph, "the loss of, or inability to use, an organ or main limb or a sense, impotence, sterility, serious deformity, or a serious somatic or mental illness" are punishable by imprisonment for a term of between six and twelve years. In the subparagraph "whoever causes genital mutilation in any of its forms" are subject to the same penalty … "if the victim is a minor or incapacitated, a sentence of between four and ten years of special disqualification from the exercise of parental authority, tutorship, guardianship, custody or sheltering will be imposed, if the judge considers that this is in the best interests of the minor or incapacitated individual". The explanatory memorandum of the law makes it clear that the precept

[5] While in countries such as Germany, Austria, Belgium, Denmark, Spain, Italy, Portugal, the United Kingdom, Romania and Sweden a specific offence of genital mutilation has been introduced, in others such as Finland, France, Holland, Hungary, Ireland, Lithuania and Luxembourg the general offence of the infliction of injury applies.

addresses the suppression of female ablation. "This is because the genital mutilation of women and girls is a practice which must be confronted with the utmost firmness, without allowing any kind of justification on alleged religious or cultural grounds". If the new paragraph of Article 149 refers, in general, to any genital mutilation, the extraterritorial prosecution of the constituent elements of the offence are restricted to ablations of female sexual organs,[6] under the Organic Law of Judicial Power.

13.3.2 Circumcision in Criminal Jurisprudence.

The analysis of criminal court decisions confirms the differing relevance of circumcision and genital mutilation in criminal law. At least in principle, jurisprudence maintains the lack of criminal content in the acts of circumcision on infants. This act is to be understood as the outpatient surgical procedure which consists of the excision of the distal portion of the foreskin or skin which covers the glans (it is part of the ritual of Jewish and Islamic religions). "When correctly carried out—as can be read in the ruling by Castellón Provincial Court of 21 September 2006, citing the medical examiner's report—it does not affect sensory-motor functionality as regards sexual intercourse or urination". So, the facts are not included in Article 149.2 of the criminal code. What is more, they lack criminal content. This difference in treatment to female genital mutilation is also extended to the potential extraterritorial prosecution of circumcision operations. By the ruling of 6 June 2008 (nº 598/2008), Barcelona Provincial Court imposed the dismissal of the preliminary proceedings opened before the lawsuit filed by the mother against the father for having hospitalised their son in Casablanca (Morocco) where he was surgically circumcised. Furthermore, in the court's opinion, the facts did not constitute an offence, insofar as the operation was carried out in a diagnosed case of phimosis, and the procedure was performed in accordance with *Lex Artis* by a doctor of the Moroccan hospital, outside national territory. The Court concludes that the Spanish courts lack jurisdiction, because the circumcision "is not within the extraterritorial offences of Article 23.4 of the Organic Law of Judicial Power".

However, the matter of the criminal transcendence of circumcision has been raised when the minor suffers harm as a result of *mala praxis* in its execution. That is to say, when the procedure is carried out by a person without experience or medical knowledge who does not use the appropriate instruments or where there is not even a minimum guarantee of asepsis. This leads to court convictions for the parents and the practitioner for the injuries caused to the child as a consequence of the negligence of the accused. The general nature of these cases indicates the clandestine nature of

---

[6] The Organic Law of Judicial Power was modified by the Organic Law 3/2005 in the sense that it allows Spanish judges the knowledge of the facts susceptible to qualifying under the penal type of genital ablation which occurs outside national territory. A paragraph was added to Article 23.4 of the Organic Law of Judicial Power stating that Spanish judges will be able to have knowledge of the facts "g) relating to <u>female genital mutilation</u>, as long as those responsible are in Spain" (own underlining).

the act of circumcision (the operations take place in private homes and are carried out by immigrants).

In the judgment of Almería Provincial Court of 3 November 2004 (nº 203/2004) the parents and the practitioner who carried out the circumcision were convicted of an offence of infliction of injury committed through negligence. The proven facts are the following. The Senegalese parents went to a compatriot's home to have their six-year old son ritually circumcised. He was forced to sit on a log and his penis was cut with a penknife in such a way that part of the glans was severed. The minor was taken to hospital and he was administered medical, sanitary and surgical treatment. It took forty-five days for him to make a complete recovery. His records state anatomical loss in the glans, although reproductive and urinary functions are preserved. In order to justify the sentence imposed in the first instance by the judge, the court emphasized the lack of medical knowledge of the person who carried out the circumcision, and also the lack of material resources, as a result of which serious harm was caused to the minor. A similar case is the judgment of Lérida Provincial Court of 1 October 2014. The circumcision of a baby in a private home carried out by a person without medical knowledge and chosen by the parents, resulting in a haemorrhage that required surgery and hospital care. The court reasoned that the parents should be convicted for an offence of serious negligence. In the hypothesis, all the constituent elements are there: They knew the risk of a person without references or qualifications carrying out the circumcision; they were aware of the lack of minimum conditions of hygiene; they were aware of the lack of appropriate instruments (the cut was made using a razor blade). The reason to have the circumcision of the baby carried out in conditions such as these, lacking material and personal resources, was purely an economic one. They did not want to spend the money necessary to have the operation done in a private hospital. The haemorrhage and the subsequent anaemia suffered by the child put the life of their son at serious risk.

Evidence that these considerations are not theoretical but real is the case, dramatic in its outcome, judged and ruled by the judgment of Zaragoza Provincial Court of 5 February 2010 (nº 8/2010). A person of Nigerian nationality carried out a circumcision on a six-month old baby with the consent of his parents. The method reflects the incompetence and the crudeness of the operation. It was carried out with a *Bic* razor blade making a jagged cut of considerable depth around the circumference of the penis, the result of which was a wound which would not stop bleeding. Startled by the haemorrhage, the mother called the person who performed the operation, who reassured her by telling her that it was normal and that she should treat the wound with *Betadine*. The next morning, on seeing that the child's condition had deteriorated, the mother took him to the health centre where he arrived unconscious and no longer breathing. At eight o´clock in the morning, the baby died as a result of hypovolemic shock caused by the haemorrhage. The Court of first instance first remanded in custody the person who performed the circumcision,[7] then convicted both this individual and the parents for a crime of negligent homicide of Article 142

[7] The ruling of Zaragoza Provincial Court 122/2009, of 25 January, considers that due to the seriousness of the offence and the fact that the defendant, who works in a rabbit slaughterhouse, frequently

of the criminal code, sentencing them to a term of eighteen months. The hearing confirmed the sentence. These events recounted demonstrate neglect of the duty of care constituting negligence, concurring with the guilt of the parents, be it conscious or unconscious. They decided to circumcise their child without consulting a doctor or having it done in an appropriate establishment; the operation was performed by a non-expert in lamentable conditions; they did not take their child to the health centre until the following morning, thus prolonging the haemorrhage for hours, which represents a resounding failure to provide assistance. What followed was the death of the child, establishing a causal link between the actions recounted and the death.[8]

13.4 Concluding Remarks. *De Iure Condendo* Contributions.

At this point, I think it is appropriate to organise all that has been presented and to offer a series of proposals on the legal situation, current and future, of the circumcision of unemancipated minors in Spain. To this effect, I believe the handling of the issue by our criminal jurisprudence is very helpful. The realism that has been shown when addressing *speciefacti* keeps us away from preconceived concepts or ideas which, to my understanding, approach problems in a somewhat obscure way. Let us summarize the ideas put forward throughout the paper in a series of numerated statements:

1. For Judaism, circumcision is an essential act of worship in the life of a believer. It symbolises the union between Yahweh and the chosen people. Derivatively, it is a widespread tradition in Islam, sometimes even obligatory in some schools or schisms within Islam.
2. The risk of this practice is very low in the case of newborns, when performed in accordance with medical *Lex Artis,* and it increases with age. In the case of children and adolescents, the operation must be performed meeting minimum conditions of asepsis and hygiene, as far as possible avoiding pain via the use of anaesthesia. Thus, it is always recommendable to have the operation performed in an authorised clinic and by medical personnel.
3. The overriding principle which instructs parent–child relationships to work in the best interests of the minor does not exclude the act of circumcision per se. In spite of its definitive nature as regards the alteration it causes to the minor's physique, it also finds justification in the need of all people to be brought up with a series of moral values which contribute in a positive way to the development of our personality. It is perfectly natural that, within the evolutionary process of human beings and while we do not have sufficient capacity of critical judgment,

---

performed circumcisions and this activity being a danger, recommended imprisonment without bail be confirmed.

[8] In any case, if the result of the defective circumcision had been impotence, sterility or serious deformity, this would constitute an offence of mutilation of Article 149.1 of the Criminal Code (Jericó Ojer 2013, 3).

our parents should be the ones to guide and direct us in accordance with their own beliefs. Such a right is recognised in international conventions and in Article 27.3 of the Spanish Constitution. In this sense, circumcision (just like the case of baptism for Christians) has a beneficial effect on the integration of the child into the complex value systems of age-old religions, as well as in a community united by the profession of a common faith. In any case, nobody is preventing the minor, once he reaches maturity, from setting his/her own course which might part or drift from those instilled by his/her parents in his/her infancy. It does not seem to be that the fact of circumcision of minors who do not have sufficient understanding goes against their future volitional autonomy. They will always be able to exercise this autonomy when they reach mental maturity.

4. Therefore, as an act protected by the freedom of worship and by the right of parents to the religious and moral upbringing of their children, and as it has not been shown that circumcision in itself has a directly adverse affect on the minor, the legality of circumcision in our Law seems to be beyond doubt. Given that the exercise of parental authority is shared by both progenitors and that circumcision is, aside from being a surgical procedure, a relevant act in the comprehensive development of the minor, it should be decided on by both parents, or by one with the explicit consent of the other.[9] If the minor has capacity of judgment, he must be heard.[10] He can also refer to a judge who can decide on what is appropriate should the minor consider he is at risk of harm.
5. In view of all this, the problem lies not in the fact of the circumcision of minors (legal per se or at least not prohibited) but in its practice. That is to say, when it is performed without knowledge, with deficient instruments or without the adequate conditions of health and hygiene. In line with the recommendations of international organisations and most doctrine and in light of the dramatic cases which our criminal courts have had to judge and rule on (which highlight cases which provoke severe injury to minors, or even their death) the need to ensure minimum medical and sanitary guarantees must be concluded. Thus, in my opinion, a series of conditions must be imposed for the performance of this operation to the benefit of the minor.

a. Circumcision should be carried out, with no exceptions, by a doctor, capable, in turn, of correctly following the evolution of the surgical procedure. The reading of the *speciefacti* of the decisions recommends that a trained medical professional perform the operation in the case of newborns as well (Moreno 2011, p. 112). This does not exclude the possibility that, through the channels of special Law, it might be determined that in the case of Judaism, the State might empower specific members of the community who have successfully undergone the corresponding training courses to allow them to be responsible for carrying out circumcisions

---

[9] See, in this sense, rulings of Castellón Provincial Court 355/2006 of 21 September and of Barcelona Provincial Court 598/2008 of 6 June.

[10] *Ex* Articles 154.3 and 158.3 of the Civil Code. And Article 9.3.c. of Law 41/2002 of 14 November, on the autonomy of the patient.

(Bioethics report Italy, 1998; Angeluci 2016, p. 25; Briones Martínez 2016, p. 54).

b. Circumcision should be carried out in establishments or clinics where there is a guarantee of asepsis, the use of appropriate instruments and adequate means of anaesthesia to incur the minimum possible suffering. Could such operations take place within the framework of the public health system? At least in principle, the fact of the non-therapeutic nature of ritual circumcision and the thrift in the public system resources exclude the carrying out of this surgical procedure in health centres or public hospitals. Arguments in favour of its inclusion would be looking out for the welfare of minors, guaranteeing medical and sanitary conditions thus avoiding clandestine operations and contributing to the integration of religious and cultural minorities. This might be one of the reasons why this practice has been admitted in certain public hospitals in countries such as the United Kingdom (De Lora 2015, p. 74, n. 37). In Spain, although it cannot be demanded from the State as a social right inherent to the exercise of religious freedom, it would in fact be useful to adjudicate co-payment methods for the surgical procedure with maximum guarantees, in the interest of the health of the minor. This recommendation is *de iure condendo* and has not come to fruition in practice.

Finally, the question remains to be asked whether the fact of ritual circumcision in itself and the conditions in which it is performed should be the object of some ad hoc regulation through a law or rules to develop a law. The hypothetical law, through the jurisprudence of the courts, will establish the framework on such aspects as the professional qualifications of the person who performs the circumcision, the place, the instruments to be used, the way the operation is carried out (which will have to include the use of anaesthesia), prior consent of the two progenitors or of the mature minor (who will have to be heard in any case if he has critical judgment), or the potential inclusion as a surgical procedure to be carried out in a centre pertaining to the social security system (Torres Fernández 2014, 173–175). The obvious positive effect of legal regulation is that it would provide certainty and legal security to male circumcisions, to the benefit of the people involved (the parents, the person who performs the circumcision, leaders of religious communities, doctors and medical staff, the minor). However, it must also be recognised that in Spain, the debate and social consensus needed to move towards a regulation which adequately balances the conflicting rights is a long way off.

References

Alicino, F. 2022. I reati culturalmente motivati fra assimilazionismo e relativismo multiculturale. (Culturally motivated crimes between assimilationism and multicultural relativism) *Stato, Chiese e pluralismo confessionale* 5: 1 ss.

Alshboul, A. 2012. La cultura del cuerpo en el Islam (nacimiento y muerte del cuerpo y la circuncisión. (The culture of the body in Islam (birth and death of the body and circumcision)) *Nómadas: revista crítica de Ciencias Sociales y Jurídicas*, 34: 13 ss.

Angeluci, A. 2016. Libertá religiosa e circoncisione in italia: una questione di specialitá confessionale. *Stato, Chiese e pluralismo confessionale* 35: 1 ss.

Borghi, A. 2019. Appunti sulla circoncisione culturale nel diritto ecclesiastico e delle religioni. (Notes on cultural circumcision in ecclesiastical law and religions) *Stato, Chiese e pluralismo confessionale* 11: 1 ss.

Briones Martínez, I. M. 2016. La circuncisión y el mejor interés del menor. Libertad religiosa y tradición. (Circumcision and the best interests of the minor. Religious Freedom and Tradition) *Revista General de Derecho Canónico y Derecho Eclesiástico del Estado* 42: 1ss.

Brusa, M. 2004. Consideraciones éticas sobre la circuncisión en España. (Ethical considerations on circumcision in Spain) *Revista española de pediatría: clínica e investigación* 60, 3: 240 ss.

Cámara Arroyo, S. 2014. La legislación y jurisprudencia penal española sobre la ablación. (Spanish legislation and criminal jurisprudence on ablation) El tipo cualificado de lesiones (Aggravated crimes of injuries) of Article 149.2. *Anuario De Derecho Eclesiástico Del Estado* 30: 829–882.

Facchi, A. 2014. Mutilaciones genitales femeninas y Derecho positivo. (Female genital mutilation and Positive Law) In *Delitos de las minorías en países multiculturales: estudios jurídicos y criminológicos comparados*, ed. L. Roca Agapito-M. M. González Tascón-J. Bernal del Castillo. Barcelona: Atelier Libros Jurídicos: 143–167.

Felix Ballesta, M. A. 2000. El régimen acordado en España sobre las peculiaridades culturales de las religiones minoritarias. (The agreed regime in Spain on the cultural peculiarities of minority religions) *Anuario de Derecho Eclesiástico del Estado*, 16: 189–192.

García Garnica, M. C. 2004. *El ejercicio de los Derechos de la Personalidad del Menor no Emancipado. Especial consideración al consentimiento a los actos médicos y a las intromisiones en el honor, la intimidad y la propia imagen.* (The exercise of personality rights of the unemancipated minor. Special consideration to consent to medical acts and to interference with honor, intimacy and personal portrayal) Cizur Menor: Thomson-Aranzadi.

Jericó Ojer, L. 2013. A vueltas con la mutilación genital (Around in circles with genital mutilation) (Article 149.2 CP): ¿aplicación exclusiva del delito sólo cuando existan motivos religiosos o culturales? (An exclusive application of the crime only when there are religious or cultural motives?) (About SAP Barcelona 135/2013, of 14 June). *Diario La Ley* 8206, 5 December: 3.

Lage, F. 2012. Polémica actual en torno a la circuncisión. (The current debate around circumcision) *Moralia: revista de ciencias morales* 35, 136: 436 ss.

Licastro, A. 2019. La questione della liceitá delle circoncisione "rituale" tra tutela dell´identitá religiosa del gruppo e salvaguardia del diritto individuale alla integritá fisica. (The question of the legality of 'ritual' circumcision between protection of the group's religious identity and safeguarding the individual's right to physical integrity) *Stato, Chiese e pluralismo confessionale* 22: 28 ss.

López Sidro, A. 2012. Circuncisión y libertad religiosa. (Circumcision and Religious Freedom) Comentario a la Sentencia del Tribunal Regional de Colonia (Comments on the sentence of Cologne Regional Court) of 7 May 2012. *Revista General de Derecho Canónico y Derecho Eclesiástico del Estado* 30: 1 ss.

Lora, P. de 2015. Cirugía de menores: el caso de la circuncisión masculina. (Surgery on minors. The case of male circumcision) *Derecho y Salud: publicación de la Asociación de Juristas de la Salud* 25, 2: 73 ss.

Maglie, C. de 2012 *Los delitos culturalmente motivados. Ideologías y modelos penales*, (Culturally motivated crimes. Ideologies and criminal models) (trad. V. M. Macías Caro). Madrid: Marcial Pons.

Márquez-García, E. Y., and García-Carvajal J. A. 2013. La circuncisión como una manifestación como una manifestación de la vulneración al libre desarrollo de la personalidad. (Circumcision as a demonstration of the infringement of the free development of personality) *Dixi* 17: 38 ss.

Moreno Antón, M. 2011. La libertad religiosa del menor en el contexto sanitario. (Religious freedom of the minor in the context of health) *Revista de la Facultad de Derecho de la Universidad Autónoma de Madrid* 15: 96 ss.

National Committee of Bioethics-Italy "La circuncisión: perfil Bioético" (Circumcision: Bioethical Profile), 25 September 1998. 1999. *Quaderni di Diritto e Política Eclesiástica*, 2: 523 ss.

Rivero Hernández, F. 2000. Límites de la libertad religiosa y las relaciones personales de un padre con sus hijos. (Limits to religious freedom and personal relationships of a parent and their children) (Comments of the STC 141/2000, of 29 May). *Derecho Privado y Constitución* 14: 265 ss.

Rivero Hernández, F. 2000. *El interés del menor*. (The best interests of the minor) Madrid: Dykinson.

Robbers, G. 2013. Recent Legal Development in Germany: Infant Circumcision and Church Tax. *Ecclesiastical Law Journal* 15: 69 ss.

Romero Coloma, A. M. 2006. *Derecho a la libertad religiosa del progenitor frente al beneficio del hijo menor. Problemática jurídica.* (The right to religious freedom of the progenitor weighed against the good of the minor. A legal dilemma) Barcelona: Bosch.

Silva Sánchez, J. 2013. Circuncisión infantil. (Child circumcision) *InDret Penal* 1: 3 ss.

Torres Fernández, M. E. 2014. Viejos Ritos, Nuevos Conflictos: la Circuncisión Masculina. Estado de la Cuestión. (Old Rites, New Conflicts: Male Circumcision. The State of the Matter). In *Delitos de las minorías en países multiculturales: estudios jurídicos y criminológicos comparados*, (Crimes of the minorities in multicultural countries: Legal and criminological contrasted studies) ed. L. Roca Agapito-M. M. González Tascón-J. Bernal del Castillo, 160 ss. Barcelona: Atelier Libros Jurídicos.

Chapter 14
Broadening Conscience: Altruism, Civil Disobedience, or (Positive) Conscientious Objection Against Migrant Healthcare Exclusion?

Rosana Triviño-Caballero

Abstract This work is aimed to analyze the difficulty of establishing clear limits between conscientious objection and civil disobedience taken as example the specific case of those healthcare professionals opposed to the Spanish Royal Decree 16/2012. The approval of this law, directed to the sustainability of the National Health System, meant a change in the previous configuration of the constitutional right to healthcare, characterized by being public and freely accessible to all the inhabitants in the country. As a consequence, undocumented migrant people had no longer a universal access to healthcare. In this situation, some healthcare professionals expressed their opposition to the law providing their services to undocumented patients. Might this behavior be considered a form of conscientious objection? Was a case of civil disobedience? Was just an act of altruism? Plausible answers to these questions will be argued along this paper.

Keywords (Positive) conscientious objection · Civil disobedience · Altruism · Migrants · Healthcare exclusion

This work was developed in the framework of the research projects *The discourse of biorights. Philosophical and legal foundations, features and implementation* (DER2014-52811-P) and *KONTUZ-2* (FFI2014-53926-R), funded by the Spanish Ministry of Economy and Competitiveness.

R. Triviño-Caballero (✉)
Department of Public Health and Maternal & Child Healthcare, Faculty of Medicine, Universidad Complutense de Madrid, Madrid, Spain
e-mail: rosanatr@ucm.es

© The Editor(s) (if applicable) and The Author(s), under exclusive license to Springer Nature Switzerland AG 2024

J.-A. Seoane and O. Vergara (eds.), *The Discourse of Biorights*, The International Library of Bioethics 109, https://doi.org/10.1007/978-3-031-66804-3_14

14.1 Introduction

Contemporary issues, as global anti-austerity movements, cyber-activism, politicized whistleblowing, or biomedical revolution are challenging the classic definitions of civil disobedience and conscientious objection from different traditions (Cooke and Petherbridge 2016). In Spain, healthcare providers appealed to the recognition of a *positive* conscientious objection against undocumented migrants' exclusion from regular healthcare services. In April 2012, Spanish government enacted the *Real Decreto-ley 16/2012, de medidas urgentes para garantizar la sostenibilidad del Sistema Nacional de Salud y mejorar la calidad y seguridad de sus prestaciones* [Law by Royal Decree 16/2012, *on urgent measures to ensure the sustainability of the National Healthcare System and enhance the quality and safety of its services*], hereinafter RDL16/2012, during a sustained period of economic crisis. Until the approval of this law, Spain had provided a great access to healthcare for its undocumented population compared with most European Union countries (Suess et al. 2014). The legal modifications involved not only a serious reduction in healthcare access for the undocumented population, but also a paradigm shift for the Spanish health system, originally modelled on the pillars of solidarity, equity and accessibility. In practice, the law implied that healthcare was no longer public, universal and freely accessible for all residents of the country, but only for those who were 'insured'.

This legislation left without access to the public healthcare system to adult undocumented migrants, excepting emergency medical treatment and other limited services, such as care for pregnant women, although even in these legal exceptions an extended denial of health assistance was detected (REDER 2017; Yo Sí Sanidad Universal 2013, 2016, 2022). The law has had serious consequences for migrants, especially for those with potentially life-threatening chronic conditions, such as HIV/AIDS, tuberculosis, and hepatitis. These patients no longer have reliable access to the medications and clinical services needed to help them manage these conditions. This healthcare deprivation has resulted in worrying rates. Between 2012 and 2015, mortality among undocumented migrants increased a 15% (Juanmarti-Mestres et al. 2021).

This situation led several professional societies and thousands of individual healthcare workers protested the RDL16/2012. They claimed that it violated their ethical duties as professionals, including (1) the physician's duty not to abandon their patients; (2) the duty to care for patient and community wellbeing; (3) the duty to avoid any kind of discrimination in their professional exercise (Rada 2012). They also denounced that the law violated several human rights conventions concerning access to healthcare for the undocumented populations (Suess et al. 2014).

The largest professional society representing general practitioners in Spain (SEMFyC) took the further step of encouraging its members to register as conscientious objectors to the law, using a provision designed for individual professionals who seek exemption from participating in specific procedures, such as abortion or euthanasia. More than two thousand healthcare professionals registered as conscientious objectors to the RDL16/2012 as a means of expressing their disagreement with the law and their intention to continue to provide healthcare to this population (SEMFyC 2012).

There have been subsequent legal initiatives to modify RDL 16/2012 measures, as the *Real Decreto-Ley 7/2018, de 27 de julio, sobre el acceso universal al Sistema Nacional de Salud* [Law by Royal Decree 7/2018, 27 July, *on the universal access to the National Health System*] and the *Anteproyecto de Ley por la que se modifican diversas normas para consolidar la equidad, universalidad y cohesión del Sistema Nacional de Salud* [Preliminary Draft Bill amending regulations to consolidate equity, universality, and cohesion of the National Health System]. The political claim has been to end healthcare exclusion. However, Spanish autonomous communities have regulated access to healthcare in such a diverse way that inequality and exclusion has been consolidated in a large part of the territory (Yo Sí Sanidad Universal 2022).

Throughout this work I will analyze healthcare professionals' recourse to conscientious objection against the denial of services to undocumented migrants, comparing it with civil disobedience and an act of altruism. First, I will review the classical definitions of civil disobedience and conscientious objection to identify the main features which might be applied to this specific case. Second, I will expose some peculiarities of the Spanish healthcare system before and after the RDL16/2012 to make more comprehensible the context in which this particular conscience claim has occurred. I will address the altruistic or mandatory nature of the claim made by these healthcare professionals, since an *action* is implied, and not an *omission*, as would be usual (i.e., the conscientious objection to abortion or to euthanasia; civil disobedience regarding taxes intended for military purposes). Then, I will analyze the most prevalent features of conscientious objection and civil disobedience, since both figures have been applied inconsistently to this case. In so doing, I will try to show that the dichotomies of *individual vs. collective*, *moral motivation vs. political motivation* and *action vs. omission* are insufficient to establish a clear frontier between conscientious objection and civil disobedience.

The ambivalent use of the concepts of civil disobedience and conscientious objection applied to the RDL16/2012 case revives the classical problem of the differences between these two figures (Raz 1979; Rawls 1999). The value of this analysis is not only theoretical, but also practical, since the legal consequences faced by healthcare professionals in this kind of situations may differ depending on the kind of normative consideration of their dissidence.

14.2 Civil Disobedience

Civil disobedience is a longstanding resource people have used to rebel against what they judge as unjust laws. Since Antigone, claiming for her duty to obey her conscience against the human law, to more recent examples, as Chelsea Manning, going through Mahatma Gandhi, Nelson Mandela, industrial workers, and women suffragists fighting for their rights, history is plenty of famous and anonymous disobedients, many of them considered as heroic human beings.

Civil disobedience has been defined by Rawls (1999) as a public, nonviolent, conscience-based, and political transgression of law aimed to change laws or policies. From his perspective, the public condition of civil disobedience implies an open claim which, additionally, has been noticed in advance to legal authorities. For Rawls, the uncovered nature of this form of dissent is a distinctive feature of civility and compliance to behave in a fairly way with authorities. As for its nonviolent nature, Rawls considers a basic condition of civility not acting violently, to the extent that violence presupposes attempting against others' civil liberties. Even if their expressions are nonviolent, according to Rawls, disobedients should be willing to accept the consequences to break the law, including punishment and criminal liability. From his point of view, these conditions—publicity, nonviolence, and responsibility for their behaviors—make the difference between civil disobedients and other kind of non-civil revolutionary agents. Civil disobedients show respect for the rule of law, although they strongly disagree about specific legal contents. Their dissent is a political commitment, but also a conscientious, honest, and genuine one that appeal to the broadly accepted notion of justice, supportive of the political order.

Joseph Raz's conception of civil disobedience expands Rawls' one. He defines it as any 'politically motivated breach of law designed either to contribute directly to a change of a law or of a public policy or to express one's protest against, and dissociation from, a law or a public policy' (Raz 1979, p. 263). Such definition includes both violent and nonviolent acts, by the one hand, and public or secret disobedience, by the other. Additionally, it openly recognizes that civil disobedience may be direct or indirect. A direct act of civil disobedience is one in which the law being broken is the same law that the person is protesting against. For instance, Rosa Parks' rejection to cede her seat on a bus to a white passenger, opposing bus segregation. Indirect disobedience involves violating a law which is not, itself, the object of protest. For example, '[t]respassing on a military base to spray-paint nuclear missile silos in protest against current military policy' (Brownlee 2007). This distinction between direct and indirect civil disobedience is not always clear. In fact, there are situation that could be seen as either direct or indirect civil disobedience. For instance, Henry Thoreau's refusal to pay the state poll taxes used to fund the war against Mexico and enforce the Fugitive Slave Law. From a strategic perspective, the more frequent acts of civil disobedience are clearly direct, expressing a correlation between the law and the active rejection of it (Brownlee 2007).

14.3 Conscientious Objection

The term conscientious objection was firstly used in the 1898 *British Vaccination Act*, which established a conscience clause to allow exemptions to smallpox compulsory vaccination (CPP 2013). Then, the concept of conscientious objector was applied to the military context, especially during the World Wars, to describe the pacifist rejection to participate in belligerent actions (Brock 2006; Brownlee 2012a). The pacifist character of conscientious objection is still applicable, although it is not so frequent to use it to define the concept. Since the military conscription has been significantly eliminated in Western societies, the most frequent scenarios for contemporary conscientious objection are related to the healthcare context, where objectors oppose to perform activities required by their professional roles or legal obligations due to reasons linked to their moral convictions (Giubilini 2016; Wicclair 2011). Typical cases are related to the refusal to provide abortion services, to supply emergency contraceptive pills, or to provide medical assistance to die.

From a legal point of view, conscientious objection requires a *violation of a law*, not any order or directive, which collides with the objector's moral beliefs (Raz 1979). The conscientious objector may consider the law either partial or totally bad or wrong. For instance, a gynecologist could be completely against an abortion law, because she is convinced of the sanctity of life, or only disagree on some abortion cases (i.e., when the reason to stop the pregnancy is due to the fetus' gender). Additionally, Joseph Raz defines conscientious objection as 'a private act, designed to protect the agent from interference by public authority' (1979, p. 276).

Expanding Raz's concept of conscientious objection, Rawls considers that it implies a conscientious-based rejection to act, not necessarily attempting against a law, but against any other normative order. In his own words, 'Conscientious refusal is noncompliance with a more or less direct legal injunction or administrative order' (Rawls 1999, p. 323). For Rawls, it is important to distinguish between *conscientious refusal* and other kind of objections, as *conscientious evasion* or *civil disobedience*. Rawls assumes that conscientious evasion is a covert behavior which has not been noticed to the authorities, for instance, '[c]overt infractions of a fugitive slave law' (1999, p. 324). Rawls separates civil disobedience from individual acts of conscientious objection, which implies a collective nature for civil disobedience and an individual one for conscientious objection. From his view, conscientious objection is not an action aimed at the 'sense of justice of the majority', publicly performed (1999, p. 324). Conscientious objection is a way of subjective rejection whose objective is not changing laws or policies. In contrast to civil disobedience, conscientious refusal is based on personal convictions which are not enough to motivate a public political action.

In the same vein than Rawls', from the dominant liberal perspective, conscientious objection is considered 'as a modest, unassuming act of deep personal conviction', while civil disobedience is 'a strategic, political act that eschews ordinary participation channels in favour of riskier, but potentially more effective, undemocratic channels' (Brownlee 2012a, p. 5). In general, from these standard views, it could be justifiable a moral right—even a legal one—to noncompliance with the law based on a private, non-communicative, conscience aimed to protect an individual's moral integrity, autonomy, and freedom of conscience. Preserving these goods is considered essential for the accommodation of different moral and philosophical perspective in pluralistic societies. Therefore, failing to guarantee them is interpreted as an imposition of a particular view on those who sustain minority moral principles (West-Oram and Buyx 2016).

Grounded on this liberal tradition, it is easy to find an increasing number of legal exemptions to avoid the accomplishment of a general law and preserve individual' conscience. For example, healthcare professionals have the possibility to not participate in abortion services thanks to the legal clauses which allow it; but, in many cases, these exemptions make difficult or even impossible the main legal purpose, i.e., guaranteeing the abortion provision for women who require it (Minerva 2013). Therefore, it can be said that recognition of conscientious objection may, in fact, provoke legal and policies changes to some extent. This point, related to the scope and goals of conscientious objection, will be further developed on this paper.

Positive Conscientious Objection

From a more descriptive perspective, Peter West-Oram and Alena Buyx (2016, p. 337) propose the following scheme which characterizes the most common context where conscientious objection is developed:

1. A duty to X is owed by all persons in group Y
2. Either the duty itself, or its likely consequences, are deemed immoral by some members of Y
3. Some members of Y will assert a conscientious objection to X, and will request an exemption from the duty to X
4. An exemption will be granted (or not) to some or all of those who objected, with or without conditions attached.

According to this overview and the previous definitions which have been exposed, conscientious objection is usually linked to an omission, not to an action. Conscientious objection is focused on the individual who refuses to participate or provide a legal service when this service collides with her moral convictions. In other words, an objector's conscience uses to say 'no'. Instead, the possibility of a *positive claim to conscience* has been traditionally underdeveloped from both a theoretical and a practical perspective—even rejected by some authors—considering that these *appeals to act* can be ascribable to civil disobedience, but not to conscientious objections (Navarro 2013; Seoane 2013; de Montalvo 2016). However, conscientious claims, specifically in the case of healthcare professionals' integrity, could be interpreted not only in terms of what one *refuses to do*, but also as the recognition of what one considers the *right thing to do*, that means, 'a positive conscientious objection' (Joffe 1995; Wicclair 2011; Harris 2012; Sepper 2012; Triviño 2012, 2014; Triviño et al. 2013; Seoane 2014; Berlinger 2016). This could be the case which has been chosen to be analyzed in this chapter. Before addressing it, I will present the Spanish healthcare context for a better understanding of the issue.

14.4 Healthcare in Spain Before and After RD 16/2012

One of the greatest achievements of democracy in Spain has been the creation and consolidation of a public healthcare system that implemented the right to health protection enshrined in the 1978 Spanish Constitution (art. 43). Its subsequent legislative development progressively secured the right to healthcare for all inhabitants residing in the country, without exception.[1] Thanks to this formulation, the Spanish National Health System has significantly contributed to the achievement of high levels of social cohesion (Fernández-García and Polentinos-Castro 2018).

Redistribution is based on the commonly shared moral assumptions that define the rules of reciprocity and define the criteria for inclusion and exclusion in the System of Social Care and Security. The basic collective norms and obligations, outlined as the '*moral economy*' of the society, refer as well which provisions should be covered and who are eligible and what are legitimate practices (Cuadra 2012). In the case of Spain, it was accepted that the full funding of the healthcare system came under the control of General State Budgets, meaning that healthcare services were decoupled from individual contributions to Social Security. The right to health protection in democratic Spain has been thus configured as a right of citizenship. The previous model, during Franco's dictatorship, of 'insured' and 'beneficiaries'—a system which left the most vulnerable populations in the hands of charities[2]—was thus superseded.

However, this situation changed dramatically since the commencement of the RDL16/2012, hastily approved after a brief debate in Congress and thanks to the parliamentary majority of the conservative *Partido Popular* (Popular Party). The law included measures related to access regulation to healthcare, prescription drug co-payment, the services portfolio of the Spanish Public Health Care System, as well as the classification of healthcare professions. The RDL 16/2012 recovered the extinct condition of 'insured' and 'beneficiaries' regarding healthcare services. According to this law, undocumented migrants were not covered by the public healthcare system, free of charge, unless they were minors, pregnant women, in an emergency situation, or suffering contagious diseases. Despite these exceptions included in the law, in practice there have been abundant cases in which adequate assistance to pregnant women, children, or people in emergency situations, among others, has not been provided (REDER 2017; Yo Sí Sanidad Universal 2013, 2016, 2022).[3]

The modifications introduced by RDL16/2012 involved not only a serious restriction of undocumented population's access to healthcare, but also a radical paradigm

---

[1] Regarding migrant people, the *Ley Orgánica 4/2000, sobre derechos y libertades de los extranjeros residentes en España y su integración social* [Organic Law 4/2000, on rights and freedoms of the resident foreigners in Spain and their social integration], reformed by the *Ley Orgánica 8/2000* [Organic Law 8/2000], included in its articles 3 and 12 foreigners' right to health protection under the same conditions as Spaniards.

[2] In relation to the evolution and success of healthcare in Spain, see Muntaner et al. 2012.

[3] According to Woodward et al. (2014, p. 818), '[w]hile EU policy supports health-care access for undocumented migrants, practices remain haphazard, with studies reporting differing interpretation and implementation of rights at regional, institutional and individual levels'.

shift in the essence of the Spanish health system, a model originally based on the pillars of solidarity, equity and accessibility (Rodríguez et al. 1999). In practice, the law implied that healthcare was no longer public, universal, and free for all residents of the country, but only for those who were insured. Under the heading of an alleged financial unsustainability, the law advocated for substantial changes in both the consideration of the recipients and the provision of benefits (Simón Lorda 2014), since many people have no choice but to pay for certain private health services not covered by the public service.

The changes introduced in the Spanish context raised the question about the regulations in force in other European countries, as well as the impact of the 2008 economic crisis on the healthcare entitlement of undocumented migrants (Suess et al. 2014). Similarly to other European countries, the legislation issued in Spain in 2012 regarding health coverage was in blunt contradiction to healthcare standards outlined in the human rights framework. Article 12 of the International Covenant on Economic, Social, and Cultural Rights affirms the right of everyone to enjoy the highest attainable standard of physical and mental health (ICESCR 1966). Other binding treaties incorporating the right to health include the International Convention of the Rights of the Child (CRC), the International Convention on the Elimination of All Forms of Racial Discrimination (ICERD), the Constitution of WHO, the Declaration of Alma-Ata, the Ottawa Charter for Health Promotion and the Bangkok Charter for Health Promotion in a Globalized World (Backman et al. 2008). The Committee on Economic, Social, and Cultural Rights, which monitors and interprets ICESCR, advised that states are 'under the obligation to respect the right to health by, *inter alia*, refraining from denying or limiting equal access for all persons, including [...] asylum seekers and illegal immigrants, to preventive, curative and palliative health services; abstaining from enforcing discriminatory practices as a State policy; [...]' (CESCR 2000, p. 34). Hence, from a human rights perspective, healthcare clearly involves primary, secondary, as well as preventive care. The Council of Europe has addressed the situation of undocumented migrants in a resolution of the Parliamentary Assembly. *Council of Europe Resolution 1509* (2006) *on Human Rights of Irregular Migrants,* article 13.2 declares that as a minimum right, emergency care should be available for irregular migrants (CE 2006). States should also 'seek to provide more holistic health care, taking into account, in particular, the specific needs of vulnerable groups such as children, disabled persons, pregnant women and the elderly' (CE 2006). In the particular case of Spain, Magdalena Sepúlveda, Special Rapporteur of the United Nations, and the European Committee on Social Rights, have warned that the 2008 financial crisis cannot serve as a pretext for restriction or denial of access to healthcare. She and the Committee underlined that the Spanish Constitution acknowledges access to healthcare as a positive duty, including obligations to migrants, regardless of their legal status (Sevillano 2014).

Although the RDL 16/2012 has been modified since 2018 by other legal initiatives to end healthcare exclusion,[4] Spanish autonomous communities have regulated

[4] *Real Decreto-Ley 7/2018, de 27 de julio, sobre el acceso universal al Sistema Nacional de Salud* [Law by Royal Decree 7/2018, 27 July, *on the universal access to the National Health System*] and

access to healthcare in such a diverse and restricted way that inequality and exclusion against undocumented migrant population has been consolidated in a large part of the territory (Yo Sí Sanidad Universal 2022). Therefore, healthcare professionals, professional associations, and NGOs are still fighting to reestablish a universal and public healthcare system.

The consideration of healthcare protection as a fundamental human right is grounded on the belief that healthcare is a minimum requirement for any person in order to attain sufficient control of her capacities and abilities, which will ensure full use of her autonomy. The duty to protect and care for human beings' health is a logical corollary to the basic and fundamental right to life, as there is no right to life without the availability of a reasonable standard of health and wellbeing, that depends—at least in a significant proportion—on the provision of social services and medical care. For these reasons, important reactions against the RDL16/2012 emerged. Various government and non-governmental institutions clearly spoke out against the measures it involved. Some argued that that the law was based on false premises and that hidden motivations could be identified to enact measures whose consequences were of concern not only for undocumented migrants, but for the Spanish society at large (Triviño et al. 2016). Moreover, a professional movement among healthcare professionals emerged from the enrooted belief that healthcare is a professional duty and a positive right that should be provided without discrimination. They considered conscientious objection as a way to defend such ethical convictions, but, as it will be shown below, this possibility was put into question with different arguments.

14.5 Healthcare Professionals Against the RD 16/2012: A Case of Altruism?

After the entry into force of RDL16/2012, some authorities argued that the law did not imply any conflict of conscience (Sahuquillo 2012). They considered the main issue not to be a healthcare-related problem, but merely a bureaucratic procedure. The administration was responsible for enforcing the law, charging for the services provided and prosecuting non-payments. From this perspective, if we consider that healthcare professionals are not disobeying the law, since they are not the persons involved in charging for their services, we could conclude that they are not objectors, but altruistic individuals willing to carry out their duties beyond what is contractually required (Murphy and Genuis 2013). In fact, the law did not explicitly forbid professionals from leaving their patients unattended.

However, the administrative requirements of RDL16/2012 did imply an unequal healthcare provision. On the one hand, access to medical or nursing offices was

---

the *Anteproyecto de Ley por la que se modifican diversas normas para consolidar la equidad, universalidad y cohesión del Sistema Nacional de Salud* [Preliminary Draft Bill amending regulations to consolidate equity, universality, and cohesion of the National Health System].

hindered or even totally obstructed—undocumented people had no access to the regular appointment system, for example—; on the other hand, access to some services was no longer free; therefore, healthcare professionals necessarily became agents in the cost charging of their services.

From a consequentialist point of view, if you do not act when (a) you have the possibility to do it, and (b) you can foresee that fact, you are causing damage; in that case, your omission is actually provoking suffering (Singer 2019). Therefore, those professionals who were taking care of undocumented people were not acting in a supererogatory way, but with an ethical responsibility towards the others, a responsibility specifically included in their professional codes.

Consequently, the law delivered significant implications, directly related to professional obligations, since it implied leaving without healthcare to those people who required it, purely because of their administrative condition. This is an act against the professional duties of healthcare providers. In this sense, the possibility of appealing to conscientious objection or becoming civil disobedients could be justified.

14.6 Healthcare Professionals Against the RDL16/2012: Civil Disobedients or Conscientious Objectors?

The active rejection of RDL16/2012 by healthcare professionals was considered by some authors a case of civil disobedience, since it was a *collective action* aimed at provoking *political change*—the revocation of measures restricting healthcare for migrants—, not preserving the integrity of their private consciences (CGOCE 2012; Navarro 2013; Seoane 2013; de Montalvo 2016). From other points of view, this reaction was seen as a possible case of conscientious objection, because it had an *individual dimension*—each professional took her own decision about what she should do– and the motivation to act may not be (purely) political, but also personal—each professional considered her own conscience and wanted to be consistent with it (Rada 2012; Triviño 2012, 2014; Triviño et al. 2013; Seoane 2014).

Civil disobedience and conscientious objection identify a sphere of personal conviction around which a liberal society and its laws tend to tread with some care. Despite the attempts to make theoretical distinctions, it is not always easy to establish a clear limit between these forms of dissent. As Kimberley Brownlee has written, '[t]here is considerable overlap between these two practices in that both are forms of sincere and serious dissent that involve some kind of principle-governed nonconformity or disobedience. Indeed, in some cases, a single act can be described as both civil disobedience and conscientious objection' (2012a, p. 532). In this sense, they could be considered as two different moments—an *individual* moment and a *political* one—within a single reality that interact in a form of symbiosis, as it was the case of the dissent against military conscription.

The relevance of the distinction between civil disobedience and conscientious objection is not merely taxonomic. In this work, my concern is related to the connection between these forms of dissent and the different degree of legitimacy that each one needs to be recognized and, eventually, to find a 'special' place in the democratic system. It is a common thought that in democratic states and just societies, civil disobedience is not necessary, since there are other forms of political participation that circumvent this kind of marginal practice (Raz 1979; Rawls 1999). Conscientious objection benefits, however, from a greater possibility of acquiring the status of a right, since it is usually characterized as an expression guided by individual motivations, and liberty of conscience is one of the most sacred principles in Western societies (Gascón 1990). Therefore, the ethical, political, and legal consequences are different depending on whether a person is considered a civil disobedient or a conscientious objector. Acts of both conscientious objection and civil disobedience are mostly defined by anachronistic legal principles more than a dialogical and communicative framework to distinguish between justifiable and non-justifiable acts of dissent (Cooke and Petherbridge 2016). From an empirical perspective, it is proved that dissent demonstration may adopt multiple forms, so it is not always easy to establish clearly with which kind of disobedience one is dealing. This is the main interest of the debate on conceptual delimitation in this case.

Number, Intention, and Kind of Behavior: Good Distinction Criteria?

Reviewing the classical definitions of conscientious objection, it is possible to identify some common features: an individual nature; a pacific expression; an ethical intentionality, aimed at avoiding a heteronomous imperative that is considered unjust; and, finally, an omissive behavior (Raz 1979; Rawls 1999; in the Spanish context, Gascón 1990). Regarding the concept of civil disobedience, we can find the following distinctive characteristics: a more collective than individual exercise; a generally non-violent demonstration; an intentionality based on the achievement of political change; and, finally, an expression that implies either an action or an omission. It is not evident, however, that these attributes are invariably met when we look at specific cases.

Number: Individual versus Collective nature

It is commonly considered that an objector' claims must not exceed the preservation of her own moral integrity, autonomy, and freedom of conscience. In the healthcare context, however, it is frequent to find situations in which conscientious objection does not occur in isolation, but in which it is a collective appeal. This is the case in many gynecological services—in Spain and somewhere else—in the case of abortion (Gracia and Rodríguez-Sendín 2008). Usually, ethical imperatives are not reduced only to the intimate sphere of the conscience. An excessive emphasis on the individual nature of conscientious objection overlooks moral conceptions not being invariably limited to a specific individual. People create and recreate their conscience in a highly intersubjective way, and its dictates can be shared by others. Therein lies the transformative potential of conscientious claims and, at the same time, the greatest danger. Thanks to their collective strength, there are occasions when disobedient consciences achieve their goals. This success results in healthcare being provided to vulnerable people, as in the case of the rejection of RDL16/2012, or in it becoming more problematic, as in the case of abortion, where patients' interests and rights are frequently violated (Tongue 2022). In both situations, the actions or omissions we assume are in the name of conscience may have a social projection. Therefore, only by denying the collective/social dimension of our ethical behavior, it is possible to establish a clear distinction between conscientious objection and civil disobedience in the *individual-collective* goals of the dissent act.

Intention: Ethical versus Political goals

As it has been established previously, civil disobedience is traditionally considered a strategic and political act, while conscientious objection is not. The argument to defend this position is that civil disobedients may act conducted by their moral convictions, but their motivation is mainly political. With their behavior, they challenge the democratic right to make collective decisions. Instead, an individual conscientious objector is not driven by the interest in questioning the way in which the democratic powers decide for the whole community (Brownlee 2012a, p. 537).

However, it is problematic determining whether the dissident' intention—either objector or civil disobedient—is to change a law or just to reject certain legal obligations for the sake of preserving their own conscience and moral duties. It is not always clear whether their interest and desire does not also include their intention to challenge a law considered deeply unjust and ethically unacceptable, to the extent that they are willing to behave against it. It is quite common for people to disagree with legal measures, but few of us are used to becoming dissenters only on the basis of disagreement.

Thus, objectors' and disobedients' goals and behaviors may be mixed. Let me recall once again the healthcare professionals who refuse to perform abortion. We can easily understand a refusal based on conscientious reasons as being in line with the intention—at varying degrees of explicitness—to challenge the legal situation to the greatest possible extent. Following Brownlee, it is wrongly assumed 'that politics and strategy do not figure into conscientious objection. Breaches carried out in secret with the aim of remaining secret are strategic acts, especially when the acts are chosen with calculation to preserve liberty from coercive interference from the law' (2012a, p. 537).

Regarding those healthcare providers against the RDL16/2012, the main purpose of breaching the law was aiding what they saw as suffering and vulnerable beings, and then, they probably also desired to change the law. In some cases, they openly communicated their opposition to the legal measures; in other cases, they may not. Based on their behavior, it can be interpreted that they were against the law and that they probably liked to change it; but what they could do, what constituted their ethical responsibility, was taking care to those people who needed them.

Insofar as non-observance of the law has supposedly no effect beyond the objector, it is possible for conscientious objection to achieve legal recognition, integrated as an exception in the democratic system. Civil disobedience, however, is attributed with a broader scope—and risk—which entail greater difficulties in achieving any recognition. Nonetheless, conscientious objection may imply political consequences since it has the capacity to modify the authority's criteria, either by initiating procedures to guarantee the possibility of appealing to conscientious objection or even by modifying the refused norm. This was the case of conscientious objection to compulsory military service in Spain,[5] for example. In the healthcare context, the limited scope of conscientious objection is questionable. Frequently, conscientious objection carries significant consequences that exceed the individual conscience of the objector. In fact, it may have a deep impact on the people who require the refused service—for instance, women seeking abortion—or the prohibited provision—as it was the case of undocumented migrants assisted by healthcare professionals—.

Kind of behavior: Action versus Omission

Usually, conscientious objection is considered a breach of a *legal positive duty*, in other words, an imperative which requires a *doing*, an action. In this sense, nature of civil disobedience has been related to either *doing* or *not-doing*, that is, an action or an omission. Nevertheless, there are situations in which people are in a position of guarantors and in which they consider it their specific *duty to act*. It is easy to imagine how healthcare professionals, who use to work in a system where universal access was provided, felt their ethical convictions compromised by a excluding law. According to Nancy Berlinger, 'in this case, conscientious objection is expressed as a double negative—a refusal to refuse to provide health care—a basic connection among an active, critically reflective conscience that says 'yes' to providing equal access to health care' (2016, p. 126).

Based on these premises, the consideration of conscientious objection in a purely negative sense—the sense of omission—does not seem very consistent (Coggon 2008; Harris 2012; Sepper 2012; Triviño 2012, 2014; Triviño et al. 2013). In the case at hand, healthcare professionals against RDL16/2012 expressed their ethical dissent through the *provision of a service* that, according to the law, should not be provided free of charge.

Is the distinction between action and omission relevant in explaining the moral responsibility of agents in the healthcare context? It has been frequently argued that we need a greater moral justification to ask or to force someone to perform an action than when requesting an omission (Sulmasy 2008; Wicclair 2011; Woollard and Howard-Snyder 2016). I defend that this is not necessarily the case, at least in relation to conscientious objection in the healthcare context. In both type of objection—negative and positive—, the beliefs that lead to the rejection of a procedure, as well as those which justify the will to provide it, are morally relevant for the people who hold them. Freedom of conscience and moral integrity may be damaged either by performing an action against one's own ethical convictions or by refraining from fulfilling a request on the basis of these convictions (Wicclair 2011; Giubilini 2016).

[5] The initial pressure contributed to the recognition of conscientious objection. Later, the resistance of the rebellious individuals, coupled with a favorable social climate, made it possible to abolish military conscription and, subsequently, to create a professional army.

For these reasons, both kind of conscientious objection should be considered, regardless of whether their origins are related to religion, secular beliefs, or any ethical commitment to the profession. Healthcare professionals develop a conscience informed by certain values, experiences, and practices that lead them to act in a consistent way. The degree of sincerity and the moral consistency of conscientious objectors become clear when we examine their willingness to undertake a charge for the sake of maintaining the consistency of their beliefs.

From a normative perspective, the lack of recognition of positive conscientious objection has important consequences at a legal level (Harris 2012). While it is possible to apply exculpatory clauses in the case of negative conscientious objection, it does not occur in relation to positive conscientious objection. Thus, the protection level between *positive* and *negative* conscientious objectors is not comparable from an empirical point of view.

14.7 Conscientious Objection and Civil Disobedience as Controverted Forms of Political Participation

In controversial issues, a certain number of people will disagree with a norm they do not consider to be ethically right. In democratic systems, we usually face this kind of disagreement in the context of the collective assumption of the vote binding condition. Based on the respect of this social contract, we have the opportunity to change an undesirable law or situation through legal channels (Savulescu 2007). If there are people who do not consider this agreement binding for them, then those others who do—accepting from the very first moment that the results could not be what they specifically chose—, would be at a comparative disadvantage, creating, in short, an unfair situation. Thus, we usually assume that the reasons to obey a law are stronger in a democratic society than elsewhere (Singer 1993).

This begs a classical question: Is defying the law legitimate in a democratic society? From a factual perspective, the possibility of derogating an unjust law by legal means in the near future is not a definitive reason to delegitimize an act of disobedience. After all, it is only a theoretical possibility, and the injustice may be inflicting specific damage and therefore cannot wait, such as is the case of undocumented migrants in Spain. According to Peter Singer, only when there is a real possibility to bring about change by legal means prior to the unwanted damage being inflicted, does this possibility become an important justification for relying solely on that path of action (Singer 1993). Additionally, it can be said that government is not always better placed than people to take better decisions, as empirical facts show. In the case of the healthcare providers, they account for all of the reasons whether and how to protect sick people, especially when it has been proved that public powers are acting under fallacies (Suess et al. 2014; Cimas et al. 2016; Triviño et al. 2016).

Therefore, the strength of the reason seems to be directly proportionate to the feasibility of change through legal means. Sometimes, dissent can correct a democratic deficit where discussion on a specific problem has been avoided or not taken into account (Markovits 2005). The spaces to challenge democratically taken decisions should not be considered as a violation of democracy, but a reflection which is only possible in a democratic framework (Brownlee 2012b).

It is important to note that any political decision should be taken in the context of collective ethical commitments. Thus, acts of disobedience must not be understood solely in legal and formal terms, but also in radical moral ones. When vulnerable people are being abandoned, individual, and professional ethics are an incentive to act. In this kind of situation, dissent can be considered not a *right*, but a *duty*. In the case of RDL16/2012, this duty preserved not only the professionals' ethical commitments, but also migrants' healthcare. It is a different matter when dissent leaves people who need a service in an unprotected situation, as in the cases of abortion, the termination of life support at the end of life, or the refusal to perform an intervention widely accepted by society. In such situations, the respect for disobedient's beliefs needs to be balanced with the concerned person's beliefs and interests.

As human beings, we have a relational nature, so our conscience does not function in isolation, but in interaction with the others (MacLeod 2013). From this perspective, the content of one's conscience is not fixed. The experience of living and reflecting has a cumulative effect on what we value, how our convictions relate to each other, and how they translate into practice and hold up when tested. Therefore, conscience can be considered as 'a living critical faculty, open to experience rather that closed off from it' (Berlinger 2016, p. 123). If this account of conscientious dissent is accepted, then we can consider it valuable to the extent that it contributes to the exchange of ideas and stimulate reflection on dominant views. Moreover, in cases where dissenters' arguments and behaviors are well grounded, they are not only a critical surveillance of power, but a stabilizing force within the society (Rawls 1999).

History shows us that conscientious objection and civil disobedience can be strong mechanisms for political participation and transformation of reality; but there are also cases in which conscience claims has been or are abusive. Therefore, it is important 'to consider civil disobedience and conscientious objection together in the debate about moral rights. Given both their intersection and their respective assertions of conscientiousness, these practices are most fruitfully considered in relation to a single proposed right to conscientious disobedience (where *disobedience* is construed broadly since not all conscientious objection is in breach of law) to determine which, if either, practice has the best case for claiming protection as a right' (Brownlee 2012a, p. 536).

14.8 Conclusions

Throughout this chapter, I have reviewed the classical definitions of conscientious objection and civil disobedience. After a brief contextualization of the Spanish healthcare system, I have used the rejection by some healthcare professionals of RDL16/2012 to critically analyze the most common distinctive criteria of these two forms of dissent. I have shown the possibility of the professionals' answer against the RDL16/2012 being only an altruistic action as doubtful, since they have ethical obligations to abandon neither their patients nor their communities, and to provide healthcare under conditions of equity. I have also tried to prove that the limits between conscientious objection and civil disobedience are not always well defined, considering the main features applied to both (individual vs. collective character, ethical vs. political goals and active vs. passive nature). I have proposed that we might distinguish two moments of a single reality that interact symbiotically: an *individual* moment and a *political* one, since we are relational beings and our consciences are constructed through interaction with others. Agreements and disagreements are very much part of our social lives and there are situations in which democratic means seem insufficient to defend the interests of the most vulnerable. In these cases, forms of dissent—conscientious objection and civil disobedience—emerge as alternative ways to transform reality.

More precisely, I have explored the *positive* dimension of claims of conscience, which in this study case appeals to the moral obligation to act to preserve the right to healthcare. The objective has been to set aside the dichotomy of action and omission to favor the legitimacy of the moral problems involved in balancing professional responsibilities and the needs of affected persons. The interest has been to draw attention to those scenarios where the agents might feel themselves a *moral obligation to act*.

Especially in difficult times, the preservation of fundamental rights is a principal means of protecting the most vulnerable populations and avoiding increases in inequality. Sometimes claims of conscience in the healthcare context have been placed at the service of sectarian interests and beliefs. In this sense, conscience clauses can be considered as ethically problematic when they offer 'too much protection' by emphasizing the rights of healthcare professionals with little or no attention to the rights of patients and to the consequences of refusal for patients seeking legal, medically appropriate, and desired healthcare (Minerva 2013; Berlinger 2016).

However, claims of conscience can also actively promote social justice. The Spanish healthcare system had hitherto proven its value in terms of sustainability, quality, and equal access (Muntaner et al. 2012). RDL16/2012 was clearly a backlash that endangers the universal access previously guaranteed. The lack of evidence of the real benefits (Suess et al. 2014; Cimas et al. 2016; Triviño et al. 2016), along with the healthcare professionals' ethical duties towards their patients, allows for the justification of positive conscientious objection as a mechanism to preserve a system sustained on the basis of solidarity.

References

Backman, Gunilla, et al. 2008. Health systems and the right to health: An assessment of 194 countries. *The Lancet* 372 (9655): 2047–2085. https://doi.org/10.1111/j.1365-2214.2009.00971_2.x.

Berlinger, Nancy. 2016. *Are workarounds ethical? Managing moral problems in health care systems*. Oxford University Press. https://doi.org/10.1093/med/9780190269296.001.0001.

Brock, Peter. 2006. *Against the draft. Essays on conscientious objection from the radical reformation to the second world war*. Toronto: University of Toronto Press. https://doi.org/10.3138/9781442627215.

Brownlee, Kimberlee. 2007. Civil disobedience. In *The stanford encyclopedia of philosophy*, ed. E. N. Zalta. http://plato.stanford.edu/entries/civil-disobedience. Accessed 30 Sept 2023.

Brownlee, Kimberley. 2012a. Civil disobedience and conscientious objection. In *The Routledge companion to philosophy of law*, ed. Andrei Marmor, 527–539. New York: Routledge. https://doi.org/10.4324/9780203124352.ch34.

Brownlee, Kimberley. 2012b. *Conscience and conviction: The case for civil disobedience*. Oxford: Oxford University Press. https://doi.org/10.1093/acprof:oso/9780199592944.001.0001.

CE-Council of Europe Parliamentary Assembly Resolution 1509. 2006. Human rights of irregular migrants. http://assembly.coe.int/nw/xml/XRef/Xref-XML2HTML-en.asp?fileid=17456&lang=EN. Accessed 30 Sept 2023.

CESCR-Committee on Economic, Social and Cultural Rights. 2000. The right to the highest attainable standard of health: 11/08/2000. E/C.12/2000/4. General Comment 14. 22nd session. Geneva. Agenda Item 3. http://www.refworld.org/pdfid/4538838d0.pdf. Accessed 30 Sept 2023.

CGOCE (Consejo General de la Organización Colegial de Enfermería). 2012. El Consejo General de Enfermería advierte a los enfermeros sobre la inviabilidad jurídica de la figura de la objeción de conciencia ante casos de no beneficiarios de la asistencia sanitaria en España [Press release]. http://www.enfermeriacanaria.com/wptfe/wp-content/uploads/12-08-09-NP-Matizacion-Consejo-Enfermeria-RD-casos-no-beneficiarios-SNS.pdf. Accessed 30 Sept 2023.

Cimas, Marta, et al. 2016. Healthcare coverage for undocumented migrants in Spain: Regional differences after Royal Decree Law 16/2012. *Health Policy* 120 (4): 384–395. https://doi.org/10.1016/j.healthpol.2016.02.005.

Coggon, John. 2008. Acts, omissions and responsibility. *Journal of Medical Ethics* 34 (8): 576–579. https://doi.org/10.1136/jme.2008.024729.

Cooke, Maeve, and Danielle Petherbridge. 2016. Civil disobedience and conscientious objection. *Philosophy and Social Criticism* 42 (10): 953–957. https://doi.org/10.1177/0191453716659522.

CPP-College of Physicians of Philadelphia. 2013. History of anti-vaccination movements. *History of Vaccines*. http://www.historyofvaccines.org/content/articles/history-anti-vaccination-movements. Accessed 30 Sept 2023.

Cuadra, Carin B. 2012. Right of access to health care for undocumented migrants in European Union—A comparative study of national policies. *European Journal of Public Health* 22 (2): 267–271. https://doi.org/10.1093/eurpub/ckr049.

Fernández-García, María, and Elena Polentinos-Castro. 2018. ¿Para cuándo la universalidad? *Atención Primaria* 50 (10): 571–573. https://doi.org/10.1016/j.aprim.2018.11.001.

Gascón, Marina. 1990. *Obediencia al Derecho y objeción de conciencia*. Madrid: Centro de Estudios Constitucionales.

Giubilini, Alberto. 2016. Conscience. In *The Stanford encyclopedia of philosophy*, ed. E. N. Zalta. https://plato.stanford.edu/archives/win2016/entries/conscience. Accessed 30 Sept 2023.

Gracia, Diego, and Juan-José. Rodríguez-Sendín. 2008. *Ética de la objeción de conciencia*. Madrid: Fundación Ciencias de la Salud.

Harris, Lisa. 2012. Recognizing conscience in abortion provision. *The New England Journal of Medicine* 367 (11): 981–983. https://doi.org/10.1097/ogx.0b013e31827bfa55.

ICESCR-International Covenant on Economic, Social, and Cultural Rights. New York: United Nations, 1966. https://www.ohchr.org/en/professionalinterest/pages/cescr.aspx. Accessed 30 Sept 2023.
Joffe, Carole E. 1995. *Doctors of conscience. The struggle to provide abortions before and after Roe v. Wade*. Boston: Beacon Press.
Juanmarti-Mestres, Arnau, Guillem López-Cassasnovas, and Judit Vall-Castelló. 2021. The deadly effects of losing health insurance. *European Economic Review* 131: 103608. https://doi.org/10.1016/j.euroecorev.2020.103608.
MacLeod, Carolyn. 2013. Taking a feminist relational perspective on conscience. In *Being relational: Reflections on relational theory and health law*, eds. Jocelyn Downie J. and Jennifer J. Llewelyn, 161–181. Vancouver: University of British Columbia Press. https://doi.org/10.59962/9780774821902-010.
Markovits, Daniel. 2005. Democratic Disobedience. *Yale Law Journal* 114 (8): 1897–1952.
Minerva, Francesca. 2013. Conscientious objection in Italy. *Journal of Medical Ethics*. https://doi.org/10.1136/medethics-2013-101656.
Montalvo Jaaskelainen, Federico de. 2016. Objeción de conciencia positiva; en particular, sobre el conflicto planteado al amparo del Real Decreto-Ley 16/2012. *Derecho y salud* 26(2): 9–20.
Muntaner, Carles, et al. 2012. *La sanidad está en venta*. Barcelona: Icària.
Murphy, Sean, and Stephen J. Genuis. 2013. Freedom of conscience in health care: Distinctions and limits. *Bioethical Inquiry* 10 (3): 347–354. https://doi.org/10.1007/s11673-013-9451-x.
Navarro, Sílvia. 2013. Las cosas por su nombre ¿Objeción de conciencia o desobediencia civil? *Revista De Bioética y Derecho* 28: 91–101. https://doi.org/10.4321/s1886-58872013000200008.
Rada, Asier. 2012. Spanish doctors protest against law that excludes immigrants from public healthcare. *British Medical Journal* 345: e5716. https://doi.org/10.1136/bmj.e5716.
Rawls, John. 1999 [1971]. *A theory of justice* (Rev. Edition). Cambridge, MA: Belknap Press.
Raz, Joseph. 1979. *The authority of law: Essays on law and morality*. Oxford: Clarendon Press. https://doi.org/10.1093/acprof:oso/9780198253457.001.0001.
REDER (Red de Denuncia y Resistencia contra el RDL16/2012). 2017. Civil society faced with healthcare exclusion: Defending our healthcare. https://reder162012.org/images/InformeOct2017/REDERsep17ENG.pdf. Accessed 30 Sept 2023.
Rodríguez, Eunice, et al. 1999. The Spanish healthcare system: Lessons for newly industrialized countries. *Health Policy and Planning* 14 (2): 164–173. https://doi.org/10.1093/heapol/14.2.164.
Sahuquillo, María R. Sanidad avisa a los médicos objetores que no pueden atender a los sin papeles. *El País*, August 2012. http://sociedad.elpais.com/sociedad/2012/08/09/actualidad/1344542144_011176.html. Accessed 30 Sept 2023.
Savulescu, Julian. 2007. The proper place of values in medicine. *American Journal of Bioethics* 7 (12): 21–22. https://doi.org/10.1080/15265160701709990.
SEMFyC. 2012. Atendemos personas, no asegurados [Statement]. https://www.semfyc.es/atendemos-personas-no-asegurados-comunicado-ante-medidas-rd-162012-registro-para-objecion/. Accessed 30 Sept 2023.
Seoane, José Antonio. 2013. Objeción de conciencia responsable. In *La bioética y el arte de elegir*, ed. A. Blanco and M.P. Núñez, 100–112. Madrid: ABFyC.
Seoane, José Antonio. 2014. Objeción de conciencia positiva. *Revista De Bioética y Derecho* 32: 34–45. https://doi.org/10.4321/s1886-58872014000300004.
Sepper, Elizabeth. 2012. Taking conscience seriously. *Virginia Law Review* 98 (7): 1501–1575. https://doi.org/10.2139/ssrn.1888375.
Sevillano, Elena G. La ONU ve 'inaceptable' la desatención sanitaria a inmigrantes en España. *El País*, April 2014. http://sociedad.elpais.com/sociedad/2014/04/29/actualidad/1398797567_706386.html. Accessed 30 Sept 2023.
Simón Lorda, Pablo. 2014. Negando la mayor. *Ética y salud pública en tiempos de crisis. Cuadernos De La Fundación Víctor Grífols i Lucas* 32: 103–125.

Singer, Peter. 1993. Civil disobedience, violence and terrorism. In *Practical ethics* (3rd edition): 256–275. Cambridge: Cambridge University Press. https://doi.org/10.1017/cbo9780511975950.012.

Singer, Peter. 2019. *The life you can safe*. Bainbridge Island/Sydney: The Life You Can Safe. https://doi.org/10.1525/9780520949454-123.

Suess, Amets, et al. 2014. The right of access to health care for undocumented migrants: A revision of comparative analysis in the European context. *European Journal of Public Health* 24 (5): 712–720. https://doi.org/10.1093/eurpub/cku036.

Sulmasy, Daniel P. 2008. What is conscience and why is respect for it so important? *Theoretical Medicine and Bioethics* 29 (3): 135–149. https://doi.org/10.1007/s11017-008-9072-2.

Tongue, Zoe L. 2022. On conscientious objection to abortion: Questioning mandatory referral as compromise in the international human rights framework. *Medical Law International* 22 (4): 349–371. https://doi.org/10.1177/09685332221119503.

Triviño, Rosana. 2014. *El peso de la conciencia: El ejercicio de la objeción en las profesiones sanitarias*. Madrid: CSIC-Plaza y Valdés.

Triviño, Rosana, et al. 2013. ¿Es moralmente relevante la distinción entre actos/omisiones en bioética? In *La bioética y el arte de elegir*, ed. A. Blanco and M.P. Núñez, 234–240. Madrid: ABFyC.

Triviño, Rosana. Conscientious Objection and Undocumented Migrants in Spain. *Hastings Bioethics Forum*, September 2012. http://www.thehastingscenter.org/conscientious-objection-and-undocumented-migrants-in-spain/. Accessed 30 Sept 2023.

Triviño, Rosana et al. 2016. Exclusion from healthcare in Spain: The responsibility for omission of due care. In *Ethical issues in poverty alleviation*, ed. Clemens Sedmark et al., 181–198. Dordrecht: Springer. https://doi.org/10.1007/978-3-319-41430-0_11.

West-Oram, Peter, and Alena Buyx. 2016. Conscientious objection in healthcare provision: A new dimension. *Bioethics* 30 (5): 336–343. https://doi.org/10.1111/bioe.12236.

Wicclair, Mark. 2011. *Conscientious objection in health care*. New York: Cambridge University Press. https://doi.org/10.1017/cbo9780511973727.

Woodward, Aniek, et al. 2014. Health and access to care for undocumented migrants living in the European Union: A scoping review. *Health Policy and Planning* 29 (7): 818–830. https://doi.org/10.1093/heapol/czt061.

Woollard, Fiona and Frances Howard-Snyder. Doing vs allowing harm. In *The Stanford encyclopedia of philosophy* (Summer 2016 Edition), ed. E. N. Zalta. http://plato.stanford.edu/archives/sum2016/entries/ng-allowing/. Accessed 30 Sept 2023.

Yo Sí Sanidad Universal. 2013. Un año de exclusión sanitaria, un año de desobediencia [Report]. https://yosisanidaduniversal.net/media/pages/materiales/informes/3042604298-1576313745/dossieraniversariordl.pdf. Accessed 30 Sept 2023.

Yo Sí Sanidad Universal. 2016. ¿Por qué rebautizamos al INSS "Instituto Nacional de la Segregación Sanitaria"? [Report]. https://yosisanidaduniversal.net/media/pages/materiales/informes/1377791722-1576313745/informeinss.pdf. Accessed 30 Sept 2023.

Yo Sí Sanidad Universal. 2022. El derecho a la asistencia sanitaria en las comunidades autónomas: Un derecho hecho pedazos [Report]. https://yosisanidaduniversal.net/media/pages/materiales/informes/informe-derecho-asistencia-sanitaria-comunidades-autonomas/1837562004-1669587030/informe_derecho-a-la-asistencia-sanitaria-en-ccaa-un-derecho-hecho-pedazos.pdf. Accessed 30 Sept 2023.

Chapter 15
Cross-Border Healthcare: The Spanish Implementation of Directive 2011/24/EU

Ana Ylenia Guerra Vaquero and Ana María Marcos del Cano

Abstract Healthcare is constituted by the services provided by healthcare professionals in order to assess, maintain or restore patients' health status. Spain adopted Directive 2011/24/EU on the application of patients' rights in cross-border healthcare, of 9 March 2011, so as to ensure patient mobility and to promote cooperation on healthcare between Member States, whilst fully respecting the responsibilities of the Member States for the definition of social security benefits relating to health and for the organisation and delivery of healthcare and medical care and social security benefits, in particular for sickness.

Keywords Cross-border healthcare · Reimbursement of costs and European Union

15.1 Introduction

European citizens, no matter where they live, have the right to choose where to receive medical treatment across the European Union (EU), and to be reimbursed for it. This right is now spelled out in the Directive on Cross-Border Healthcare, which entered into force in the whole EU in October 2013.

Under current EU law, citizens benefit from their own countries' national social security scheme if they fall sick while travelling in another Member State. However, for planned cross-border care, a Member State is able to require patients apply for prior authorisation. In this case, the Member State is only compelled to grant the authorisation if patients cannot be treated at home within a time limit considered medically justified.

The organisation, management, financing and delivery of healthcare constitute a responsibility for the EU Member States, according to article 168 of The Treaty on the

A. Y. Guerra Vaquero (✉) · A. M. Marcos del Cano
Universidad Nacional de Educación a Distancia, Madrid, Spain
e-mail: anaguerravaquero@gmail.com

A. M. Marcos del Cano
e-mail: amarcos@der.uned.es

© The Editor(s) (if applicable) and The Author(s), under exclusive license to Springer Nature Switzerland AG 2024

J.-A. Seoane and O. Vergara (eds.), *The Discourse of Biorights*, The International Library of Bioethics 109, https://doi.org/10.1007/978-3-031-66804-3_15

Functioning of the European Union (TFUE), that states: "*The Union shall encourage cooperation between the Member States in the areas referred to in this Article and, if necessary, lend support to their action. It shall in particular encourage cooperation between the Member States to improve the complementarity of their health services in cross-border areas*".

However, several judgments of the European Court of Justice confirm that patients have in certain cases the right to access healthcare products and services in a Member State other than their own, with the cost being borne by their own health system.

15.2 Legislative and Case-Law Development

The phenomenon of globalisation is no longer unequivocal of the tendency towards the homogenisation of several aspects in the international prism and, particularly, in the case of Europe. As European and national regulations demonstrate, healthcare is one of the aspects calling for a "Europeanisation". Evidence of this European and, later, Spanish regulation is cross-border healthcare.

It can be said that the vast majority of patients in the European Union receive healthcare in their own country by their own choice, but in some circumstances they may seek certain forms of assistance in other countries. It can be a very specialized attention, or of border areas in which the closest appropriate centre is located in the neighbouring country.

In the 1990s, several citizens seek the Court of Justice of the European Union to demand their right to reimbursement of the healthcare received in other Member States. In consequence, the Court had to define the conditions of the reimbursement of the healthcare received by patients in other Member States, rather than their own, becoming the true promoter of this kind of healthcare rights.

The Court of Justice of the European Union began to introduce in this field in view of the need to interpret and clarify the scope of the regulations on coordination in social security. However it progressively accepted the impact in this particular area of activity that two great freedoms of the acquis communautaire have: the freedom of movement that people have, and the freedoms of economic agents about the establishment and provision of services.

In 1998, the European Court of Justice stated that European citizens have the right to benefit from healthcare services in a different Member State. The doctrine was established in its landmark pronouncements in the Kohll and Decker cases in 1998. These principles created an uncertain legal situation during their application. The reason was the diversity of healthcare systems, especially regarding the reimbursement aspects and the delivery of health-care services.

According to Fotinopoulou Basurko (2011: 329–352), the contrast or the conflict between social norms and community economic freedoms began in this specific context, which– concerning the jurisprudence issued by the Court of Luxembourg—caused them to happen later.

Thanks to this jurisprudential work, European citizens have been able to decide, in many cases, the place where they receive healthcare and, in certain cases, they have also obtained the right to reimbursement of the expenses they previously had to pay for healthcare in a different Member State. According García Murcia and Rodríguez Cardo (2014: 309–329), this jurisprudence, which has been developed fundamentally since 2001 and which supposed the recognition of a kind of right to "free movement of patients", generated legal uncertainty and financial problems due to the absence of clear and direct normative support.

Attending to these reasons, the European Commission Directorate-General for Health and Consumer Protection in 2006 launched a public consultation on this issue, with its final report concluding on the need establish a general legal framework.

In this sense, it is important to state that in June 2007 the International Health Regulations entered into force. They are an international legal instrument that is binding on 196 countries across the globe, including all the Member States of the World Health Organization. Their aim is to help the international community prevent and respond to acute public health risks that have the potential to cross-borders and threaten people worldwide.

The International Health Regulations require countries to report certain disease outbreaks and public health events to the World Health Organization. Building on the unique experience of the World Health Organization in global disease surveillance, alert and response, the International Health Regulations define the rights and obligations of countries to report public health events and establish a number of procedures that the World Health Organization must follow in its work to uphold global public health security.

The year after, in July 2008, the Commission adopted a proposal for a directive of the European Parliament and of the Council on the application of patients' rights in cross-border healthcare. The proposal aims at establishing a Community framework for the provision of cross-border healthcare within the EU, for those occasions where the care patients seek is provided in a Member State other than their home country. This is structured around three main areas:

- the establishment of common principles in all EU health systems, clearly defining the Member States' responsibilities;
- the development of a specific framework for cross-border healthcare, providing clarity on the patients' entitlements to have healthcare in another Member State;
- the promotion of EU cooperation in healthcare, in areas like the recognition of prescriptions issued in other countries, European reference networks, health technology assessment, data collection, quality and safety.

Therefore, and respecting the principles of universality, access to quality care, equity and solidarity, the objectives of this framework would be, on the one hand, to offer sufficient clarity on the reimbursement rights for the healthcare received in other Member States and, on the other hand, to ensure that the necessary requirements for quality, safe and effective healthcare are also ensured in the case of cross-border care (European Union Commission, 2008).

15.3 Directive 2011/24/EU on the Application of Patients' Rights in Cross-Border Healthcare

The European Parliament adopted its position at the second reading the 19th of January 2011 and published in the EU's Official Journal on 9 March 2011. It was DIRECTIVE 2011/24/EU ON THE APPLICATION OF PATIENT' RIGHTS IN CROSS-BORDER HEALTHCARE that entered into force on the 25th of October 2013. The aims were to guarantee patients' mobility, the establishment of rules in order to facilitate their access to safe and high-quality healthcare in the European Union, and the promotion of cooperation in healthcare between Member States, fully respecting the responsibilities of these in the organisation and provision of such assistance. The Directive provides a detailed legal framework focused on three main areas: rules concerning the reimbursement of the costs of cross-border healthcare; responsibilities of the Member States with regard to cross-border healthcare and cooperation between healthcare systems.

The new Directive introduces three major changes, focusing on patients' rights: Firstly, citizens have the right to choose and be reimbursed for treatment, either public healthcare or private healthcare, anywhere in the EU. Secondly, prior authorisation for cross-border healthcare will become the exception rather than the rule.

Finally, citizens have the right to make informed decisions about treatment options. They are, therefore entitled to receive any relevant information from national contact points, established under the new Directive, and information from healthcare and treatment providers directly.

In order to increase transparency on quality and safety standards across the EU, the Directive advocates mutual assistance and cooperation between Member States in particular on the interoperability of eHealth tools and the use of health technology assessment. It also facilitates the recognition of prescriptions for medical products in every Member State.

Eventually, the Directive will provide for the development of European reference networks, to encourage the pooling of knowledge and maximise the cost-effective use of resources in highly specialised healthcare, such as the diagnosis and treatment of rare diseases.

This new law marks a real breakthrough for European citizens: not only for European citizens to be able to take more control over their own healthcare, but also to help patients associations promote higher quality and safety of care. Let us now analyse the Spanish case.

15.4 Spanish Royal Decree

The climate, the diet, the level of prices and the quality of life in Spain makes the country a destination for tourism but also a highly appealing place of residence, especially for European pensioners. This causes a significant public expense for the healthcare provided to citizens of other countries of the European Union, either as residents of our country or during a temporary stay. For the purposes of applying the legislation, the relevant aspect is the provision of healthcare in a State different from that in which the citizen has the right to receive such benefit.

On the other hand, many Spanish citizens have migrated to other Member States, especially after the economic crisis of the last decade, that caused situations such as a Spanish citizen who was working and affiliated with the Social Security system of another State, if this person had the need to be attended during a temporary stay (for family reasons for example) in Spain would be included in the compensation system provided. It would also happen to a Spanish emigrant who had generated the right to their pension in a European country at the time of their returning to Spain and establishing their residence here. (Relaño Toledano and Infante Campos, 2009).

In response to the diversity of situations that may arise as a result of the latest migratory movements, Spain adopted Directive 2011/24/EU on the application of patients' rights in cross-border healthcare, of 9 March 2011, so as to ensure patient mobility and to promote cooperation on healthcare between Member States, whilst fully respecting the responsibilities of the Member States for the definition of social security benefits relating to health and for the organisation and delivery of healthcare and medical care and social security benefits, in particular for illness.

On February 7th 2014, the Cabinet approved the Royal Decree transposing Directive 2011/24/EU on the application of patients' rights in cross-border healthcare into the Spanish legal system and amending Royal Decree 1718/2010 of 17 December on medical prescriptions and dispensing orders at the proposal of the Minister of Health, Social Services and Equality.

According to this Directive, patients of European Union countries can go to a Member State other than their own to receive healthcare. They will have to pay in advance for the services they receive and subsequently request reimbursement in their country under certain conditions which, in the case of some kinds of treatment, will require prior authorisation. The spirit of this Directive responds to the free movement of persons, goods and services in the EU.

The aims of the Royal Decree are as follows:

1. To ensure access to safe and high-quality cross-border healthcare.
2. To guarantee patient mobility.
3. To facilitate cooperation on healthcare between Spain and the rest of the EU.

According to article 3 of the Royal Decree, healthcare consists of health-related services provided by healthcare professionals to patients in order to assess, maintain or restore their health status, including the prescription, dispensing and provision of medicines, medical devices and dietetic foods for special medical purposes. The particularity of cross-border healthcare is that the healthcare is provided or prescribed in a Member State other than the Member State of affiliation.

In consequence, it is necessary to guarantee general principles, taking into account that it will be provided in accordance with the regulations of the Member State of treatment, including the standards and guidelines on quality and safety, and with European Union legislation in the field of safety standards, and also taking into account the principles of universality, access to high quality care, equity and solidarity. If healthcare is provided in Spain to patients whose State of affiliation is another Member State, the principle of non-discrimination based on nationality will also apply.

15.4.1 Reimbursement and Authorisation

According to this legislation, patients may go to another country in order to receive healthcare, which may be provided by either public or private services.

Patients will have to pay in advance, which will then be reimbursed to them through their country's competent health authority (in Spain, the regional authorities, INGESA and mutual societies for civil servants, as appropriate).

The cost of the benefits included in the National Health System's common portfolio of services and, as appropriate, in the complementary portfolio of the relevant regional authority, will be reimbursed in our country. Healthcare is defined in the broadest possible way and includes medicinal products and medical devices. Long-term healthcare, organ transplants and public vaccination programs are excluded.

Reimbursement will be according to the official rates of each health service, as if the treatment had been delivered in Spain.

Royal decree also establishes the necessity of requesting prior authorisation from the regional authority, INGESA (regional authority for Ceuta and Melilla) or mutual societies for civil servants in two cases:

- Where the healthcare involves hospital accommodation for at least one night.
- When the treatments require highly specialised or cost-intensive technology or equipment.

15.4.2 Patients' Rights

The Royal Decree also guarantees a series of rights for Spanish patients:

1. They may have a copy of any clinical reports, diagnostic tests and therapeutic procedures.
2. They will be ensured continuity of treatment after having received healthcare in another country.
3. Protection of their personal data will be guaranteed.
4. They will have all the necessary information at their disposal through the National Contact Point. The National Contact Point has already been set up at the Ministry of Health, Social Services and Equality through the Citizens' Advice Sub-Directorate.

Nevertheless, cross-border healthcare does not guarantee the coverage of all medical assistance in other States. There are certain services that are excluded from the scope of application of the Royal Decree:

(a) Long-term care services, whose purpose is to help those who require assistance when performing routine and daily tasks;
(b) The allocation of organs and the access to them for transplant purposes;
(c) Public vaccination programmes against infectious diseases, whose sole purpose is to protect the health of the population in Spanish territory and which are subject to specific planning and execution measures, without prejudice to the cooperation between Spain and the other Member States within the European Union.

Indeed, these exceptions constitutes a reflection of the biggest Spanish problems with healthcare and evidence the current discussions about long-term and end-of-life decisions, organ transplants and public vaccination programmes.

But what rights do citizens from other States have if they receive healthcare in Spain?

Before seeking healthcare, they will be entitled to receive information on quality and safety standards and on the healthcare providers in Spain and whether these have been duly authorised to provide healthcare according to Spanish regulations. Providers have to inform them about the different treatment options available, provide them with clear information about prices and give them a copy of the report on the treatment they have received.

European citizens may not be discriminated against relative to Spanish citizens. They will have the same rights and the legislation and regulations which apply in Spain will be applied to them for both their treatment and the conditions of access to that treatment. These patients may not be deprived of the most beneficial rights ensuing from the Regulations on the coordination of social security systems (for example, using the European Health Card) if they have not explicitly opted for the framework laid down by the Directive.

If they opt for this new legislation, European citizens will have to pay for the costs of the healthcare they have received, which will subsequently be reimbursed in their own country. In order to so, they will receive a clear invoice in the country of treatment, which includes patient data, centre or service, the treatment in detail and the amount actually paid. (Ministry of Health, Social Services and Equality 2014).

15.4.3 European Cooperation

This Royal Decree establishes measures aimed at promoting cooperation between Spain and the rest of the European Union Member States.

Information on health professionals will be shared. The Directive regulates the establishment of a European Reference Network, that the centres, services and units of reference of the National Health Service will join (currently 187 units for 42 pathologies or procedures). This will be especially beneficial for people suffering from rare diseases, who will be able to attend a specialised centre in another country.

In this sense, the Royal Decree states in its article 21 that it is the Ministry of Health, Social Services and Equality's responsibility, given the agreement at the Interterritorial Council of the National Health Service, on a proposal of the Reference Centres, Services and Units Project (CSUR) Designation Committee, to establish the procedure for the CSUR of the NHS designated according to Royal Decree 1302/2006, of 10 November, to be able to become a European Reference Network member or a collaborator with the network.

The Commission Implementing Decision of 10 March 2014 states in its article 3.3 that the membership application shall be accompanied by a written statement from the healthcare provider's Member State of establishment certifying that its participation in the proposal to establish a Network is in accordance with the Member State's national legislation (Agreement to provide healthcare providers access to European reference networks (ERNs), 2016).

Spain also plays an active role in the European eHealth Network. Spain leads the European Union's eHealth project, thanks to the highly successful implementation of eHealth in Spain (today 20 million Spaniards already have interoperable health records and more than 70% of prescribing and dispensing in our country is done electronically).

Spain also takes part in the European Health Technology Assessment Network, which will promote scientific information transfer between States.

Additionally, the Royal Decree amends Royal Decree 1718/2010 in order to facilitate the recognition of medical prescriptions issued in another State. Thus, medical practitioners will be able to issue valid "European prescriptions" across the Union. These prescriptions have to include the medicinal product's active substance.

To sum up, the Directive which is being transposed by the Royal Decree constitutes an opportunity to strengthen and unify health criteria and requirements, safety and healthcare by ensuring equal access to healthcare to citizens of any regional authority and citizens from other Member States. Spain is one of the leading countries in matters having to do with cross-border healthcare and is at the same time taking a further step to improving the healthcare of the people needing the most specialised treatments, such as the ones suffering from rare diseases. (Ministry of Health, Social Services and Equality 2014).

15.5 Health Tourism *Versus* Cross-Border Healthcare

Once the regulatory framework on cross-border healthcare has been presented, we proceed to reflect on one of the paradoxes that, we believe, derive from it. While the movement of European citizens to receive health care in another State has been a historical practice, its delimitation from an economic point of view has taken place at a difficult time. In this way, the Spanish Health Administration encourages the possibilities of its members, as patients, while being able to attract members from other Member States who demand their healthcare in Spain. It is then, paradoxically, an incentive for a practice framed more in the tourist field than in the welfare one.

In this sense, it should be noted that, from an academic point of view, the definition of health tourism is not clear. Some authors, such as Helble (2010) have a very broad view of this phenomenon and describe it as any medical act that occurs outside the place of residence, whether intentional or not. For others, like Lizarralde (2013) the concept is much more restrictive and would only cover those acts intentionally received by the patient-tourist, so, for us to talk about health tourism, it is a necessary condition that there is an a priori will to travel to receive medical treatment.

The World Tourism Organization defines a tourist as a visitor who travels to a main destination different from their usual environment for a duration of less than one year, with any main purpose, leisure, business or other personal reason, other than that of being employed by a resident entity in the country or place visited. A visitor (internal, receiver or issuer) is classified as a tourist (or overnight visitor), if their trip includes an overnight stay, or as a day-visitor (or hiker) otherwise.

Medical tourists elect to travel across international borders to receive some form of medical treatment. Treatments may span the full range of medical services. The most common are dental care, cosmetic surgery, elective surgery, and fertility treatment.

However, there isn´t an agreed definition of medical tourism; as a result, the methods applied by countries vary substantially, some countries count foreign patients' visits to hospitals whereas others count the entry of individual patients into the country. Other countries record nationality but not place of residence of patients, which can be problematic when migrants return to their home country for treatment. (World Health Organization, 2011).

Giraldo Chapaprieta and Méndez Pérez (2015) define a health tourist as a person who, fulfilling the above characteristics, whose main purpose of their trip is to receive medical treatment. It is important to highlight, therefore, that two conditions must be met simultaneously: intentionality in the reception of the service and displacement and overnight stay outside the place of origin.

Spain promotes, through its regulation on cross-border healthcare, patients´choice in order to receive healthcare outside Spain which is charged to public funds, being able to choose for that purpose the health centre, either a centre belonging to the public health network, or to private healthcare (Lomas Hernández, 2014). This is curious, much more so in a country where there are administrative obstacles to the healthcare of citizens who want to move to other Autonomous Communities, and even when there are bureaucratic complications for patients who, within their own Autonomous Community, want to choose another public health centre to be seen at.

15.6 Conclusions

1. Directive 2011/24/EU on patients' rights in cross-border healthcare is an important achievement of the 'patient empowerment' policy of the European Commission and an essential requirement enabling European citizens to benefit from

cross-border healthcare services. It is a natural extension of the fundamental freedoms included in the EU Treaties.

2. However, the development of the Directive concerns the Member States. Thus, the technologies and economic resources are not at the same level in all the countries and, moreover, the healthcare assistance will follow the Member State of treatment legislation. So, it is evident that the cross-border healthcare development will have different perspectives depending on the healthcare provider Member State.
3. The spirit of the Spanish regulation on cross-border healthcare is similar to the European one. Thus: to provide sufficient clarity about the right to be reimbursed for healthcare provided in other Member States, and to ensure that the necessary requirements for high-quality, safe and efficient healthcare are ensured for cross-border care.

The Directive is aimed at facilitating access to high-quality cross-border healthcare, ensuring patient mobility and cooperation among States in health matters. But, from our point of view, this is a paradox, because, in their own country there are many restrictions if you change the Autonomous Community of treatment.

4. Every citizen is a potential patient who may need timely, specific and high-quality care, even across the border. Good cross-border cooperation may help to contribute a better organisation of healthcare services, anticipating the current and future challenges concerning patients' rights.

References

Bacigalupe, A., U. Martín, R. Font, Y. González-Rábago, and N. Bergantiños. 2016. Austeridad y privatización sanitaria en época de crisis: ¿existen diferencias entre las comunidades autónomas. *Gaceta Sanitaria* 30 (1): 47–51.

Comisión de las Comunidades Europeas. 2008. *Marco comunitario para la aplicación de los derechos de los pacientes en la asistencia sanitaria transfronteriza.* Bruselas: Comisión de las Comunidades Europeas.

EUR-Lex. 2011. Healthcare in other EU countries—patients' rights http://eur-lex.europa.eu/legal-content/EN/TXT/HTML/?uri=URISERV:sp0002&from=ES. Accessed September 2023.

Fotinopoulou Basurko, O. 2011. El reembolso de gastos médicos y la directiva sobre asistencia sanitaria transfronteriza. *Lan Harremanak: Revista De Relaciones Laborales* 25: 329–352.

García Murcia, I., and I.A. Rodríguez Cardo. 2014. Asistencia sanitaria transfronteriza en el ámbito de la Unión Europea: De la seguridad social de trabajadores migrantes a una regulación específica". *Foro, Nueva Época* 17 (1): 309–329.

Giraldo Chapaprieta, A., and E. Méndez Pérez. 2015. El turismo sanitario en España: Mitos y realidades. *Revista Internacional De Trabajo Social y Ciencias Sociales* 9: 91–118.

Helble, M. 2010. The movement of patients across borders: challenges and opportunities for public health. *Bulletin of the World Trade Organization.* 89 (1): 68–72.

Jutten, K., and Janssens, P. 2016. Patients without borders. Cross-border patient flows in the Benelux. General Secretariat of the Benelux Union.

Lizarralde, E., and Auren. 2013. *Turismo de Salud.* Madrid: Ed. Fundación EOI.

Lomas Hernández, V. 2014. Comentario sobre el Real Decreto 81/2014, de 7 de febrero por el que se establecen normas para garantizar la asistencia sanitaria transfronteriza, y por el que se modifica el Rd 1718/2010, de 17 de diciembre, sobre receta médica y órdenes de dispensación. *Revista CESCO De Derecho De Consumo* 9: 177–186.

Ministry of Health. 2023. Social Services and Equality: https://www.sanidad.gob.es/en/pnc/ciudadanoUE/home.htm. Accessed March 2023.

Ministry of Health, Social Services and Equality. 2016. Agreement to provide healthcare providers access to european reference networks (ERNs). chrome-extension://efaidnbmnnnibpcajpcglclefindmkaj/https://www.sanidad.gob.es/fr/profesionales/CentrosDeReferencia/docs/Access_ERNs_Agreement.pdf. Accesed September 2023.

Navarro López, V. 2007. ¿Cómo está evolucionando la situación social de la Unión Europea? *Mediterráneo Económico* 12: 417–437.

Pérez Menayo, V. 2002. La Tarjeta Sanitaria Europea. *La Mutua* 8: 75-90.

Relaño Toledano J., and Infante Campos, A. 2009. Asistencia sanitaria transfronteriza del Sistema Nacional de Salud. Tipos y repercusión económica. *Revista de Administración Sanitaria Siglo XXI* 7 (4): 619–630.

Requejo, M.T. 2014. Cross-border healthcare in Spain and the implementation of the directive 2011/24/EU on the application of patient's rights in cross-border healthcare. *European Journal of Health Law* 21: 79–96.

Tena Reif, S. 2016. Influencia de la crisis económica del 2008 en la salud en España. *XII Congreso Español de Sociología.*

World Health Organization. 2013. Medical Tourism. World Health Organization.

Chapter 16
Comparative Review of National Regulatory Frameworks in the Context of Secondary Use of Data for Research Across Europe

Olga Tzortzatou-Nanopoulou, Alexandra Ziaka, Carla Barbosa, Gauthier Chassang, Aliuska Duardo-Sánchez, Silja Elunurm, Christine Dalebø Gjerdevik, Radek Halouzka, Mette Hartlev, Ragnhild Angell Holst, Dorota Krekora-Zajac, Jan Kuráň, Teodora Lalova—Spinks, Maria Luisa Lavitrano, Matteo Macilotti, Marina Makri, Signe Mežinska, Fruzsina Molnár-Gábor, Susanne Rebers, Jane Reichel, Santa Slokenberga, Tom Southerington, and Ruth Vella Falzon

Abstract Scientific research is a crucial tool for advancing healthcare and public health. In cross-border research collaborations, researchers need to navigate a complex pool of different requirements, which potentially hamper scientific research. This chapter aims to map the current legal landscape in seventeen Member States of the European Economic Area in the context of the secondary processing of health and

---

O. Tzortzatou-Nanopoulou (✉) · A. Ziaka · M. Makri
Biomedical Research Foundation of the Academy of Athens, 4 Soranou Efesiou Street, 11527 Athens, Greece
e-mail: otzortzatou@bioacademy.gr; olgananop@gmail.com

A. Ziaka
e-mail: a.ziaka@tilburguniversity.edu

M. Makri
e-mail: makrimarina@yahoo.gr

O. Tzortzatou-Nanopoulou · R. Halouzka · D. Krekora-Zajac · S. Mežinska
ELSI Services and Research, Biobanking and BioMolecular Resources Research Infrastructure—European Research Infrastructure Consortium (BBMRI-ERIC), Graz, Austria
e-mail: halouzka@mou.cz

D. Krekora-Zajac
e-mail: d.krekora@wpia.uw.edu.pl

S. Mežinska
e-mail: signe.mezinska@lu.lv

Present Address:
A. Ziaka
Tilburg Institute on Law, Technology & Society, Tilburg University, Tilburg, Netherlands

© The Editor(s) (if applicable) and The Author(s), under exclusive license to Springer Nature Switzerland AG 2024

J.-A. Seoane and O. Vergara (eds.), *The Discourse of Biorights*, The International Library of Bioethics 109, https://doi.org/10.1007/978-3-031-66804-3_16

genetic data for scientific research purposes. It critically assesses the transposition of GDPR in the national legal order of each State and its interplay with other applicable legislations. Our research findings show that only a handful examined Member States have a dedicated Act on secondary use, as the majority rely on provisions of different

C. Barbosa
Biomedical Law Center, University of Coimbra, Coimbra, Portugal
e-mail: cbarbosa@fd.uc.pt

Jean Monnet Center of Excellence "Building the Age of a Lawful and sustainable Data-Use" (BALDUS), Universitá Degli Studi di Perugia, Perugia, Italy

Department of Health, Ethics & Society—CAPHRI School, FHML, Maastricht University, Maastricht, Netherlands

G. Chassang
Inserm UMR1295 Centre for Epidemiology and Research in Population Health (CERPOP), Faculty of Medicine, University of Toulouse III Paul Sabatier, Toulouse, France
e-mail: gauthier.chassang@gmail.com

Unesco Chair "Ethics Science and Society", E2S, Federal University of Toulouse, Toulouse, France

Present Address:
Ethics and Biosciences Platform—Genotoul Societal, GIS Genotoul, Toulouse, France

A. Duardo-Sánchez
Department of Public Law, Social and Legal Sciences Applied to New Technosciences, University of the Basque Country (UPV/EHU), Basque Country, Spain
e-mail: aliuskad@gmail.com

Present Address:
Department of Legal Philosophy, Faculty of Law, Universidad Nacional de Educación a Distancia (UNED), Madrid, Spain

S. Elunurm
Secondary Data Use, Estonian Next Generation National Health Information System development project, Estonian Ministry of Social Affairs, Tallin, Estonia
e-mail: silja.elunurm@healthfounders.ee

Present Address:
Regulatory and Legal, Migrevention, Tartu, Estonia

Health Founders Estonia Consortium, Tartu, Estonia

C. D. Gjerdevik
PwC, Oslo, Norway
e-mail: c_gjerdevik@hotmail.com

R. Halouzka
Masaryk Memorial Cancer Institute, Brno, Czech Republic

Faculty of Medicine, Masaryk University, Brno, Czech Republic

National Centre of Nursing and Other Health Professions, Brno, Czech Republic

M. Hartlev
Faculty of Law, University of Copenhagen, Copenhagen, Denmark
e-mail: mette.hartlev@jur.ku.dk

laws. Consent, which has been traditionally relied upon for the processing of health and genetic data for scientific research purposes, still remains the most commonly used legal basis. However, there is an increasingly common stance among experts towards the lack of appropriateness of consent as legal basis and a preference over using it as additional safeguard. Most Member States have enabled the derogation from the exercise of data subject rights under art 89(2) GDPR, while providing a series

National Committee on Health Research Ethics, Copenhagen, Denmark

R. A. Holst
Norwegian Directorate of Health, Oslo, Norway
e-mail: Ragnhild.Angell.Holst@helsedir.no

D. Krekora-Zajac
Zając & Partners Law Firm L.P. Advocates and Legal Counsels, Warsaw, Poland

Department of Comparative Civil Law, Faculty of Law and Administration, University of Warsaw, Warsaw, Poland

J. Kuráň
Masaryk Memorial Cancer Institute, Brno, Czech Republic
e-mail: jan.kuran@mou.cz

T. Lalova—Spinks
Clinical Pharmacology and Pharmacotherapy research group, Department of Pharmaceutical and Pharmacological Sciences, KU Leuven, Leuven, Belgium
e-mail: teodora.spinks@kuleuven.be

Center for IT & IP law (CiTiP), KU Leuven, Leuven, Belgium

M. L. Lavitrano
School of Medicine and Surgery, Universita' Degli Studi di Milano—Bicocca, Milan, Italy
e-mail: marialuisa.lavitrano@unimib.it

M. Macilotti
Faculty of Law, University of Trento, Trento, Italy
e-mail: matteo.macilotti@gmail.com

Italian node, Biobanking and BioMolecular resources Research Infrastructure of Italy (BBMRI.it), Milan, Italy

Present Address:
M. Makri
Faculty of Medicine, Aristotle University of Thessaloniki, Thessaloniki, Greece

S. Mežinska
Faculty of Medicine, University of Latvia, Riga, Latvia

Institute of Clinical and Preventive Medicine, University of Latvia, Riga, Latvia

F. Molnár-Gábor
Faculty of Law/BioQuant, University of Heidelberg, Heidelberg, Germany
e-mail: Fruzsina.Molnar-Gabor@hadw-bw.de

S. Rebers
Netherlands Cancer Institute, Amsterdam, Netherlands
e-mail: s.rebers@nki.nl

ELSI, Health-RI, Utrecht, Netherlands

of appropriate safeguards, mostly including anonymisation, pseudonymisation and encryption.

Keywords GDPR · Genetic data · Health data · Research ethics committee · Scientific research · Secondary use

16.1 Introduction

Although data reuse might greatly benefit healthcare and research, the full deployment of data originating from the healthcare sector raises challenging legal, ethical and social implications (ELSI) and questions[1] which need careful consideration. Indeed, cultural diversity, applicable legislation and operational implementation in national context form a heterogeneous canvas, that researchers are called to navigate.[2]

The divergences in national regulatory frameworks maintain for decades a fragmented legal landscape across EU, even after the General Data Protection Regulation (GDPR)[3] entered into force.[4] This is due partly to the flexibility that GDPR offers to European Economic Area (EEA) States to maintain or introduce their own additional conditions for processing special categories of data (GDPR, art 9(4)). There are many voices calling for the development of a common ethico-legal framework that will enable the compliance with international and national laws and policies.[5]

J. Reichel
Faculty of Law, Stockholm University, Stockholm, Sweden
e-mail: jane.reichel@juridicum.su.se

Center for Research Ethics & Bioethics, Uppsala University, Uppsala, Sweden

S. Slokenberga
Faculty of Law, Uppsala University, Uppsala, Sweden
e-mail: santa.slokenberga@jur.uu.se

T. Southerington
School of Law, University of Turku, Turku, Finland
e-mail: tomsou@utu.fi

Finnish Biobank Cooperative—FINBB, Turku, Finland

Medical Research Ethics Committee, Turku University Hospital, Turku, Finland

R. Vella Falzon
University of Malta, Msida, Malta
e-mail: ruth.vella-falzon@um.edu.mt

[1] Nuffield Council on Bioethics (2015).

[2] Eugenia Lamas, et al. (2015).

[3] European Parliament and Council Regulation 2016/679 of Apr. 27 (2016).

[4] Olga, Tzortzatou and others (2021).

[5] Rebecca Branum and Susan Wolf (2015).

The European Commission's 1 + MG Initiative[6] aims to enable the cross-border access to genomic data of more than one million EU citizens for research purposes and clinical applications. However, a joint cross-border genome initiative appears to be complicated, due to the abovementioned heterogeneity. In that context, the European Commission's Beyond 1 Million Genomes (B1MG) project aims to establish an acceptable ELSI framework for secure data sharing across EU.[7]

Despite the already distinguished work on the comparative assessment of national legislations on health research,[8] this chapter aims to critically assess seventeen countries' reaction to GDPR. It relies on the findings presented in the Report 'D2.3—Analysis of legal framework and development of common minimum standard', which was prepared for the B1MG Project. The findings collected during four workshops organised in 2021–2022, reflect the national experts' interpretation based on their expertise and practical experience.

16.2 Comparative Review of National Regulatory Frameworks

16.2.1 National Regulatory Framework

The GDPR commonly applies alongside national law in regulating secondary processing of health and genetic data for scientific research purposes.

Traditionally Nordic countries value scientific research, reflected in how they regulate secondary data use. ***Finland*** and ***Norway*** are the only ones with dedicated Acts on secondary use.[9] In Finland, additional laws govern relevant issues, including the Biobank Act[10] and the Finish Data Protection Act.[11] The Norwegian applicable framework also includes the Health Registries Act,[12] the Health Personnel Act,[13] the

[6] European Commission. European '1 + Million Genomes' Initiative. https://digital-strategy.ec.europa.eu/en/policies/1-million-genomes. Accessed 25 May 2024.

[7] B1MG project. https://b1mg-project.eu/. Accessed 25 May 2024.

[8] DG Health and Food Safety (2021).

[9] Act on the Secondary Use of Health and Social Care Data No 552/2019 *Laki sosiaali- ja terveystietojen toissijaisesta käytöstä 552/2019;* Act 2008-06-20-44 (Health Research Act) *Lov 20. juni 2008 nr. 44 om medisinsk og helsefaglig forskning (helseforskningsloven).*

[10] Biobank Act 688/2012 *Biopankkilaki 688/2012.*

[11] Data Protection Act No 1050/2018 (Finnish Data Protection Act) *Tietosuojalaki (1050/2018),* particularly Sects. 4 and 6.

[12] Act 2014-06-20-20 (Health Registries Act) *Lov 6. juni 2014 nr. 20 om helseregistre og behandling av helseopplysninger (helseregisterloven).*

[13] Act 1999-07-02-64 (Health Personnel Act) *Lov 2. juli 1999 nr. 64 om helsepersonell m.v. (helsepersonelloven),* para 29.

Act relating to the application of biotechnology in medicine[14] and the Personal Data Act.[15] Although ***Denmark*** and ***Sweden*** lack specialized laws on secondary use, they have a set of applicable laws regulating this area. The Danish legal framework consists of the Health Act,[16] the Danish Data Protection Act[17] and the Act on Research Ethics Review of Health Research Projects.[18] In Sweden, these issues are regulated by the Patient Data Act,[19] the Ethical Review Act[20] and the Public Access to Information and Secrecy Act (PAISA).[21] An initiative has been taken to review the legislation in order to facilitate secondary use of health data, with a public survey presented in November 2023.[22]

The examined ***South European countries*** have no dedicated Act. In particular, the ***Greek*** applicable legal framework includes Law 2619/1998,[23] the Code of Medical Ethics/Deontology,[24] the Ministerial Decision DYG 3/89292/2003 implementing Directive 2001/20/EC,[25] Law 4386/2016 on Regulations for Research, and other provisions,[26] as well as the data protection legislation, including some provisions of pre-GDPR Law 2472/1997,[27] and Law 4624/2019.[28] The ***Italian*** legal framework consists of GDPR, the Legislative Decree no 196/2003 (as modified by Legislative

[14] Act 2003-12-05-100 relating to the application of biotechnology in medicine *Lov 5. juli 2003 nr. 100 om humanmedisinsk bruk av bioteknologi m.m. (bioteknologiloven)*, para 5-8 Sect. 3.

[15] Act 2018-06-15-38 (Norwegian Personal Data Act) *Lov 15. juni 2018 nr. 38 om behandling av personopplysninger (personopplysningsloven).*

[16] Consolidated Act on Health (Health Act) *Lovbekendtgørelse nr. 247 af 12. March 2024 om sundhed (Sundhedsloven).*

[17] Consolidated Act on supplementary provisions to the regulation on the protection of natural persons with regard to the processing of personal data and on the free movement of such data (Danish Data Protection Act) No. 289 *Lovbekendtgørelse nr 289 af 8. marts 2024 (Gældende)*, Sect. 10.1.

[18] Consolidated Act No. 1338 on Research Ethics Review of Health Research Projects *Lovbekendtgørelse nr. 1338 af 1. September 2020 om videnskabsetisk behandling af sundhedsvidenskabelige og sundhedsdatavidenskabelige forskningsprojekter (Komiteloven).*

[19] Patient Data Act No 2008:355 *Patientdatalag (2008:355).*

[20] Ethical Review Act No 2003:460 *Lag (2003:460) om etikprövning av forskning som avser människor (2022:49).*

[21] Public Access to Information and Secrecy Act No 2009:400 (PAISA) *Offentlighets- och sekretesslagen (2009:400).*

[22] Ministry of Social Affairs (2023).

[23] Law 2619/1998 *Νόμος 2619/1998 (ΦΕΚ Α'132/19.6.1998).*

[24] Code of Medical Deontology, Law 3418/2005 *Κώδικας Ιατρικής Δεοντολογίας Νόμος 3418/2005 (ΦΕΚ Α' 287/28.11.2005)*, art 24(2) d.

[25] Ministerial Decision DYG 3/89292/2003 implementing Directive 2001/20/EC *Υπουργική Απόφαση ΔΥΓ 3/89292/2003 Εναρμόνιση της Ελληνικής Νομοθεσίας προς την Κοινοτική (Οδηγία 2001/20) (ΦΕΚ Β'1973/31.12.2003).*

[26] Law 4386/2016 on Regulations for Research and other provisions *Νόμος 4386/2016 για την έρευνα και άλλες διατάξεις (ΦΕΚ Α' 83/11.5.2016).*

[27] Law 2472/1997 Νόμος 2472/1997 (ΦΕΚ Α' 50/10-4-1997).

[28] Law 4624/2019 *Νόμος 4624/2019 (ΦΕΚ Α' 137/29.8.2019).*

Decree no 101/2018) (Italian Personal Data Protection Code)[29] and the Provision of the Italian Privacy Authority no 146/2019.[30] In ***Malta***, apart from the Data Protection Act,[31] there is no specific legislation regulating scientific research, except for some provisions in the Clinical Trial Regulation[32] and laws regulating higher education and health. Malta has been quite proactive by enacting the secondary processing (health sector) regulations in 2019,[33] and establishing an ad-hoc task force competent to propose a regulatory framework for biobanks. In ***Portugal***, the applicable law consists of Genetic Information Law 12/2005 and regulatory diploma (Decree-Law 131/2014)[34] and Law 58/2019.[35] Deliberation 227/2007 of the National Data Protection Commission also remains relevant. Ahead of other Southern European countries, ***Spain's*** regulatory framework includes the Spanish Constitution,[36] the Organic Act 3/2018 (Spanish Data Protection Act),[37] the Act 14/2007 on Biomedical Research,[38] the General Act 14/1986 on health,[39] the Act 41/2002,[40] and the Royal Decree 1716/2011.[41] Thus, Malta and Spain are gradually progressing, moving towards Nordic countries and approaching a common European standard.

---

[29] Personal Data Protection Code Legislative Decree 196/2003 (Italian Data Protection Code) *Codice in materia di protezione dei dati personali, del d.lgs. 196/2003.*

[30] *Provision of the Italian Privacy Authority on the Processing of Particular Categories of Personal Data* no 146/2019 (Provision of the Italian Privacy Authority) *Provvedimento recante le prescrizioni relative al trattamento di categorie particolari di dati, ai sensi dell'art 21, comma 1 del d.lgs. 10 agosto 2018, n. 101, n. 146 del 5 giugno 2019.*

[31] Chapter 586 of the Laws of Malta, Data Protection Act.

[32] Subsidiary Legislation 458.43, Clinical Trials Regulation.

[33] Subsidiary Legislation 528.10, Processing of Personal Data (Secondary Processing) (Health Sector) Regulations 2019.

[34] Act on Personal Genetic Information and health information No 12/2005 *Lei n.º 12/2005, de 26 Janeiro, regulated by* Decree-Law 131/2014) *Decreto-Lei n.º 131/2014, de 29 de agosto.*

[35] Law No 58/2019 *Lei n.º 58/2019, de 8 de agosto*, particularly art 31.

[36] Spanish Constitution *Constitución Española «BOE» núm. 311, de 29/12/1978*, art 44(2).

[37] Organic Law on the Protection of Personal Data and Guarantee of Digital Rights No 3/*Ley Orgánica 3/2018, de 5 de diciembre, de Protección de Datos Personales y garantía de los derechos digitales «BOE» núm. 294, de 06/12/2018.*

[38] Act on Biomedical Research No 14/2007 *Ley 14/2007, de 3 de julio, de Investigación biomédica «BOE» núm. 159, de 04 de julio de 2007.*

[39] General Act on Health No 14/1986 *Ley 14/1986 de 25 de abril General de Sanidad «BOE» núm. 102, de 29 de abril de 1986.*

[40] Law 41/2002 of 14 November, Regulating Patient Autonomy and Rights and Obligations Regarding Clinical Information and Documentation. *Ley 41/2002, de 14 de noviembre, básica reguladora de la autonomía del paciente y de derechos y obligaciones en materia de información y documentación clínica «BOE» núm. 274, de 15 de noviembre de 2002.*

[41] Royal Decree No 1716/2011 of November 18, establishing the basic requirements of authorization and functioning of biobanks for biomedical research and the management of human biological samples, and regulating the functioning and organization of the National Registry of Biobanks for biomedical research *Real Decreto 1716/2011, de 18 de noviembre, por el que se establecen los requisitos básicos de autorización y funcionamiento de los biobancos con fines de investigación biomédica y del tratamiento de las muestras biológicas de origen humano, y se regula el funcionamiento y organización del Registro Nacional de Biobancos para investigación biomédica.*

Eastern European countries are more reserved. ***Latvia*** is already working towards a Law on secondary use and a Biobank Law. The applicable framework comprises the Oviedo Convention,[42] the Law on the Rights of the Patients,[43] the Pharmaceutical Law[44] and the Cabinet Regulation 289 of 23 March 2010[45] that have specific provisions regulating clinical trials of medicinal products, the Human Genome Research Law[46] and data protection law including GDPR and the Personal Data Processing Law.[47] Also, the Cabinet Regulation No 134 of 11 March 2014[48] regulates some further data sharing aspects within medical care. ***Estonia*** is a notable example. The secondary use of health data from the national health information system or the national health registries is regulated by the Health Services Organisation Act,[49] the Public Health Act[50] and the Personal Data Protection Act.[51] The latter together with the Oviedo Convention govern the secondary processing of genetic data specifically for scientific research purposes. Additionally, the Human Genes Research Act (HGRA) regulates the establishment, maintenance and research within the Estonian Biobank.[52] The framework for registries is quite fragmented, lacking an 'umbrella' Act, besides the Public Information Act[53] that prescribes the main rules for state databases/registries. In the ***Czech Republic*** the legal landscape is quite fragmented. Secondary processing is mainly governed by GDPR and the Personal Data Processing Act[54] but there are also some provisions in the Act on Health Services

---

[42] Convention for the protection of Human Rights and Dignity of the Human Being with regard to the Application of Biology and Medicine, Apr. 4, 1997 ETS 164 (Oviedo Convention) *Konvencija par cilvēktiesību un cieņas aizsardzību bioloģijā un medicīnā - Konvencija par cilvēktiesībām un biomedicīnum, "Latvijas Vēstnesis", 205, 30.12.2009.*

[43] Law on the Rights of Patients *Pacientu tiesību Latvijas Vēstnesis, 205, 30.12.2009,* particularly Sect. 10.

[44] Pharmaceutical Law *Farmācijas likums Latvijas Vēstnesis, 103, 24.04.1997.*

[45] Cabinet Regulation No. 289 of 23 March 2010 *Ministru kabineta 2010 gada 23 marta noteikumi Nr.289, Latvijas Vēstnesis, 51/52, 31.03.2010.*

[46] Human Genome Research Law *Cilvēka genoma izpētes likums Latvijas Vēstnesis, 99, 03.07.2002.*

[47] Personal Data Processing Law (Latvian Personal Data Processing Law) No 132 *Fizisko personu datu apstrādes likums Latvijas Vēstnesis 132, 04.07.2018,* particularly Sect. 31.

[48] Cabinet Regulation No. 134 of 11 March 2014 *Ministru kabineta 2014. gada 11. marta noteikumi Nr.134* Latvijas Vēstnesis, 52, 13.03.2014.

[49] Health Services Organisation Act Tervishoiuteenuste korraldamise seadus RT I 2001, 50, 284.

[50] Public Health Act *Rahvatervise seadus* RT I 1995, 57, 978.

[51] Personal Data Protection Act (Estonian Personal Data Protection Act) *Isikuandmete kaitse seadus* RT I, 04.01.2019, 11.

[52] Human Genes Research Act (HGRA) *Inimgeeniuuringute seadus RT I 2000, 104, 685,* particularly Sect. 1.

[53] Public Information Act *Avaliku teabe seadus RT I 2000, 92, 597,* particularly Chap. 5.

[54] Act No. 110/2019 Coll., on Personal Data Processing, as amended (Czech Personal Data Processing Act) *Zákon č. 110/2019 Sb., o zpracování osobních údajů, ve znění pozdějších předpisů,* particularly Sect. 16.

regarding the access to data contained in medical records.[55] The situation in ***Poland*** is less evolved, due to the lack of specific legal regulations on Biobanking and biomedical research related to personal data processing. The Personal Data Protection Act,[56] lacks special provisions on secondary use. Therefore, despite the lack of specialized legal framework, the abundance of national provisions and the significant steps of Latvia and Estonia hold potential for further contributing to a more unified European approach.

Central European countries lack a common approach. In ***the Netherlands*** the processing of health and genetic data for invasive research is governed by a Specific Act for trials.[57] In the absence of a specific Act on observational research, some more general laws apply, like the Medical Treatment Agreement Act.[58] The lack of clarity has been compensated by two Codes of Conduct by the Committee on Regulation of Health Research.[59] Following to GDPR's transposition through the Dutch Data Protection Act,[60] a newly published Code of Conduct governs the re-use of health data.[61] Additionally, ongoing discussions are in place about the adoption of a new law on biosamples. Despite ***Belgium's*** lack of a dedicated Act on secondary use, its biobank framework is quite rich, including the Law of 19 December 2008 on obtaining and using human body material (HBM) for human medical applications or scientific research purposes,[62] the Royal Decree on biobanks of 9 January 2018,[63] the Law of 30 October 2018 modifying the Law of 19 December 2008[64] as well as

---

[55] Act No. 372/2011 Coll., on Health Services and Conditions of Their Provision (Act on Health Services), as amended *Zákon č. 372/2011 Sb., o zdravotních službách a podmínkách jejich poskytování (zákon o zdravotních službách), ve znění pozdějších předpisů,* particularly Sect. 65.

[56] Personal Data Protection Act (Polish Data Protection Act) No 10 *Ustawa o ochronie danych osobowych z dnia 10 maja 2018 r. Dz.U. z 2019 r., poz. 1781,* art 2.

[57] Medical Research Involving Humans Act *Wet Medisch-Wetenschappelijk onderzoek met mensen BWBR0009408 (WMO).*

[58] Medical Treatment Agreement Act *Wet geneeskundige behandelingsovereenkomst BWBR0007021(WGBO).*

[59] Code of Conduct on Health Research Gedragscode Gezondheidsonderzoek (2004); Code of Good Use Code Goed Gebruik (2011).

[60] Dutch GDPR Implementation Act *Uitvoeringswet Algemene verordening gegevensbescherming BWBR0040940.*

[61] Code of Conduct on Health Research Gedragscode Gezondheidsonderzoek (2022).

[62] Law of 19 December 2008 regarding the procurement and use of human body material destined for human medical applications or for scientific research purposes *Loi relative à l'obtention et à l'utilisation de matériel corporel humain destiné à des applications médicales humaines ou à des fins de recherche scientifique.*

[63] Royal Decree on biobanks in implementation of Article 22 of the Act of December 2008 on the acquisition and use of human body material for the purpose of medical application to humans or scientific research *Arrêté royal relatif aux biobanques 9 Janvier 2018.*

[64] Law of 30 October 2018 modifying the Law of 19 December 2008 regarding the procurement and use of human body material destined for human medical applications or for scientific research purposes Loi modifiant la loi du 19 décembre 2008 relative à l'obtention et à l'utilisation de matériel corporel humain destiné à des applications médicales humaines ou à des fins de recherche scientifique 30 Octobre 2018.

the Compendium on biobanks (20.07.2018),[65] expected to be adapted soon. Further adaptations of the Belgian biobank law were recently approved in 2022.[66] The Data Protection Act,[67] also applies. In ***France***, the Data Protection Act, "Loi Informatique et Libertés" (LIL)[68] introduced simplified procedures. The LIL provisions on data processing for health research are further specified by the Commission for Information Technology and Liberties (CNIL) within methodologies of reference (MR) (LIL, art 66(II) and 73), depending on the health research type defined by French law. The applicable framework includes provisions in the Public Health Code,[69] the Civil Code[70] and the Penal Code.[71] In ***Germany***, the legal landscape is complex due to the federal state structure and the co-existence of general and specific laws. The applicable legal framework includes the Patient Data Protection Act,[72] State hospital laws, State data protection laws, the Federal Data Protection Act,[73] Civil Law provisions and professional secrecy rules. The newly adopted Health Data Use Act (GDNG) is intended to make health data easier and faster to use for public welfare purposes.[74] To this end, a decentralized health data infrastructure with a central data access and coordination office will be established at the Federal Institute for Drugs and Medical Devices. This law takes the first steps towards preparing the German healthcare system for a European connection to the European Health Data Space.

---

[65] Compendium on Biobanks *Compendium biobanken/biobanques/biobanks 20.07.2018.*

[66] Law of 23 February 2022 on provisions regarding human body material and embryos and gametes *Loi portant des dispositions en ce qui concerne le matériel corporel humain et les embryons et gametes 23 Fevrier 2022;* Law of 18 May 2022 providing various urgent health provisions *Loi portant des dispositions diverses urgentes en matière de santé (1) 18 Mai 2022.*

[67] Law of 30 July 2018 on the protection of natural persons with regard to the processing of personal data (Belgian Data Protection Act) *Loi relative à la protection des personnes physiques à l'égard des traitements de données à caractère personnel 30 Juillet 2018.*

[68] Law No 78-17 1978 relating to data processing, files and freedoms *Loi n° 78-17 du 6 janvier 1978 relative à l'informatique, aux fichiers et aux libertés (ou Loi Informatique et Libertés).*

[69] Public Health Code *Code de la Santé Publique* Part I, Book I, Title II Biomedical research, art L1121-1 to L1128-12.

[70] Civil Code *Code Civil,* Book I Title I Civil Rights *Des droits civils*, particularly Chap. III, art 16-10 to 16-13 on genetic data processing.

[71] Penal Code *Code Penal,* Book II Title II, Chap. VI Personality breach *Des atteintes à la personnalité*, art 226-1 to 226-32.

[72] Patient Data Protection Act *Patientendaten-Schutz-Gesetz (PDSG) vom 14. Oktober 2020 (BGBl. I 2020 S. 2115).*

[73] Federal Data Protection Act *Bundesdatenschutzgesetz vom 30. Juni 2017 (BGBl. I S. 2097), das zuletzt durch Artikel 10 des Gesetzes vom 23. Juni 2021 (BGBl. I S. 1858; 2022 I 1045) geändert worden ist.*

[74] Act on the Improved Use of Health Data, *Gesetz zur verbesserten Nutzung von Gesundheitsdaten (BGBl. 2024 I Nr. 102 vom 25.03.2024).*

16.2.2 Legal Basis

The choice over the legal basis indicates whether a country is more reserved to data re-use for research due to data protection considerations.

Nordic countries seem to be the most progressive. In ***Denmark*** generally, no consent is required for data and tissue samples transfers, and Research Ethics Committees (RECs) will normally grant an exemption from consent. Unlike tissue samples from research biobanks, there are some opt-out options for tissue samples from clinical biobanks taken in clinical situations as well as for genetic data storage in the National Genome Centre (Health Act, Sect. 29). Under the Act on Research Ethics Review of Health Research Projects, informed consent is necessary for sample collection. However, the Act allows the derogation from informed consent for secondary use of samples when the research project poses no health risk or burden, or obtaining consent is impossible or disproportionately difficult. Yet, for very comprehensive genetic analysis and very sensitive issues, RECs can still require consent, and based on new legislation, RECs can also make exemption of consent conditional to providing information to the person concerned about the intention of secondary use of samples or genetic data. When research involves tissue samples collected directly from research participants, both informed consent and REC authorization are necessary. In ***Finland***, under the Act on Secondary Use of Health and Social Care Data, there is no obligation to obtain informed consent, nor to undergo REC review for purely data based research. Personal data processing for scientific research can be based on public interest (Finnish Data Protection Act, Sects. 4 and 6). Processing personal data for biobank purposes may fall under the public interest, although an (ethical) biobank consent or opt-out will still be required. In ***Norway***, the legal basis for secondary processing of health and genetic data from patient records or health registries (Health Registries Act, Sect. 19a) for scientific research can be either consent or an administrative decision granting exception from professional secrecy. Administrative decision is the preferred legal basis in registry studies where a large number of data subjects are included. Thus, the processing is based on the public interest and supplemental legal basis in the administrative decision. Administrative decisions can be made by either the Norwegian Directorate of Health, the Norwegian Institute of Public Health or REC, depending on the source from where the data is collected and the purpose (Health Personnel Act Sect. 29, Health Registries Act Sect. 19e and Health Research Act Sect. 33). However, if data is limited to indirectly identifiable data from National Health Registries, no administrative decision granting exemption from confidentiality is required and the controller may decide to disclose data for scientific research inter alia. REC can decide that biological material shall be used in scientific research without consent (Health Research Act Sect. 28). Lastly, if there is another data source, the processing is regulated under the Personal Data Act, requiring compliance with art 89 GDPR and prior DPO consultation (Norwegian Personal Data Act, para 9). In ***Sweden***, public interest is the default legal basis for secondary processing in publicly-run research. Private research institutions can rely on legitimate interest for private-run research. For samples in biobanks, informed consent is always needed, but the 2023 Biobank Act enables using patients' consent to receive care, as long as relevant information is provided.[75] Although Nordic countries still use consent, they lean towards public interest, displaying a common culture of data exchange for scientific research.

Conversely, ***South European*** countries seem prima facie, to rely on consent. In ***Greece***, informed consent remains the main legal basis. However, public authorities may process health and genetic data for different purposes than the original one if necessary for the public interest, provided that one of the art 9(2) GDPR legal basis applies (Law 4624/2019, art 22(2)). Additionally, it is possible to transfer health data from public entities to private ones under the same conditions (Law 4624/2019, art. 26). Similarly, in ***Malta*** consent is the main legal basis. According to the Secondary Processing (health sector) Regulations, personal data may be also processed where the scientific research activities are in the public interest. Consent remains the general rule in ***Portugal***. However, in retrospective research of health information extracted from personal data, other than samples, e.g. clinical records, in the absence of consent, the data controller has the obligation to carefully weigh whether to grant authorisation, only upon a favourable REC opinion. In tandem, under Law 12/2005, consent can be overcome for retrospective sample use or in special situations, provided that it is substantially demonstrated why obtaining consent is impossible (Law 12/2005, art 19(6)). In ***Spain***, the Additional Provision 17 of the Spanish Data Protection Act prescribes that the legal basis can include consent, reasons of public interest in the field of public health, archiving purposes in the public interest, scientific or historical research purposes or statistical purposes, and reasons of essential public interest (art. 9(2)a, i, j. g GDPR). Consent can be broad, in the sense that it may not be necessarily limited to specific research. However, the public interest in public health can be used only when health authorities and public institutions with competence in public health matters, conduct research, and only in extraordinary situations of special relevance and seriousness. Although in ***Italy***, consent remains the general legal basis, there are several exceptions. Italian Personal Data Protection Code provides that consent is not necessary when the research is carried out based on provisions of law or regulation or EU law in accordance with art 9(2)j GDPR, including the case in which research is part of a biomedical or health research program regulated by Legislative Decree no 502/1992 and on condition that a Data Protection Impact Assessment (DPIA) is prepared. Also, consent is not deemed necessary, when it is impossible or it would require disproportionate effort to inform the data subject, or it would render the achievement of research purposes impossible or seriously affected (Italian Data Protection Code, art 110 (1)). In these cases, the research project has attained a prior favourable opinion by the local Ethics Committee, and the Data Controller must respect the ethical standards issued by the Italian Privacy Authority for this case (Italian Personal Data Protection Code, art 110(2)). For health data, consent is not necessary, when the research conducted based on legal or regulatory provisions or EU law (Provision of the Italian Privacy Authority no 146/2019, art 5(3)). It is also possible to overcome consent, if the data

[75] Biobank Act No 2023:38 *biobankslag (2023:38)*, Chap. 7 Sect. 4.

controller documents the exceptional reasons for not informing the data subject. In the context of biological samples and genetic data, while consent is generally required (Provision of the Italian Privacy Authority no 146/2019, art 4(5)), Provision no 146/2019 outlines some exceptions, like in art 4(11)3 and when consent cannot be obtained despite reasonable efforts and when certain requirements are met, e.g. no possibility of data subject's identification through further processing (Italian Personal Data Protection Code, art 110 (2)). All in all, although South European countries still prefer consent, they tend to be more open to the idea of public interest, following Malta's example.

Eastern European countries follow a similar trajectory. In ***Latvia***, similarly to the pre-GDPR period, consent is the main legal basis. The secondary processing of health data from patient medical records for scientific research purposes, apart from consent, can be also based on public interest under five conditions, among which the patient has not opted out, unobtainable consent by reasonable means and a proportionate public health benefit (Law on the Rights of the Patients, Sect. 10 para 8). Interestingly, the Human Genome Research Law has been interpreted as enabling broad consent in establishing project-related biobanks (Human Genome Research Law, Sect. 10). In ***Poland***, consent is also the main legal basis. Consent is the basis for secondary use of data from medical records.[76] Data from medical records may be transferred to a university or research institute without consent, only if the patient cannot be identified (Act on Patient Rights and Patient Ombudsman, art 26 Sect. 4). Given the lack of specific provisions on scientific research in the Personal Data Protection Act, BBMRI-PL is developing a Code of Conduct under art 40 GDPR. The Code recommends obtaining a tiered or dynamic consent for biobanks. It suggests that consent can be overcome if obtaining it is impossible or requires extraordinary measures. In that case, obtaining the competent Bioethics Committee's opinion is recommended. Although, consent remains the main legal basis in the ***Czech Republic***, the national legal framework offers exceptions, prescribing the scientific research as alternative legal basis (GDPR, art 9(2)j and 89; Czech Personal Data Processing Act, Sect. 16). According to the national experts, patients' explicit consent may not be required in most cases where public health providers also serve medical research purposes, however in practice consent as legal basis prevails. ***Estonia*** has been particularly progressive. Secondary processing of health data for scientific research purposes is possible without consent if the data is either pseudonymized or placed in a format providing equivalent protection. Interestingly, health data that can lead to data subject identification can still be processed without consent under certain conditions, like when there is overriding public interest (Estonian Personal Data Protection Act, Sect. 6(3)). Processing genetic data collected to the Estonian Biobank for scientific research purposes requires informed consent (HGRA, Sect. 12). The HGRA introduces broad consent (HGRA, Sect. 12). The secondary use of health data for various studies can be based on public interest upon the approval of the Estonian Committee on Bioethics and Human Research. However, there is an ongoing debate

[76] Act on Patient Rights and the Patient Ombudsman *Ustawa o prawach pacjenta i Rzeczniku Praw Pacjenta z dnia 6 listopada 2008 r. Dz.U. z 2023, poz. 1545*, art 26.

on whether HGRA prescribes a public interest or consent model. Therefore, Eastern European countries keep embracing consent as legal basis, except Estonia, which has a forward-looking strategy.

Central European countries stand somewhere in between. In the ***Netherlands***, the Medical Treatment Agreement Act provides that consent is the standard procedure. This consent is generally considered as an 'ethical informed consent', rather than a GDPR one. However, an opt-out procedure can be used when consent cannot reasonably be asked from the patient, given the study's nature and purpose, and when certain conditions are met, including that research serving the general interest, being impossible without this data and having no expressed objection (Medical Treatment Agreement Act, art 458). The Code of Conduct on Health Research establishes a layered consent system for health data re-use (Code of Conduct on Health Research, Chap. 5). Although GDPR consent is the general requirement, the law acknowledges practical limitations, and therefore offers hospitals regularly re-using data for research, the option to require ethical consent. Under certain conditions, opt-out procedure is also allowed. For the re-use of genomic data, however, GDPR consent is always necessary. In ***Belgium***, consent is not the sole legal basis for the secondary processing, which can be also based on a provision under EU or Member State law, a positive outcome of the compatibility assessment (GDPR, art 6(4)), or when the presumption of compatibility applies. According to the Belgian Council of University Hospitals, when real world data is processed for scientific research, compatibility is presumed, limiting the compatibility test to safeguard assessment (e.g., pseudonymization).[77] An exemption under art 9(2) GDPR remains needed, the most relevant being medicine, substantial public interest and public interest in the area of public health, research and informed consent. In the Biobanking context, the national legislation requires informed consent as an ethical requirement (Belgian Biobank law, art 20(1)). In ***France***, although consent can be a legal basis, it is not generally preferred due to its challenging nature. Data controllers can notably rely on art 9(2)j GDPR. Also, French law prescribes that secondary processing of health data for health research may only take place in consideration of their public interest purposes (LIL, art 66(I)). With the Bioethics Law, consent is only required for processing constitutional genetic data.[78] In this case, consent must be specific, separate and potentially multi-layered. However, the general rule for research on somatic genetic data is an opt-out procedure, which is also applicable on the reuse of biological samples for any genetic research. Interestingly, in ***Germany*** broad consent is an option, pursuant to Recital 33 GDPR. Although German law implementing GDPR lacks sufficient details on broad consent, an opinion of the conference of all state level data protection supervisory authorities prescribes specific safeguards for its use and can thus be considered as an expression of administrative practice.[79] Although

[77] Belgian Council of University Hospitals (2022).

[78] Bioethics Law *Loi n° 2021-1017 du 2 août 2021 relative à la bioéthique*, art 16.

[79] Independent data protection supervisory authorities of the federal and state governments (2019). Resolution of the 97th Conference on the interpretation of the term 'certain areas of scientific

hotly debated, public interest in the area of public health (GDPR, art 9(2)i) can be considered both as an exception to the prohibition of processing special categories of data and as a legal basis (GDPR, art 6(1)e). Scientific research serves as an alternative exception to explicit consent (GDPR, art 9(2)j), which is also highly debated due to the (only slightly changed) implementation of Art. 9(2)(j) GDPR in federal and state level laws. Beyond consent, Art. 9(2)(j) GDPR is implemented by the Federal Data Protection Act (Federal Data Protection Act, Sect. 27(1)). The federal states have directly implemented Art. 9(2)(j) GDPR in conjunction with Art. 89(1) GDPR in their state data protection laws. The GDNG does not provide for consent as the only possible legal basis for the processing of health data in the field of research. This is evidenced by various research provisions of the law, which define a legal basis for the processing of health data in the field of research.[80] Therefore, Central European countries offer a broader scope of consent and provide alternative legal basis, including the public interest.

16.2.3 Data Subject Rights—Reaction to Derogations

Here we examine the participating countries' approach towards the leeway provided under art 89(2) GDPR, which allows derogations from the rights of access, rectification, restriction of processing and objection (GDPR, art 15, 16, 18, 21), when personal data are processed for scientific research purposes, and the protection of such rights would likely render impossible or seriously impair these purposes. In such cases, the derogation depends on the adoption of appropriate safeguards under art 89(1) GDPR.

All ***Nordic*** countries enable the derogation under art 89(2) GDPR. ***Denmark*** and ***Finland*** allow the derogation from all data subject rights mentioned therein. ***Norway*** enables the derogation from the right to access, right to rectification and the right to restriction under certain conditions (Norwegian Personal Data Act, para 17), except when processing has legal effects or direct actual effects on the data subjects. ***Swedish*** legislation lacks a specific provision. However, GDPR derogations directly apply.

South European countries share a common approach. ***Greece*** allows the derogation from all four rights (Law 4624/2019, art 30(2)). RECs conduct this challenging assessment. Similarly, ***Portugal*** follows the same example, when the rights' exercise is impossible (Law 58/2019, art 31(2)). Although, the ***Maltese*** national legislation does not prescribe any specific derogations, the relevant GDPR provisions directly apply. The ***Spanish*** Data Protection Act, allows the derogations from the four rights,

research' in recital 33 of the GDPR. https://www.bfdi.bund.de/SharedDocs/Downloads/DE/DSK/DSKBeschluessePositionspapiere/97DSK_BeschlussEG33.pdf;jsessionid=4EA01CC14D23EE86E1758E4A4EE2CF8C.intranet242?__blob=publicationFile&v=4. Accessed 25 May 2024.

[80] This is also demonstrated by a reverse conclusion to Sect. 8 sentence 1 GDNG, which contains provisions for the event that health data is processed for research purposes in a research project on the basis of this law without the consent of the data subjects.

setting though specific requirements (Additional Provision 17 Spanish Data Protection Act, art 2(e)). The ***Italian*** Personal Data Protection Code prescribes that the Privacy Authority has the power to promote deontological rules (Italian Personal Data Protection Code, art 106(2)f), that also govern the cases where derogations from data subject rights can take place.

All ***Eastern European*** countries have a specific provision on derogations, except Poland. Although ***Latvia*** enables the derogation from the four rights (Latvian Personal Data Processing Law, Sect. 31), the practical implementation may be restricted by old laws that require specific conditions, like the Human Genome Research Law. The ***Czech Republic*** enables the derogation from data subject rights as well (Czech Personal Data Processing Act, Sect. 16(3)), similarly to ***Estonia*** which dictates that the processing objectives would otherwise be rendered impossible. Lastly, ***Poland*** stands out as there is no specific provision on derogations. Nevertheless, when the secondary processing involves data derived from medical records or clinical trials, derogations from art 15 and 16 GDPR can be allowed under the Constitution, the Act on the Patients' Rights and Patient Ombudsman. Interestingly, Polish law does not permit derogations from art 18 and 21 GDPR, and it is silent on derogations when the data does not derive from medical records or clinical trials.

Central European countries also embrace derogations. The ***Dutch*** Implementation Act of GDPR allows the derogation from art 15, 16 and 18 GDPR, leaving aside art 21 (Dutch GDPR Implementation Act, art 44). ***Belgium*** enables the derogation from the exercise of the four rights, subject to specific conditions and safeguards (Belgian Data Protection Law, Title 4). In ***France*** too, these derogations are possible (LIL, art 78)[81] but must be justified on scientific or practical grounds and subject to specific conditions. Prior review of the Committees of Protection of Persons (CPP) for prospective health research, or review of Ethics and Scientific Committee for Research, Studies and Evaluations in the field of Health (CESREES) for retrospective health research is required, while prior CNIL authorisation may be necessary. Apart from the four rights, ***Germany's*** Federal Data Protection Act also allows derogations from the right to be forgotten under art 17(3)d GDPR (Federal Data Protection Act, Sect. 27(2), 35(1)).

[81] Gauthier Chassang, Michael Hisbergues, Emmanuelle Rial-Sebbag. 2021. Research Biobanking, Personal Data Protection and Implementation of the GDPR in France. In *GDPR and Biobanking Individual Rights, Public Interest and Research Regulations across Europe*, eds. Olga Tzortzatou, Santa Slokenberga, Jane Reichel, 257-276. Law, Governance and Technology Series 43, Springer.

16.2.4 Appropriate Safeguards

Another important issue is the provision of appropriate safeguards, as a form of compensation for the restriction of the data subjects' right to data protection. GDPR provides limited guidance on what these safeguards should include.[82]

All ***Nordic countries*** have adopted appropriate safeguards. In ***Denmark***, the Data Protection Act enlists specific safeguards mainly for further processing (Danish Data Protection Act, Sect. 10.2–10.4). The basic rule is that data must not be subsequently processed for purposes other than scientific ones, while a specific provision requires prior authorisation of the supervisory authority for data disclosure to third parties (Danish Data Protection Act, Sect. 10.3). When a research is exclusively based on personal data, normally a REC authorisation will not be necessary, contrary to cases where the research project entails a risk of secondary findings (Act on Research Ethics Review of Health Research Projects, Sect. 21a–21b). Furthermore, according to the Act on Research Ethics Review of Health Research Projects, REC's authorisation is necessary for conducting research on tissue samples. ***Finland*** has risk-based approach, having a list of specific safeguards, including encryption, pseudonymisation, DPIA, Data Protection Officer (DPO) designation etc. (Finnish Data Protection Act, Sect. 6). The Act on Secondary Use of Health and Social Care Data also prescribes security measures, while the Biobank Act includes other safeguards, like material/data transfer agreements and pseudonymization. A new permissions authority, called "Findata", has been established for covering cases where data from more than one public, or any private social or healthcare providers are needed (Act on Secondary Use of Health and Social Care Data, Sect. 44). Although ***Norway*** has not listed specific safeguards under art 89(1) GDPR into Norwegian law, it still has safeguards in place through other regulations, like requiring a specific purpose for the permission to process and the exemption from secrecy (Act on Health Personnel, Sect. 29 and Act on Health Registries, Sect. 19 a), technical and organisational measures under a risk-based approach (Act on Health Registries, Sect. 21), and provisions on research transparency (Health Research Act, Chap. 8). REC authorisation is necessary before initiating a health research project (Health Research Act, Sect. 33). In ***Sweden***, REC authorisation is necessary for every research involving sensitive data (Ethical Review Act, Sect. 6). Health and genetic data must be kept confidential, unless it is deemed that disclosure will not harm the individual or someone close to them (PAISA, Chap. 25, Sect. 1). If safeguards, such as ethical approval, confidentiality or pseudonymisation are in place, the data may be released to researchers (PAISA, Chap. 10, Sect. 14, Chap. 21, Sect. 7). RECs usually require consent as additional safeguard, which can be waived though if privacy risk is low. Individuals may themselves waive confidentiality (PAISA, Chap. 12, Sect. 2).

South European countries pursue a relatively similar path. In ***Greece***, Law 4624/2019 includes safeguards, like pseudonymisation, encryption and anonymisation on

[82] Ciara Staunton, Santa Slokenberga, Andrea Parziale and Deborah Mascalzoni. 2022. Appropriate Safeguards and Article 89 of the GDPR: Considerations for Biobank, Databank and Genetic Research. Frontiers in Genetics 13: 719317.

condition that it is permitted by the scientific purposes, and there is no conflict with data subjects' legitimate interests (Law 4624/2019, art 30(3)). The competent ethics committee conducts deontological screening of the data processing for scientific research.[83] Besides scientific and ethics check, it also checks data protection compliance. In ***Italy***, the data controller must take appropriate measures under art 89(2) GDPR, when informing the data subject is impossible or requires disproportionate effort. In this case, the research project requires the local REC's favourable opinion and the Data Controller must respect the ethical standards issued by the Italian Privacy Authority for this case (Italian Data Protection Code, art 106, Sect. 2, Clause d). The same applies where consent could not be obtained for the conservation and further use of biological samples and genetic data in research programs different than the original. In ***Malta***, the Data Protection Act provides a set of appropriate safeguards, e.g. pseudonymisation and measures compliant to data minimisation principle (Data Protection Act, art 6(4)). Another safeguard for processing sensitive data for scientific research in the public interest, requires prior consultation with the Office of the Information and Data Protection Commissioner (IDPC), that in turn must consult with a REC. When academics, students or NGOs assisting patients in the health sector conduct research, they must obtain REC and IDPC authorisation. Data should be pseudonymised, or if not possible, other safeguards should be employed until data are anonymised after having achieved the research purpose. In ***Portugal***, although Law 58/2019 lacks specific data protection provisions for scientific research, it requires compliance with the data minimisation principle, and other safeguards, like anonymisation or pseudonymisation, as long as objectives are met. ***Spain*** has introduced safeguards for public health research, including, DPIA, quality standards and measures ensuring data subject identification protection. The issuance of prior REC report is required (Additional Provision 17 Spanish Data Protection Act, art 2(g)), whose lack can be substituted by a DPO report. Pseudonymised data can be used for research without consent if re-identification is prevented through appropriate technical measures. In this case, the research requires REC's prior favourable opinion (Additional Provision 17 Spanish Data Protection Act, art 2(g)).

Eastern European countries share a common approach. In ***Czech Republic,*** the Personal Data Processing Act includes an indicative list of special measures, including DPO designation, encryption, pseudonymisation, limited data access, regular testing etc. (Czech Personal Data Processing Act, Sect. 16). Although not mandatory, Data Transfer Agreements are commonly used as additional safeguard. Interventional research projects require independent examination of an Ethics Committee.[84] Even in non-interventional retrospective research, REC approval is sometimes requested as a means of appropriate safeguard. In ***Latvia***, no direct link exists between art 89(1) GDPR and national law on the safeguards' content. However, the authorisation by an authority required under the Law on the Rights of Patients for the secondary use of data without consent, could serve as a safeguard (Law

[83] Law 4521/2018 *Νόμος 4521/2018 (ΦΕΚ Α΄ 38/02.03.2018)*, art 21, 23.

[84] Additional Protocol to the Convention on Human Rights and Biomedicine, concerning Biomedical Research, Jan. 25, 2005, CETS 195, art 9.

on the Rights of Patients, Sect. 10 para 8). Also, there is no systemic approach regarding the RECs' role. Besides the Oviedo Convention, there is no general law requiring scientific and ethical approval for research. Nevertheless, specific laws mandate REC ethics review, e.g. in clinical trials for medicinal products (Cabinet Regulation No. 289 of 23 March 2010, para 31). Additionally, the Central Medical Ethics Committee undertakes the ethics review of genetic research (Human Genome Research Law, Sect. 22). Prior REC authorisation is required for student research using data from medical documents (Law on the Rights of Patients, Sect. 10 para 8^1 cl 5). ***Poland*** lacks a provision for appropriate safeguards. Similar to Latvia, prior REC authorisation is not legally required. However, it is a common safeguard. Also, Bioethics Committee consent is required for human biological sample research. ***Estonia*** has several legal provisions regulating REC's role. The secondary use of health data from the national health system or the national health registries, which is based on the Health Services Organisations Act, the Public Health Act and the Personal Data Protection Act is allowed to take place for scientific research purposes upon an Ethics Committee approval. Also, the secondary processing of health data for scientific research purposes requires an Ethics Committee compliance verification (Estonian Personal Data Protection Act, Sect. 6(4)), or if not possible, by the Estonian Data Protection Inspectorate. Under HGRA, researchers can process health and genomic data for research studies upon the approval of the Estonian Committee on Bioethics and Human Research, which also assesses re-contact and interviews with biobank participants (HGRA, Sect. 24(2)4). Generally, the Ethics Review Committee on Human Research of the Ministry of Social Affairs reviews[85] all research projects involving Estonian Biobank data or biological material. Moreover, Estonian law provides extensive safeguards, e.g. prohibiton of using genetic data and biological material in civil or criminal proceedings or for surveillance (HGRA, Sect. 16). Pseudonymisation or alternative methods providing equivalent protection, are considered sufficient.

Finally, ***Central European countries*** also share a common approach. ***Belgium*** divides safeguards into general application for both primary and secondary use, those for data directly collected from the data subject, and those for further processing. General safeguards include DPO designation and adding elements to the record of processing activities (Belgian Data Protection Law, art 190–191, 204). When data is collected directly from the data subject, data controllers must also inform them about potential anonymisation and explain why the exercise of their rights may impact scientific research purposes (Belgian Data Protection Law, art 193). For further processing, many obligations and safeguards apply (Belgian Data Protection Law, art 194–195, 197, 198–203). Data should generally be anonymised when used for research. If not possible, pseudonymisation is the next step. When scientific research goals cannot be met otherwise, non-pseudonymised data can be used

[85] Estonian Personal Data Protection Act; Minister of Social Affairs, Regulation on 'Establishment of the Research Ethics Committee, its rules of procedure, number of members and procedure for their appointment, and fees for the examination of a research application', Sect. 6.

exceptionally. Additionally, when data is shared with a new controller, an agreement with the original controller is obligatory, while specific rules on anonymisation and pseudonymisation apply. REC approval is required for scientific research use of health data in biobanking. Under Law of 2008 on HBM, a positive REC opinion is necessary when obtaining consent is impossible or exceptionally inappropriate.[86] Like Belgium, ***France*** distinguishes safeguards into State-level and data controller/processor levels. On State-level, RECs, CPP, CESREES and CNIL experts assess and approve research projects involving personal data processing, depending on the project's legal qualification. On the data controller/processor level, safeguards include DPO designation, DPIA, accountable data management, data minimisation principle measures, pseudonymisation etc. In ***the Netherlands***, there are appropriate safeguards, but they are not specifically outlined in national legislation. The Code of Conduct provides guidance on this. While not regulated by specific legislation, REC approval is common practice in most academic hospitals. In ***Germany***, additional rules specify technical and organisational measures adopting a risk-based approach (Federal Data Protection Act, Sect. 22(2)). For broad consent, additional safeguards emphasize transparency and the ethical review's role.[87] The GDNG helps to create the appropriate infrastructure for the processing of health data for research purposes and thus contributes to technical and organizational measures in this context.

16.3 Discussion

As indicated above not all European countries have specific legislation for the secondary use of health and genetic data for scientific research purposes, unlike Finland and Norway. Some, like Spain, Portugal and Malta have adopted sector-specific legislation. Provisions in different laws combined with the data protection legislation, regulate this area. Belgium and France have taken significant steps forward in standardizing procedures. Also, Latvia is taking promising steps as it is working on the introduction of rules on secondary use and a Biobank Law, similarly to the Netherlands, where a new law on Biobanking and biomedical research is vividly discussed.

It is apparent that consent remains the most common legal basis for secondary use of health and genetic data for scientific research purposes. However, its scope varies substantially across Europe, which can further impede cross-border data transfers. Concerns exist regarding the appropriateness of using consent as a legal basis. First, the right to withdraw consent could undermine research based on data linked to individuals.[88] Second, fulfilling validity requirements under art 4(11) GDPR is

[86] Law of 19 December 2008 regarding the procurement and use of human body material, art 20(1), see also art 21.

[87] Independent data protection supervisory authorities (n 79).

[88] Article 29 Working Party (2018). Guidelines on consent under Regulation 2016/679.

challenging.[89] Also, it is very often impossible to obtain specific consent as identifying the processing purpose at the data collection time can sometimes be difficult. Although Recital 33 GDPR allows data subjects to consent to certain areas of research or parts of a research project, the obligation for specific consent is not disapplied.[90] Literature suggests researchers could request consent as an additional ethical safeguard instead of legal basis,[91] similarly to Nordic countries. Nevertheless, it cannot be overlooked that several countries also consider the public interest under certain conditions.

All examined countries use art 89(2) GDPR, with some divergences though. Norway and the Netherlands do not apply derogations to the right to object. Sweden, Poland and Malta lack specific provisions for derogations, but enable them through other means. France is cautious about broad derogations, while Germany extends derogations to the right to be forgotten.

European countries prioritize appropriate safeguards, often listing them in their legislation. Some common safeguards are pseudonymisation, anonymisation, encryption, DPO designation and security measures. In most countries RECs continue to play a significant role, although their role may not always be regulated under national law, like in Latvia and the Netherlands.

16.4 Conclusion

The chapter aimed to map the current legal landscape on the secondary processing of health and genetic data for scientific research purposes across Europe. An abundance of different laws, either dedicated or more general, has been identified. The comparative overview of seventeen countries has indicated elements that might affect the cross-border exchange of health and genetic data in the EU from the healthcare context to the research context and vice versa.

Acknowledgements Dr. Olga Tzortzatou wishes to make a special acknowledgement to Alexandra Ziaka for her indispensable support and Dr. Regina Becker for her critical spirit during the whole process of research and drafting of this paper.

Aliuska Duardo-Sánchez gratefully acknowledges the financial support of Project AIMOFGIFT funded by the Basque Government, Department of Economic Development, Sustainability and Environment, through the program of aid for Collaborative Research in strategic areas—Elkartek 2022.

Dorota Krekora-Zajac acknowledges that her work was conducted under the research project no. UMO-2016/23/D/HS5/00411 financed by the National Science Center in the context of her affiliation with the Department of Comparative Civil Law, Faculty of Law and Administration of the University of Warsaw, Poland.

[89] Mark Taylor and Tess Whitton (2020).

[90] EDPB (2020).

[91] Edward Dove (2018).

Dr. Teodora Lalova-Spinks participated in the workshops and drafting of this paper during her PhD project at KU Leuven (2019-2023). Her PhD was supported with a scholarship awarded by the Research Foundation–Flanders (FWO), Project No. 11H3720N.

Funding This publication was funded within B1MG project that has received funding from the European Union's Horizon 2020 research and innovation programme under grant agreement No. 951724.

Ethical Approvals Not applicable.

Conflict of Interest The authors declare that they have no conflict of interests.

References

National Regulatory Frameworks (per Country in Alphabetical Order)

Belgium

Belgian Council of University Hospitals. 2022. Common position establishing a framework for secondary on secondary use of real-world data collected in hospitals. https://www.univ-hospitals.be/common-position-establishing-a-framework-for-secondary-use-of-real-world-data-routinely-collected-in-hospitals/. Accessed 25 May 2024.

Compendium on Biobanks *Compendium biobanken/biobanques/biobanks 20.07.2018.*

Law of 18 May 2022 providing various urgent health provisions *Loi portant des dispositions diverses urgentes en matière de santé (1) 18 Mai 2022.*

Law of 19 December 2008 regarding the procurement and use of human body material destined for human medical applications or for scientific research purposes *Loi relative à l'obtention et à l'utilisation de matériel corporel humain destiné à des applications médicales humaines ou à des fins de recherche scientifique.*

Law of 23 February 2022 on provisions regarding human body material and embryos and gametes *Loi portant des dispositions en ce qui concerne le matériel corporel humain et les embryons et gametes 23 Fevrier 2022.*

Law of 30 July 2018 on the protection of natural persons with regard to the processing of personal data (Belgian Data Protection Act) *Loi relative à la protection des personnes physiques à l'égard des traitements de données à caractère personnel 30 Juillet 2018.*

Law of 30 October 2018 modifying the Law of 19 December 2008 regarding the procurement and use of human body material destined for human medical applications or for scientific research purposes *Loi modifiant la loi du 19 décembre 2008 relative à l'obtention et à l'utilisation de matériel corporel humain destiné à des applications médicales humaines ou à des fins de recherche scientifique 30 Octobre 2018.*

Royal Decree on biobanks in implementation of Article 22 of the Act of December 2008 on the acquisition and use of human body material for the purpose of medical application to humans or scientific research *Arrêté royal relatif aux biobanques 9 Janvier 2018.*

Czech Republic

Act No. 110/2019 Coll., on Personal Data Processing, as amended (Czech Personal Data Processing Act) *Zákon č. 110/2019 Sb., o zpracování osobních údajů, ve znění pozdějších předpisů.*
Act No. 372/2011 Coll., on Health Services and Conditions of Their Provision (Act on Health Services), as amended *Zákon č. 372/2011 Sb., o zdravotních službách a podmínkách jejich poskytování (zákon o zdravotních službách), ve znění pozdějších předpisů.*

Denmark

Consolidated Act on supplementary provisions to the regulation on the protection of natural persons with regard to the processing of personal data and on the free movement of such data (Danish Data Protection Act) No. 289 *Lovbekendtgørelse nr 289 af 8. marts 2024 (Gældende).*
Consolidated Act No. 1338 on Research Ethics Review of Health Research Projects *Lovbekendtgørelse nr. 1338 af 1. September 2020 om videnskabsetisk behandling af sundhedsvidenskabelige og sundhedsdatavidenskabelige forskningsprojekter (Komiteloven).*
Consolidated Act on Health (Health Act) *Lovbekendtgørelse nr. 247 af 12. marts 2024 om sundhed (Sundhedsloven).*

Estonia

Health Services Organisation Act *Tervishoiuteenuste korraldamise seadus* RT I 2001, 50, 284.
Human Genes Research Act (HGRA) *Inimgeeniuuringute seadus RT I 2000, 104, 685.*
Minister of Social Affairs, Regulation on 'Establishment of the Research Ethics Committee, its rules of procedure, number of members and procedure for their appointment, and fees for the examination of a research application'.
Personal Data Protection Act (Estonian Personal Data Protection Act) *Isikuandmete kaitse seadus* RT I, 04.01.2019, 11.
Public Health Act *Rahvatervise seadus* RT I 1995, 57, 978.
Public Information Act *Avaliku teabe seadus RT I 2000, 92, 597.*

Finland

Act on the Secondary Use of Health and Social Care Data No 552/2019 *Laki sosiaali- ja terveystietojen toissijaisesta käytöstä 552/2019.*
Biobank Act 688/2012 *Biopankkilaki 688/2012.*
Data Protection Act No 1050/2018 (Finnish Data Protection Act) *Tietosuojalaki (1050/2018).*

France

Bioethics Law *Loi n° 2021–1017 du 2 août 2021 relative à la bioéthique.*
Civil Code *Code Civil,* Book I Title I Civil Rights *Des droits civils.*
Law No 78–17 1978 relating to data processing, files and freedoms *Loi n° 78–17 du 6 janvier 1978 relative à l'informatique, aux fichiers et aux libertés (ou Loi Informatique et Libertés).*
Penal Code *Code Penal,* Book II Title II, ch VI Personality breach *Des atteintes à la personnalité.*
Public Health Code *Code de la Santé Publique* Part I, Book I, Title II Biomedical research.

Germany

Act on the Improved Use of Health Data *Gesetz zur verbesserten Nutzung von Gesundheitsdaten (BGBl. 2024 I Nr. 102 vom 25.03.2024).*

Federal Data Protection Act *Bundesdatenschutzgesetz vom 30. Juni 2017 (BGBl. I S. 2097), das zuletzt durch Artikel 10 des Gesetzes vom 23. Juni 2021 (BGBl. I S. 1858; 2022 I 1045) geändert worden ist.*

Patient Data Protection Act *Patientendaten-Schutz-Gesetz (PDSG) vom 14. Oktober 2020 (BGBl. I 2020 S. 2115).*

Greece

Code of Medical Deontology, Law 3418/2005 *Κώδικας Ιατρικής Δεοντολογίας Νόμος 3418/2005 (ΦΕΚ Α' 287/28.11.2005).*

Ministerial Decision DYG 3/89292/2003 implementing Directive 2001/20/EC *Υπουργική Απόφαση ΔΥΓ 3/89292/2003 Εναρμόνιση της Ελληνικής Νομοθεσίας προς την Κοινοτική (Οδηγία 2001/20) (ΦΕΚ Β'1973/31.12.2003).*

Law 4386/2016 on Regulations for Research and other provisions *Νόμος 4386/2016 για την έρευνα και άλλες διατάξεις (ΦΕΚ Α' 83/11.5.2016).*

Law 2472/1997 Νόμος 2472/1997 (ΦΕΚ Α' 50/10-4-1997).

Law 2619/1998 *Νόμος 2619/1998 (ΦΕΚ Α'132/19.6.1998).*

Law 4521/2018 *Νόμος 4521/2018 (ΦΕΚ Α΄38/02.03.2018).*

Law 4624/2019 *Νόμος 4624/2019 (ΦΕΚ Α' 137/29.8.2019).*

Italy

Personal Data Protection Code Legislative Decree 196/2003 (Italian Data Protection Code) *Codice in materia di protezione dei dati personali, del d.lgs. 196/2003.*

Provision of the Italian Privacy Authority on the Processing of Particular Categories of Personal Data no 146/2019 (Provision of the Italian Privacy Authority) *Provvedimento recante le prescrizioni relative al trattamento di categorie particolari di dati, ai sensi dell'art 21, comma 1 del d.lgs. 10 agosto 2018, n. 101, n. 146 del 5 giugno 2019.*

Latvia

Cabinet Regulation No. 134 of 11 March 2014 *Ministru kabineta 2014. gada 11. marta noteikumi Nr.134* Latvijas Vēstnesis, 52, 13.03.2014.

Cabinet Regulation No. 289 of 23 March 2010 *Ministru kabineta 2010 gada 23 marta noteikumi Nr.289, Latvijas Vēstnesis, 51/52, 31.03.2010.*

Convention for the protection of Human Rights and Dignity of the Human Being with regard to the Application of Biology and Medicine, Apr. 4, 1997 ETS 164 (Oviedo Convention) *Konvencija par cilvēktiesību un cieņas aizsardzību bioloģijā un medicīnā - Konvencija par cilvēktiesībām un biomedicīnum, "Latvijas Vēstnesis", 205, 30.12.2009.*

Human Genome Research Law *Cilvēka genoma izpētes likums Latvijas Vēstnesis, 99, 03.07.2002.*

Law on the Rights of Patients *Pacientu tiesību Latvijas Vēstnesis, 205, 30.12.2009.*

Personal Data Processing Law (Latvian Personal Data Processing Law) No 132 *Fizisko personu datu apstrādes likums Latvijas Vēstnesis 132, 04.07.2018.*

Pharmaceutical Law *Farmācijas likums Latvijas Vēstnesis, 103, 24.04.1997.*

Malta

Chapter 586 of the Laws of Malta, Data Protection Act.
Subsidiary Legislation 458.43, Clinical Trials Regulation.
Subsidiary Legislation 528.10, Processing of Personal Data (Secondary Processing) (Health Sector) Regulations 2019.

Netherlands

Code of Conduct on Health Research *Gedragscode Gezondheidsonderzoek (2004).*
Code of Conduct on Health Research *Gedragscode Gezondheidsonderzoek (2022).*
Code of Good Use *Code Goed Gebruik (2011).*
Dutch GDPR Implementation Act *Uitvoeringswet Algemene verordening gegevensbescherming BWBR0040940.*
Medical Research Involving Humans Act *Wet Medisch-Wetenschappelijk onderzoek met mensen BWBR0009408 (WMO).*
Medical Treatment Agreement Act *Wet geneeskundige behandelingsovereenkomst BWBR0007021(WGBO).*

Norway

Act 1999–07–02–64 (Health Personnel Act) *Lov 2. juli 1999 nr. 64 om helsepersonell m.v. (helsepersonelloven).*
Act 2003-12-05-100 relating to the application of biotechnology in medicine *Lov 5. juli 2003 nr. 100 om humanmedisinsk bruk av bioteknologi m.m. (bioteknologiloven).*
Act 2008-06-20-44 (Health Research Act) *Lov 20. juni 2008 nr. 44 om medisinsk og helsefaglig forskning (helseforskningsloven).*
Act 2014-06-20-20 (Health Registries Act) *Lov 6. juni 2014 nr. 20 om helseregistre og behandling av helseopplysninger (helseregisterloven).*
Act 2018-06-15-38 (Norwegian Personal Data Act) *Lov 15. juni 2018 nr. 38 om behandling av personopplysninger (personopplysningsloven).*

Poland

Act on Patient Rights and the Patient Ombudsman *Ustawa o prawach pacjenta i Rzeczniku Praw Pacjenta z dnia 6 listopada 2008 r. Dz.U. z 2023, poz. 1545.*
Personal Data Protection Act (Polish Personal Data Protection Act) No 10 *Ustawa o ochronie danych osobowych z dnia 10 maja 2018 r. Dz.U. z 2019 r., poz. 1781.*

Portugal

Act on Personal Genetic Information and health information No 12/2005 *Lei n.º 12/2005, de 26 Janeiro, regulated by* Decree-Law 131/2014) *Decreto-Lei n.º 131/2014, de 29 de agosto.*
Law No 58/2019 *Lei n.º 58/2019, de 8 de agosto.*

Spain

Act on Biomedical Research No 14/2007 *Ley 14/2007, de 3 de julio, de Investigación biomédica «BOE» núm. 159, de 04 de julio de 2007.*

General Act on Health No 14/1986 *Ley 14/1986 de 25 de abril General de Sanidad «BOE» núm. 102, de 29 de abril de 1986.*

Law 41/2002 of 14 November, Regulating Patient Autonomy and Rights and Obligations Regarding Clinical Information and Documentation. *Ley 41/2002, de 14 de noviembre, básica reguladora de la autonomía del paciente y de derechos y obligaciones en materia de información y documentación clínica «BOE» núm. 274, de 15 de noviembre de 2002.*

Organic Law on the Protection of Personal Data and Guarantee of Digital Rights No 3/*Ley Orgánica 3/2018, de 5 de diciembre, de Protección de Datos Personales y garantía de los derechos digitales «BOE» núm. 294, de 06/12/2018.*

Royal Decree No 1716/2011 of November 18, establishing the basic requirements of authorization and functioning of biobanks for biomedical research and the management of human biological samples, and regulating the functioning and organization of the National Registry of Biobanks for biomedical research *Real Decreto 1716/2011, de 18 de noviembre, por el que se establecen los requisitos básicos de autorización y funcionamiento de los biobancos con fines de investigación biomédica y del tratamiento de las muestras biológicas de origen humano, y se regula el funcionamiento y organización del Registro Nacional de Biobancos para investigación biomédica.*

Spanish Constitution *Constitución Española «BOE» núm. 311, de 29/12/1978.*

Sweden

Biobank Act No 2023:38 *biobankslag (2023:38).*

Ethical Review Act No 2003:460 *Lag (2003:460) om etikprövning av forskning som avser människor (2022:49).*

Patient Data Act No 2008:355 *Patientdatalag (2008:355).*

Public Access to Information and Secrecy Act No 2009:400 (PAISA) *Offentlighets- och sekretesslagen (2009:400).*

Other Resources

Additional Protocol to the Convention on Human Rights and Biomedicine, concerning Biomedical Research, Jan. 25, 2005, CETS 195.

Article 29 Working Party. 2018. Guidelines on consent under Regulation 2016/679.

B1MG project. https://b1mg-project.eu/. Accessed 25 May 2024.

Branum, Rebecca, and Susan Wolf. 2015. International policies on sharing genomic research results with relatives: Approaches to balancing privacy with access. *Journal of Law, Medicine & Ethics* 43: 576–593.

Chassang, Gauthier, Hisbergues, Michael, and Rial-Sebbag, Emmanuelle. 2021. Research biobanking, personal data protection and implementation of the GDPR in France. In *GDPR and biobanking individual rights, public interest and research regulations across Europe,* eds. Olga Tzortzatou, Santa Slokenberga, Jane Reichel, 257–276. Law, Governance and Technology Series 43, Springer.

DG Health and Food Safety. 2021. Assessment of the EU Member States' rules on health data in the light of GDPR. https://health.ec.europa.eu/system/files/2021-02/ms_rules_health-data_en_0.pdf. Accessed 25 May 2024.

Dove, Edward. 2018. The EU general data protection regulation: Implications for international scientific research in the digital era. *Journal of Law, Medicine and Ethics* 46: 1013–1030.

EDPB. 2020. Guidelines 05/2020 on consent under Regulation 2016/679. https://edpb.europa.eu/sites/default/files/files/file1/edpb_guidelines_202005_consent_en.pdf. Accessed 25 May 2024.

European Commission. European '1+ Million Genomes' Initiative. https://digital-strategy.ec.europa.eu/en/policies/1-million-genomes. Accessed 25 May 2024.

European Parliament and Council Regulation 2016/679 of Apr. 27, 2016, Protection of natural persons with regard to the processing of personal data and on the free movement of such data, and repealing Directive 95/46/EC (GDPR), 2016 O.J. (L 119) 1.

Independent data protection supervisory authorities of the federal and state governments. 2019. Resolution of the 97th Conference on the interpretation of the term 'certain areas of scientific research' in recital 33 of the GDPR. https://www.bfdi.bund.de/SharedDocs/Downloads/DE/DSK/DSKBeschluessePositionspapiere/97DSK_BeschlussEG33.pdf;jsessionid=4EA01CC14D23EE86E1758E4A4EE2CF8C.intranet242?__blob=publicationFile&v=4. Accessed 25 May 2024.

Lamas, Eugenia, Anna Barh, Dario Brown, and Marie-Christine. Jaulent. 2015. Ethical, legal and social issues related to the health data-warehouses: Re-using health data in the research and public health research. *European Federation for Medical Informatics* 210: 719–723.

Ministry of Social Affairs. 2023. Re-use of health data for healthcare and clinical research, SOU 2023:76 Vidareanvändning av hälsodata för vård och klinisk forskning.

Nuffield Council on Bioethics. 2015. The collection, linking and use of data in biomedical research and health care: ethical issues. https://www.nuffieldbioethics.org/wp-content/uploads/Biological_and_health_data_web.pdf. Accessed 25 May 2024.

Staunton, Ciara, Slokenberga Santa, Andrea Parziale, and Deborah Mascalzoni. 2022. Appropriate safeguards and article 89 of the GDPR: Considerations for biobank, databank and genetic research. *Frontiers in Genetics* 13: 719317.

Taylor, Mark, and Tess Whitton. 2020. Public Interest, health research and data protection law: Establishing legitimate trade-off between individual control and research access to health data. *Laws* 9: 6.

Tzortzatou, Olga, et al. 2021. Biobanking across Europe post-GDPR: A deliberately fragmented landscape. In *GDPR and biobanking individual rights, public interest and research regulation across Europe*, ed. Santa Slokenberga, Olga Tzortzatou, and Jane Reichel, 397–419. Law, Governance and Technology Series: Springer.

Chapter 17
Privacy, Big Data and eHealth Profiling in European Law: Rights & Wrongs

Maria Leonor Teixeira

Abstract This *brave new world* of big health data it´s an incognito. The purpose of this paper is to analyze the European legal framework in the transdisciplinary field of eHealth, personal data, privacy values and potential eHealth profiling abuses. Advancement and improvement of information and communication technology have changed health care system. Electronic health sector (eHealth) is a sensitive issue, demanding therefore the same level of innovation and security, not only to collect, store and analyze health data, but also in any regards related to medical care and investigation. The development, implementation and use of Electronic Health Records system has been especially stimulated, giving raw material to big health databases. In this sense, it's secure to say that its growth raises tremendous concerns regarding privacy rights. Especially when it comes to correlate sets of personal health data and extract them attributes, biometric features and characteristics to identify a person (personalized profiling), to predict his future behavior or attitudes (eHealth profiling). It's a critical challenge with rights and wrongs.

Keywords Privacy · Big health data · Electronic health data · eHealth profiling · European health data space

17.1 Introduction

In today's world of advancing technology and science, we find ourselves in a constant flux between exaltation and vigilance. We strive for progress with innovations in data acquisition, virtual reality, and artificial intelligence, yet are wary of the safety and security surrounding their implementation. The ease and aid of digital access has blurred the lines between work, family, and personal spaces. It has created an expectation of immediate gratification effectively shortening gaps of distance and

M. L. Teixeira (✉)
Public Prosecutor, Porto, Portugal
e-mail: mleonorteixeira@gmail.com

© The Editor(s) (if applicable) and The Author(s), under exclusive license to Springer Nature Switzerland AG 2024

J.-A. Seoane and O. Vergara (eds.), *The Discourse of Biorights*, The International Library of Bioethics 109, https://doi.org/10.1007/978-3-031-66804-3_17

time. "*My home is my castle and fortress*" has become a utopian concept as digital life and digital time are a never-ending history.

In this *brave new world*, datafication of our lives and bodies are challenges, especially concerning the big health data legal framework. Collection, storage, and algorithmic analysis of a vast volume of health data promise the *El Dorado* in health and medical care. However, it has relevant counterpoint restrictions on fundamental rights such as privacy, freedom, autonomy and data protection. That's why we believe that an effective policy change to ensure proper protection should be drawn, in order to minimize the misuse of health data.

An example of this was during the COVID-19 pandemic, and subsequent containment measures implemented by governments worldwide. During this time, paradigmatic cases of massive digital surveillance, self-isolation, quarantines, and use of drones to monitor people's movements and communications opened the *pandora's box* of data collection and user's privacy. According to the *World Health Organization (WHO)* surveillance in relation to public health is the "ongoing, systematic collection, analysis and interpretation of health-related data essential to the planning, implementation and evaluation of public health practice". All over the world, big health data collecting and the disclosure of sensitive data have enabled the development of mHealth—mobile health, which refers to mobile devices and apps used to control body functions (Tzanou 2021, p.8). However, apps that track body functions and performances are no longer enough. There has become a sense of urgency to track citizens and their communications, even to the point of profiling social behaviors, paving the way for new apps emerging to meet these expectations. This includes the "digital and biometric surveillance technologies that track "viral footprints" of Covid-19 across bodies, homes, streets and borders". In this sense, it's logical to deduce that COVID-19 pandemic created "new cultures of surveillance" (Lyon 2022, p.12), raising questions about fundamental rights such as privacy, autonomy, freedom and data protection.

European data strategy and European Health Data Space aim to build a "European way of living in a data driven economy" rooted in the protection of fundamental rights.

Therefore, the main purpose of this chapter is to point out the dialectic tension among the use and misuse of Big Health Data analyzing, and the risk of unwanted outcomes such as personal eHealth profiling.

17.2 Privacy and Personal Data: The Moving Way

Conceptualizing privacy is like walking in shifting sands, given the cultural, spatial, chronological, and personal influences to which it is subjected to. Privacy is a puzzle word, with several meanings and different approaches. We can talk about physical privacy, informational privacy, proprietary privacy, decisional privacy and so forth. Privacy as a concept, in its essence, is a fundamental right that underpins personal freedoms within a social framework, and therefore requires security and legal protection.

In classical legal literature, Edward Lawrence Godkin (1890, pp. 65–66) was the first one referring to privacy as a right: "Personal dignity is the fine flower of civilization, and the more of it there is in a community, the better off the community is. It is the only form of self-respect which does not "take on airs" and which is constantly compelled to justify itself by suitable living. But without privacy its cultivation or preservation is hardly possible". In the same year, Samuel Warren and Louis Brandeis (1890) recognized the existence of a general right to privacy, a right to intimacy—"the person, his private and domestic life should be preserved from intrusion from others". Their article *The Right to Privacy* is a milestone in the legal construction of the concept of privacy in a triple-tier sense. First, by emerging in the context of private law, with a view to ensure that citizens are adequately protected in the event of unwanted intrusion into their private lives. This includes the most intimate sphere of their feelings, thoughts and attitudes, and it aims to establish control from the subject himself, with a view to prevent the unauthorized disclosure of personal data. Secondly, this right is not a property right but a broader subjective right, "the right to be let alone", the right of each citizen to his or her own personality and freedom. Thirdly, this right could be protected by an innominate tort and precautionary measures or civil liability actions appropriate to prevent or likely to compensate non-pecuniary damages arising from the violation of the right to privacy or the right to be let alone.

Indeed, the concept of privacy differs depending on the society in question, being a legal, philosophical, but also a cultural issue. That's why it's understandable for instance, that the conceptual difference conveyed by North American doctrine differs from that of Europe. In one way, privacy revolves around freedom, and in another way, privacy is anchored in dignity (Whitman 2004). In the U.S., they have a construct based on jurisprudence, while in Europe they are constitutionally recognized and protected as a right, such that "American privacy law is a body caught in the gravitational orbit of liberty values, while in Europe law caught in the orbit of dignity". The U.S. Supreme Court held, in several cases, that although the Constitution does not expressly refer to privacy, this right is implicit throughout the first, third, fourth, fifth and ninth amendments of the Bill of Rights. Here lies the origin of decisional privacy; the freedom of each individual to decide and act as he or she pleases in private matters, without being subject to the interference of third parties in his or her decision making. Developing this perspective, the U.S. Supreme Court, *in Roe v. Wade* (1973) held that the right to privacy, to individual autonomy concerning the body, required that the decision whether or not to end a pregnancy in the first twelve weeks of gestation should be taken solely by the pregnant woman. Recently, in *Dobbs v. Jackson Women's Health Organization* the U.S. Supreme Court overturned the Roe v. Wade decision, stating that the right to abortion has no constitutional protection, threatening, on one hand, the right to privacy and, on the other, posing relevant questions regarding data protection, namely with information related with personal reproductive health data.

Moreover, the substantial impact of information and communication technology (ICT) in human affairs, namely in health issues: with the use of electronic applications (eHealth), mobile health applications (mHealth), big health data analytics, electronic health records (EHR), artificial intelligence (AI) or blockchain, highlights the need to protect physical privacy (personal isolation or seclusion, intimate sphere) and informational privacy (conversation about more or less secret or intimate data or facts, that includes health information). Which leads us to a debate not only on the efficiency of such ICT health apps and devices, but also about the fact that they collect, store, and use sensitive personal data. Those ICT health apps and devices are supported in someone´s singular health information. Users should know for whom their health information will be delivered, where it will be stored, the duration, and what purposes are given to them. Also, equally relevant, is the justification or the reasons behind all of that.

Digital health and healthcare context has its own singularities, arousing legal and ethical questions namely in privacy as a concept. It should be perceived that privacy has emerged and developed as a fundamental right linked to human dignity. The aim being to ensure and safeguard the reserved and somewhat secretive nature of certain aspects of one's intimacy, health, or genetics. Human dignity, privacy and personal identity, faces a critical dialectical tension: massive collection of personal data versus potentially damaging to the space and values of each individual.

The technological development enabled the rapid rise of computerized record-keeping and, consequently, big databases increased vulnerability for hackers and data breaches. Neglecting those vulnerabilities is to ignore some of the most profound challenges situated within binomial big data analytics and fundamental rights. Clearly, human rights express the recognition of the power of the citizen, drawing the boundaries of the power of the states. Fundamental rights are (a) universal—all human beings are entitled to fundamental rights, (b) fundamental—they aim to ensure the basic interests and needs of human beings, (c) abstract, needing to be concretized (d) moral—their validity depends solely on their existence, (e) priority—they express expectations or faculties of all and define the substantial connotations of democracy, being constitutionally exempt from the discretion of majorities: right to life, liberty, health, education, privacy, data protection. Thus, privacy must be seen as a fundamental right even when it is at stake. "Unpopular privacy", as Anita Allen (2011) denotes the dichotomy of popular privacy, the "one that people tend to want, believe they have a right to, and expect government to secure" *vs.* unpopular privacy "with intended beneficiaries and targets (…) the class of people whose conduct is directly regulated by particular privacy protection standards. Physicians, nurses, and hospitals are among the intended targets of U. S. Federal privacy statutes. Privacy law can be unpopular with its intended targets".

The COVID-19 pandemic legal framework is a typical example of "unpopular privacy law", imposing constraints on human rights; lockdowns occurred, doctor's offices, courts, and stores went remote, distancing was required. The wearable trackers, phone apps, drones, remote body temperatures checkers have been adopted, all of them, under the aegis of the common good: the public health. Systematically political and power relations decide whatever integrates personal or public sphere, personal or public health. Personal health data-collection imposes confidentiality (secrecy) for members of the scientific community (doctors, nurses, pharmacists, researchers, governments) or anyone who may collect, store, manage or analyze health data and information. "Patients" are the data subject, and are always the owner of their own personal and sensitive data. Thus, individuals have a moral obligation to respect not only other people´s privacy but also their own (Allen 2013).

Likewise, personal health data collection must be based on a well informed and express consent. Individual freedom can only be assured when the data subjects can fully dispose of the files concerning themselves, maintaining their management at their disposal, whether by authorizing their use or by ordering their deletion. It should be noted, data protection, is a fundamental right with two incisive vectors, the right of limited access to personal information and the right to control personal data and information. On one side, needing to safeguard relevant and intimate data from public domain, and on the other side, allowing the subject to have full control over their own data publication or access by third parties (self-determination).

Today, privacy rights and data protection co-exist. Article 8 European Convention on Human Rights (ECHR) and Article 7 Charter of Fundamental Rights of the European Union (CFREU), provides a principle of prohibition of interferences with the individuals private and family life, home and communications. It protects the individual´s privacy and autonomy. On the other hand, Article 8 CFREU, provides regulation for processing of personal data. It guarantees the control, openness, accountability and transparency of the processing of personal data. Even though the processing of personal data is allowed and legal, a number of exceptions exists. For instance, "sensitive data": data relating to racial or ethnic origin, political opinions, religious or philosophical beliefs, trade union membership or data concerning health or sexual preference. The underlying motive is that the processing of such sensitive data bears a supplementary risk of discrimination. The prohibition is nonetheless never absolute, but derogations are only possible in strictly defined circumstances, for example for reasons of public health. In the same sense, decision making affecting persons solely on the basis of profiles are allowed based on the data subject´s explicit consent (22–2 c) GDPR). We must remember that our personal data is a part of us and we should not give it away without knowing what use it will be put to. Big databases provide enough raw material, that when algorithmically analyzed, are able to expose everything we are, including our "most intimate thoughts". Therefore, while the usefulness of privacy is questioned, privacy protection is fading away.

17.3 Big Health Data and the "Electronic Eye"

17.3.1 Medical Big Data

Long gone are the days when Alan Turing (1950, p. 460), claimed "We may hope that machines will eventually compete with men in all purely intellectual fields". Since then, the development of telecommunications systems associated with digital and disruptive technology has revolutionized communication and human coexistence. New technologies enhance scientific development in multiple areas.

Information and communication technologies are part of our daily lives. They are intertwined, interrelated, dynamic, and in constant evolution. Cloud computing, big data, IoT, artificial intelligence, robots, and algorithms, assume a leading role in the storage, processing, transmission and use of information and knowledge. ICT's have definitely changed relational, personal, social, work, and coexistence dynamics. Nowadays, communication is at the click of a button, a touch of a fingertip, facial recognition, iris pattern, or voice command. They have the particular susceptibility to expedite the transmissibility and reuse of sensitive personal data, including digital individual identity, health data, and, sometimes, even without the knowledge or consent of the data subject. This is why ICTs are particularly important in the process of shaping and designing the character, the personality, the way of being, and the ethical principles of every human being. Their immersion in the daily life of each citizen goes far beyond factories or smart homes, like Alexa or Siri, or any other home automation or programming. They present evolving solutions on health information technology (HIT), blockchain technology for healthcare, telemedicine, 3D printing for healthcare, storage and collection of medical big data into areas such as diagnosis, drug research, and virtual clinical trials.

Focusing on big data, we can say that they are the databases of structured or unstructured data collection of everything we think, wish, dream, feel, write, listen, plan, buy, sell, research and so on. To note, big data preeminent characteristics and attributes are: (i) Volume—very large amount of data (health, geolocation, travel, social networks); (ii) Velocity—proliferation of new data in real time; (iii) Variety—multiple sources and origins of data; (iv) Veracity—the possible truth of the data imposing its filtering in order to make the results credible; (v) Validity—correct and perceptible; (vi) Volatility—data should be stored only in the period necessary to achieve the purpose for which they were collected; (vii) Value—economic value, profit, towards which all the previous characteristics converge. Big data algorithmic analysis aims, above all, to maximize the results by enhancing knowledge of target content, that is, the desired information depending on the purpose (health, consumption, geo-location, hobbies). Neutrality of big data processing is only apparent, since the "simple" design of the algorithms may be imbued with the peculiar and specific characteristics of the programmer, who is typically a human being, and who influences the result obtained. As Danaher (2017, p. 2) mentioned: "No human being can make sense of this data unassisted. Hence there is significant reliance on algorithms to mine, parse, sort and configure the data into useful packages. Oftentimes these systems are maintained and tweaked by human designers and engineers, and the information is then utilized by humans in traditional corporate and bureaucratic decision-making systems. But there is also a growing willingness to outsource decision-making authority to algorithm-based decision-making systems. (…) Whether we like it or not, algorithms are increasingly being used to nudge, bias, guide, provoke, control, manipulate and constrain human behaviour."

Medical big data can derive from traditional (health information, electronic health records, clinical information) or nontraditional sources (costumer purchasing records, social network, Facebook likes). The use of those databases have proven to be an invaluable asset. Health and data are the building blocks that ensure big health data, and the *electronic eye* given by sophisticated analytic techniques leads to find connections and relationships between data that are particularly easy to monetize in healthcare context.

17.3.2 Electronic Health Records

Clinicians, like other professionals, use computers as a method to record and display medical files and clinical documentation, consolidating each patient´s medical information in electronic health record (EHR), processed for healthcare purposes.

Since the beginning of the twenty-first century, personal health data has been almost entirely stored in EHR systems. This includes a patient's medical history, diagnoses, treatments, laboratory tests, and medical or drug prescriptions. Using EHR systems makes it possible to collect and display a very large number of personal health data as well as to process and share them almost instantaneously. This is done through electronic communication and connectivity—whether authorized by patients, as it is legally required, or accidental or even in a fraudulent way- allowing the crossing of information between clinical sector operators (medical team members, laboratories, patients, clinicians) in real time. This allows the streamlining of procedures for faster response and resolution of concrete clinical situations as well as enhancing the maximization and efficiency of the concrete results obtained. EHR systems can improve clinical practice. This can be in terms of diagnosis, medication, or treatments, as it allows association, interconnection, and immediate analysis. It can do so electronically (through previously elaborated algorithms) with a patient's past medical history, family history, medication list, lab test results, drug interactions, allergies, and advance directives. Furthermore, it can even help reduce medical errors and associated health care costs. EHR systems have many more functionalities, namely: Clinical documentation and health information display; Results management; Computerized provider order entry and management (CPOE); Clinical decision support (CDS); Electronic communication and connectivity; Patient support; Administrative processes; Reporting and population health management (Hoffmann 2016, pp. 10–13).

Obviously, EHR regarding each patient, belongs to one another (data subject), even though health data is stored in large databases owned by the health institutions who collect them (hospitals, doctor's' offices, pharmacists). That kind of personal health data has an exponential economic and scientific value. They are the mortar product of big health data, an essential tool for healthcare providers, pharmaceuticals and logistics, genetics, biomedical and so on. It is through the cross-sharing of these anonymized data between various players in the scientific community (doctors, pharmacists, laboratories), and their analysis using predefined algorithms with different variables (age, sex, diseases, treatments) that the goals (e.g., new drugs, vaccines) and purposes sought by data controller can be achieved.

Public health has been tracking, monitoring, recording and analyzing certain types of contagious diseases using traditional statistical methods (sampling) since the eighteenth century. Though the purpose has been in order to discover their origin and prevent them from spreading, we should bear in mind that the COVID-19 pandemic has highlighted the use of EHR systems, and the need of sharing personal and non-personal electronic health data under FAIR (Findability, Accessibility, Interoperability, Reusability) health data principles. Synergies between dataveillance, monitoring citizens action, and communications and mobile contact tracing, in real time, gave the healthcare system access to the identification of COVID patients and their interactions. This enabled the surveillance and control of large populations to contain the pandemic.

17.3.3 Big Challenges

It's improbable to expect that some level of health data isn't shared by a patient, potentializing the escalation of the accumulation of data, particularly regarding healthcare and biomedical research. Electronic Health Records, most of the time, are acquired for a specific purpose, clinical or administrative, which generate electronic traces. Accordingly, it is appropriate to assess the nature of the challenges thrown by contemporary use of medical big data and personal electronic health records, bringing challenges both to medical big data analysis and to privacy and data protection rights.

Nevertheless, data-driven economy maximizes all the data that is collected; economically, financially (profit), and socially (even those that are apparently irrelevant and innocuous) by reusing it ad infinitum, extracting all possible information from it, even if it is invisible or unnoticeable. "Data-driven economy serves as an umbrella term for business that perform the (re)use as their core activity. (…) the focus of the data-driven economy is always on the secondary use of data, e.g. business models that seek to utilize the existing data in innovative and profitable ways" (Vrabec 2021, p. 25). This permanent use and reuse of data generates, as we all know, a kind of permanent dataveillance, which is especially relevant and even worrying in the healthcare sector, when using personal health data.

The uninterrupted use of eHealth and mHealth technologies has a threefold effect. Firstly, they provide the user up-to-date, real-time information on their own health and well-being (weight, height, heart rate, calories consumed…). Secondly, they also enable the data subjects to monitor and control themselves at all times. Lastly, this allows permanent surveillance and control by third parties like the data controller, the owners of big databases, hospitals, pharmacists, healthcare sector, or the state itself. Consequently, it leads the state to collaborate with private health sectors (doctors, hospitals, pharmacists), as Schneier (2015, p. 95) pointed "Governments don't conduct surveillance, censorship, and control operations alone. They are supported by a vast public–private surveillance partnership". They urge these private health sectors to share the data that is generated. This includes the personal electronic health data, non-personal electronic health data, and the research data, in order to develop ways to investigate, diagnose, and treat the patients. Though these eHealth technologies, medical devices, mobile apps and wearables could represent significant advances in the healthcare evolution, unintentional consequences quickly ascend, because, despite the fact that citizens are the data subjects, the difficulty to access their own EHR is still a maze. The advancement in these categories makes it difficult to effectively exercise the FAIR health data principles and patient's rights over their electronic health data, raising some privacy and data protection concerns. The *European Health Data Space Regulation (Proposal)* was drafted in order to more concisely legislate these concerns. It was built under the EU Charter on Fundamental Rights principles and GDPR provisions. It defines common rules as well as standards and practices for the primary and secondary use of electronic health data. Its purpose is to be the cornerstone of coherent implementation support for privacy and data protection rights as applied to electronic health data.

The uncertainties surrounding the impact of medical big data analytics, the untraceable secondary use of personal electronic health data and the daily advance of eHealth technologies, make us believe there is still a long way to go to dodge privacy breaches and negative consequences for the free movement of personal electronic health data.

17.4 eHealth and Privacy Relationship: The Legal Framework

17.4.1 Ubiquitous Digital Health

Since the beginning of the twenty-first century, citizens have been encouraged to use personal technologies in lifestyle and healthcare context, self-monitoring their daily lives. In 2001 G. Eysenbach held that eHealth is "an emerging field in the intersection of medical informatics, public health and business, referring to health services and information delivered or enhanced through the Internet and related technologies. In a broader sense, the term characterizes not only a technical development, but also a state-of-mind, a way of thinking, an attitude, and a commitment for networked, global thinking, to improve health care locally, regionally, and worldwide by using information and communication technology."

This emerging field of eHealth and mHealth solutions has been implemented and developed either in national or in international organizations and nations. In 2005, WHO, considered eHealth as "the cost-effective and secure use of information and communications technologies in support of health and health-related fields, including health-care services, health surveillance, health literature, and health education, knowledge and research." Adding, in 2013, the need of "standardization and interoperability of health data" and considered to be necessary to establish the precise boundaries of ".health" internet domain". Also, in 2015, highlighting the relevance of "mHealth", because "the use of mobile wireless technologies for public health (…) has been shown to increase access to health information, services and skills, as well as to promote positive changes in health behaviors and disease management". Moreover, in 2018, it was considered that digital health "with the development of digital technologies in health should be prioritized."

The symbiosis between digitization of health sector and the development of ICT tools regarding the healthcare, with new forms of doctor and patient interaction and observation (telemedicine, EHR, 3D printing for healthcare), allied to collection and analysis of personal health data of healthy citizens, leads to a rapid and continuous improvement of an equitable, effective and efficient health system that enables good clinical practice, cost reduction and maximization of results that are needed to satisfy the "physical, psychological and social well-being" of each citizen. Still, as has been stated, due to this digitalization of the health sector, we are in an urgent need of the development of a legal framework that can streamline the use of personal health data and information from EHRs, mobile apps and other electronic devices. The important factors to consider in doing so, are to adequately safeguard privacy and autonomy of the data subject. This is done by guaranteeing the protection of personal data, and holding the data controller, or any other person who may have access to the data, to being held fairly responsible for the primary or secondary use, as well as access or sharing of personal health data in an improper or unauthorized way. For this reason, the globalization of eHealth horizons has to be based on multi-level strategic planning which, in addition to the WHO's intervention, involves international and national legal systems.

17.4.2 eHealth and Privacy Under the GDPR on European Union Data Space

Aware of the importance of the digital world, the European Union has approved the "European Strategy for Data", which aims to implement a single data market that guarantees competitiveness in the digital world while safeguarding fundamental rights, specifically privacy and data protection, of the data subjects and data processors. It also draws up appropriate legislation on data governance, access and reuse, and cloud computing infrastructures. Thus, creating availability to data, making it possible in some cases to reuse it free of charge while also developing data processing infrastructures and data sharing.

The pursuit of these objectives requires a robust and cohesive legal framework designed with respect for the values and principles of the European Union. It was this need that gave rise to *Regulation (EU) 2022/868 of the Parliament and of the Council of 30 May 2022 on European data governance (Data Governance Act)*. This regulation has been in force since September 24th of 2023. It is one of the pillars of the new EU data map and aims to provide the essential legal mechanisms for greater and better use, sharing and reuse of data between the various public and private economic operators. Specifically regarding the field we've been discussing, this piece of legislation could also enable the anonymized reuse of health data and therefore boost the development of research and consequently improve healthcare. Alongside this line of thought, entered into force, on 11 January 2024, the *Regulation (EU) 2023/2854 of the European Parliament and of the Council of 13 December 2023 on harmonised rules on fair access to and use of data and amending Regulation (EU) 2017/2394 and Directive (EU) 2020/1828 (Data Act)* which establishes procedures for the use of data generated by the various IoT devices.

As foreseen in that strategy, the European Union is implementing a common area for all Member States aimed to protect the health of EU citizens, making a coordinated and joint effort to improve the prevention, treatment and monitoring of diseases. As stated by the *European Health Data Space*, this space is "one of the central building blocks of the European Health Union and a milestone in EU's digital transformation, aims to:—improve across the EU, by empowering people to control their health data in their home country or in other EU countries;—offer a consistent, secure, trustworthy and efficient framework for the use of health data. Under strict conditions, researchers, innovators, public institutions or industry will have access to large amounts of high-quality health data, crucial to developing life-saving treatments, vaccines or medical devices;—foster a genuine single market for digital health services and products."

The European Health Data Space is built on rigorous data privacy, interoperability and security requirements, including cybersecurity, which is the key for the trust of citizens and the robustness of the project". In that context on May 3rd 2022, is born a *Proposal for a Regulation of the European Parliament and of the Council on the European Health Data Space* (EHDS) submitted by the European Commission. EHDS "will address health-specific challenges to electronic health data access and sharing (…) EHDS will create a common space where natural persons can easily control their electronic health data. It will also make it possible for researchers, innovators and policy makers to use this electronic health data in a trusted and secure way that preserves privacy. (…) It also aims to ensure a legal framework consisting of trusted EU and Member State governance mechanisms and a secure environment. This would allow researchers, innovators, policy-makers and regulators at EU and Member State levels to access relevant electronic health data to promote better diagnosis, treatment and well-being of natural persons, and lead to better and well-informed policies. It also aims to contribute to a genuine single market for digital health products and services, by harmonising rules, and so boost healthcare system efficiencies…The EHDS will also promote better exchange and access to different types of electronic health data, including electronic health records, genomics data, patient registries etc. Not only will this support healthcare delivery (services and personnel involved in providing health care or primary use of electronic health data), it will also support health research innovation, policy-making, regulatory purposes and personalised medicine purposes (secondary use of electronic health data). It will also establish mechanisms for data altruism in the health sector. The EHDS will help to attain the Commission's vision for EU's digital transformation by 2030, the Digital Compass aim of providing 100% of natural persons with access to their medical records and the Declaration of Digital Principles."

However, it should be noted that this space was not created alone but was based on legislation such as the Regulation (EU) 2016/679 (General Data Protection Regulation -GDPR), on the Regulation (EU) 2018/1725 (EU Data Protection), on the Regulation (EU) 2017/745 on medical devices (Medical Devices Regulation), on the Regulation (EU) 2017/746 on in vitro diagnostic medical devices (In Vitro Diagnostics Regulation), on the proposed Artificial Intelligence Act, on the Regulation (EU) 2022/868 (Data Governance Act), on the proposed Data Act, on the Directive 2016/1148 on security of network and information systems (NIS Directive), on the Directive 2011/724/EU and on the application of patient's rights in cross-border healthcare (CBHC Directive).

All the above-mentioned EU legislative frameworks were created on fundamental values and rights that shaped the EU. It is therefore understandable that the EHDS imposes the application of digitized health data (eHealth, EHR systems) of the rights and guarantees conferred by the Charter of Fundamental Rights of the European Union and for GDPR; namely, data subject rights, referring to the group of rights that data protection law grants to individuals, such as the rights to access, to portability, to be forgotten or the right to object. In short, the aim of legal framework regarding digital health context is to strengthen the interoperability and data portability of EHR systems, enabling effective control of eHealth data and ensuring respect for the privacy and data protection rights of data subjects.

17.5 eHealth Profiling

17.5.1 Profiling: Variances and Inconsistencies

When we speak of data, it encompasses the structure of multiple data, meaning, as Mittelstadt and Floridi said, (2018, p. 431) "any meaningful occurrence data are invariably plural. A single datum functions, perhaps, only like the Cartesian cogito: a signal that there is something rather than nothing. Data as they appear are always composed and configured in sets (and, therefore, potentially open to decomposing and recomposing in different ways)".

The problem is that the same set of data can be used and reused. All data can have secondary uses. Health data is no exception. Personal medical big data and electronic health records are automatically recorded and stored, during a certain period of time, while also processed and monitored in a proper technological way. This means the data is algorithmically identifying patterns and trends and checking whether new data fit the pattern therefore providing data processors raw material skilled to profile (identify and represent) a natural person or a specific group of data subjects. Which in principle enables a permanent real-time analysis of the conduct of citizens and the affirmation of evaluations and predictions about their behaviour, sensibilities, preferences, identity and choices. The aforementioned profiled data subject can be regarding a person (personalized profile), an organization, a group, a category (group profile), or a "thing". Our concerns will only regard the use of profiling technologies to identify and represent the identity of a person and her or his health status.

In the European Union legal data protection framework, profiling "means any form of automated processing of personal data consisting of the use of personal data to evaluate certain personal aspects relating to a natural person, in particular to analyse or predict aspects concerning that natural person's performance at work, economic situation, health, personal preferences, interests, reliability, behaviour, location or movements;" (4–4, GDPR).

Although, most of the time, the goal of profiling is not to find the identity of the data subject but that individual's special characteristics, interests or behaviour. Whereas, data user targeting often attempts to evaluate the assessment of opportunities or risks and offer to the data subject a *tailor-made suit,* a product or service that fits him perfectly. Nevertheless, interests of the data subject and the data user aren't always coincident, so when sensitive personal data is at stake, profiling can represent a big risk and consequently some damages to the data subject, the natural person to whom the data belongs.

Data concerning health is a special category of sensitive "personal data related to the physical or mental health of a natural person, including the provision of health care services, which reveal information about his or her health status" (4–15; 9–1, GDPR). Their relevance and value are highly dependent on the epistemic context of their collection, purposes and treatment. Before the processing of the data, the controller must, carry out an assessment for the impact of the envisaged processing operations on the protection of personal data which is mandatory in case of "systematic and extensive evaluation of personal aspects relating to natural persons which is based on automated processing, including profiling" (4–4; 22, GDPR) and in case of "processing in a large scale of special categories of data, it's also necessary the advice of the data protection officer, if it exists (9–1; 35–1–2–3 a) b), GDPR). Alongside the supervisory authority shall establish and make a list of processing operations which are subject to the requirement for a data protection impact assessment (Recitals 9, 71, 75; 35–4 9, GDPR), following the "Guidelines on Data Protection Impact Assessment (DPIA) and determining whether processing is "likely to result in a high risk" for the purposes of GDPR or not. Those Guidelines (WP248-rev.01.29-Revised and Adopted on 4 October 2017) include: Evaluation or scoring, like profiling and predicting, especially from "aspects concerning the data subject's performance at work, economic situation, health, personal preferences or interests, reliability or behavior, location or movements. Examples of this could include "a biotechnology company offering genetic tests directly to consumers in order to assess and predict the disease/health risks, or a company building behavioural or marketing profiles based on usage or navigation on its website."

Moreover, GDPR states that the data subject should be informed about data processing operation, its purposes, the period it will occur, the circumstances and context of processing, the existence of profiling and the consequences of such profiling. It also confers to the natural person the right to access his personal data, in order to verify the lawfulness of the processing, including personal health data, regardless of where they are stored or from where they were obtained. This includes medical records, electronic health records, diagnoses, treatments or interventions provided. Furthermore, the data subject has the right to be informed of the logic involved in any automatic personal data processing, at least when based on profiling and the consequences of such processing. Namely when it predicts aspects concerning the natural person's health or produces direct effects on said health (24, 60, 63, 71 GDPR). As we see, profiling and its foreseeable eternity can be extremely damaging to the human dignity principle, as it encourages the acceptance of human beings as objects—in Günter Dürig's (2003 (1958), pp. 17) conceptualization "Objektformel". To avoid this risk, profiling should only be allowed in limited contexts, previously subject to a proportionality test between dignity and the purpose of profiling.

Although a profile is always different from the original, there are kinds of specific data or sets of data, properly achieved, algorithmically treated, influenced by the environment and perspective of the programmer, enabling the data processor to draw someone's personality, political options, beliefs or even health status. In this circumstance, profiling means a set of correlated data that is able to portray a person in a cartoon that is not they're real portrait. This in turn having potential consequences to that citizen either in performance at work, employment opportunities, health risks, insurance risks, and so on, putting in peril his privacy, autonomy and non-discrimination rights.

17.5.2 Digitalized Risk Assessment of Health e-profiling

Data is power and profit. Citizens (data subjects) are permanently under observation happily spreading their data in networked environments. Data controllers "clap their hands" happily acquiring and processing that enormous amount of data, tracking in real time, users behavior's in a digital environment. Yet, the purpose of data collection should be taken into account by the user as this determines a profile that emerges from their web surfing habits.

In an Era of ubiquitous computing, the collecting and recording of terabits of information imposes a selection of the relevant data and the correlation between data or data sets through the use of data mining techniques. Those strategies produce an uninterrupted stream of profiles that can be used by the profiled one (receiving personalized services or accessing personalized risk assessment), or by enterprises, organizations or governments agencies (to assess risks and opportunities concerning e.g. consumers, potential terrorists, diseases or pandemics).

Regardless of the purpose of said profiling, it represents a particular importance because the results may become an assessment of risks and opportunities of the data subject. In this regard, it should be stated that personalized profiling means, to appreciate attributes, biometric features (physiological or passive: like face image, fingerprint, hand geometry, iris pattern) and behavior (or active biometrics, these are characteristics represented actions or functions performed by an individual at a specific time for a specific reason), in a digital environment and when or if necessary, correlating that data with the one from analogical (off line) databases, who generates inferences about the user and about data subject. If the profiling directly impacts a citizen, it may be able to identify and represent them. This knowledge will be used to predict future behavior, impelling the user to act in the best interests of the data controller, most of the time, unknowingly, neglecting their own needs and well-being.

Similarly, data healthcare context allows the provider, to have a suitable understanding of the emerging patterns, therefore maximizing the potential of offering products (medicines, food supplements, slimming products, vaccines) or services (therapies, complementary diagnostic tests, X-rays) to the target person. That suggestion of products and services is the result of the user's eHealth behavior correlated with his clinical records and electronic health records, and his social behavior in digital environment. Profiling gives guidelines to define the data subject and the knowledge of some of their personal characteristics, resulting in helping to predict diseases and/or health risks. On the other hand, it gives public authorities raw material to foresee diseases and pandemics proving a fundamental help to public health. Nevertheless, we should be aware that at the same time it poses relevant ethical and legal issues. Predicting someone's behavior, character, health risks or diseases could impact and influence a person's life. It seems difficult to know when decision-making reflects a person's free-will and autonomy (meaning that the citizen is capable of ruling their own life) or, instead, is oriented on the basis of "a profile". Personalized profiling is able to identify a person or, "profiling built on sameness in the sense of unique identification or continuity with oneself. (…) the term identity refers to the concept of *ipse* or self. This concept overlaps with the idem-identity as it depends on a sense of the continuity of one's own existence (…) *ipse*-identity also concerns the *sense of self* that is constitutive of human subject." Hildebrand (2008). Identifying a person has consequences on his private sphere, on his privacy in the sense of "intimacy, anonymity, reserve, solitude" (Westin 1968).

Profiling technologies cannot identify "*the sense of self*" of each one but they can identify similitudes, e.g. preferences or attitudes, on a comparison with other persons information in their social digital environment, which may impact "*the sense of self*". This personalized profiling may lead to manipulation either of the citizen profiling or of the behavior of the profiled individual citizen. In it turn, this kind of hidden manipulation is able to produce relevant changes in power relationships between individual citizens and between citizens and organization.

The biopolitical Era studied by Foucault, based on the human being as an economic agent, has evolved into biopower. This makes the individual believe that their actions are free, spontaneous and voluntary. When in fact their behaviour is predictable and conditioned, the computer "chip" is subcutaneous and invisible, the great social influencers are the holders of personal big databases (Hun 2014).

17.6 A Critical Challenge with Rights and Wrongs

The starting point of this paper´s discussion was the dialectic tension between privacy as a fundamental right, its need of preservation, the use or abuse of big health data analysis and the risks that eHealth profiling may represent.

The increasing influence of computers, ICT, IoT's, eHealth technologies, EHR, mHealth wearables and apps, in contemporary societies, has been seen as an excellent promise for the future, however, as we showed, there is another side to that story, since it also should be seen as menacing. In as much as they present evolving solutions in healthcare while are also able to expand their surveillance capacity of all forms of organization influencing privacy and data protection rights.

Data can be used and reused. Personal medical big data and electronic health records provide data broker a valuable asset. In an Era of ubiquitous computing, health provides data processors data sets of correlated personal health data skilled to extract knowledge. As mentioned by Foucault (1963, tl.2003, 196), "For clinical experience to become possible as a form of knowledge, a reorganization of the hospital field, a new definition of the status of the patient in society, and the establishment of a certain relationship between public assistance an medical experience, between help and knowledge, become necessary; the patient has to be enveloped in a collective homogeneous space. It was also necessary to open up language to a whole new domain: that of a perpetual and objectively based correlation of the visible and the expressible". That metaphor is still applicable nowadays. Personalized profiling is personal knowledge, appreciating attributes, biometric features, characteristics, represented actions or functions performed by an identified person in a digital environment with his own boundaries.

It seems that ICT's gave upsurge to a different way of individual health knowledge. It´s results may become an assessment of risks and opportunities for the data subject, the "patient" or the "patient-consumer". This is what eHealth profiling means. The most dangerous part of it all is that this knowledge will be used to predict future behavior, to weave an invisible spider's web around the user that pushes them to act in the best interests of the data controller, most of the time, unknowingly, and therefore, neglecting their own needs and well-being. Hence, we must be aware of the data we are giving, to whom we are given and under what circumstances we are giving.

References

Allen, Anita L. 2011. *Unpopular privacy: What must we hide?* New York: Oxford University Press Inc.

Allen, Anita L. 2013. An ethical duty to protect one's own information privacy?. 65 *Ala. L. Rev.* 845. Faculty Scholarship at Penn Carey Law. 451. https://scholarship.law.upenn.edu/faculty_scholarship/451 Accessed 23 Aug 2020.

Danaher, John et al. 2017. Algorithmic governance: Developing a research agenda through the power of collective intelligence. Big Data & Society July-December: 1–21. https://journals.sagepub.com/doi/pdf/https://doi.org/10.1177/2053951717726554 Accessed 23 June 2025.

Dürig, Günter. 2003 (1958) *Grundgesetz: Kommentierung der Artikel 1 und 2 Grundgesetz, in* Maunz-Dürig (Hrsg.) Grundgesetz. München: C.H. Beck.

Eysenbach, G. 2001. What is e-health? *Journal of Medical Internet Research* 3: 2–20. https://www.jmir.org/2001/2/e20/PDF Accessed 23 Aug 2023

Foucault, Michel. 1963. Naissance de la Clinique. Presses Universitaires de France. Foucault, Michel. 2003. *The Birth Of The Clinic An Archaeology of Medical Perception.* (trans: M. Sheridan). London: Routledge Taylor & Francis e-Library.

Godkin, Edward Lawrence. 1890. "The Rights of the Citizen. IV - To his own reputation". *Scribner's Magazine.* VIII- July-December.

Hun, Byung-Chul. 2014. Psychopolitik: Neoliberalismus und die neuen Machttechniken. Frankfurt Am Main: S. Fisher Vellag GmbH.

Hildebrandt, Mireille, 2008. Profiling and the Identity of the European Citizens in *Profiling the European Citizens Cross-Disciplinary Perspectives*, ed. Hildebrandt, Mireille and Serge Gutwirtt. Springer.

Hoffman, Sharona. 2016. *Electronic health records and medical big data, law and policy.* Cambridge: Cambridge University Press.

Lyon, David. 2022. *Pandemic surveillance.* Cambridge: Polity Press.

Mittelstadt, Brent Daniel, and Luciano Floridi. 2018. *The ethics of biomedical big data.* Springer.

Schneier, Bruce. 2015. *Data and Goliath the hidden battles to collect your data and control your world.* New York: W.W. Norton & Company.

Turing, A.M. I. 1950. Computing machinery and intelligence. *Mind* LIX: 236: 433–460. https://doi.org/10.1093/mind/LIX.236.433.

Tzanou, Maria. 2021. *Health data privacy under the GDPR big data challenges and regulatory responses.* New York: Routledge Taylor & Francis.

Vrabec, Helena U. 2021. *Data subject rights under the GDPR.* Oxford: Oxford University Press.

Warren, Samuel D. and Brandeis, Louis D. The Right to Privacy. 1890. Harvard Law Rev. Dec. 15. Vol. 4. No 5.:193- 220. The Harvard Law Review Association. https://openyls.law.yale.edu/bitstream/handle/20.500.13051/806/Right_of_Privacy__The.pdf.

Westin, Alan F. (1968). Privacy and Freedom. *Wasington & Lee Law Rev*iew 166. https://scholarlycommons.law.wlu.edu/wlulr/vol25/iss1/20/.

Whitman, James Q. 2004. The two western cultures of privacy: Dignity versus liberty. *The Yale Law Journal* 113(6): 1151–1221. https://www.yalelawjournal.org/article/the-two-western-cultures-of-privacy-dignity-versus-liberty. Accessed 23 Oct 2010.

U. S Supreme Court. https://www.supremecourt.gov/opinions/21pdf/19-1392_6j37.pdf.

European Health Data Space. https://health.ec.europa.eu/ehealth-digital-health-and-care/european-health-data-space_en. Accessed 23 Aug 2023.

Chapter 18
Euthanasia and Assisted Suicide: The Public Provision of Death as a New Bio-Right?

Carolina Pereira-Sáez

Abstract In certain countries, the public authorities have shaped the provision of death on request, in certain circumstances, as a legal right, implying a public obligation to dispense death. Death is thus the provision to be supplied, the object of the right. Spain's latest legislation on euthanasia and assisted suicide is a paradigmatic case. The purpose of this paper is to consider this bio-right as a *new* right, belonging to a new and distinct category of rights –not just a further generation of rights continuing the previous ones. To this end, it firstly focuses on the claim that this new bio-right is grounded on classic rights, of previous generations –a claim found both in the academic discourse and in recent Spanish legislation. Secondly, therefore, it tries to analyse the relevant features of this new bio-right that can also be found in other new rights, in order to confirm a previously launched proposal for the differentiation of this new category of rights. Finally, in conclusion, it points out some aspects of the understanding of the Law that these new rights imply: new rights form part of a Law that is also new.

Keyword Assisted suicide · Euthanasia · New rights

This chapter is one of the results of the research project "Los nuevos derechos humanos: teoría jurídica y praxis política (NDH)", PID2019-111115GB-100, financially supported by the Spanish Ministry for Science and Innovation, and of the *Philosophy, Constitution and Rationality* Research Group within the Programme for research groups with growth potential (ED431B 2023/59), financially supported by the Xunta de Galicia (Spain).

C. Pereira-Sáez (✉)
Universidade da Coruña, A Coruña, Spain
e-mail: c.pereira.saez@udc.es

© The Author(s) 2024

J.-A. Seoane and O. Vergara (eds.), *The Discourse of Biorights*, The International Library of Bioethics 109, https://doi.org/10.1007/978-3-031-66804-3_18

18.1 Introducing Intended Death as the Object of a New Bio-Right

The aim of this paper is to study euthanasia and assisted suicide as a new bio-right. In some countries, most recently Spain, the dispensation of death on request (either through the provision of suicide essential assistance or through the execution of euthanasia by the public authorities through their health care system) is legally recognised as a service right. Thus, in Spain, for example, people in what is called a "euthanasic context" (a situation of suffering related to some specific types of disease) can request from the public authorities the dispensation of death or essential assistance to commit suicide. Well, it is this particular regulation (in contrast, for instance, to forms of decriminalising compassionate killing and assisted suicide) that will be used to test the hypothesis, sustained elsewhere (Pereira-Sáez 2017) that we are facing a new generation of rights, rights that are viewed in a transformative way (Arosemena 2020), significantly detached from previous generations of rights. To this end, we will first present an understanding of the new rights. We will then examine whether the right to euthanasia and assisted suicide is indeed a case of this new generation of rights. Although euthanasia and assisted suicide have been understood in Spanish Law and in academic debates mainly as a demand for respect for autonomy,[1] the argument here is that the right to euthanasia and assisted suicide is not simply a new development of an existing right to autonomy. To this end, the novel elements of this right will be examined. The conclusion to be drawn is that this is indeed a new right, which shares some features of this new generation of rights, most notably that of promoting the slippage of human being in Law, from subject to object. It is possible that this feature, like others typical of the new rights, is not present in all cases of the new rights, which sometimes seem, as we shall see, to be just new versions of old rights. But it is, in my view, interesting for a philosophical analysis of the Law, because it implies a relevant change in rights, which in turn is significant for a new Law in which they live.

We have said that not all seemingly new rights are really new rights; if this is the case, why should the right to euthanasia and assisted suicide be considered truly a new right? In Spain, the latest Organic Law 3/2021, of 24 March, regulating euthanasia, "introduces into our legal system a new individual right such as euthanasia. Euthanasia is understood as an action that produces the death of a person directly and intentionally by means of a unique and immediate cause-effect relationship, at the informed, express and reiterated request of that person, and which is carried out in a context of suffering due to an incurable illness or suffering that

[1] I use this term because it is the usual one in the academic discourse on this right, but I think that it is not autonomy—giving oneself rules to guide one's own free action- that is at stake. Nor would it be self-determination—the making of oneself– given the decisive external intervention in dispensing death. Rather, it would be about demanding that a third party carry out a person's will as regards her or himself, which is what autonomy is in this context understood to mean. On the other hand, not all legal systems explicitly include a fundamental right to autonomy or self-determination: this is the case in Spain, although, in practice, judicial interpretation endorses it.

the person experiences as unacceptable and which has not been mitigated by other means" (preamble of Organic Law 3/2021, of 24 March, regulating euthanasia). This law was appealed before the Spanish Constitutional Court as violating constitutional rights, especially the right to life. However, the Constitutional Court ruled that the right to life does not apply to voluntary death and based that right to euthanasia and assisted suicide on the right to physical and moral integrity, understood as means for self-determination (STC 19/2023, 22 March, FJ 6). This would seem to be reason enough for any reader with a minimum of legal positivist background to recognise it as a right. What then is the point of the question is this right really new and really a right? Both questions are interesting, and it seems to me that the second one is the most important for our understanding of the Law.[2] However, my interest in this paper is limited to answering the first question because, as I said, it helps us understand the new rights, which in turn helps our understanding of the features of the Law of our times.

In the Spanish case, it seems undeniable that the right to euthanasia and assisted suicide is a *new* right. It is a service that the citizen can request from the public authorities, a service that is part of the public health system's portfolio of services; and it is a new service that could not be requested before the enactment of Organic Law 3/2021. In other cases, new rights are the result of case Law interpretations, citizens' demands, non-binding declarations of rights, lobbies' claims, etc., which makes it more interesting to analyse the extent to which these are really new rights. But, in this case and for Spanish Law, the new right is introduced by the legislature itself, with the support of the interpretation given by the rulings of the Constitutional Court. One does not have to be an obstinate positivist to consider this *pedigree* sufficient to understand such a claim as a right in a relevant sense, so it can be brought before the judges and to which they must respond on the basis of the Law.

However, the fact that the service provided could not be required until the enactment of Organic Law 3/2021 may not be sufficient for it to be a truly new right. Indeed, the Spanish legislature presents the new provision as a requirement of old rights (of privacy, integrity and ideological freedom, in addition to human dignity and the higher value of freedom).[3] The Spanish Constitutional Court, on the other hand, has made it clear that the new provision is based on the right to physical and moral integrity contained in Article 15 of the Spanish Constitution understood as

[2] Cf. Zambrano (2024), where the author argues that it is a right that undermines its own foundations.

[3] "Euthanasia is linked to a constitutionally protected fundamental right of the person, such as life, but which must also be reconciled with other rights and goods, equally constitutionally protected, such as the physical and moral integrity of the person (art. 15 EC), human dignity (art. 10 EC), the higher value of freedom (art. 1.1 EC), ideological freedom and freedom of conscience (art. 16 EC) or the right to privacy. When a fully capable and free person is faced with a life situation which, in her or his opinion, violates her or his dignity, privacy and integrity, such as that which defines the euthanasia context described above, the good of life may decline in favour of the other goods and rights with which it must be weighed up, given that there is no constitutional duty to impose or protect life at all costs and against the will of the holder of the right to life" (preamble to Organic Law 3/2021, of 24 March, regulating euthanasia).

a means of self-determination.[4] Thus, it could be understood that euthanasia has been in the Spanish Constitution from the start, like an unpolished stone which only now is fully realised. It is true that we could see this question as a purely technical one, depending on whether constitutional rights are understood as *numerus clausus* or *apertus*. In no case, however, would this exclude new legal rights, which, in the Spanish case, need not derive from the Constitution, only not contradict it[5]. It could also be understood as a political strategy on the part of the legislature to prevent a future legislative assembly from suppressing this right; however, this explanation does not justify the interpretation of the Constitutional Court, which does not have positive legislative power, but only negative power as guarantor of the Constitution.[6] To conclude: given that, according to the Constitutional Court's rulings, not guaranteeing these benefits would mean violating old constitutional fundamental rights, it seems difficult to argue that we are dealing with a significantly new right.

In my view, however, the right to euthanasia and assisted suicide is indeed a truly new right, and not only on its own, insofar as it is intended for a new service, but as indicative of a new generation of rights. And although this is not the first time that the understanding of rights has undergone a change, justifying their classification into different generations, this time the novelty could imply a change of paradigm, mainly because of its favouring a shift of the position of the human being in the Law, from subject to object. I do not claim that this is always the case, but depends on countries, legal traditions, branches of Law, etc., but it does not, in my opinion, seem any less relevant for that reason. However, we must first clarify what is meant by a new right in order to assess whether, and to what extent, this is true.

18.2 A Brief Proposal on New Rights

Although the ground beneath our feet is still shifting, and they are not a consolidated legal reality that allows for definitive conclusions, I have argued elsewhere (Pereira-Sáez, 2017) that it is possible to identify a latest generation of rights featuring some traits that decisively distinguish them from previous generations, to the extent that they cannot be considered as just another step in an evolution that begins with civil and political rights, passes through social and solidarity rights and reaches our times with no interruption.

Different authors propose alternative criteria (probably more acute than mine) to identify new rights (Serna 2024). I understand that not all rights that are enunciated as such for the first time in a legal text, including soft Law texts, are substantially new rights. Thus, new rights would not be really new if they were necessary to guarantee old rights that were de facto not respected (such as the obligation to assume reasonable accommodation in the new version of the right to education for disabled people), or

[4] Cf. STC 19/2023, 22 March, FJ 6.

[5] Cf. STC 19/2023, of 22 March, FJ 6 and dissenting opinion of Judge Concepción Espejel Jorquera.

[6] Cf. *ibid*.

just covering new responsible subjects (so the recognition of the horizontal effect of old rights would not give rise to new rights), or proposed to address new threats to old rights (such as the protection of personal data in the digital environment). Nor would they be new rights that identify among their holders a particular group that was, strictly speaking, already included (as the rights of disabled people, because they were included among the holders of earlier declarations proclaiming these same rights). Indeed, the new threats to the goods protected by the Law are sometimes of such a different nature that we can think we are dealing with a truly new right: thus, advances in technoscience make it possible to threaten human goods that until recently were intangible, such as the integrity of the mind (Andorno 2024), or make us realise that something (for example, human treatment, as opposed to treatment by an artificial intelligence) is a good that we may not have been aware of before. In these cases, the good at stake was already recognised and protected by Law, such as privacy (albeit not mental), or was simply beyond its reach. At the same time, and in a different sense, it should also be borne in mind that legislatures and judges, (especially the latter, since their function is to guarantee an old Law rather than to design a new one) link new rights with old rights, as we saw for the Spanish version of the right to euthanasia—even when they are really new, to the point of depriving the old right they are reinterpreting of its meaning. So, what makes new rights new?

Of course, all these cases we have referred to (new tools, responses to new threats, etc.) are new rights understood in a literal sense. However, in some way, insofar as the good to which the right responds—from which the right is specified[7]—does not basically change, nor does the holder,[8] nor does the intervention of the Law regarding that human good, we would not be dealing with a significantly new right. To support this, I rely on proposals that understand the nature of rights from basic human goods, as opposed to alternatives such as choice or benefit, which I find less robust, although this is not the place to develop their defence (Massini 2020, pp. 32–35 and Finnis 2011, pp. 203–205). This would imply that, as specifications of basic human goods, the range of rights will be limited, hence, at least in this respect, it would not be easy to find new rights.[9] In the following, we will see whether there are any relevant novelties in the right to euthanasia and assisted suicide in these regards.

---

[7] To Finnis, "modern rights-talk amplifies the undifferentiated reference to the 'common good' by providing a usefully detailed listing of the various aspects of human flourishing and fundamental components of the way of life in community that tends to favour such flourishing in all" (Finnis 2011, p. 221).

[8] However, the recent Spanish animal welfare law presents animal rights as rights derived from their nature, i.e. natural (cf. Law 7/2023 of 28 March, on the protection of animal rights and welfare, art.1.2: "Animal rights are understood as their right to good treatment, respect and protection, inherent and derived from their nature as sentient beings"); rights that, in a way, were already there. Thus, it would seem that the Spanish legislature does not really intend to be *creating* rights: either they find them in old rights (euthanasia, in physical and moral integrity, understood as an instrument of self-determination) or inherent in nature (animal rights).

[9] Cf. Finnis and the difference between concept and conceptions of a right (Finnis 2011, pp. 219–220). On the other hand, this makes especially interesting studies on new rights that address the consideration of declarations of rights as *numerus apertus* or *numerus clausus* (Toller 2024), the *pedigree* necessary to argue that the new right is part of the parent legal system (Vergara 2024) or the

18.3 What is New in the New Bio-Right to Euthanasia and Assisted Suicide?

Although, as I have said, the right to euthanasia and assisted suicide is often presented as a new specification of a general right to autonomy, I think that it can be understood as a significantly new right in that it involves a genuinely new judgement about the goods at stake—in particular life. I will try to support this in what follows.

As far as the service provided by the right is concerned, it seems that the novelty is clear: it is the provision of death, directly and intentionally, or of the essential means for suicide. The object of the right is thus a direct and intentional assault on the hitherto-recognised basic good of life. Thus, we would be dealing with a new right that denies an old good (life) or identifies a new good (the provocation of death). However, it could be objected that (as in the argumentation of the Spanish legislature and Constitutional Court), the good to which the right responds is simply a different one: self-determination. Thus, it is not denied that life—a classic good—is a good, but only that it is an absolute good. Nor would there be a new good (the provocation of death), but a new, broader interpretation of an old good (self-determination), because what is considered good is the fulfilment of the person's will with regard to him or herself (and so involuntary euthanasia is excluded). The protected good therefore, would be an old one, and the Law would not be changing its operation regarding this good, but merely identifying a new specification of it. Moreover, such a specification would be justified by the new risks to self-determination (dysthanasia and therapeutic overkill) and, on the other hand, it would not be radically different -again, in the opinion of the Spanish legislature and the Constitutional Court- from classical interpretations of this good, which already accepted the assumption of the risk of death in the exercise of self-determination.[10]

However, I think this is not enough to reject the novelty of the right to euthanasia and assisted suicide. It must be borne in mind that, in this case, the Law assumes the public authorities' legal obligation to carry out the person's will with regard to him or herself. As we know, the Law does not always assume that our right to self-determination means that someone, or the public authorities, must carry out our will for us (even if they only affect oneself, and even if the third party's action is essential, as in amputations or agreed cannibalism, but not always in dispensed death). And, if it does so in this case, it is precisely because it is based on a judgement about the goodness of causing death—a judgement which, on the other hand, is not excluded by the fact that involuntary euthanasia is ruled out, because rights are exercised in freedom, and this does not exclude a judgement about the goodness of their object.[11] This is in line with a type of argument that repeatedly appears in

importance of the transformative paradigm as a converter of old rights into new rights (Arosemena 2024).

[10] Cf. STC 19/2023, 22 March, FJ 6.

[11] Thus, for example, the right to vote be must freely exercised, but voting is protected because political participation is a good. This means, as Keown explains, that the reasons that justify voluntary euthanasia also justify non-voluntary euthanasia, because voluntary euthanasia is not based on

debates on euthanasia, such as the following: if we have accepted death as good when self-determination brings it about in other contexts, why not do so in this one, taking it to the point that, if death does not occur, we should provoke it? Moreover, is it not necessary to do so, in order to avoid unfair discrimination? Thus, to the Spanish Constitutional Court, the right to be killed is part of the right to physical and moral integrity for the same reason that this right protects the refusal of treatment even if it implies death.[12] In other cases[13] it is argued that, if those who are plugged into a machine can die, if they want to, because the action of unplugging them is not prohibited, is it not unjust that those who are not plugged in but also want to die, cannot die? Quite apart from the confusion these arguments create about the role of intention in shaping free action (Finnis 1995), it should be noted that the same argument could imply the injustice of both a terminally ill person and a healthy person wanting to die and only the ill one dies: the desired death would be an unjustly distributed good. It could be argued that what is considered fair in this case is just the fulfilment of one person's will but not the other's, whatever he or she wants, but, as we have already said, this is not how the Law reasons in other similar cases (Keown 2022b, p. 34). Therefore, this right guarantees not only respect for autonomy, but also the fulfilment of a duty of beneficence, on the basis of a judgement about the goodness of voluntary intentional homicide in certain cases (Keown 2022a). Ultimately, this could lead us to understand that if something is a right, it is because it is a good. Is it not, then, a matter of justice that it should be enjoyed by all (the non-dying sick, the mentally ill, children or persons lacking capacity, and in fact all of us)?

So, what we mean is that euthanasia and assisted suicide is a new right because it significantly changes the appreciation of human goods. However, it could be argued – looking specifically at Spanish Law–, that the Spanish Constitutional Court expressly refers to life as a good, which would exclude our right from being new because it denies the old good of life. But what the Constitutional Court specifically states is that mere life is not the object of a right, but a good[14]: it is voluntariness that delimits the right to life. Thus, respect for the right to life does not require respect for life, but respect for the will to live. Let us not forget, however, that when life leaves the scope of the right, the subject—the human person—also leaves it, because it is not possible to dissociate life from the subject (unlike what can happen in other rights). Life (the subject) is thus a good, at one's disposal (in principle, for oneself, but at disposal, with all that this implies: cf. Serna and Rivas 2000, and Sandel 2005, pp. 113–116). In fact, its impact as a good in the reasoning about the right we are considering is very limited: to the Spanish Constitutional Court, life is a good that does not exclude that homicide can be a right; its effectiveness is restricted to limiting voluntary homicide

---

pure autonomy, but also on a judgement about the value of life in the euthanasic situation (Keown 2022a).

[12] Cf. STC 19/2023, of 22 March, FJ 6. Taking this argument to its limit would allow us to understand the right to the dispensation of death as, for example, a development of religious freedom, that leads martyrs not to renounce their faith even if it costs them their lives.

[13] Cf. Keown (2022a), pp. 92–93.

[14] Cf. STC 19/2023, 22 March, FJ 6.

to cases of life "in a euthanasic context". Only a healthy life without suffering (the health necessary for a happy life, not life) is a good enough.

In the end, the right would not protect life, but rather self-determination with respect to life (which, regarding the *nuda* life, is reduced to procuring death, since it cannot have the aim of procuring life). Indeed, this self-determination is usually limited to situations of serious illness and suffering, which, as we have seen, implies a substantive judgement on life; but it seems that the legislature could do without this judgement (as suggested by the magistrate of the Spanish Constitutional Court María Luisa Balaguer for the case of Spanish Law[15]). We could agree or not with the legislature who adopts this position, and guarantees euthanasia and assisted suicide to all citizens, regardless of suffering or illness, and perhaps find reasons to criticise it; but it seems difficult to understand that such a right would be new because it involves a new judgement on the good of life. In other words, this would seem a euthanasia right version based solely on autonomy, that in its turn, is a right already known. Is this the case?

18.4 Just Autonomy? the Foundations of the Right to Euthanasia and Assisted Suicide

As we have seen, the most frequently invoked grounds for proposing euthanasia and assisted suicide are beneficence and autonomy (Keown 2022a). Beneficence would justify euthanasia, in order to alleviate suffering (Finnis 1995, pp. 23–24), and autonomy would justify assisted suicide, in order to fulfil the person's will for him or herself. This difference is blurred when it is understood that unwanted life is the cause of suffering (thus, autonomy would be decisive in defining what is beneficence); or that, if someone wants to die, he or she will have their reasons (thus, once again, autonomy determines the scope of beneficence, because no one better than the person concerned can judge in which cases the avoidance of suffering justifies death). Thus, in today's frequent convergence between the two grounds, it seems that autonomy has the greater influence; pain or illness would be relevant insofar as their absence would cast doubt on the authenticity of the will, since no one wants to die for no reason (cf. BVerfG of 26 February 2020). However, this is not the only possible association of these two reasons: the presence of suffering and illness can lead us to believe that no person would want to continue living in such circumstances, hence the proposals for involuntary euthanasia for children, people with dementia, etc. In the Spanish regulation, too, the balance between autonomy and beneficence favours autonomy. It certainly restricts this right to people in a euthanasic situation, but it does not explain

[15] Cf. the dissenting opinion of Judge María Luisa Balaguer Callejón to STC 19/2023, of 22 March, which understands that "the vital situations in which a person can decide to end their life in dignified and non-violent or degrading conditions" are not reduced to euthanasic contexts but include all those in which "self-determination of the will is produced and expressed in conditions of full recognition of personal autonomy and freedom".

why (in fact, as we have seen, there is another possible reading, according to the dissenting opinion of Judge María Luisa Balaguer) and, in any case, it justifies this right as a development of the right to integrity, understood as self-determination. In order to assess the extent to which autonomy is indeed the basis of the right we are examining, let us first look at the services it guarantees.

At first glance, it seems difficult to see death or suicide as a right. Death, rather than being a right, is a universal fact that nature grants to all of its creatures with unquestionable certainty, so the "right to die" would be an absolutely guaranteed right for all of us. We could understand that it is in fact the right to a painless death, but in that case the object of the service would have to be a palliative or analgesic benefit rather than the dispensation of death; indeed, it would fit better into a general right to live without pain, since only the one who is alive can experience pain. Could we then understand it as a right to suicide? Suicide, as a strictly individual act, does not seem to make sense as a right, since a right always refers to a behaviour owed by another: the right to suicide would then mean the claim that no one may prevent us from committing suicide, which is not what is at stake in our case. Finally, we could understand it as a right to self-determination, the exercise of which consists in fulfilling the person's will with regard to him or herself. The inducement of death would be just one instrument among others (depending on the person's will) for this purpose. However, this understanding does not hold, because, as we have seen, it is the public authority that decides, through the Law, when the will of the person concerned must be carried out, and it also considers itself essential to ensure that it is carried out correctly.[16]

So it is not a right to die, nor, it seems, a right not to suffer, nor a general right to have one's own will respected. So what is at stake? It must be borne in mind that the service which is the object of this right is specifically to kill the person or to contribute in a decisive way to his or her suicide. In my view, the spirit of this claim is more akin to a kind of right not to live (which is impossible), similar to that asserted in wrongful life claims, where the person who did not eliminate life in its very beginnings is held responsible for an unwanted life. Here, in the right to euthanasia and assisted suicide, the Law would hold the public authorities responsible for the fact that a person who (rightly, according to the Law) wants to die, has not yet died. Thus, the argument that typically supports euthanasia and assisted suicide claims that no one can be forced to live,[17] as if not killing[18] someone were forcing him or her to live. It is true that a similar argument—inaction implies responsibility—is typical of economic and social rights, for example, but it is based on the idea that we are somehow responsible for the injustice of the baseline situation. Such an argument, applied to our case, would assume that the injustice is being alive without wanting to be alive (with sufficient

[16] Cf. STC 19/2023, 22 March, FJ 6, where the Court upholds the existence of a public duty to give effectiveness to this right of lethal self-determination.

[17] Cf. STC 19/2023, 22 March, FJ 6.

[18] It should be borne in mind that the person who is held responsible for life is not preventing death, as could be the case in connection to life support mechanisms, which is a different situation from the one we are considering here.

reason, hence the euthanasia context); an injustice in the face of which the public authorities would take responsibility for ending the unwanted life.

The right to euthanasia and assisted suicide would thus become the right to self-determination over life itself. Since in fact no one has chosen to live (our life is always the choice of others[19]; of fate or nature, if you like, but not of ourselves), the illusion that life is voluntary[20] would end up being reduced to the guarantee of the voluntariness of death, backed up by the power of public authorities. But in the end, no one is responsible for his or her own existence, and no one has the capacity to fully assume that responsibility. That is to say, the desire to guarantee self-determination over one's own life in the most radical sense would mean making us responsible for life, yet we are unable to assume this responsibility because no one can give a justification of his or her own existence. Finally, the State would assume the obligation to account for the meaning of life for all of us and, by means of this right, would define it for us: in a euthanasic context, none, beyond one's own will. What, then, is the human being reduced to in the name of autonomy?

18.5 Bio-Right as the Fading of the Subject in the Name of Autonomy

What, then, can be said about the right to euthanasia and assisted suicide, configured as a new right in the way proposed by the Spanish law?

The first thing that could be said is that it does indeed appear to be a significantly new right. Whatever the reasons that lead judges, legislatures and scholars to link it to old rights, the radical novelty of the service it guarantees seems to imply judgements about the human goods at stake, especially life, that are so novel that they can hardly be understood as a mere development of previous rights. And this seems to be the case even if we try to understand it as detached from any judgment about the good of life but exclusively linked to a right to self-determination. As we have seen, this is not a general right to self-determination, because the Law does not guarantee us whatever we want for self-determination. Rather, it seems to be a right to self-determination only in relation to death, and in specific cases: in the Spanish regulation, in euthanasic contexts. This would have two consequences: firstly, such self-determination would not really be self- but hetero-determination, both because it is someone else (the

[19] In any case, it would be the parents who "force" a child to live when they bring it into the world. But parents are not really responsible for the life of that particular person, because they choose to be parents, but not to be parents of that particular person.

[20] As we have seen, the Spanish Constitutional Court understands that it is voluntariness that delimits the right to life, which is actually the right not to be killed involuntarily. It makes no sense, then, that this Court has taken the trouble to clarify in previous rulings that the right to life does not include the right to death, since we cannot understand that by "right to death" it is designating non-voluntary death. It is clear that when the Constitutional Court stated that the right to life does not include the right to death, it was thinking of voluntary death, and that it was excluded not by any consideration of its voluntariness, but because of death (i.e. because of attacking life).

public authority) who determines when the decision to die has to be carried out, and because it is understood that it has to be carried out by a third party in order to be really effective, i.e. it is the public authority that dispenses death. Secondly, it is based on a certain judgement about the good of human life, which is far from its classical understanding.

Although the approach to the right to euthanasia and assisted suicide that we are studying is not exclusively autonomist, and therefore the dispensation of death is not guaranteed in all cases, but only in euthanasic contexts, the importance of autonomy as the basis of this right may lead us to consider a regulation of the right to euthanasia and assisted suicide different from the one we are studying, but based solely on autonomy, in order to assess whether or not in this case we would likewise be dealing with a significantly new right. In other words, would a right to euthanasia and assisted suicide that is not conditioned by illness and suffering, but is free and based solely on autonomy, really be new? Could it be understood as a development of an old generic right to self-determination? Well, in my view that would not be easy. The Law does not recognise such a generic right to self-determination, but rather first makes a judgement on the concrete object of each claim to self-determination. That is to say, this supposedly free right to euthanasia and suicide would imply an obligation on the part of the public authorities to fulfil our wish for self-determination whenever it consists of death being granted, but not, for example, when it involves mutilating healthy limbs or signing a cannibalism pact. Our self-determination would then remain, in a relevant sense, hetero-determined, in relation to life, but not, for example, in relation to the integrity of our limbs. Once again, we would be faced with a substantive judgement about the goods at stake—especially life—which I think is new compared to the classical one.

On the other hand, considering that it would be an exclusively lethal right of self-determination allows us to glimpse the understanding of life that would underlie such a right; an understanding that, I think, would be significantly different from the previous one. It is a subtle change, and the reflections on it, which are only hypothetical, would be as follows: through this right the Law would, paradoxically, dictate to us to "be free". That is to say: "live only if you want to" (the conditions of health and suffering, we understand, will determine this will); in order for this to be the case, the public authorities make available the dispensation of death at will. And even if it seems an option, it would in fact be a prescription: living would now be free, whether we want it or not, and therefore our responsibility: there is no reason to live outside our own will. But faced with the public offer of the dispensation of death, we will need a (publicly defensible?) reason to go on living; our life, hitherto spontaneous, absolutely given, without need of any cause or will to support it, would now have to be justified, if only by our own will. That is to say, the public authorities, which would guarantee the freedom of our life through the right to provoke death, would "condemn" us, perhaps unconsciously, to the absence of meaning: the answer to the question of the meaning of life offered by the public authorities would be that there is no answer, because if there were an answer, it would "own" our life and we would not be truly free. But the absence of meaning will make it more difficult to offer (even to ourselves) a reason to go on living, because it does not exist (the public authorities have told us) beyond our own will.

In my view, then, we can say that we are dealing with a truly new right, which implies a new understanding of the human good and, to some extent, of the person him or herself. With the approach we have outlined, self-determination would become hetero-determination and, as paradoxical as it may seem, would favour the weakening of the subject who is to self-determine. Thus, despite its claim to guarantee autonomy, this new right would facilitate the slippage of the human being from the position of subject to that of object in the Law. In this way, for example, physical and moral integrity, which in the case of Spanish Law underpins the right to euthanasia and assisted suicide, would not be the starting point for the Law, but rather the arrival point: our physical and moral integrity would require the decisive intervention of a third party; in fact, it would be something to be constructed, and not by the individual alone, but with the essential support of the public authorities. In the same way, the subject's actions, free and responsible, would ultimately, paradoxically, lose their relevance, because understanding ourselves as responsible for what we are not (our life) and cannot assume (because we are unable to justify our existence) favours the perception that free and responsible behaviour is, in fact, almost irrelevant. That is, the approach reflected in this right would imply a kind of responsibility for life, derived from the fact that we have not killed ourselves (or others who wish to do so). In a sense, we would become responsible for states of affairs (the existence of lives that are justifiably unwanted by their protagonists), and we understand that we have a legal duty to respond to them (by killing those who wish to do so). As we have already mentioned, something similar happens in those classic cases where the Law is obliged to act in the face of a situation (poverty, illiteracy, etc.), but the duty to act to alleviate this situation is explained by the injustice of this situation: it is much more complicated to understand oneself as responsible for the unequal distribution of the meagre will to live. In this way, the affirmation of a responsibility that does not really belong to us ends up rendering our free and responsible action useless: if we are responsible for everything, including conditions that are not the result of our free action, then our intentional action is irrelevant.

As I said, I think that these features favoured by the new rights (especially the one we are studying here) help us to understand some characteristics of contemporary Law. One of them would be the trend towards a change in the way the normative function of Law is exercised, which some authors have identified: a function that now seems to refer more to states of affairs than to behaviours, although this is not only due to the features of new rights, but is also explained by other typical phenomena of contemporary Law: for example, the introduction of weighting in judges' decisions, which makes it seem as if their function is to choose between good (value-fulfilling) but incompatible states of affairs.[21] This would make it easier for the Law to end up as an instrument to bring about different states of affairs rather

[21] On weighing, which does not evaluate the conduct that led to the conflict of rights but reflects the axiological importance of the rights, and the notion of reasonable accommodation, which serves the agency of the right-holders, as an alternative, see Arosemena and Torres (2024). In other cases it seems that, on the contrary, the Law clearly (and unjustifiably, one might think) attends to intent:

than to regulate the free and voluntary action of human beings. This would favour the nihilistic drift identified by some authors, in which "man, the subject of the Law, becomes the object of the rules, and thus matures the progression towards 'perfect' legal nihilism" (Romano 2006, p. 86), where Law is a mere device at the service of an extrinsic end; a mere procedure, governed by a purely technical reason that resides in a single rule: functional success, which nullifies its capacity to resist a power of which the State is sometimes no more than a manager.

It could be the case that some of the characteristics of this new generation of rights point in this nihilistic direction. However, in order to avoid these reflections turning out to be only particular and hasty assessments, it would be necessary to study more closely and systematically other cases of new rights, which could help to complete the picture and achieve a more accurate vision of the characteristics of the new Law within which they live. Given the purpose of this paper, this will have to be left to another work; it is hoped that the suggestions made here will prove useful.

References

Andorno, Roberto. 2024. Los «neuroderechos» como respuesta a los desafíos de las neurotecnologías. La iniciativa de la UNESCO. In *Los nuevos derechos humanos: Teoría jurídica y praxis política*. Ed. Jorge Crego and Carolina Pereira, 285–296. Granada: Comares.

Arosemena, Gustavo. 2020. Freedom or transformation? Conflicting tendencies in United Nations human rights discourse. In *European populism and human rights*. Ed. Jure Vidmar, 165–189. Leiden: Brill.

Arosemena, Gustavo. 2024. El paradigma transformador de los derechos humanos: Rasgos estructurales y consecuencias paradójicas. In *Los nuevos derechos humanos: Teoría jurídica y praxis política*. Ed. Jorge Crego and Carolina Pereira, 51–70. Granada: Comares.

Arosemena, Gustavo and Torres, Ana María. 2024. Conflicto de derechos, ponderación y ajustes razonables". In Los nuevos derechos humanos: teoría jurídica y praxis política. Ed. Jorge Crego and Carolina Pereira, 205-255. Granada: Comares.

Finnis, John. 1995. A philosophical case against euthanasia, In *Euthanasia Examined*. In *Ethical, clinical and legal perspectives*. Ed. John Keown, 23–35. Cambridge: Cambridge University Press.

Finnis, John. 2011. *Natural law and natural rights*, 2nd ed. Oxford: Oxford University Press.

Keown, John. 2022a. The logical link between voluntary and non-voluntary euthanasia. *Cambridge Law Journal* 81 (1): 84–108.

Keown, John. 2022b. Desmond Tutu, George Carey and the legalization of Euthanasia: A response. *Christian Bioethics* 28(1): 25–40.

Massini, Carlos Ignacio. 2020. *Dignidad humana, derechos humanos y derecho a la vida. Ensayos sobre la contemporánea ética del derecho*. Mexico: UNAM.

Pereira-Sáez, Carolina. 2017. Los nuevos derechos: ¿la clausura de un ciclo?. *Persona y Derecho* 75: 93–114.

Romano, Bruno. 2006. *Scienza giuridica senza giurista: il nichilismo «perfetto». Trenta tesi per una filosofia del diritto 2005–2206*. Torino: Giappichelli.

---

for example, in criminalising hatred. However, hate crimes presuppose hatred: since they cannot prove it, they dissociate it from intention. In the end, the Law seems to forget that its protagonist is a free subject, who thinks, reasons and makes decisions, and who can judge in a sphere of his or her conscience into which the Law does not enter.

Sandel, Michael. 2005. *Public philosophy. Essays on morality and Politics.* Harvard: Harvard University Press.
Serna, Pedro. 2024. El discurso de los nuevos derechos. Perspectiva genético crítica. In *Los nuevos derechos humanos: teoría jurídica y praxis política.* Ed. Jorge Crego and Carolina Pereira, 17–49. Granada: Comares.
Serna, Pedro, and Pedro Rivas. 2000. ¿Debe una sociedad liberal penalizar la euthanasia? Consideraciones entorno al argumento de la autonomía de la voluntad. *Revista De Derecho* 1 (1): 137–152.
Toller, Fernando. 2024. Los derechos humanos no enumerados: Historia, sentido, dificultades, posibilidades. In *Los nuevos derechos humanos: Teoría jurídica y praxis política.* Ed. Jorge Crego and Carolina Pereira, 227–262. Granada: Comares.
Vergara, Óscar. 2024. La solera de los derechos. Una aproximación lógico-sistemática al proceso de producción de nuevos derechos humanos. In *Los nuevos derechos humanos: teoría jurídica y praxis política.* Ed. Jorge Crego and Carolina Pereira, 71–90. Granada: Comares.
Zambrano, Pilar. 2024. Un nuevo derecho llamado «eutanasia», un nuevo derecho sin derechos, o la progresiva disolución del Derecho. In *Los nuevos derechos humanos: Teoría jurídica y praxis política.* Ed. Jorge Crego and Carolina Pereira, 395–413. Granada: Comares.

Open Access This chapter is licensed under the terms of the Creative Commons Attribution 4.0 International License (http://creativecommons.org/licenses/by/4.0/), which permits use, sharing, adaptation, distribution and reproduction in any medium or format, as long as you give appropriate credit to the original author(s) and the source, provide a link to the Creative Commons license and indicate if changes were made.

The images or other third party material in this chapter are included in the chapter's Creative Commons license, unless indicated otherwise in a credit line to the material. If material is not included in the chapter's Creative Commons license and your intended use is not permitted by statutory regulation or exceeds the permitted use, you will need to obtain permission directly from the copyright holder.

Chapter 19
Biorights at the End of Life: Achievements and Open Questions in the Italian Context

Patrizia Borsellino

Abstract The theme of rights at the end of life has received increasing attention in Italian bioethical, biojuridical and biopolitical reflection since the last decades of the last century, when the model of a medicine, which, while firmly pursuing the objective of restoring health, does not take the burden of relieving from suffering, guaranteeing care that respects their wishes, as well as their needs, those who cannot be cured, but whose survival can be prolonged and whose dying process can be modulated, became the object of increasingly widespread critical consideration. Taking that reflection into consideration, the chapter highlights the important outcome represented by the deontological and juridical, as well as ethical, recognition of the right of subjects who cannot recover, not only to receive all treatments capable of alleviating psycho-physical suffering, but also the right to refuse life-saving treatments that they consider unsustainable. On the other hand, the chapter also highlights how the persistent absence in Italy of a legislative framework for assisted suicide and euthanasia compromises the right to a dignified death of those for whom active assistance in dying constitutes the only way out of the captivity of survival in conditions no longer tolerable for them.

Keywords Bio-rights · End of life · Italian regulatory framework · Advances in medicine · Relief from suffering

19.1 The End of Life as a Bioethical and Biojuridical Issue on the Background of the Transformation of Dying Scenarios

For several years now, the final phase of life has become a central or even privileged object of bioethics and biolaw.

P. Borsellino (✉)
University of Milano-Bicocca, Milan, Italy
e-mail: patrizia.borsellino@unimib.it

© The Editor(s) (if applicable) and The Author(s), under exclusive license to Springer Nature Switzerland AG 2024

J.-A. Seoane and O. Vergara (eds.), *The Discourse of Biorights*, The International Library of Bioethics 109, https://doi.org/10.1007/978-3-031-66804-3_19

This has been a growing focus, which has interested not only theoretical reflection, but also public opinion and institutional political debate, in the context of numerous countries, including Italy. In order to understand the reasons for this, it is appropriate not to lose sight of the profound transformations in the scenarios of dying that, in relatively recent times—it is the history of a few decades, not centuries, and it does not concern all areas of the world, but only the developed ones—have occurred also, though not exclusively, as a result of the extraordinary progress in the biomedical field that has taken place since the mid-twentieth century.

These transformations have consisted in subtracting the event of death from the horizon of 'chance and necessity' in order to subject it to an increasing possibility of control, relating not to the 'if' (given that death will remain inescapable for human beings, as for all living beings), but to the 'when' and the 'how', that is to say the times and ways in which the event will occur.

For a long stretch of human history, the time span separating death from the onset of disease or from the occurrence of accidental events, that were its cause, was very short, and this was due to the inability of medicine to offer effective responses to pathological conditions that today we would find hard to consider fatal. In the space of a few decades, the ever-increasing availability of therapeutic strategies and methods, with a more or less high level of technology, has created the conditions for a prolongation of survival that has nothing 'natural' about it, depending on the medical interventions themselves, and has meant that death, as the outcome of the "dying process", has, in turn, lost its naturalness.

It could be argued that death remains the most natural of all events, if by 'natural' we mean an event that affects everyone, that is bound to occur and that connotes human beings to the point of justifying their qualification as 'mortal'. But death is no longer such if we identify the characterising element of naturalness in its indifference to human choices and actions.

The scenarios of dying, that have been transformed thanks to medicine's increased capacity to intervene, are, for example, those in which death occurs as a result of chronic degenerative, oncological and other pathologies, the evolution of which is accompanied by an increasingly severe deterioration in the quality of life and the manifestation of situations of worsening suffering. Or those in which individuals, belonging to an increasingly long-lived population, spend the final part of their lives in a worsening condition of polypathology, often associated with cognitive decline, which precludes any relational dimension. Or, again, those in which, because of very serious injuries resulting from accidents, people, often still young, do escape death, thanks to the implementation of resuscitative techniques and life-support treatments, but find themselves in situations of true suspension between life and death, such as the permanent vegetative state, while in other cases their cognitive faculties are not impaired, but they experience a condition of motor and sensory deprivation, as well as exposure to suffering, of such severity that the continuation of life appears to them as an unbearable imprisonment.[1]

[1] To exemplify these conditions, see, in the following pages of this contribution, the references to the cases of Eluana Englaro, Piergiorgio Welby and Fabio Antoniani.

If reference is made to the above-mentioned scenarios of prolonged survival, which are characterised by the implementation of medical interventions capable of modulating the dying process, but not of counteracting it, by removing the causes of pathologies, it is easy to understand how the conditions have been created to place the end of life within a horizon of possible, indeed, inevitable choices, and to make it a privileged area for ethics and law (Borsellino 2010, pp. 1–2).

The availability of therapeutic methods and aids, that can significantly affect the time and manner in which life ends, raises the question of whether, and to what extent, recourse to those methods and aids is justified, and it also, and even more importantly, raises the question of the subjects entitled to make such choices. In order to address and resolve these issues, it is not enough to have recourse to the necessary clinical-scientific knowledge, but it is indispensable to have recourse to the guiding criteria of practices represented by the principles, values and rules that find their main containers in ethics and law.

19.2 Advances in Medicine, New Scenarios of Dying and Old Ethical Paradigms

From above considerations it follows, therefore, that the emergence of the final phase of life as an ethical and legal issue in the twentieth century went, hand in hand, with a decisive change in the direction of medicine, which became a dynamic context, characterised by its increased ability to successfully intervene in a significant number of pathologies and, in any case, to affect human life in the various phases of its development, modulating, above all, the times and modes of its conclusion, in discontinuity with a medical practice that, for centuries, had been devoid of effective therapeutic strategies.

One would be mistaken, however, if one believed that discontinuity on the technical-clinical level was (promptly) accompanied by discontinuity on the level of the conceptual and ethical paradigm underlying medical activity, in general, and its repercussions on the end of life, in particular.

To understand this, it is useful to refer to a famous passage by one of the fathers of modern thought, Francis Bacon, who, at the beginning of the seventeenth century, wrote:

«*And further, we esteem it the office of a physician to mitigate the pains and tortures of diseases, as well as to restore health; and this not only when such a mitigation, as of a dangerous symptom, may conduce to recovery; but also, when there being no further hopes of recovery, it can only serve to make the passage out of life more calm and easy.... But the physicians of our times make a scruple of attending the patient after the disease is thought past cure, though, in my judgment, if they were not wanting to their own profession and to humanity itself, they should here give their attendance to improve their skill, and make the dying person depart with greater ease and tranquility*». (Bacon 2013, 190).

Vibrant words, with which the great English philosopher pronounced a harsh condemnation of a medicine incapable of taking charge of the sick person for whom there was no hope for recovery, and identified the relief of suffering until the end of life as an inescapable duty that the physician must fulfill in order not to betray his mandate.

Of course, the medicine of Bacon's time was, and would have remained for a long time, as previously observed, a medicine that was on the whole ineffective and incapable of dealing with the majority of pathologies, so much so as to make it seem plausible to hypothesise that it was the scarcity of therapeutic instruments available that fuelled the attitude of physicians towards the incurable sick and caused Bacon's warning to go unheeded.

But was it really only the unavailability of therapeutic remedies that caused the sick persons, near the end of their lives, to remain, de facto, outside the reach of medicine?

Towards the negative answer leads the observation that, not differently from the ineffective pre-modern medicine, the modern and effective technological medicine did not promptly take charge of the specific treatment needs of the incurable ill, whose survival it prolonged, nor did it identify the relief of physical pain and psychological suffering as the specific and direct task that not only physicians, but health workers, in general, are invested with, in relation to these ill patients. With regard to individuals suffering from pathologies, no longer responsive to therapies capable of positively influencing their evolution, the response of modern medicine has, in fact, continued to be either that of doing nothing, or, on the contrary, that of doing too much, but in the wrong direction. In any case, sick persons left alone with their suffering. In the first case, because, in fact, abandoned. In the second case, because subject to obstinate interventions aimed at to prolong their life at all costs, not to improve its quality.

I believe that the reasons for the persistent disregard for patients approaching the end of life are to be sought and can be found elsewhere (Borsellino 1999, pp. 171–178).

First of all, in the fact that modern medicine has taken as a paradigm of reference the so-called bio-mechanistic model, which has overcome the foggy 'qualitative' approach of pre-scientific medicine, allowing the acquisition of important therapeutic results, but at the price, as it was written, of relating to the disease as "a kind of mechanical failure to be repaired" (Wulff et al. 1987). A model, this one, which leaves in the background the consideration of the psycho-physical symptoms and, in general, of the subjective states of the sick, making the practitioners, who adopt it, run the risk of forgetting that they are dealing with persons, and not only with diseased organs.

But the scant importance attributed to the patient's experience, as an element to be taken into account in the diagnosis and treatment of diseases, and the consequent lateralisation of the problem of suffering, especially at the end of life, have also found an appropriate context in the configuration of the therapeutic relationship of paternalistic imprint, re-proposing which the traditional medical ethics has, for a long time, rooted the conviction that the patient cannot have any role in the decisions on treatments, these being the exclusive responsibility of the doctors (Borsellino 2018, pp. 111–116).

Modern technological medicine has by no means promptly freed itself from those beliefs related to treatment decisions, nor has it rapidly distanced itself from the model that identifies the "*sanare*" and, in any case, the "*serbare vitam*", as the almost exclusive objectives in the direction of which the physician must direct his interventions. On the contrary, the persistent deference paid to the so-called 'therapeutic privilege', has entrenched the conviction that the availability of a treatment, especially if it is life-saving, makes its administration, always and in any case, not only justified but also due, and this regardless of the patient's will for or against, as well as any consideration of the impact of the treatments on her/his overall condition.

It was, therefore, methodological assumptions, together with ethical convictions, that hindered the overcoming of a vision of medicine that was as firm in considering death the burning failure, in which the doctor would never want to be involved, as it was reluctant to recognise in death the outcome of a phase of life, the final one, which requires to enter fully into the range of action of a medicine rethought in its assumptions and remodelled in its objectives.

19.3 Towards a Medicine that Cures Even When It Cannot Recover. Relief of Suffering and Palliative Care

In order to reverse the trend and ensure that, albeit centuries later, Francis Bacon's warning would finally be heeded, it was, on closer inspection, necessary to break the link, taken for granted, between cure and recovery and between cure and prolongation of survival, emphasising that the duty of care extends far beyond the duty to restore health or to extend life at all costs. In other words, as Bacon thought, it was a matter of affirming and spreading the idea that one can, indeed must, cure even when one cannot recover.

This was precisely the apparently simple idea, but in reality of extraordinary innovative scope, which, first in the countries of the Anglo-Saxon area, around the mid-1960s, and subsequently in an increasing number of contexts, including Italy, has shaped the healthcare model of palliative care, understood—according to the definition given at the beginning of the 1990s by the National Council for Hospice and Palliative Care Services of the World Health Organisation (WHO)—as «active and global care of the sick, suffering from advanced chronic illness, who no longer respond to specific treatments» (World Health Organization 1990).

Palliative care has intercepted the need for care that is detached from the no longer achievable objective of healing and restoring health, and has ensured that the "sick people given up for dead" (to use Bacon's strong expression), enter the medical scene as subjects deserving no less attention than that reserved for the sick persons who can recover.

Making them the recipients of specific and targeted care interventions, has meant distancing ourselves from a medicine which, having remained insensitive to the problem of suffering for too long, has ended up by putting in place a forgetfulness or, perhaps better, a "removal", with regard to the dying process and the peculiar needs of the individuals for whom it is taking place.

On the one hand, palliative care, thus, tore away the veil of removal, exercising a disruptive function of breaking a 'taboo', the taboo of death, which, from being an event destined to remain outside the doctor's work, had to become an event up to which the doctor was obliged to extend his action. While, on the other hand, they broadened the possibilities of treatment and, therefore, the therapeutic/assistance choices available to practitioners, offering the sick the option of being relieved of suffering, which lost the connotation of a high price to be paid 'necessarily' for the disease.

What made palliative care a caring approach with the credentials to bring about a real paradigm shift in medical practice and, even earlier, in medical ethics, was not, however, only the focus on the problem of suffering. It was also the relevance of the quality of life, which, in the case of patients no longer responsive to treatments aimed at recovery, replaced health in the role of fundamental criterion for guiding treatment choices. And so was the consequent reappraisal of the 'centrality of the sick person', to be guaranteed by means of an axistential practice carried out in accordance with the needs of the sick persons, and, above all, in constant reference to the wishes and desires manifested by them.

The quality of life cannot, in fact, be determined solely from the outside, and in exclusively clinical-objective terms, but has an ineliminable subjective connotation, which justifies, indeed, makes reference to the patient's point of view essential (Borsellino 1999, pp. 171–178).

Palliative care, on the other hand, on closer inspection, also laid the foundations for a change in care relationships and in the roles of the various parties involved, starting with doctors. From being the exclusive decision-makers in the management of the illness and, for the most part, unwilling to discuss treatment not only with the patients, but also with the other professionals involved in care, because they were little or not at all prepared to question the position of supremacy traditionally occupied in the therapeutic relationship, doctors were called upon to take on a different guise. That of professionals who make themselves available to the sick in order to offer the treatment options best suited to their needs, collaborating with various professional figures, whose involvement is justified by the conviction that the peculiar condition of the suffering of the terminally ill, for which the expression "total pain" has been coined (Saunders 1984), makes it necessary to intervene on the painful physical manifestations of the illness, as well as on the serious alterations on the psychological, relational and spiritual levels that are linked to it.

19.4 Sick Persons at the End of Life as Holder of Rights

The palliative care model, with its highly innovative elements, required and implied that individuals suffering from fatal and/or irreparably disabling illnesses should be considered (legitimately) bearers of expectations and aspirations supported by good reasons, which can be referred to as "rights in the moral sense".

These were expectations and aspirations that drew strength from the disenchanted consideration of the scenarios in which in Italy, as in other national contexts, patients suffering from incurable pathologies (above all, though not only oncological), and close to death, continued, even in the last decades of the last century, to spend the last phase (weeks, days or hours) of their existence. The scenarios in question were, in some cases, those which saw the sick subjected, mostly in a hospital setting, to often very invasive treatments aimed at prolonging, even slightly, their survival. In other cases, those of the substantial abandonment of the sick by care structures designed and organised with a view to the goal of recovery, not of a cure aimed at alleviating not only the physical but also the psychological suffering of those who cannot recover. And again, in both cases, patients with little or no information and, consequently, excluded from the possibility of expressing their wishes regarding treatment, but also deprived of the possibility of voicing their needs and expressing their emotions.

In this context, in which the inadequate commitment to the relief of suffering went, hand in hand, with the failure to recognise that only the sick person can be the legitimate judge of his suffering and the quality of his life, the emergence of the lexicon of rights, in relation to the final phase of life, represented a winning strategy to initiate that change of perspective at the cultural level, without which the battle in favour of the spread of care aimed at 'curing when one cannot heal' could not only not have been won, but could not even have been undertaken.

'Right'—wrote Uberto Scarpelli, an authoritative legal philosopher and father of Italian bioethics with a secular orientation—is a word that «has been charged in the history of culture with a favourable and intense emotional force» (Scarpelli 1992, 40), thanks to which it can well serve to «call others to one's side, to make oneself animated with them, not wanting to be alone or lonely in a struggle to be sustained» (Scarpelli 1992, 41). In a word, it can well serve to influence ethical and political choices and, more generally, actions, making them functional to the needs and interests of certain categories of subjects.

This is what, certainly not without encountering difficulties and resistance, has happened thanks to the activation of private individuals operating within Foundations, such as the Floriani Foundation and the VIDAS, which for decades have remained points of reference in the Italian context.[2] These private institutions have made available to the sick, discharged from hospital, because they were incurable, the first free home care services, thus making up for the shortcomings of healthcare facilities, but,

[2] Both Foundations, still operating mainly in the North of Italy, were established, the first, the Floriani Foundation, in 1977 and the second, VIDAS, in 1982, on the initiative of people, such as Mr and Mrs Floriani and Mrs Giovanna Cavazzoni, made sensitive to the problem of incurable patients by painful personal experiences.

at the same time, and first and foremost, they made their own an ambitious and challenging cultural project aimed at raising awareness among citizens and institutions, but, first and foremost, at removing the obstacles to the acceptance and dissemination of the palliative care model, which were posed by the inadequate training of healthcare workers.

Aiming to contribute to this cultural project, the Committee for ethics at the end of life, a body set up in 1992 within the Floriani Foundation, produced and disseminated the "Charter of the Rights of the Dying" (Comitato per l'etica di fine vita 1997), a document whose twelve articles set out a precise identikit of the model of care capable of satisfying the needs and improving the condition of the sick who cannot recover.

The model in question was that of a non-standardised care, organised in such a way as to be able to meet, in a specific and targeted manner, not only the physical, but also the psychological needs of each individual patient, with the aim of guaranteeing, at the highest possible level, the quality of life of the sick person, not prolonging the dying process. But, above all, it was the model of care that never forgets that the approach of death must not compromise dignity, which is recognised in an individual, whatever his or her condition, only if he or she is enabled to participate consciously in the decisions that affect him or her and is respected as a person.

This was a model whose easy implementation in practice would have been unrealistic to envisage, but which would, at the very least, have received institutional attention and regulatory approval. This is confirmed by the legislative measures which, since 1999, have provided for the funding of a national programme for palliative care for the terminally ill (both in the form of home care and through the creation or adaptation of appropriate in-patient facilities, such as hospices) and, above all, by law no. 38 of 15 March 2010, whose "Provisions to guarantee access to palliative care and pain therapy" were marked by the idea of the inseparability of the commitment to the relief of suffering from the enhancement of the autonomy and dignity of the sick person.

This important piece of legislation, followed by regulations and implementation plans aimed at enabling the construction of palliative care and pain therapy networks, as well as, a few years later, by a decree that included palliative care for all patients suffering from diseases with an inauspicious prognosis among the 'Essential Levels of Assistence', charged to the National Health System, represented, in Italy, a turning point, after which it would have been reductive to continue to speak of patients close to the end of life as bearers of rights only in the 'moral sense', instead of recognising them as holders of those prerogatives attributed and guaranteed by norms of positive law, to which one refers when speaking of rights in the 'juridical sense'.

19.5 The New Framework of Principles and Rules for the Care Relationship and the Rights of Sick Persons Until the End of Life.

It is true that the care model of palliative care appeared on the scene of a medicine still strongly marked by ethical and juridical criteria which put in the background, or did not consider at all, the rights of the sick, in general, and of the sick at the end of life, in particular. It is, however, also true that its not uncontested, but progressive rooting, as well as the above-mentioned recognition of the rights, which that care model required, took place in the background and concomitantly with the incisive transformations which have affected the overall Italian regulatory framework on the matter of the care relationship and of the mandate of medicine.

The transformations I am referring to are those that have undermined the cornerstones of the traditional paternalistic and objectivist-vitalist conception of the doctor-patient relationship, in the defence of which medical deontology and law have long been aligned in the Italian context, not differently from the context of many other countries. The former, like the latter, firm in attributing to the physician the (exclusive) power to decide not only whether and how to intervene, but also whether and how much to inform the patient of his condition, on the assumption of a sort of 'self-legitimation' of medical activity, which finds in health and, in any case, in life, the objective goods whose protection represents an absolute and unconditional duty for the physician.

It must be acknowledged that this conception fostered attitudes that even today cannot be considered completely eradicated from medical practice. However, the acceptance, even in principle, that it received at a deontological and legal level, has appeared, since the last decades of the last century, to be difficult to defend, not only for cultural reasons and for reasons related to developments in medicine, but also, in Italy, for strictly legal reasons.

When I speak of 'cultural' reasons, I am referring to the increasingly widespread subscription, by members of society, to a pluralistic system of values, in which the consideration of autonomy as a priority ethical criterion of reference, in relation to choices, decisions and actions that affect an individual's life, was accompanied by a changed sensitivity towards suffering—especially that due to illness—no longer accepted as an ineluctable destiny, but considered a condition on which it is not only possible, but a duty, to intervene.

On the other hand, the image of medicine as a sphere of certainty, never touched by the doubt on the identification of the good (the safeguard of life), to which the interventions should be aimed, far from being strengthened by the increased availability of therapeutic strategies, was, on the contrary, weakened by the diversification of the scenarios resulting from the implementation of the possible interventions or the choice not to resort to them, as well as by the evidence of the possible problematic outcomes, as well as of the potentialities, of modern technological medicine.

Lastly, with regard to the legal reasons for the progressive erosion, to which the paternalistic model of the care relationship would have gone against, what provided them with a solid foundation was, first and foremost, the presence in the Italian legal system, at the highest normative level, the one of the Constitution that came into force in 1948, of the provisions contained in Article 32.

This article, after qualifying health as a "fundamental right of the individual and an interest of the community", states, in fact, in its second paragraph, that "no one may be obliged to undergo a given medical treatment, except by provision of law…", thus identifying in respect of the patient's will a limit, to which the power/duty of treatment is subject, as a rule, mandatory, and susceptible to exception only in restricted and well-specified situations, when there is a motivated clinical urgency, not otherwise manageable, to intervene on a subject to protect health and/or public safety, as well as his health.[3]

In spite of attempts, by conservative legal doctrine, to reduce its scope (Borsellino 2018, 126), art. 32 has become a fundamental reference provision, from which the remodelling of the care relationship derives, while the principle of the voluntariness of health treatments, enshrined therein, has been confirmed as a pivotal criterion of healthcare activity also in subsequent important supranational normative documents signed by Italy, such as, first and foremost, Council of Europe, Convention on Human rigths and Biomedicine (Oviedo 1997) and Parliament, Council and Commission of Europe, European Charter of Fundamental Rights (Nice 2000), whose belonging to the national legal system can no longer be doubted after the entry into force, in 2005, of a law[4] that strengthened the guarantee of Italy's fulfilment of its obligations deriving from Community and European Union acts signed by the Italian government.

These documents also made explicit mention of the instrument for implementing the principle of the voluntary nature of treatments, the informed consent expressed by the patient, which is, moreover, identified, as a rule, as a necessary condition for the legitimacy of any intervention on an individual's body, both in various legislative interventions on health matters that have followed one another since the end of the 1970s, first and foremost Law no. 833/78, establishing the National Health Service, and in the reformulations of the ethical codes of health professionals, doctors and nurses, carried out from the 1990s onwards.

The reconstruction of the pathway through which a regulatory framework has been defined to recognise the sick person as the holder of rights, first and foremost of the right to self-determination with regard to treatment, and at the same time the framework of principles and rules has been created to rethink the prerogatives of the sick person near the end of life, would not, however, be adequate if one did not mention the decisive role played by important judicial decisions, also adopted by the Constitutional Court and the higher courts, without which it would not have been possible to have tangible signs of a change of course with respect to treatment practices, that disregarded the wishes of the sick and were little, or not at all, sensitive to the problem of their suffering.

---

[3] Law No 180 of 13 May 1978, "Voluntary and Compulsory Health Assessments and Treatment".

[4] Law No 11 of 4 February 2005, 'General rules on the participation of Italy in the European Union's legislative process and on the procedures for implementing Community obligations'.

In spite of some fluctuations and counter-trend decisions, thanks to the consistent jurisprudence of the last few decades, the recognition that no invasive act of a therapeutic or non-therapeutic nature in the physical sphere can take place, without or against the consent of the person concerned, has been consolidated and, above all, the barrier traditionally placed in the way of not activating and, even more, of suspending life-support treatments, has been broken down (Borsellino 2015), not only when this is directly refused by a competent patient, in conditions of unbearable suffering, as in the case of Piergiorgio Welby, but also when it is the legal representative who expresses, as the spokesman and guarantor of an incompetent patient, the refusal of a treatment functional to a survival not compatible with the conception of the dignity of life referred to the patient himself, as in the case of Eluana Englaro.[5]

These were two cases that remained in the news for a long time, whose point of arrival at the judicial level was represented by judgments[6] after which, on the one hand, the assimilation of the suspension of life-saving treatment to homicide no longer appeared sustainable, while, on the other hand, was imposed, as inescapable, the question of guaranteeing, also to the incompetent patient, decisions on treatment in conformity with his wishes, either expressly manifested by him when capable, or—as we read in the judgement of the cassation on the Englaro case—inferable "from his personality, his lifestyle and his convictions".

But was there really, at this point, on a regulatory level, all that was needed to ensure that every individual, who is ill and up to the end of his or her life, receives care that is appropriate to his or her condition and needs and always respectful of his or her wishes?

Towards the negative answer directs the observation that these judicial decisions had undoubtedly marked fundamental steps in a traced and hardly reversible path, and were destined to represent a precedent capable of influencing possible future decisions. However, they did not protect against the risk that the recognition of rights would still pass, as had happened in the Welby and Englaro cases, through lengthy court proceedings. On the other hand, the initiatives taken, also at a political level (Borsellino 2018, pp. 424–433), in the aftermath of the conclusion of the Englaro case, to downgrade, in the name of the unavailability of life, the right to self-determination of the sick person, made it clear that the legal basis, for a clear and uncontroversial definition of the rights of the sick person in all care situations, could not, in a civil law context, such as the Italian one, only be provided by the interventions of the judges, but required a legislative measure, that would regulate, in a general way, the roles of the subjects involved in the therapeutic relationship and clearly define the mandate of medicine, addressing the problematic knots to be unravelled to ensure the best care until the end of life.

[5] On the Welby and Englaro cases, see references in (Borsellino 2018, pp. 67–69).

[6] Respectively, in relation to the Welby case, the judgment of the Court of Rome no. 2049 of 23/7/2007, and in relation to the Englaro case, the judgment of the Court of Cassation no. 21748 of 16/10/2007.

After a long and arduous journey, started on 2004 and continued for several legislatures, this measure was achieved thanks to the approval, in 2017, of Law No 219 "Rules on informed consent and advance treatment dispositions".

In a relationship of full consistency with the principles and values already embodied in the rules of law, deontological codes and judicial decisions previously referred to, this law has struck a decisive blow to the "paternalistic" exclusion of the patient from treatment decisions, and, at the same time, has outlined the design of a care paradigm in which attention to the suffering of the sick persons takes the place of maintaining, at any cost, survival as the guiding criterion of healthcare practices.

This is confirmed by provisions from which a table of rights emerges clearly defined, in the strong sense of uncontested prerogatives recognised by norms of positive law to all recipients.

Firstly, the right to have the final word on all treatments, to be implemented or already implemented and intended to continue over time, which Article 1 of Law 219/2017 attributes to the recipients of the interventions, by virtue of an autonomy, qualified as 'decisional', which is theirs alone and cannot be placed on the same level of the autonomy, justified by professional competence, which makes healthcare professionals the subjects entitled to identify and propose, but certainly not to impose, the treatment paths appropriate to the patients' conditions.

Secondly and relatedly, the right, also enshrined in Article 1, to refuse any diagnostic assessment and/or medical treatment, including artificial hydration and nutrition, after having been adequately informed, in the case of life-saving treatment, of the consequences of refusal. This is a right that the law requires health professionals to respect, while also explicitly exempting them from civil and criminal liability.

Thirdly, the right, enshrined in the second article, to be relieved of suffering, even in the case of refusal of the treatment indicated by the doctor, by receiving appropriate pain therapy and palliative care, including the last frontier of treatment represented by deep palliative sedation, as well as the right not to undergo, in the presence of pathologies with an inauspicious prognosis and in the imminence of death, a prolongation of the dying process due to the administration of unnecessary and disproportionate treatments.

Lastly, the list of rights cannot overlook reference to the detailed provisions with which the law has sought, in Article 3, to emphasise, as far as possible, respect for the wishes of minors and incapacitated persons in the decisions that concern them, as well as to the detailed regulation, in the articles 4 e 5, of the instruments, the 'Advance Treatment Dispositions" and of 'Shared care planning', based on the idea that, despite the onset of incapacity, it is still possible to have voice in decisions on treatment that concern us, avoiding that others take them, perhaps in contrast with our convictions and values.

19.6 Rights at the End of Life Recognised but not Fully Implemented and Rights Still in the Balance

The above considerations make it possible to affirm that the transformations that have taken place in recent decades have created in Italy, on a regulatory level, the premises for recognising to each person, with incurable and/or irreparably invalidating pathologies, rights that can have an important and positive impact on the way life is concluded.

However, we must agree with the observation that, in the early 1990s, Norberto Bobbio, one of the greatest exponents of twentieth century Italian legal philosophy and politics, formulated in a book entitled *L'età dei diritti* (Bobbio 1990, p. 16), underlining how the basic problem with which human rights must be confronted is often, and even more than that of their justification, that of their protection.

It would be wrong to believe that this problem has not concerned the substantial set of prerogatives attributed today to the sick, in general, and to the sick at the end of life, in particular, by the law (in substantial harmony with the deontology of health professionals) and, above all, as noted above, by Law No 219/2017.

It was the law itself that envisaged, in the ninth and tenth paragraphs of its first article, actions aimed at providing patients, and all those who might become patients, with adequate information on the tools (informed consent, advance dispositions, shared care planning) made available for the implementation of their rights. It also calls for the adoption, by healthcare structures, of organisational interventions and initiatives aimed at the in-depth and continuous training of physicians and other healthcare workers, not only on technical-clinical aspects, but also on profiles pertaining to the relationship and communication with the patient, as well as on pain therapy and palliative care, without which it was unrealistic to think of the new paradigm of care, and respect for the rights that are its distinguishing features, taking root in practice.

Although undertaken after the law came into force, these actions and initiatives did not have the capillary diffusion that would have been necessary, and when the Covid epidemic19 came along, which led to its freezing, it became evident that the care paradigm based on respect for rights represented a construction that was as precious as it was fragile. And became also evident that, due to its inadequate assimilation, for many patients, who died as a result of Covid or during the Covid epidemic, the end of their lives was worse than what the heavy emergency situation could have justified (Borsellino et al. 2023).

There is, therefore, still a lot of work to be done to ensure that the rights at the end of life, already recognised on the deontological and juridical plane, are translated into solid and undisputed guiding criteria for care practices.

With regard to rights at the end of life, today it is not, however, only that relating to implementation the open question in the Italian context. There is also the one raised by the qualification of the aid to die, in the modality of euthanasia or assisted suicide, provided to subjects in a condition of suffering assessed by them as unbearable.

Such interventions, which have always been the subject of lively controversy in the national and international bioethical and biojuridical debate, were not contemplated by Law No. 219/2017, and, even after the advanced regulation introduced by it, continued to be considered crimes, provided for and heavily sanctioned, respectively by Article 579 (Murder of the consenting person) and Article 580 (Instigation and aid to suicide) of the Italian Criminal Code.

It is, however, undoubtedly that, once the right to refuse life-saving treatment had been recognised for every individual, thus escaping the imprisonment of existences protracted, in the name of the unavailability of life, in irretrievably compromised conditions, it would not have been possible to close one's eyes for long in the face of a wide range of situations of suffering to which the solution, assessed as adequate by people in these situations, could not be offered by the paths that law and ethics had already made practicable, namely the non-activation and withdrawal of treatment and the simultaneous implementation of deep palliative sedation.

This was confirmed when the Constitutional Court was called upon to rule on the question of the constitutionality of Article 580 of the Criminal code, raised in the criminal judgment brought against the political activist Marco Cappato, for having helped Fabiano Antoniani, the young DJ known by the pseudonym DJ Fabo, who, thanks to suicide assistance obtained in Switzerland, was able to be freed from a survival made unbearable for him by the devastating and unrelievable consequences of a serious car accident.

Circumscribing its decision to situations defined as "unimaginable" at the time when the Italian Criminal code came into force, the 1930s, and closely linked to developments in medicine that had become increasingly capable of snatching death away, but sometimes not of restoring a "sufficiency of life conditions", the Court held that the absolute ban on aiding suicide entailed an unreasonable and unjustified restriction on the freedom of the sick person to self-determine with respect to any treatment, based on Articles 2, 13 and 32(2) of the Constitution.

Consequently, in Judgment No. 242 of 22 November 2019, the Constitutional Court ruled that Article 580 of the Criminal Code is constitutionally illegitimate, insofar as it does not exclude the punishability of acts carried out to facilitate the suicide of persons kept alive by life-supporting treatment and with an irreversible pathology, source of intolerable psycho-physical suffering for them, who have consciously developed and manifested a will to that effect.

That one adopted by the Constitutional Court was an innovative and courageous decision, especially if assessed in the specific Italian context, in which any openness towards the legal recognition of the lawfulness of aid in dying, albeit subject to strict limits and conditions, found, until the eve of the sentence, strong opposition mainly, but not only, in the Catholic sphere.

To many, including myself, who have, instead, formulated a positive assessment (Borsellino 2020), the decision seemed worthy of appreciation for the arguments with which the Supreme Court upheld the need for further steps at the regulatory level, to be taken going beyond the results in the field of rights, moreover firmly established, marked by the law that governed the instruments for the expression of the patient's will on treatment. But also because the Court, overcoming the opposition, in the abstract, between availability and unavailability of life, has linked the need to continue the path of transforming the rules, that affect the final phase of life, to the goal of protecting the dignity of life, recognised as a right, and not as a duty, as well as a value, in its biographical and not only biological value, starting from the awareness that, in the case of subjects kept alive thanks to medical interventions, it is impossible to achieve that goal, if adequate responses are not prepared for to the specificity of their conditions.

There is no doubt that Judgment No. 242/2019 laid the groundwork for broadening the group of persons suffering from incurable diseases and in an irreparably disabling condition for whom the possibility of escape from a survival perceived as detrimental to their dignity seems to be opening up. But can it also be considered that, since the judgment, aid in dying has become the object of a right granted by law to all those for whom it represents the only viable way to escape the captivity of their unbearable condition?

It is impossible to give an adequate answer without emphasising that the Court ruled, as it was required to do, on the case of assisted suicide, i.e. on the help given to a person who, despite his compromised condition, is still capable, as DJ Fabo was, of performing by himself the last act leading to death, thus investing, albeit implicitly, this residual 'self-sufficiency' as a requirement in the absence of which, as well as the further requirement represented by dependence on life-support, an individual irreparably suffering, requesting to be helped to die, would not have been able to avail himself of the very significant transformation of the legal framework on end-of-life initiated by the decision.

After the sentence of the Constitutional Court, a number of other pronouncements of the ordinary judiciary have intervened and have appropriately distanced themselves from a restrictive interpretation of the requirement of dependence on life-support. But, on the other hand, the problem of subjects who, due to physical incapacity, cannot themselves activate the process that leads to death with a suicidal act, but need the intervention of a third party with a properly euthanasic act, has remained to be addressed and resolved. This is an act whose discontinuity, first and foremost from an ethical point of view, with respect to assisted suicide, can be strongly resized, if it is considered as the most complete form of 'assistance' in dying and, therefore, we could say, reversing the traditional representation, as the hypothesis of suicide assistance appropriate to the situations of persons unable to perform any action.

I think we can, therefore, justifiably state that the right to be helped to die, when the dramatic situations occur, in which such help becomes a condition for ending one's life with dignity, is still, in Italy, a sort of 'right in the balance'.

The situation is that of a 'work in progress', initiated but not yet fully realised, which will be completed if, as has happened in the case of other rights at the end of life, it will be possible to have, as has been repeatedly requested by the Constitutional Court itself, a legislative discipline, capable of providing solid guarantees to the sick and, at the same time, safe orientation criteria also for healthcare workers, who are called upon to perform acts well set within the framework of the mandate of care redefined by the centrality acquired by the relief of suffering, but still subject to a prohibition by long tradition reaffirmed by medical deontology, starting from Hippocratic ethics.

Good laws, in which rights find their foundation and the guarantee of their implementation, require ethical and political sensitivities of which, from 2019 to date, the Italian Legislator has not been able to demonstrate by intervening with a law on the subject. But there are the virtuous examples of the disciplines introduced in other countries, even those culturally close to Italy, such as Spain,[7] and there is the impulse that comes from below, from civil society, in the presence of which it is reasonable to think that the result will be achieved, although perhaps not in the short term, as would be desirable.

References

Bacon, F. 2013. *On the Dignity and Advancement of Learning and Novum Organum: And Novum Organum.* London: Reprint Forgotten Books.
Bobbio, N. 1990. *L'età dei diritti.* Torino: Einaudi.
Borsellino P. 1999. *Bioetica tra autonomia e diritto*, Zadig, Milano.
Borsellino P. 2010. *Le questioni etiche del fine vita*, www.timeoutintensiva.it, Focus n° 14, 26 luglio.
Borsellino, P. 2015. Limitation of the therapeutic effort: Ethical and legal justification for withholding and/or withdrawing life sustaining treatments. *Multidisciplinary Respiratory Medicine* 10: 5.
Borsellino, P. 2018. *Bioetica tra "morali" e diritto. Nuova edizione aggiornata*, Cortina editore, Milano.
Borsellino, P. 2020. La sentenza della Corte costituzionale n. 242/2019: Presupposti, punti fermi e questioni aperte. In *La corte costituzionale e il fine vita*, ed. G. D'Alessandro and O. Di Giovine, 39–58. Torino: Un confronto interdisciplinare sul caso Cappato-Antoniani, Giappichelli.
Borsellino, P., Forni L., Gallucci M. and Others,2023. *I diritti dei morenti in diversi setting di cura al tempo del Covid-19*, Rivista italiana di cure palliative 25: 121–132.
Comitato per l'etica di fine vita. 1997. Carta dei diritti dei morenti, https://www.comitato-finevita.it/documenti/carta-dei-diritti-dei-morenti.
Saunders, C. (ed), 1984^2. *The management of Terminal Malignant Disease*, Arnold Publications, London.
Scarpelli U., *Diritti positivi, diritti naturali. Un'analisi semiotica* in Caprioli S., Treggiari F.. Diritti umani e civiltà giuridica. Perugia: Centro Studi Giuridici e Politici.
World Health Organization. 1990. *Cancer pain relief and palliative care—Report of a WHO expert committee.*
Wulff, R., S.A. Pedersen, and R. Rosenberg. 1987. *Philosophy of medicine: An introduction.* Oxford: Blackwell.

[7] Country in which a 'Ley orgánica de regulacion de la eutanasia' was approved in March 2021.

SPRINGER NATURE

GPSR Compliance

The European Union's (EU) General Product Safety Regulation (GPSR) is a set of rules that requires consumer products to be safe and our obligations to ensure this.

If you have any concerns about our products, you can contact us on ProductSafety@springernature.com

In case Publisher is established outside the EU, the EU authorized representative is:

Springer Nature Customer Service Center GmbH
Europaplatz 3
69115 Heidelberg, Germany

The manufacturer's authorised representative in the EU is Springer Nature Customer Service Centre GmbH, Europaplatz 3, 69115 Heidelberg, Germany. If you have any concerns regarding our products, please contact ProductSafety@springernature.com

Printed and bound by CPI Group (UK) Ltd, Croydon, CR0 4YY
01/10/2026
02225906-0010